Rod and Staff Books

(Milestone Ministries)

800-761-0234 or 541-466-3231

www.RodandStaffBooks.com

Mathematics for Christian Living Series

Mathematics for Christian Living Series

Working Arithmetic

Grade 2

Teacher's Manual

(Units 3–5)

Rod and Staff Publishers, Inc.
Hwy. 172, Crockett, Kentucky 41413
Telephone: (606) 522-4348

Acknowledgments

We are indebted to God for the vision of the need for a *Mathematics for Christian Living Series* and for His enabling grace. Charitable contributions from many churches have helped to cover the expenses for research and development.

This revision was written by Sisters Miriam Rudolph and Marla Martin. The brethren Marvin Eicher, Jerry Kreider, and Luke Sensenig served as editors. Most of the illustrations were drawn by Lois Myer. The work was evaluated by a panel of reviewers and tested by teachers in the classroom. Much effort was devoted to the production of the book. We are grateful for all who helped to make this book possible.

—The Publishers

This book is part of a course for grade 2 arithmetic and will be most effective if used with the other parts of the course. *Working Arithmetic* includes the following items:

Teacher's Manual, part 1 (Units 1, 2)
Teacher's Manual, part 2 (Units 3–5)
Pupil's Workbook, Unit 1
Pupil's Workbook, Unit 2
Pupil's Workbook, Unit 3
Pupil's Workbook, Unit 4
Pupil's Workbook, Unit 5
Blacklines

Rod and Staff Publishers, Inc.

Hwy. 172, Crockett, Kentucky 41413

Printed in U.S.A

ISBN 978-07399-0461-9

Catalog no. 13293.3

9 10 11 12 13 — 16 15 14 13 12 11

CONTENTS

Materials for This Course

Books and Worksheets

5 Pupil's Workbooks
2 Teacher's Manuals
Blacklines

Teaching Aids

Addition and Subtraction Flash Cards 1–18
  Individual Student Flash Cards 11–18
* Boat Poster
* Clover Patch Poster
* Blossom Charts
* 1,000 Book
Number Line 0–100
Large coins
Large clock
Cup, pint, quart, gallon

* See pages 12–14 for further instructions.

An Overview of This Course

Understanding the Teacher's Manual

In the Teacher's Manual, each lesson is outlined under three main headings: *Before Class, Class Time,* and *After Class.*

Before Class lists the things to do before school in the morning.

(1) Gather the materials that are listed.

(2) Put your chalkboard samples and exercises on the board.

Class Time is the second heading. *Class Time* tells you what to do during your teaching session. This section contains the core of the lesson. Begin with number 1 and proceed step by step to the last point. Bold type indicates what is spoken or recited. An ellipsis (. . .) usually means to continue with more of this same drill. The last point always reads: Assign Lesson (number)

SAMPLE (Lesson 5)

Get your arithmetic book. Tear out Lesson 5. Pause until the books have been put away again.

Begin with the first whole and parts. Trace and write the first facts. Then move on to the next whole and parts, and facts.

We understand how to do the second page. Tell me what you will do at the top of the third page. Tell me what you will do at the water lilies.

When you have completed and checked over these three pages, you may do the Extra Activity. How many rows will you fill today?
We will fill all the rows that have equal lines.

Your teaching session does not include doing the workbook lesson. Your teaching and chalkboard samples prepared the children to work. They are eager to begin. The exercises are repetitious. A running look at each page is sufficient.

However, if the children ought to be more particular in number formation or rechecking their work, tell them before they begin the day's work.

After Class is the last heading. These exercises are like the gravy on the potatoes. They add flavor for today and savor for tomorrow.

After Class gives further practice with new material, and it also previews concepts that are taught in succeeding lessons. Thus, new material is introduced by stages: first in *After Class,* then in *Class Time,* and finally in the pupil's lesson. A pupil is usually exposed to a new concept several times before he actually uses it in a written assignment.

When should you use *After Class*? Near the end of your arithmetic period or in the afternoon. Try to cover each point. Some individual drills can be done in other free time, such as lunch time.

The Pupil's Workbook

Each workbook lesson has two perforated sheets. Allow the children to keep the books inside their desks. They can tear out one lesson each day.

Tear-out pages will make checking more convenient for you. It will help to keep the parent abreast with his child's daily performance because the child will take arithmetic work home every day, not just when the book is completed.

The first three pages of a lesson contain the core of the child's seatwork for that lesson. The fourth page is an Extra Activity or a Speed Drill.

Use the Extra Activity *only* after the rest of the lesson is completed. If you need to choose between Extra Activity and Blacklines, choose Extra Activity.

Many pages have a line of fine print at the bottom. Use these thoughts as is suitable for your class, to develop an atmosphere of God-consciousness in relation to the lesson. The line can be read and discussed at the beginning of the assignment. Able students can be encouraged to look up the references and read the account after the assignment is finished. When there is not time to discuss the bottom line in class, it can be a silent influence to think of God in the sphere of arithmetic class.

Grading Arithmetic

Since the arithmetic lesson is the core of the child's work, his arithmetic grade should be derived from the lesson. The number of answers will vary from one lesson to another. But the total value of each lesson will not vary.

The total value of each lesson has been established as 50 points. Therefore, if you use an E-Z Grader, always set it at 50 to determine the child's score.

In most lessons the actual number of answers is more than 50. But each lesson has some review exercises. With the E-Z Grader set at 50, the child will lose more points if he gets a review exercise wrong. This is realistic, for the child should have a thorough mastery of that exercise.

Speed Drills

This course has 81 Speed Drills in the pupil's workbooks. Speed Drills appear on the fourth page of Lessons 6, 8, and 10. They begin again in Lesson 16 and continue every two lessons through Lesson 170.

Give the Drill right after the teaching session before the children begin the workbook lesson.

(1) Their minds will be fresh.

(2) They will not have had an opportunity to mentally answer the Drill beforehand.

Administering the Speed Drill:

Tear out the two pages for today's lesson. Pause until the books have been put away again. **Find the Speed Drill. Look at me. Pencils up!** Each child will raise his pencil above his head. **Ready, set, go!**

After 1 minute: **If you are not finished, circle the problem you are working on, and then finish.**

Check the completed Drills immediately. The child will write the number of correct answers inside the bee. If he has any fact wrong, he will write it correctly in the boxes below.

Extra Activity

This course has Extra Activity pages in the pupil's workbook. Extra Activity appears on the fourth page of Lessons 1–5, 7, 9, 11–15, 17, 19; and continues every two lessons through Lesson 169.

Extra Activity is not a part of the lesson core. Use Extra Activity *only* after the core of the lesson is done. The children should complete the Extra Activity before they work on the Blacklines for a particular lesson.

The type of work on the Extra Activity page will vary throughout the year.

Rocky Bluff

In Lesson 1-40 the Extra Activity is a rocky bluff where the facts are written. The child begins at the top.

In Lesson 1 he fills two rows.

In Lesson 2 he fills three rows.

In Lesson 3 he fills four rows.

In each lesson the screened equal lines show the child how far to write the facts.

The illustrations below show in what order the facts will be written. Facts with 0 are not written.

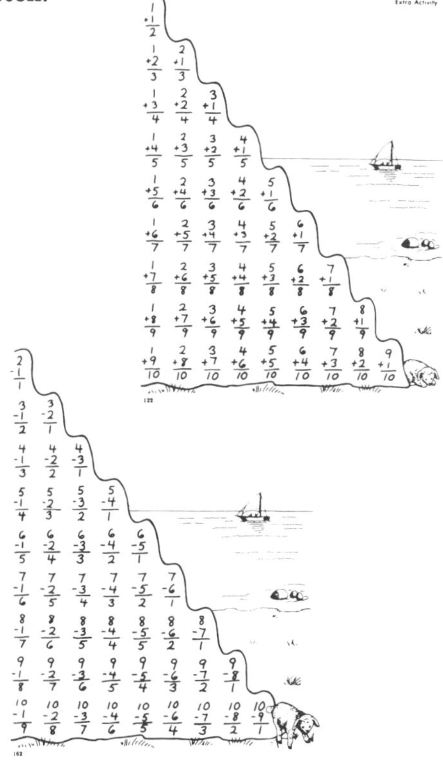

Beehive

In Lessons 41–159 the Extra Activity is a skep (straw hive).

When there is one triplet, fill all the clovers and bees with that triplet.

When there are two or more triplets, make the triplets take turns as you fill the clovers and bees.

The small bee inside a skep ring shows which facts shall be written in this ring.

Miniature Blossom Charts

In Lessons 161-169 the Extra Activity is a review of Blossom Charts 11–18. The whole number will be written in the blossom. The parts will be written in the bees.

Blacklines

Since the amount of work a class needs will vary from year to year, this course includes Blacklines. These Blacklines may be reproduced as needed in teaching the course.

The Teacher's Manual lists the Blacklines that correlate with each lesson. The Blacklines are listed in order of importance. For example, Lesson 8:

Blacklines
- Number Facts #2
- Form B
- Missing Numbers #4

Select Number Facts #2 before Form B. Use the Blacklines as masters. Make as many copies as you need for your class.

A lesson number is in the upper righthand corner of most Blacklines.

means use in Lessons 8, 9, and 10.

means this is a form. There are four forms in all: A, B, C, and D. They will be used in many lessons.

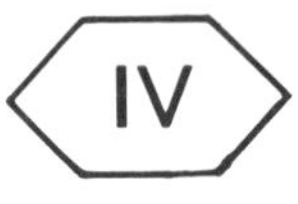

means this is a fact form. There are twelve fact forms in all: I–XII. They will be used in many lessons.

You may ask, "Why the same worksheet again and again?" This is the way second graders learn. "Line upon line, line upon line." (Isaiah 28:10).

The Blacklines are not confined to these specific lessons. For example, your children may need drill in writing numbers in sequence for Lesson 3, but Form A is not listed with Blacklines in Lesson 3. You may copy Form A and give it to your children again.

A handy way to file your Blackline masters is to put them in a 1½" D-Ring Binder. Since the forms will be used often, put those at the front of your notebook. Keep each skill set together. *Multiply and Divide* is optional; put this set at the back of the notebook. File the other sets in alphabetical order as they are in the box or in the order they are introduced in the course.

(This order is listed below.)

Forms A-D
Forms I-XII

1. Missing Numbers
2. Number Facts
3. 2-Place Computation
4. Skip Counting
5. Money
6. Reading Problems
7. Fact Hives
8. Missing Whole or Parts
9. Triplets With Facts
10. Number Triplets
11. Number Words
12. Mixed Computation
13. Equations
14. Multiply and Divide

Directions for Blackline Forms

Form A—— *Number Grid.* Turn the paper sideways to write numbers in the rows. Use this form to make a blank copy of *My 1,000 Book* for each child. Have the children fill in the numbers to write their own 1,000 books as they are able in spare time.

Form B—— *Addition and Subtraction Facts.* Write the facts up to the family currently being studied.

Form C—— *Flash Card Drill.* Use the pictures in the left margin to identify which row you are working on. As you flash a fact card, the children will write the answer in a box.

Form D—— *Blank Fact Form.* Use this form for special drill on problem combinations. Prepare the sheet by filling it with facts for the combination that needs to be drilled.

Fact Forms—Use these sheets often as progress checks and refresher drills.

Directions for Blacklines

Equations—Complete each equation. The word box on the right will help the child to spell his words correctly.

Fact Hives—The triplet at the first skep in each row tells which facts shall be written in that row. Write the facts in order.

Missing Numbers—Write the numbers that are missing.

Missing Whole or Parts—Fill in the missing whole number or the missing part.

Mixed Computation—Figure the answer to the first two numbers; then add or subtract the third number. Write the answer.

Money Identification—Write the name of the coin on the blank and the value in the box.

Number Facts—Answer the facts.

Number Triplets—Write the whole number on the clover blossom. Write the parts on the bee's wings.

Number Words—Write the numerals for the number words.

Reading Problems

#1 Read the story. Write the numbers in the beehive. Write the label words on the lines.

#4 Read the sentence. Write the problem in the box.

Skip Counting—Read the directions. Start with that number in the first blank and continue counting until the blanks are full. Have the children use *My 1,000 Book* for help.

#3 Count 25-100 again and again.

Triplets With Facts—What triplet must the child think of to complete the fact? Write the whole number in the clover; write the parts on the bee's wings. Complete the fact.

2-Place Computation—Answer the problems.

Multiply/Divide (Optional)

Multiply Form. Copy a multiplication table from a key four times.

Divide Form. Copy a division table from a key four times.

#1 Each child will use his multiplication key to answer the facts.

#2 Each child will use his division key to answer the facts.

The Whole Number and Its Two Parts

In Grade 1, the child learned that addition is putting two or more numbers together to see how many there are in all. He learned that subtraction is taking a part away, then discovering how many are left. Addition and subtraction facts were learned by families.

In Grade 2 Lessons 1-40 are basically review.

Addition—Lessons 1-10
Subtraction—Lessons 11-20
Addition—Lessons 21-30
Subtraction—Lessons 31-40

In this review the child sees that each number fact has a whole number and two parts. The whole and parts are illustrated with sailboats on a poster.

After Lesson 40 new addition and subtraction facts are introduced in the same lesson. They are introduced by the whole number and its two parts. They are illustrated with clover blossoms and bees on a poster.

The whole number and two parts are called a triplet. Example: (11) 6 5. This method of introducing facts is valuable for these eight reasons:

1. The whole number is seen first.
2. The two parts are seen second.
3. Memorizing the triplet (11) 6 5 helps the child to know four facts:
   11−6=5, 11−5=6, 6+5=11, 5+6=11.
4. The triplet helps the child realize that no matter if he adds or subtracts, (11) 6 5 must stay together.
5. The child can clearly understand the interrelationship of addition and subtraction.
6. It helps the child comprehend reading problems. He determines which is missing, the whole or a part. If the whole is missing, he adds. If the part is missing, he subtracts.
7. It breaks the crutch of tapping out answers with the fingers.
   The child sees 5+6=__.
   He taps 6, 7, 8, 9, 10, **11**.
   He sees 11−5=__.
   He taps 10, 9, 8, 7, **6**.
   With the "whole number and two parts" method *the child does not tap at all.*
8. When a child knows the triplet (11) 6 5, he can quickly answer all these combinations:

5+6=__	6+__=11	11−__=5
6+5=__	5+__=11	11−__=6
__+5=11	11−5=__	__−5=6
__+6=11	11−6=__	__−6=5

Hand Signals

Develop a healthy combination of verbal and visual teaching. It helps a teacher and a group of children to count and recite with one voice because everyone starts together, stays together, and stops together.

The first day, introduce a few hand signals.

1. One downward sweep of your hand means "begin together or answer together."
2. A cupped hand at your ear means "speak up."
3. A wide-spread hand means "stop."

Following are illustrations of other hand signals you will find sprinkled through the Teacher's Manual.

The teacher will motion and say:

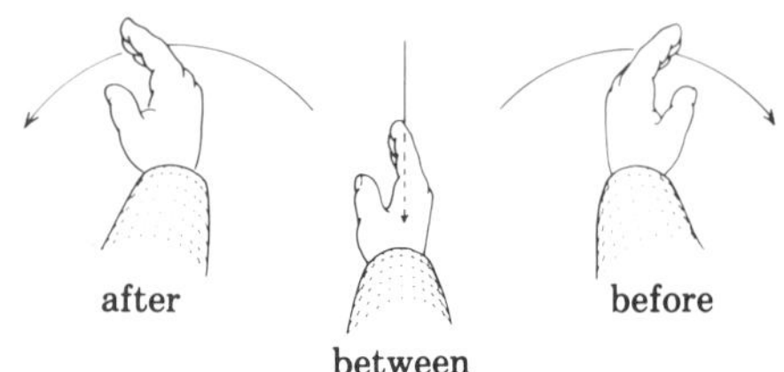

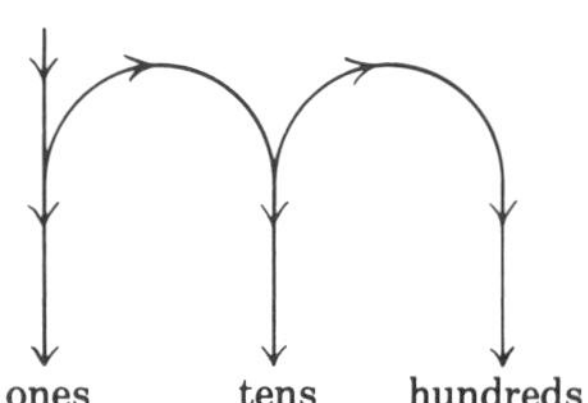

Since the children are facing you, their motions will mirror yours. When you motion to your right, they will motion to their left. This is why the ones, tens, hundreds motion proceeds from left to right for you.

Scheduling Arithmetic Class

Arithmetic is one of the basic subjects in second grade. A basic subject should be taught in the morning when a child is most alert. Aim to have each child complete the day's assignment. Reading, English, and recess will also need to be scheduled during these morning hours. You may circle back in the afternoon and complete unfinished seatwork or *After Class* activities.

A suggested order:

1. Conduct *Class Time* period.
2. Do the Speed Drill—if the lesson has one.
3. Assign the lesson.
4. Work on Extra Activity—if the lesson has one.
5. Do *After Class* activities.
6. As children finish their seatwork, some may have time to do a Blackline copy.

Multiplication and Division

Multiplication and division are optional in Grade 2. If you teach them, begin no earlier than Lesson 124. You may begin later than Lesson 124. The outline below shows the scope of multiplication and division in this course. Each table is used for nine lessons, six lessons with multiplication and three lessons with division.

Multiply and divide by 2

Lessons *Activities*

124, 125, 126—Copy the multiplication facts.
127, 128, 129—Answer the multiplication facts.
130, 131, 132—Copy and answer the division facts.

Multiply and divide by 10

133, 134, 135—Copy the multiplication facts.
136, 137, 138—Answer the multiplication facts.
139, 140, 141—Copy and answer the division facts.

Multiply and divide by 5

142, 143, 144—Copy the multiplication facts.
145, 146, 147—Answer the multiplication facts.
148, 149, 150—Copy and answer the division facts.

Multiply and divide by 1

151, 152, 153—Copy the multiplication facts.
154, 155, 156—Answer the multiplication facts.
157, 158, 159—Copy and answer the division facts.

In Grade 2, Multiplication and Division are optional because

- the Addition and Subtraction facts are to be taught, drilled, or reviewed daily.
- some children need all their time for Addition and Subtraction facts.
- Multiplication and Division are taught as new concepts in Grade 3.

Therefore

- the *Class Time* will continue to center around Addition and Subtraction.
- the children will continue to carry their Addition and Subtraction flash cards home each evening to practice.
- the ring of keys with Multiplication and Division tables will not be carried home to practice.
- no Multiplication or Division exercises are in the workbook. They are on Blacklines.
- the keys will introduce the children to the signs (× ⟌) and operations.
- the children will learn to read and copy the facts. They will not master the facts until Grade 3.

Multiplication and Division Keys

Making the Keys

Materials

Heavy paper, file-folder weight is ideal

1 metal ring that opens and closes for each child (Look for them in a bookstore or office supply store.)

Key patterns can be found in the Multiply/Divide set of the Blacklines.

1. Copy the keys onto heavy paper.
2. You may have each child cut out his own key.
3. Fasten the key to the ring.

Using the keys

1. Use them during *After Class* activities.
2. Use them for referral during seatwork.

TEACHING AIDS

My 1,000 Book

In the set of Blacklines for this course are masters for *My 1,000 Book.* Before the school term opens, copy a 1,000 book for each child in second grade. A clear plastic report cover with a backbone spine will make a nice book.

The book will be used during *Class Time* for counting beyond 100. It will be used during seatwork for writing beyond 100. It will be used for counting by 1's, 2's, 5's, and 10's.

The book will be used first in Lesson 3 during *Class Time* and seatwork.

Number Line

A Number Line is a long runner-type chart showing large, clear, easy-to-read numbers. You will find a Number Line with numbers 0–100 very helpful in second grade.

Mount the Number Line high on the wall before the school year begins. If you do not have space to put it in one continuous line, divide the line at number 50. Mount 1–50 above and 51–100 beneath.

You may purchase a Number Line at a local school supply store or order it from

Kurtz Bros.
Clearfield, PA 16830
PA: 800-252-3811
Other States: 800-441-8223

Money

In second grade, pennies, nickels, dimes, and quarters are reviewed, and half dollars are introduced. Counting different kinds of coins is directly related to different kinds of rote counting.

- Count by 1's for pennies
- Count by 5's for nickels
- Count by 10's for dimes
- Count by 25's for quarters

The children will count and add money. They will learn how to change 115¢ to $1.15.

Real coins will be used during *After Class.* Giant coins will be used to drill and review money. You may purchase giant coins at a local school supply store or order them from the address above.

Boat Poster

In lessons 1–40 you will use this poster to illustrate the "whole and parts" concept.

Making the poster

Materials:

41" × 22" blue poster board
Blue crayon
White poster board
Black construction paper
Patterns—See Appendix, page 212.

1. Lay the bottom edge of the wave pattern flush with the bottom edge of the blue poster board. Trace the waves. Flip the pattern end for end. Trace more waves. Continue to flip and trace until you have 10 "dips."
2. Outline the waves with blue crayon.
3. Cut a 2½" slit in the "dip" of each wave.

4. Trace 10 sailboats on white poster board. Paste black construction paper on the back of the white poster board. Cut out the boats. When the boats are finished, they will be black on one side and white on the other side.
5. Optional: Add a cloud and birds.
6. Optional: The sailboats may be laminated to make sliding in and out of slots easier. When cutting out the boats, be careful to keep a sealed edge around the paper.

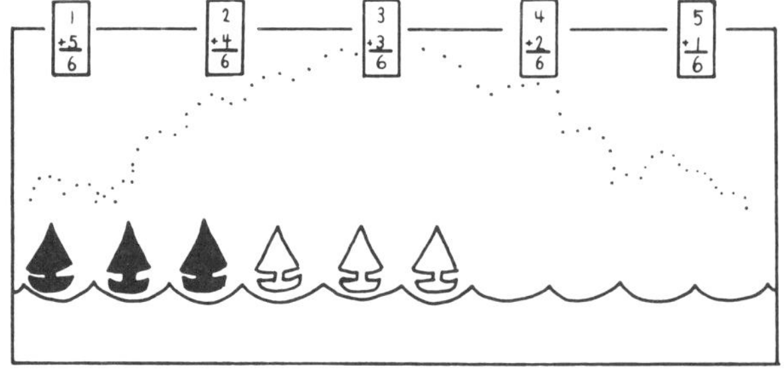

Mounting the poster

Mount the poster on the wall with E-Z Clips. E-Z Clips will hold the poster away from the wall, making it easier to slide the boats in and out of the slots.

Using the poster

1. *Always* place the first boat in the first wave on the left.
2. *Always* have the dark boats first and the light boats last. Never mix the dark and light boats.
3. When you want to exchange a dark boat for a light boat, pull the dark boat out, flip it over and slide it back into the same slot.
4. Tack your flash cards above the poster with E-Z Clips.
5. Follow these rules for addition and subtraction.

Clover Patch Poster

In Lessons 41–159 you will use this poster to illustrate the whole and parts concept.

Making the poster

Materials:

44¼″ × 14″ light green poster board
White poster board
Patterns—See Appendix, page 212
Green marker (broad-tipped)
Ruler | Crayons
Pencil | Scissors
Razor blade | Paste

1. Draw a light horizontal line 5 inches above the bottom of the green poster board.
2. Begin at the left end of the line and mark ¾″, 1½″, ¾″, 1½″ . . . until you reach the right end of the line.
3. With the green marker, draw a tall grass clump in every ¾″ section. Draw a short grass clump in every 1½″ section.
4. Cut a horizontal slit through each 1½″ (short grass) section.

Making the blossoms

1. Use pink. Color 10 blossoms without bees. Paste these blossoms on white poster board.
2. Use pink. Color 9 blossoms with bees. Paste these on the back of 9 blossoms that you made in point 1.
3. Use red-violet. Color 8 blossoms without bees. Paste these blossoms on white poster board.
4. Cut out the blossoms. Slide them into the slots in the grass.
5. Optional: Add treetops and more grass.
6. Optional: The clover blossoms may be laminated to make sliding in and out of slots easier. When you cut out the blossoms, be careful to keep a sealed edge around the paper.

Mounting the poster

Mount the poster on the wall with E-Z clips when you are ready for Lesson 41. Preceding Lesson 41 is an explanation on using the Clover Patch Poster, page 148.

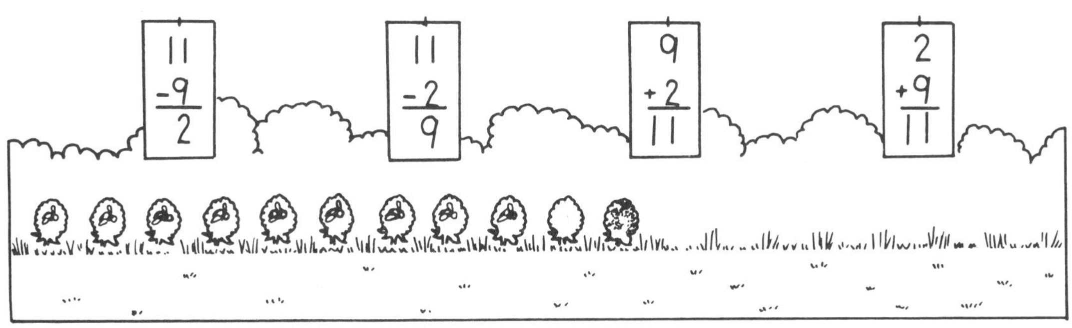

Blossom Charts

In lessons 47–170 you will use Blossom Charts to drill the triplets.

Making the charts

Materials:

8 (13″ × 16″) pieces of posterboard
8 large clover blossoms—See Appendix page 217.
20 bees—See Appendix, page 216.
Black marker (broad-tipped)
Green marker (broad-tipped)
Crayons

1. Color the clover blossoms pink, red, purple, white, red-violet, or yellow.
2. Color the bees yellow and brown. Do not color the wings.
3. Use the black marker to write the *whole* numbers on the clover blossoms.
4. Use the green marker to write the *parts* on the bees' wings.

(11) 9 2
(11) 8 3
(11) 7 4
(11) 6 5

(12) 9 3
(12) 8 4
(12) 7 5
(12) 6 6

(13) 9 4
(13) 8 5
(13) 7 6

(14) 9 5
(14) 8 6
(14) 7 7

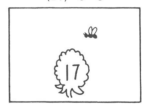

(15) 9 6
(15) 8 7

(16) 9 7
(16) 8 8

(17) 9 8

(18) 9 9

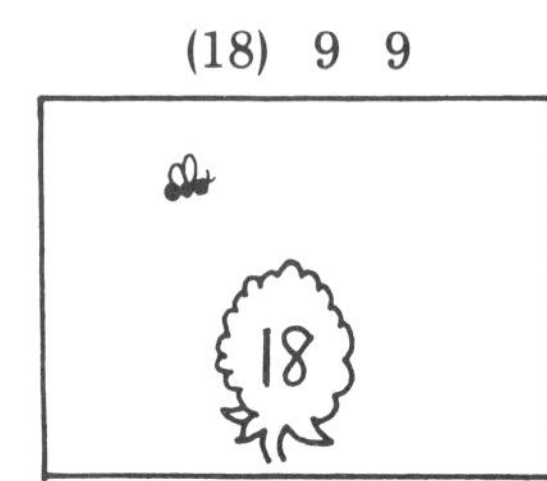

Why are subtraction facts first? The (11) 9 2 facts are taught, drilled, and written in this order:

$$\begin{array}{r} 11 \\ -9 \\ \hline 2 \end{array} \qquad \begin{array}{r} 11 \\ -2 \\ \hline 9 \end{array} \qquad \begin{array}{r} 9 \\ +2 \\ \hline 11 \end{array} \qquad \begin{array}{r} 2 \\ +9 \\ \hline 11 \end{array}$$

We begin with 11−9=2 because

- the numbers in the problem are in the same order as the triplet.
- we say the *whole* number first—11.
- we say the greater *part* next—9.
- the clover patch poster illustrates the greater *part* and then the lesser *part*.

Using the Blossom Charts

1. Blossom 11 Chart is first used in Lesson 47.
2. The Teacher's Manual tells you when to add each new bee.
3. The Teacher's Manual tells you when to mount a new Blossom Chart.
4. *Drill, drill, drill the triplets.* Always say the *whole* number first, the greater *part* second, the smaller *part* last: (11) 9 2.
5. Add bee after bee to a Blossom Chart. Add chart after chart to the wall until Blossom Charts 11–18 are all displayed.

New Skills Listed by Lessons

Teacher's Manual

Lesson Number	New Skills
1	Addition Families 2 and 3 Whole and parts concept Largest number Counting by 1's
2	Addition Family 4
3	Addition Family 5 After numbers
4	Addition Family 6 Before numbers
5	Place value: 1's, 10's, 100's
6	Reading Problem: key word—in all 2 digits + 2 digits
7	Addition Family 7 Penny
8	2 digits + 1 digit
9	Skip counting by 10's
10	
11	Subtraction families 2 and 3 Smallest number
12	Subtraction Family 4 Before and After numbers
13	Subtraction Family 5 2 digits − 2 digits

Pupil's Book

Lesson Number	New Skills
1	Addition Families 2 and 3 Whole and parts concept After numbers Counting by 1's
2	Addition Family 4
3	Addition Family 5 Largest numbers
4	Addition Family 6
5	
6	Place value: 1's, 10's, 100's Before numbers
7	Addition Family 7
8	2 digits + 2 digits Reading Problem: key word—in all Penny
9	
10	2 digits + 1 digit
11	Subtraction Families 2 and 3 Skip counting by 10's
12	Subtraction Family 4
13	Subtraction Family 5 Smallest number

New Skills Listed by Lessons

Teacher's Manual

Lesson Number	New Skills
14	Subtraction Family 6 Reading Problem: key word—left Dime
15	2 digits − 1 digit
16	
17	Subtraction Family 7
18	
19	Dimes + pennies Before and After numbers by 10's
20	
21	Addition Family 8 Skip counting by 5's
22	Nickel
23	Reading Problem: key word—altogether
24	Addition Family 9
25	3 digits + 3 digits
26	

Pupil's Book

Lesson Number	New Skills
14	Subtraction Family 6
15	2 digits − 2 digits
16	Dime
17	Subtraction Family 7 2 digits − 1 digit
18	
19	Dimes + pennies Reading Problem: key word—left
20	
21	Addition Family 8 Before and After numbers by 10's
22	
23	Skip counting by 5's
24	Addition Family 9 Nickel
25	
26	

New Skills Listed by Lessons

Teacher's Manual

Lesson Number	New Skills
27	Addition Family 10 Nickels + pennies
28	3 digits + 2 digits
29	
30	Reading Problem: key word—both
31	Subtraction Family 8 Skip counting by 25's Before and After numbers by 5's
32	Quarter
33	Reading Problem: no key word
34	Subtraction Family 9
35	3 digits − 3 digits
36	Quarters + pennies
37	Subtraction Family 10 3 digits − 2 digits
38	1 digit + 1 digit + 1 digit Find total cents
39	Skip counting by 2's

Pupil's Book

Lesson Number	New Skills
27	Addition Family 10 3 digits + 3 digits
28	
29	Nickels + pennies 3 digits + 2 digits
30	
31	Subtraction Family 8 Before and After numbers by 5's
32	
33	Skip counting by 25's
34	Subtraction Family 9 Quarter
35	
36	3 digits − 3 digits
37	Subtraction Family 10 Quarters + pennies
38	3 digits − 2 digits
39	

New Skills Listed by Lessons

Teacher's Manual

Lesson Number	New Skills
40	
41	(11) 9 2 triplet and facts
42	Before and After numbers by 2's
43	Clocks—:00 Missing whole or part
44	Reading Problem: missing part
45	
46	(11) 8 3 triplet and facts
47	
48	Equation: 60 minutes = 1 hour
49	Dimes + nickels
50	
51	(11) 7 4 triplet and facts

Pupil's Book

Lesson Number	New Skills
40	
41	(11) 9 2 triplet and facts Skip counting by 2's
42	
43	Find total cents
44	1 digit + 1 digit + 1 digit Missing whole or part Clocks—:00
45	Before and After numbers by 2's
46	(11) 8 3 triplet and facts
47	
48	
49	
50	Reading Problem: no key word Dimes + nickels
51	(11) 7 4 triplet and facts

New Skills Listed by Lessons

Teacher's Manual

Lesson Number	New Skills
52	
53	2 digits + 2 digits + 2 digits
54	
55	Equation: 30 minutes = ½ hour
56	(11) 6 5 triplet and facts Clocks—:30 2 digits + 2 digits + 1 digit
57	
58	Missing Signs
59	
60	
61	(12) 9 3 triplet and facts Skip Counting by 100's Mental arithmetic
62	Place value: 1's, 10's, 100's, 1,000's
63	

Pupil's Book

Lesson Number	New Skills
52	Reading Problem: key word—altogether
53	
54	
55	2 digits + 2 digits + 2 digits
56	(11) 6 5 triplet and facts
57	Clocks—:30
58	
59	
60	
61	(12) 9 3 triplet and facts 2 digits + 2 digits + 1 digit
62	
63	

New Skills Listed by Lessons

Teacher's Manual

Lesson Number	New Skills
64	Reading Problem: 2-digit computation Reading Problem: ¢
65	Carrying: 2 digits + 2 digits
66	(12) 8 4 triplet and facts
67	
68	
69	
70	
71	(12) 7 5 triplet and facts
72	Clocks—:15
73	
74	
75	
76	(12) 6 6 triplet and facts
77	

Pupil's Book

Lesson Number	New Skills
64	Place value: 1's, 10's, 100's, 1,000's
65	
66	(12) 8 4 triplet and facts
67	Carrying: 2 digits + 2 digits
68	
69	
70	
71	(12) 7 5 triplet and facts
72	
73	
74	Clocks—:15
75	
76	(12) 6 6 triplet and facts
77	

New Skills Listed by Lessons

Teacher's Manual

Lesson Number	New Skills
78	
79	(13) 9 4 triplet and facts Clocks—:45
80	
81	
82	
83	Shapes: circle, square
84	Column addition—carrying Shape: triangle
85	
86	
87	(13) 8 5 triplet and facts Shape: rectangle
88	Borrowing: 2 digits − 2 digits
89	
90	
91	

Pupil's Book

Lesson Number	New Skills
78	Reading Problem: key word—both
79	(13) 9 4 triplet and facts
80	
81	Clocks—:45
82	
83	
84	Column addition—carrying Shapes: circle, square
85	Shape: triangle
86	
87	(13) 8 5 triplet and facts Shape: rectangle
88	
89	
90	Borrowing: 2 digits − 2 digits
91	

New Skills Listed by Lessons

Teacher's Manual

Lesson Number	New Skills
92	
93	
94	
95	(13) 7 6 triplet and facts
96	
97	$ sign and decimal point
98	Fraction: ½
99	
100	Reading Problem: how much more
101	
102	
103	(14) 9 5 triplet and facts
104	

Pupil's Book

Lesson Number	New Skills
92	
93	
94	
95	(13) 7 6 triplets and facts
96	
97	
98	$ sign and decimal point
99	
100	Fraction: ½ Reading Problem: missing part
101	
102	
103	(14) 9 5 triplet and facts
104	

New Skills Listed by Lessons

Teacher's Manual

Lesson Number	New Skills
105	
106	Fraction: ¼
107	
108	½ of a number
109	
110	
111	(14) 8 6 triplet and facts
112	
113	Reading Problem: how much less
114	Carrying twice: 3 digits + 3 digits
115	Equation: 12 things = 1 dozen Equation: 6 things = ½ dozen
116	
117	Reading Problem: 1 dozen Equation: 7 days = 1 week
118	

Pupil's Book

Lesson Number	New Skills
105	
106	
107	
108	Fraction: ¼
109	
110	
111	(14) 8 6 triplet and facts
112	Reading Problem: 2-digit computation
113	
114	
115	Carrying twice: 3 digits + 3 digits
116	Reading Problem: ¢
117	Equation: 12 things = 1 dozen Equation: 6 things = ½ dozen
118	

New Skills Listed by Lessons

Teacher's Manual

Lesson Number	New Skills
119	(14) 7 7 triplet and facts Equation: 12 months = 1 year
120	
121	
122	(15) 9 6 triplet and facts
123	Reading Problem: ½ dozen
124	2 × table (optional)
125	Equation: 12 inches = 1 foot
126	
127	
128	Even and odd numbers Equation: 3 feet = 1 yard
129	
130	(15) 8 7 triplet and facts Divide by 2 (optional)
131	
132	Skip Counting by 50's

Pupil's Book

Lesson Number	New Skills
119	(14) 7 7 triplet and facts
120	
121	
122	(15) 9 6 triplet and facts
123	
124	
125	
126	
127	Reading Problem: 1 dozen Equation: 12 inches = 1 foot
128	
129	Equation: 3 feet = 1 yard
130	(15) 8 7 triplet and facts
131	
132	

New Skills Listed by Lessons

Teacher's Manual

Lesson Number	New Skills
133	Half dollar 10× table (optional)
134	Half dollar + dimes
135	
136	
137	
138	(16) 9 7 triplet and facts Half dollar + pennies
139	Divide by 10 (optional)
140	Fraction: ⅓
141	
142	Finding the sum 5× table (optional)
143	
144	
145	
146	(16) 8 8 triplet and facts

Pupil's Book

Lesson Number	New Skills
133	
134	
135	Half dollar + dimes
136	
137	
138	(16) 9 7 triplet and facts Half dollar + pennies
139	
140	
141	Fraction: ⅓
142	
143	
144	
145	
146	(16) 8 8 triplet and facts

New Skills Listed by Lessons

Teacher's Manual

Lesson Number	New Skills
147	Equation: 2 cups = 1 pint
148	Divide by 5 (optional)
149	(17) 9 8 triplet and facts
150	Equation: 2 pints = 1 quart
151	$1\times$ table (optional)
152	
153	Reading Problem: difference Equation: 4 quarts = 1 gallon
154	
155	
156	
157	(18) 9 9 triplet and facts Equation: 16 ounces = 1 pound
158	
159	
160-170	Review

Pupil's Book

Lesson Number	New Skills
147	
148	
149	(17) 9 8 triplet and facts Equation: 2 cups = 1 pint
150	
151	Equation: 2 pints = 1 quart
152	
153	
154	
155	Equation: 4 quarts = 1 gallon
156	
157	(18) 9 9 triplet and facts
158	Equation: 16 ounces = 1 pound
159	
160-170	Review

Unit 3

Lessons 61–102

61

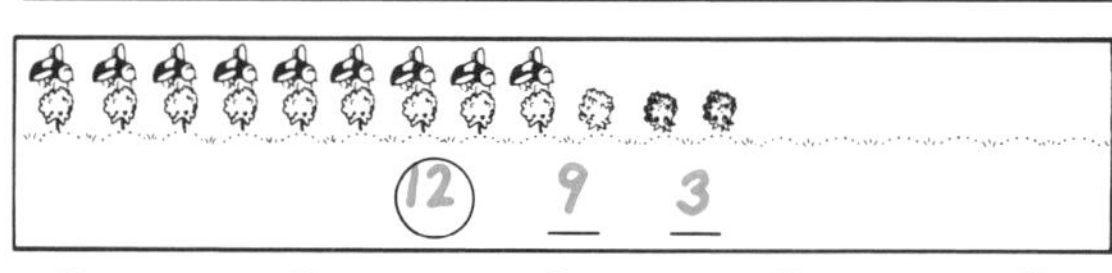

Trace and fill in the whole and parts.

Trace, answer, and write the facts.

"The law of the Lord is . . . sweeter . . . than honey." Psalm 19:7, 10
7

Before Class

Make (12) 9 3 flash cards for each child.

Tack the (12) 9 3 flash cards above the clover patch in this order:

12	12	9	3
−9	−3	+3	+9
3	9	12	12

Materials

12 blossoms, 9 with bees

Large clock

Chalkboard

92	32	45	63	23
33	65	32	53	12
+ 3	+31	+42	+ 2	+94

Class Time

1. **Count by 2's from 100 to 200.**
2. Point to Blossom 11 Chart.
   Say each triplet 3 times.
3. Stand near the clover patch.

(12) 9 3

   a. **How many pink clovers are in the patch?** 10
      We think—10 pink.
      2 more make __ altogether. 12
      We think—10 pink.
      1 less makes __ clovers with bees. 9
   b. Circle the clover with your finger.
      12 clovers in the patch;
      12 is the whole number.
      What part of the 12 has bees? 9
      What part of the 12 has no bees? 3
      The whole number is 12.
      Its parts are 9 and 3.
   c. **The triplet is (12) 9 3;**
      (12) 9 3 . . .

61

Extra Activity

Answer these facts.

9 +3 12	12 -9 3	12 -3 9	3 +9 12	12 -9 3	9 +3 12	12 -9 3	12 -3 9
12 -3 9	3 +9 12	12 -9 3	9 +3 12	12 -3 9	3 +9 12	9 +3 12	12 -9 3
12 -3 9	12 -9 3	3 +9 12	12 -9 3	9 +3 12	12 -3 9	12 -9 3	3 +9 12
12 -9 3	9 +3 12	12 -3 9	3 +9 12	12 -9 3	12 -3 9	9 +3 12	12 -9 3
12 -9 3	12 -3 9	12 -9 3	12 -3 9	12 -9 3	9 +3 12	3 +9 12	12 -9 3
		12 -9 3	3 +9 12	12 -3 9	12 -9 3	9 +3 12	12 -3 9

8

d. Point to the flash cards. **The facts are 12−9, 3; 12−3, 9; 9+3, 12; 3+9, 12 . . .**

4. **Say the triplets as I fill the bees.**
   (12) 9 3; (12) 9 3 . . .

5. Point to the (12) 9 3 flash cards again. **Say the triplet; then say the answer.**

6. Do the Column Addition samples.

7. Review time. Use the large clock.
   Answer together as I move the hands.

5:00	**5:30**	**7:00**	**7:30**
10:00	**10:30**	**12:30**	**2:00**
3:30	**6:00**	**8:30**	**11:30**

8. Assign Lesson 61.

Note: Make Blossom 12 Chart for Lesson 62.

Answer these problems.

32	33	33	64	74	22
53	22	21	32	21	14
+24	+62	+65	+33	+32	+93
109	117	119	129	127	129

14	44	55	23	35	42
53	31	32	72	60	55
+ 2	+ 2	+ 2	+ 4	+ 2	+ 2
69	77	89	99	97	99

Write the time.

9

Blacklines

Fact Hives #8

Triplets With Facts #3

Form A: 500–599

After Class

1. Give each child his (12) 9 3 flash cards.
2. Mixed Computation: **Think. Raise your hand to answer.** (Speak slowly.)

10−5+4=	9	**2+8−7=**	3
6+3−2=	7	**12−9+4=**	7
11−8+3=	6	**3+7−2=**	8
4+7−2=	9	**6+5−4=**	7
11−6+5=	10		

3. **Begin with 100. Count by 100's as I write. 100, 200, 300, 400, 500, 600, 700, 800, 900, 1,000.**

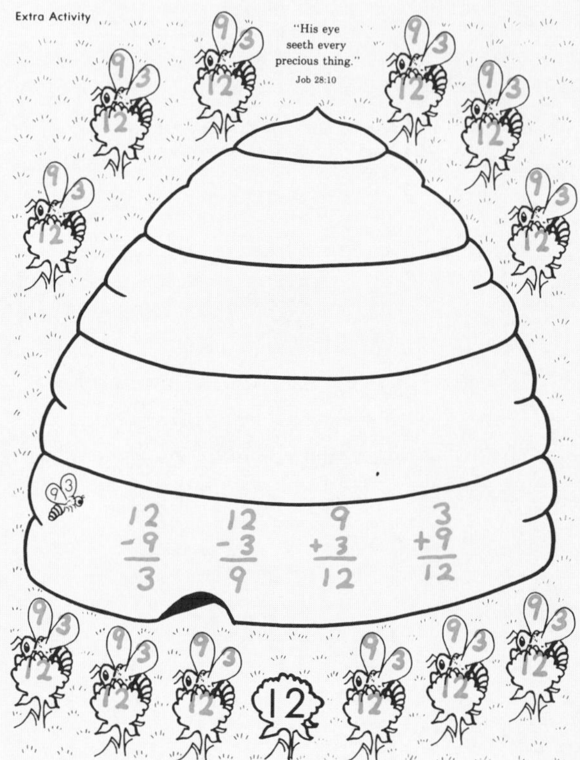

62

Fill in the whole and parts.

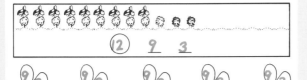

Trace, answer, and write the facts.

62
(12) 9 3
"The law of the Lord is . . . sweeter . . . than honey." Psalm 19:7, 10
11

Before Class

Tack bee (12) 9 3 on Blossom 12 Chart.
Mount it on the wall.

Materials

Addition and Subtraction 9–11 flash cards
9–11 and (12) 9 3 flash cards

Chalkboard

(ones)	569	703	4	152	87	630
(tens)	95	832	92	404	211	346
(hundreds)	943	185	362	79	667	801

Note: Encourage the children to refer to the Blossom Charts while working. Referral will cement *correct* answers in the child's mind and help solid learning to take place.

Class Time

1. Stand near the clover patch.

(12) 9 3

   Circle the clover with your finger.
   12 clovers in the patch;
   12 is the whole number.
   What part of the 12 has bees? 9
   What part of the 12 has no bees? 3
   12 is the whole number.
   Its parts are 9 and 3.
   a. **The triplet is (12) 9 3 . . .**
   b. **The facts are 12−9, 3; 12−3, 9; 9+3, 12; 3+9, 12 . . .**
2. Stand near the Blossom Charts.
   a. Drill the 11 triplets.
   b. Drill the 12 triplet.
   c. **Jump back and forth.**
   Drill (11) 9 2 and (12) 9 3.
3. Flash Addition and Subtraction 9–11 cards.
   Girls, answer the addition.
   Boys, answer the subtraction.

62

Answer these problems.

124 − 93 = 31	93 + 32 = 125	126 − 34 = 92	125 − 91 = 34	36 + 92 = 128	128 − 36 = 92
96 + 33 = 129	129 − 98 = 31	32 + 95 = 127	127 − 34 = 93	93 + 35 = 128	127 − 92 = 35
34 + 91 = 125	128 − 97 = 31	127 − 93 = 34	127 − 35 = 92	129 − 37 = 92	94 + 34 = 128
127 − 96 = 31	97 + 32 = 129	128 − 35 = 93	34 + 93 = 127	129 − 94 = 35	91 + 37 = 128
129 − 35 = 94	32 + 93 = 125	128 − 92 = 36	93 + 31 = 124	32 + 90 = 122	128 − 33 = 95
		31 + 91 = 122	126 − 31 = 95	129 − 93 = 36	94 + 30 = 124

12

4. Stand near the Place Value samples.
   a. **Read the numbers with me.**
   b. **Which place has the greatest numbers?**
      hundreds' place
   c. Have the children do the samples.
5. Review time.
   a. **60 minutes=__.** 1 hour
      30 minutes=__. ½ hour
   b. **1 hour has __.** 60 minutes
      ½ hour has __. 30 minutes
6. Do the Speed Drill in Lesson 62.
7. Assign Lesson 62.

Circle the numeral
in ones' place,
in tens' place,
in hundreds' place.

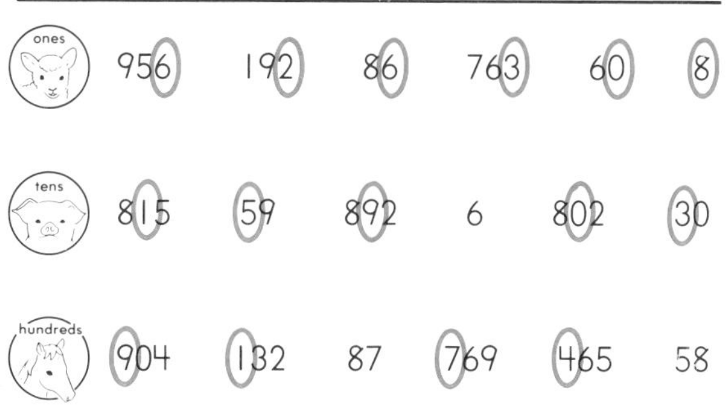

Write the time.

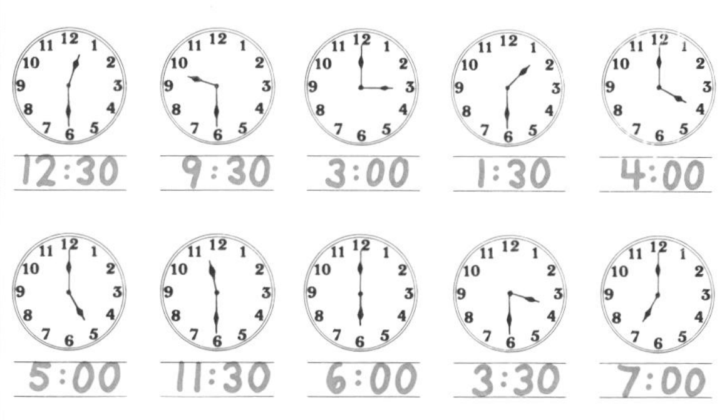

13

Blacklines

Fact Hives #8

Triplets With Facts #3

Number Words #1

After Class

		hundreds	tens	ones
1573	,			
1264	,			
1318	,			
1440	,			
1729	,			
1635	,			
1157	,			

1. Circle Drill: 9–11 and (12) 9 3 flash cards.
2. Stand near the grid on the board.
   a. Review the meaning of
      - •1 one—1 apple
      - •1 ten—1 bag of apples
      - •1 hundred—1 bushel of apples
   b. **Ones, tens, hundreds . . . Do you know what place comes next?** Write *thousands*.
   c. **Say each number and place as I fill the grid. 3 ones, 7 tens, 5 hundreds, 1 thousand . . .**

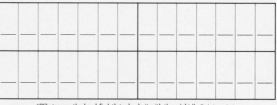

Speed Drill
3 + 9 = 12; 12 − 3 = 9; 9 + 3 = 12; 12 − 9 = 3; 9 + 3 = 12; 12 − 3 = 9
9 + 3 = 12; 3 + 9 = 12; 12 − 9 = 3; 3 + 9 = 12; 12 − 3 = 9; 12 − 9 = 3
3 + 9 = 12; 12 − 9 = 3; 12 − 3 = 9; 3 + 9 = 12; 12 − 9 = 3; 9 + 3 = 12; 12 − 3 = 9; 9 + 3 = 12
12 − 9 = 3; 9 + 3 = 12; 12 − 9 = 3; 12 − 3 = 9; 3 + 9 = 12; 12 − 9 = 3; 9 + 3 = 12; 3 + 9 = 12
"Whatsoever thy hand findeth to do, do it with thy might." Ecclesiastes 9:10
14

63

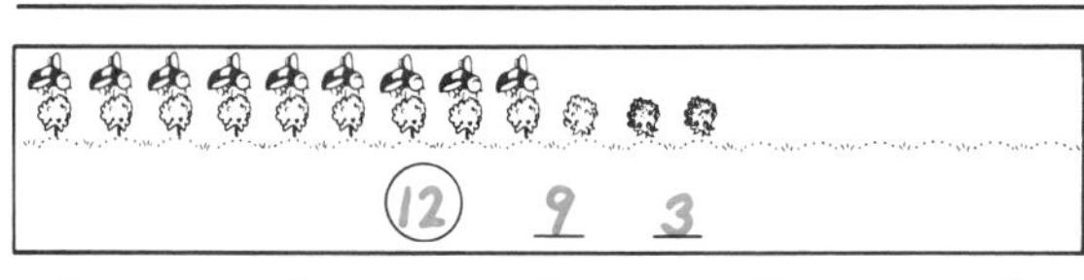

Fill in the whole and parts.

Trace, answer, and write the facts.

12 − 9 = 3 | 12 − 3 = 9 | 9 + 3 = 12 | 3 + 9 = 12

12 − 9 = 3 | 12 − 3 = 9 | 9 + 3 = 12 | 3 + 9 = 12

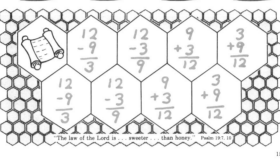

12 − 9 = 3 | 12 − 3 = 9 | 9 + 3 = 12 | 3 + 9 = 12

"The law of the Lord is . . . sweeter . . . than honey." Psalm 19:7, 10

15

Before Class

Materials

Large coins

11's and (12) 9 3 flash cards

Chalkboard

	thousands	hundreds	tens	ones
1000	,			
1470	,			
1568	,			
1824	,			
1399	,			
1612	,			

11	3	4	6	12	9
5	9	7	5	9	2
6	12	11	11	3	11
11	9	5	7	11	12
7	3	6	4	6	3
4	12	11	11	5	9

Class Time

1. Story Problems
   a. **Father had 12 steers. He sold 3. How many steers does he have now? Who can give us the whole problem?**
      12 steers − 3 steers = 9 steers.
   b. **9 cats drank milk from a green dish. 3 cats drank milk from a blue dish. How many cats were at both dishes? Who . . . ?**
      9 cats + 3 cats = 12 cats.
2. Stand near the clover patch.

   (12) 9 3

   Circle the clovers with your finger.
   12 clovers in the patch;
   12 is the whole number.
   What part of the 12 has bees? 9
   What part of the 12 has no bees? 3
   12 is the whole number.
   Its parts are 9 and 3.
   a. **The triplet is (12) 9 3 . . .**

63

Extra Activity

Count the first row.
Write the total.
Count the second row.
Write the total.
Add the two totals.

b. **The facts are 12−9, 3; 12−3, 9; 9+3, 12; 3+9, 12 . . .**

3. Drill the triplets on the Blossom 11 and 12 Charts.
4. Do the Computation samples. **Can you fill in the missing sign?**
5. Place Value
   a. **Ones, tens, hundreds,** (Drop your voice comma), **thousands . . .**
   b. Ask individuals to fill the grid as everyone says each number and its place.
      0 ones, 0 tens, 0 hundreds, 1 thousand . . .
   c. **Read the numbers together.**
      1,000, 1,470 . . .
6. Flash the large coins.
   a. **Quarter, penny, dime, nickel . . .**
   b. **25¢, 1¢, 10¢, 5¢ . . .**
7. Assign Lesson 63.

Answer these facts.

9	11	12	6	12	9	11	11
+3	−6	−3	+5	−9	+3	−6	−5
12	5	9	11	3	12	5	6

12	5	12	6	12	3	9	12
−3	+6	−9	+5	−3	+9	+3	−9
9	11	3	11	9	12	12	3

11	11	3	12	5	12	11	3
−5	−6	+9	−9	+6	−3	−6	+9
6	5	12	3	11	9	5	12

Write the time.

5:30 9:00 4:30 8:00 3:30

8:30 11:00 7:30 10:00 6:30

17

Blacklines

Fact Hives #8

Missing Whole or Parts #5

Number Words #1

After Class

1. Flash the 11's and the (12) 9 3 cards. **Say the triplet; then say the answer.**
2. Chalkboard Drill: **Write the number you hear.**
   - **The king of Canaan had 900 chariots of iron.** (Judges 4:3)
   - **King Pharaoh's 600 chariots were covered in the Red Sea.** (Exodus 14:7)
   - **The Syrians had 700 chariots.** (2 Samuel 10:18)
   - **King David took 1,000 chariots.** (2 Samuel 8:4)
   - **King Solomon had 1,400 chariots.** (2 Chronicles 1:14)

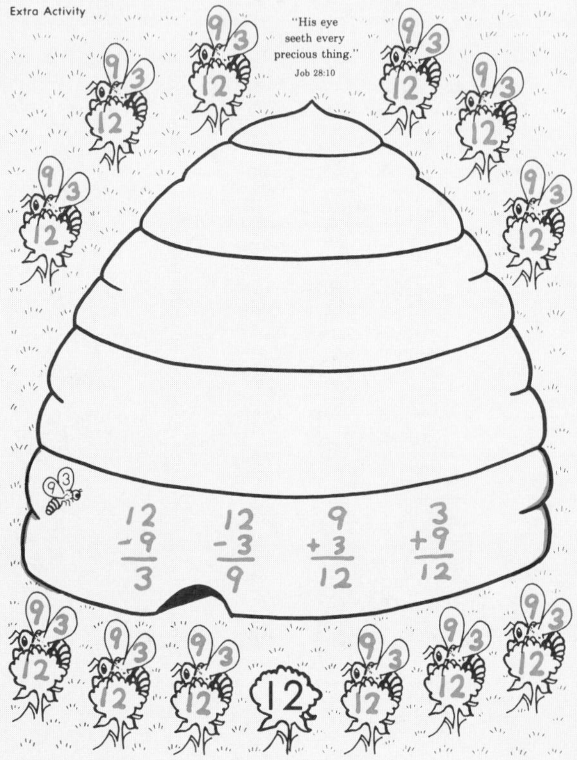

64

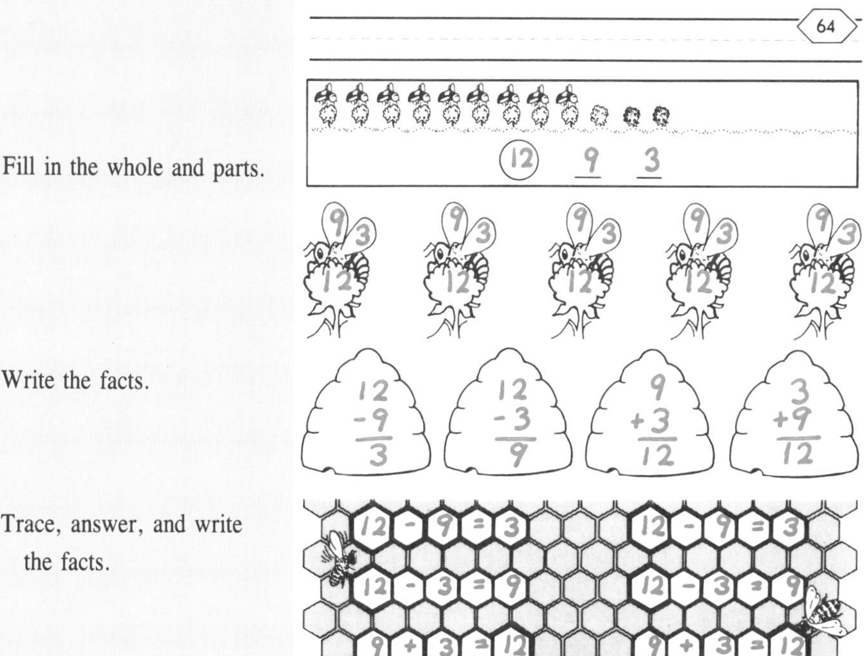

Fill in the whole and parts.
Write the facts.
Trace, answer, and write the facts.
"The law of the Lord is . . . sweeter . . . than honey." Psalm 19:7, 10
19

Before Class

Materials

Large clock

Chalkboard

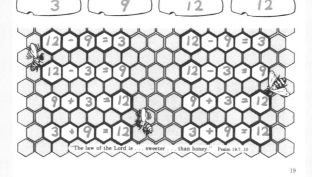

	thousands	hundreds	tens	ones
975	,			
1234	,			
1350	,			
892	,			
1764	,			
1458	,			

Class Time

1. Stand near the clover patch.

   While some worker bees fly out to the clover patch to sip nectar, other worker bees guard the hive.

   Who is the bees' enemy? A mouse is an enemy. He wants to steal honey from the hive. If a mouse dares to come in, the bees will sting and sting him until he dies.

2. | (12) 9 3 |
   |---|

   12 clovers in the patch;
   12 is the whole number.
   What part of the 12 has bees? 9
   What part of the 12 has no bees? 3
   12 is the whole number.
   Its parts are 9 and 3.

   a. **The triplet is (12) 9 3 . . .**
   b. Point to the first flash card.
      Close your eyes; say it 3 times.
      Drill each fact.

64

Fill in the missing whole or parts.

9 + 3 = 12	12 - 9 = 3	12 - 3 = 9
3 + 9 = 12	3 + 9 = 12	3 + 9 = 12
12 - 9 = 3	12 - 9 = 3	12 - 9 = 3
12 - 3 = 9	12 - 3 = 9	12 - 3 = 9
3 + 9 = 12	3 + 9 = 12	3 + 9 = 12
12 - 9 = 3	9 + 3 = 12	12 - 9 = 3

Speed Drill

Answer these problems.

6	3	1	4	8	3	7	1
3	2	2	5	1	6	2	1
+3	+5	+9	+2	+3	+3	+3	+9
12	10	12	11	12	12	12	11

5	9	2	4	5	1	1	2
4	0	7	5	3	8	6	1
+2	+3	+3	+3	+3	+3	+3	+9
11	12	12	12	11	12	10	12

20

3. Place Value
   a. **Read the numbers. 975 . . .**
   b. Have individuals fill the grid.
4. Review time. **Read the time as I move the hands on the clock. 12:00, 12:30, 4:30, 7:00, 8:30, 10:30, 11:00 . . .**
5. Do the Speed Drill in Lesson 64.
6. Assign Lesson 64.

Write the numbers in the correct places.

	thousands	hundreds	tens	ones
1583	1,	5	8	3
1815	1,	8	1	5
80	,		8	0
293	,	2	9	3
1325	1,	3	2	5
1784	1,	7	8	4
1623	1,	6	2	3

	thousands	hundreds	tens	ones
1639	1,	6	3	9
1298	1,	2	9	8
20	,		2	0
1315	1,	3	1	5
290	,	2	9	0
1324	1,	3	2	4
1816	1,	8	1	6

Write the time.

21

Blacklines

Missing Whole or Parts #5

Fact Form IV

Number Words #2

After Class

1. Have individuals count by 5's from 100 to 200.
2. Chalkboard Drill: **Write the problem you hear.**
   a. **Mother paid 45¢ for a plant and 53¢ for a flower pot. How much did Mother pay for both?**

      45¢ + 53¢ = 98¢

   b. **Father paid 72¢ for a pencil and 46¢ for a pen. How much did Father pay for both?**

      72¢ + 46¢ = 118¢

   c. **Joel and Nathan made cards for poor old Mrs. Smith. Joel pasted 34¢ in his card. Nathan pasted 95¢ in his card. How much money is that altogether?**

      34¢ + 95¢ = 129¢

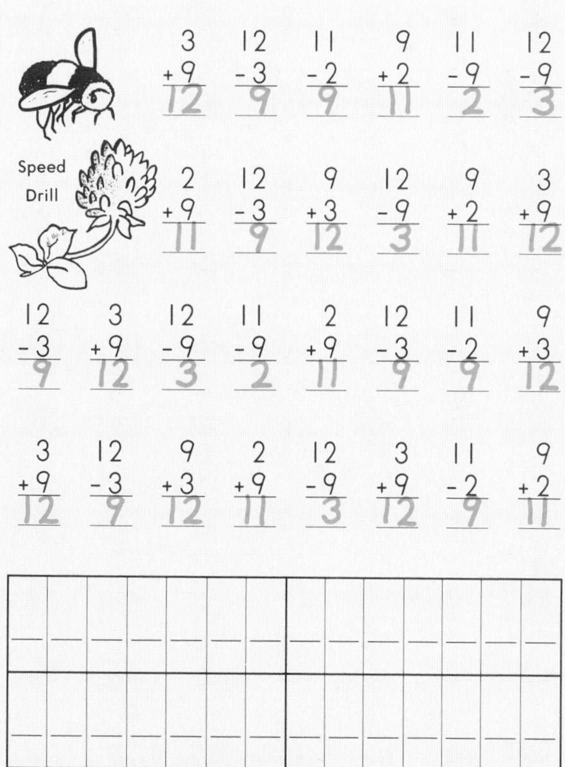

		3 + 9 = 12	12 - 3 = 9	11 - 2 = 9	9 + 2 = 11	11 - 9 = 2	12 - 9 = 3
		2 + 9 = 11	12 - 3 = 9	9 + 3 = 12	12 - 9 = 3	9 + 2 = 11	3 + 9 = 12
12 - 3 = 9	3 + 9 = 12	12 - 9 = 3	11 - 9 = 2	2 + 9 = 11	12 - 3 = 9	11 - 2 = 9	9 + 3 = 12
3 + 9 = 12	12 - 3 = 9	9 + 3 = 12	2 + 9 = 11	12 - 9 = 3	3 + 9 = 12	11 - 2 = 9	9 + 2 = 11

"Whatsoever thy hand findeth to do, do it with thy might." Ecclesiastes 9:10

22

65

65

Write the whole and parts.

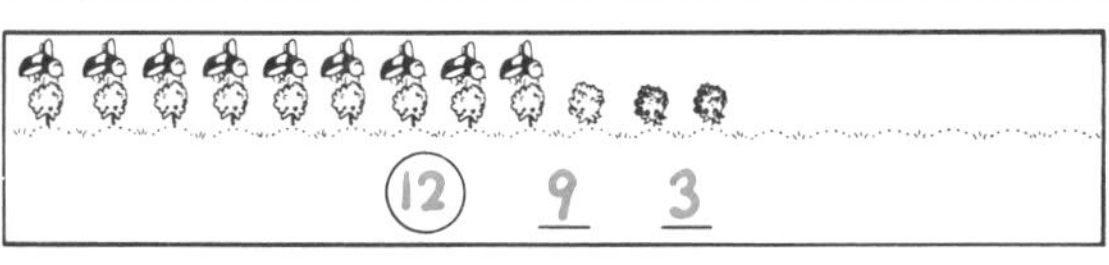

Write the facts.

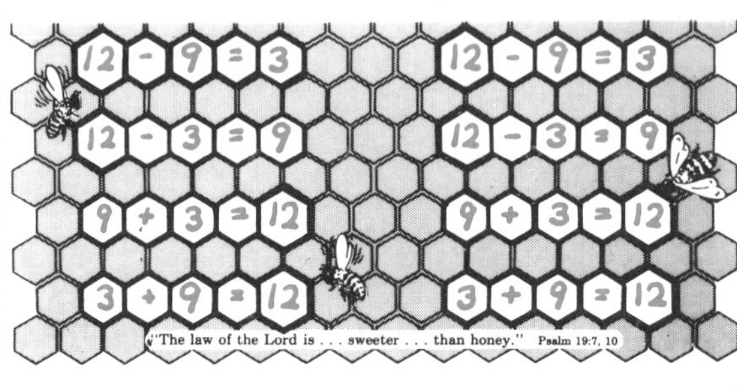

Trace, answer, and write the facts.

12 − 9 = 3　　12 − 9 = 3
12 − 3 = 9　　12 − 3 = 9
9 + 3 = 12　　9 + 3 = 12
3 + 9 = 12　　3 + 9 = 12

"The law of the Lord is . . . sweeter . . . than honey." Psalm 19:7, 10

23

Before Class

Materials

11's and (12) 9 3 flash cards

Large clock

Chalkboard

23	64	33	46	32	93
12	52	25	20	43	33
+94	+ 3	+61	+52	+42	+ 3

Class Time

1. Flash the 11's and (12) 9 3 cards. **Answer together.**
2. Do the Column Addition samples.
3. Stand near the clover patch.

(12) 9 3

   12 clovers in the patch;
   12 is the whole number.
   What part of the 12 has bees? 9
   What part of the 12 has no bees? 3
   12 is the whole number.
   Its parts are 9 and 3.

   a. **The triplet is (12) 9 3 . . .**
   b. **The facts are 12−9, 3; 12−3, 9; 9+3, 12; 3+9, 12 . . .**
4. Point to the Blossom 11 and 12 Charts. Drill all the triplets.

Extra Activity

Read the story.
Write the numbers in the beehive.
Write the label words on the lines.
Answer the problem.

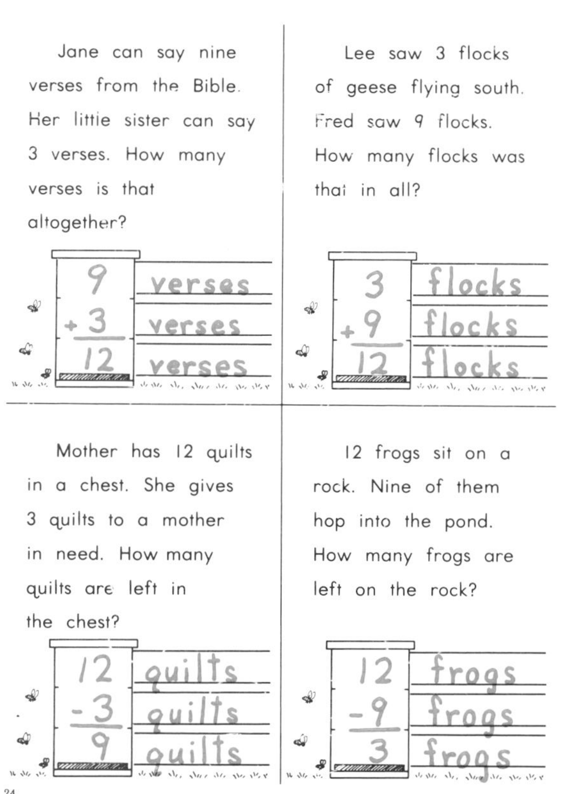

Jane can say nine verses from the Bible. Her little sister can say 3 verses. How many verses is that altogether?

9 verses
+3 verses
12 verses

Lee saw 3 flocks of geese flying south. Fred saw 9 flocks. How many flocks was that in all?

3 flocks
+9 flocks
12 flocks

Mother has 12 quilts in a chest. She gives 3 quilts to a mother in need. How many quilts are left in the chest?

12 quilts
-3 quilts
9 quilts

12 frogs sit on a rock. Nine of them hop into the pond. How many frogs are left on the rock?

12 frogs
-9 frogs
3 frogs

24

5. Review hour and half hour.
   a. Set the large clock at 3:00.
      In one hour it will be __. 4:00
      One hour ago it was __. 2:00
      In two hours it will be __. 5:00
      Two hours ago it was __. 1:00
      In ½ hour it will be __. 3:30
   b. Set the clock at 9:00 and ask the same questions.

6. Point to the Number Line.

a.	**10+1**	**10+4**	**10+7**
	10+2	**10+5**	**10+8**
	10+3	**10+6**	**10+9**
b.	**10+6**	**10+1**	**10+5**
	10+2	**10+4**	**10+3**
	10+9	**10+7**	**10+8**

7. Assign Lesson 65.

Note on ***After Class:*** Today addition and place value converge into the carrying process. The term "carry *over*" will be used to help the child remember which way to go when he carries. A ones' place number is carried over to tens' place when adding.

"Carry *over*" is a directional term that guides the child through this complex step in addition. Saying "*over*" as he does the calculation will help the child to establish the proper direction of transfer.

Answer these facts.

7	12	12	3	11	5	12	11
+4	-9	-3	+9	-7	+6	-9	-5
11	3	9	12	4	11	3	6

11	3	11	9	11	3	9	11
-4	+9	-6	+3	-4	+9	+3	-6
7	12	5	12	7	12	12	5

11	12	6	11	9	12	12	4
-5	-9	+5	-7	+3	-3	-9	+7
6	3	11	4	12	9	3	11

Write the numbers in the correct places.

	thousands	hundreds	tens	ones
1295	1,	2	9	5
37	,		3	7
1315	1,	3	1	5
290	,	2	9	0
1324	1,	3	2	4
1816	1,	8	1	6

	thousands	hundreds	tens	ones
1815	1,	8	1	5
380	,	3	8	0
1293	1,	2	9	3
1325	1,	3	2	5
1784	1,	7	8	4
1623	1,	6	2	3

25

Blacklines

Missing Whole or Parts #5

Fact Form IV

Number Words #2

After Class

33	26	12	68	39	54
+69	+95	+99	+23	+53	+47

1. Call the children to the Addition samples.
   a. **3+9=__.** Write 2.
      Carry *over* 1. 1+3=__; 4+6=__.
      Write 10.
   b. **6+5=__.** Write 1.
      Carry *over* 1. 1+2=__; 3+9=__. Write 12.
   c. Have the children say **carry *over* 1** as they complete the samples.
2. Have individuals count by hundreds to 1,000.

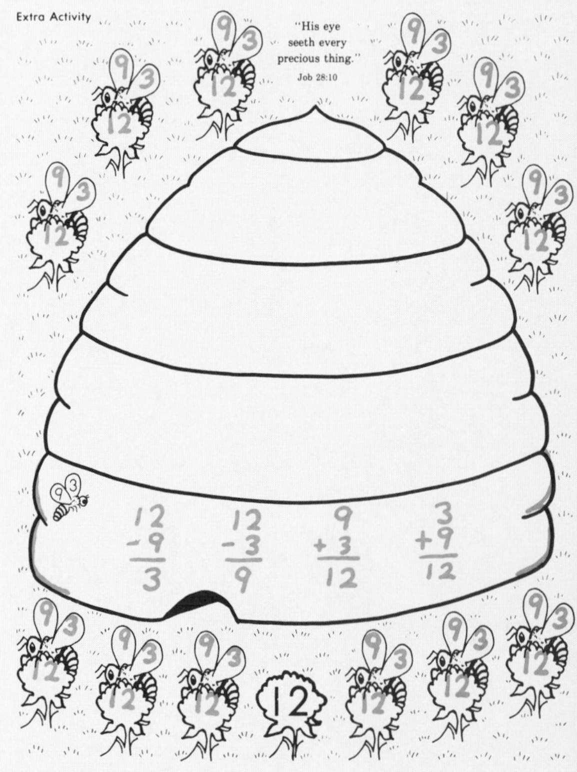

66

Trace the whole and parts.

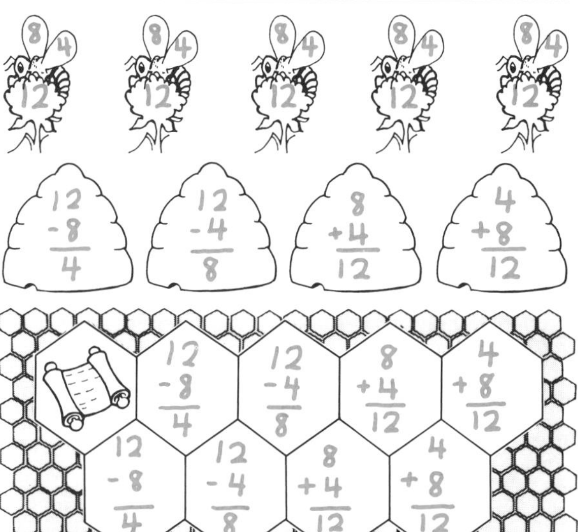

Trace, answer, and write the facts.

"The law of the Lord is . . . sweeter . . . than honey." Psalm 19:7, 10

27

Before Class

Make (12) 8 4 flash cards for each child.

Tack (12) 8 4 flash cards above the clover patch in this order:

12	12	8	4
−8	−4	+4	+8
4	8	12	12

Materials

12 blossoms, 8 with bees

Large clock

Chalkboard

43	82	36	27	49	45
+69	+39	+74	+94	+53	+66

Class Time

1. **Count by 2's to 250.** Have responsive counting. **I will say 2; you say 4 . . .**
2. Stand near the clover patch.

   (12) 8 4

   a. **How many pink clovers are in the patch?** 10
   We think—10 pink.
   2 more makes __ altogether. 12
   We think—10 pink.
   2 less makes __ with bees. 8

   b. Circle the clover with your finger.
   12 clovers in the patch;
   12 is the whole number.
   What part of the 12 has bees? 8
   What part of the 12 has no bees? 4
   12 is the whole number.
   Its parts are 8 and 4.

66

Answer these facts.

4 + 8 = 12	12 − 8 = 4	12 − 4 = 8	8 + 4 = 12	12 − 8 = 4	4 + 8 = 12	12 − 4 = 8	12 − 8 = 4
12 − 4 = 8	8 + 4 = 12	12 − 8 = 4	4 + 8 = 12	12 − 4 = 8	8 + 4 = 12	4 + 8 = 12	12 − 8 = 4
12 − 8 = 4	12 − 4 = 8	8 + 4 = 12	12 − 8 = 4	4 + 8 = 12	12 − 4 = 8	12 − 8 = 4	8 + 4 = 12
12 − 4 = 8	4 + 8 = 12	12 − 8 = 4	8 + 4 = 12	12 − 8 = 4	12 − 4 = 8	4 + 8 = 12	12 − 8 = 4
12 − 8 = 4	12 − 4 = 8	12 − 8 = 4	12 − 4 = 8	12 − 8 = 4	4 + 8 = 12	8 + 4 = 12	12 − 8 = 4
		12 − 8 = 4	8 + 4 = 12	12 − 4 = 8	12 − 8 = 4	4 + 8 = 12	12 − 8 = 4

28

c. **The triplet is (12) 8 4 . . .**

d. Point to the flash cards. **The facts are 12−8, 4; 12−4, 8; 8+4, 12; 4+8, 12 . . .**

3. **Say the triplets as I fill the clover and bees. (12) 8 4 . . .**
4. Point to the flash cards again. **Say the triplet; then say the answer.**
5. **Say the (12) 9 3 and (12) 8 4 facts as I fill the beehive.**
6. Do the Carry *over* samples.
7. Do the Speed Drill in Lesson 66.
8. Assign Lesson 66.

66

Write the numbers in the correct places.

	thousands	hundreds	tens	ones
1948	1,	9	4	8
306	_,	3	0	6
1680	1,	6	8	0
93	_,	_	9	3
1945	1,	9	4	5
1784	1,	7	8	4
1623	1,	6	2	3

	thousands	hundreds	tens	ones
639	_,	6	3	9
1582	1,	5	8	2
607	_,	6	0	7
1315	1,	3	1	5
1290	1,	2	9	0
324	_,	3	2	4
1816	1,	8	1	6

Write the time.

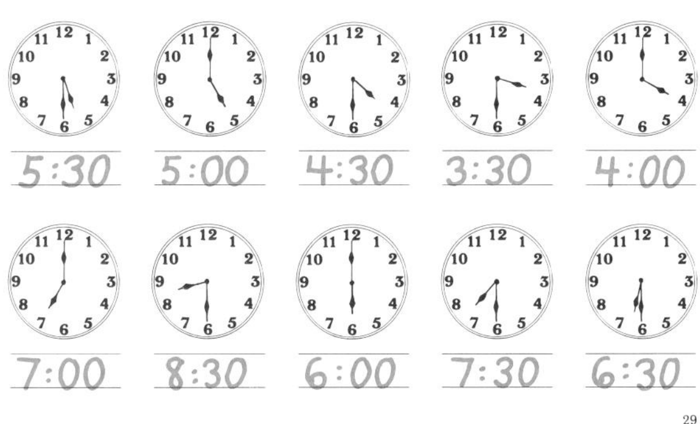
5:30 5:00 4:30 3:30 4:00

7:00 8:30 6:00 7:30 6:30

29

Blacklines

Fact Hives #9

Triplets With Facts #4

Number Facts #8

After Class

1. Give each child his (12) 8 4 flash cards.
2. Half hour
   a. Set the large clock at 8:00.
   In ½ hour it will be __. 8:30
   b. Move the hands to 8:30.
   It is ½ hour from 12 down to 6.
   It is a ½ from 6 up to 12.
   c. Set the clock at
   - 9:00 **In ½ hour it will be __.**
   - 9:30 **In ½ hour it will be __.**
   - 10:00 **In ½ hour it will be __.**

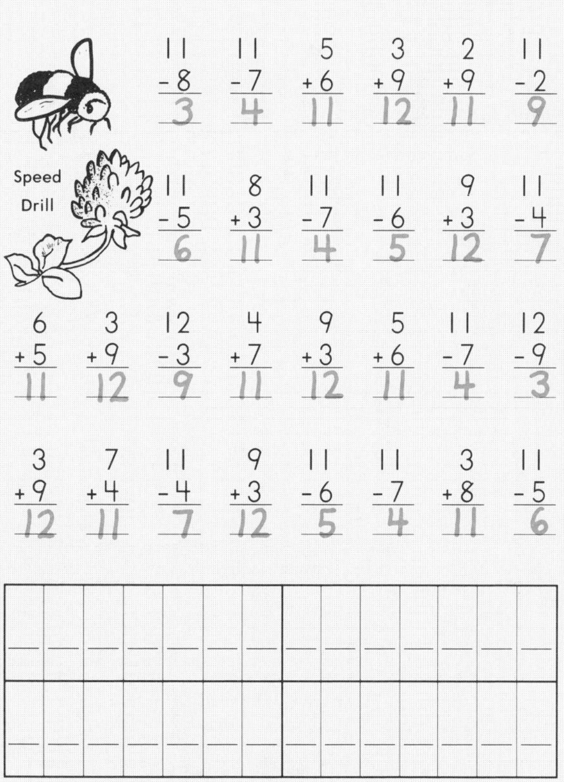
Speed Drill

11	11	5	3	2	11
-8	-7	+6	+9	+9	-2
3	4	11	12	11	9
11	8	11	11	9	11
-5	+3	-7	-6	+3	-4
6	11	4	5	12	7

6	3	12	4	9	5	11	12
+5	+9	-3	+7	+3	+6	-7	-9
11	12	9	11	12	11	4	3
3	7	11	9	11	11	3	11
+9	+4	-4	+3	-6	-7	+8	-5
12	11	7	12	5	4	11	6

"Whatsoever thy hand findeth to do, do it with thy might." Ecclesiastes 9:10

30

67

67

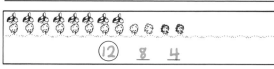

Fill in the whole and parts.

(12) 8 4

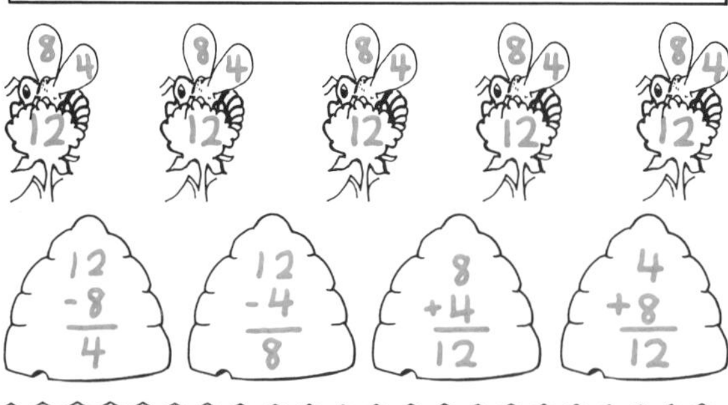

Trace, answer, and write the facts.

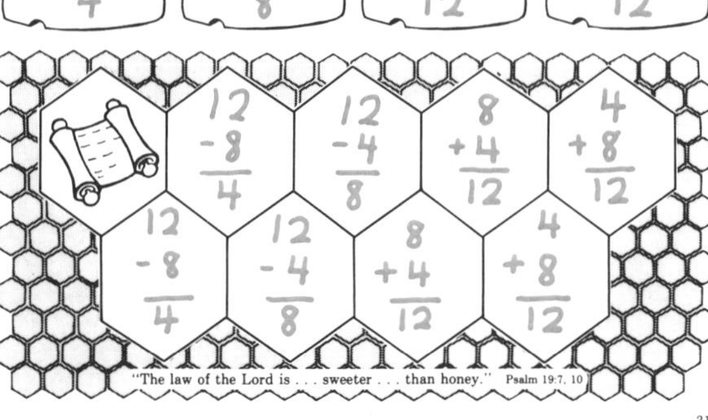

"The law of the Lord is . . . sweeter . . . than honey." Psalm 19:7, 10

31

Before Class

Add (12) 8 4 bee to Blossom 12 Chart.

Materials

*11's and 12's flash cards

Addition and Subtraction 9's–12's flash cards

Chalkboard

36	53	77	43	25	49
+85	+49	+44	+67	+95	+53

__+8=12	__−3=9
6+__=11	__+5=11
12−__=4	11−6=__
__+9=12	4+__=12

*When no particular flash cards are specified, use those you have introduced thus far.

Class Time

1. Stand near the clover patch.

   (12) 8 4

   12 clovers in the patch;
   12 is the whole number.
   What part of the 12 has bees? 8
   What part of the 12 has no bees? 4
   12 is the whole number.
   Its parts are 8 and 4.

   a. **The triplet is (12) 8 4 . . .**
   b. **The facts are 12−8, 4; 12−4, 8; 8+4, 12; 4+8, 12 . . .**

2. Stand near the Blossom Charts.

   a. Point to Blossom 11 Chart.

      (11) 9 2
      (11) 8 3
      (11) 7 4
      (11) 6 5 . . .

   b. Point to Blossom 12 Chart.

      (12) 9 3; (12) 8 4 . . .

67

Extra Activity

Answer these problems.

129 − 88 = 41	84 + 45 = 129	129 − 46 = 83	127 − 83 = 44	42 + 86 = 128	129 − 42 = 87
83 + 43 = 126	128 − 83 = 45	43 + 82 = 125	129 − 46 = 83	85 + 42 = 127	129 − 83 = 46
48 + 81 = 129	128 − 87 = 41	128 − 84 = 44	128 − 45 = 83	128 − 41 = 87	88 + 40 = 128
129 − 84 = 45	42 + 84 = 126	128 − 45 = 83	81 + 44 = 125	128 − 82 = 46	43 + 84 = 127
129 − 89 = 40	82 + 42 = 124	128 − 48 = 80	44 + 83 = 127	86 + 42 = 128	129 − 88 = 41
		43 + 85 = 128	125 − 84 = 41	127 − 47 = 80	82 + 45 = 127

32

3. Flash the 11's and 12's cards.
   Answer together.
4. Do the Missing Whole or Parts samples.
5. Do the Carry *over* samples.
6. Story Problems
   a. **John hung a bird feeder in the tree. 12 birds came to eat. 4 of them were blue. How many birds were not blue?**
      12 birds − 4 birds = 8 birds.
   b. **The 12 birds ate and ate. Some ate seeds from the feeder. Some ate seeds from the ground. Then a black cat came. 8 birds flew away. How many birds did not fly away?**
      12 birds − 8 birds = 4 birds.
7. Assign Lesson 67.

Answer these problems.
Carry *over* in every problem.

58 + 44 = 102	35 + 86 = 121	84 + 36 = 120	39 + 63 = 102	77 + 43 = 120	27 + 94 = 121
43 + 69 = 112	18 + 92 = 110	66 + 45 = 111	74 + 38 = 112	24 + 87 = 111	35 + 75 = 110

Read the story.
Write the numbers in the beehive.
Write the label words on the lines.
Answer the problem.

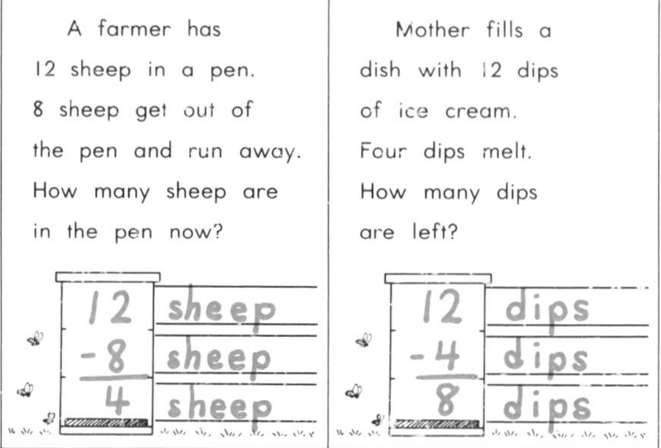

A farmer has 12 sheep in a pen. 8 sheep get out of the pen and run away. How many sheep are in the pen now?	Mother fills a dish with 12 dips of ice cream. Four dips melt. How many dips are left?
12 sheep − 8 sheep 4 sheep	12 dips − 4 dips 8 dips

33

Blacklines

Fact Hives #9
Triplets With Facts #4
Number Facts #8

After Class

1. Circle Drill: Addition and Subtraction 9–11 and 12's flash cards.
2. Chalkboard Drill: **Write 546. Change it to 946, 943, 913, 713, 703, 707, 607, 677, 1,677, 1,277, 1,274.**

Extra Activity
"His eye seeth every precious thing."
Job 28:10
12 − 8 = 4
12 − 4 = 8
8 + 4 = 12
4 + 8 = 12
12 − 9 = 3
12 − 3 = 9
9 + 3 = 12
3 + 9 = 12
34

68

Fill in the whole and parts.

Trace, answer, and write the facts.

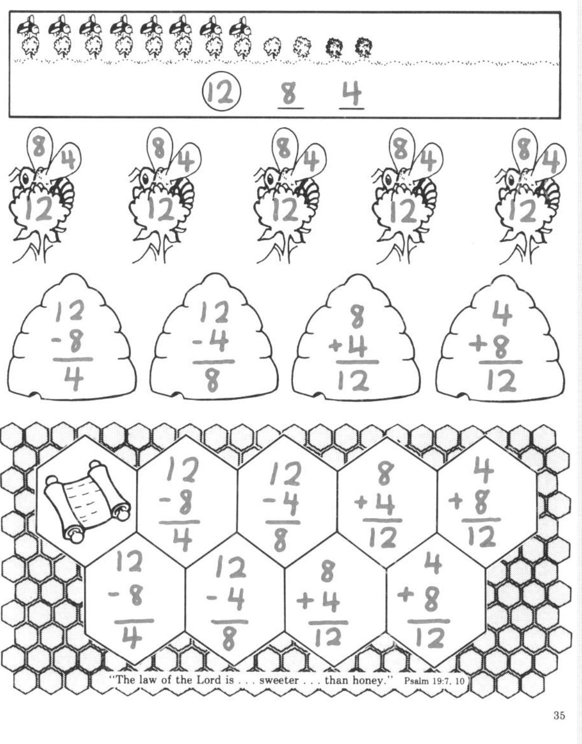
68
(12) 8 4
"The law of the Lord is . . . sweeter . . . than honey." Psalm 19:7, 10
35

Before Class

Chalkboard

(25¢)( )( ) (1¢)( )( )( )( ) ____

(10¢)( )( ) (5¢) + ____

(10¢)( )( )( )( )( )( ) (5¢) ____

(25¢) (1¢)( )( )( )( )( )( ) + ____

____	243	____	____	____	247	____
____	____	100	____	____	____	120
88	____	____	____	96	____	____
____	180	____	____	____	220	____

Class Time

1. **Count by 100's to 1,000.**
   100, 200 . . .
2. Do the Missing Number samples.
   Decide if you should count by 1's, 2's, 5's, or 10's.
3. Stand near the clover patch.

(12) 8 4

   Circle the clover with your finger.
   12 clovers in the patch;
   12 is the whole number.
   What part of the 12 has bees? 8
   What part of the 12 has no bees? 4
   12 is the whole number.
   Its parts are 8 and 4.
   a. **The triplet is (12) 8 4 . . .**
   b. **The facts are 12−8, 4; 12−4, 8; 8+4, 12; 4+8, 12 . . .**

68

Count the first row.
Write the total.
Count the second row.
Write the total.
Add the two totals.

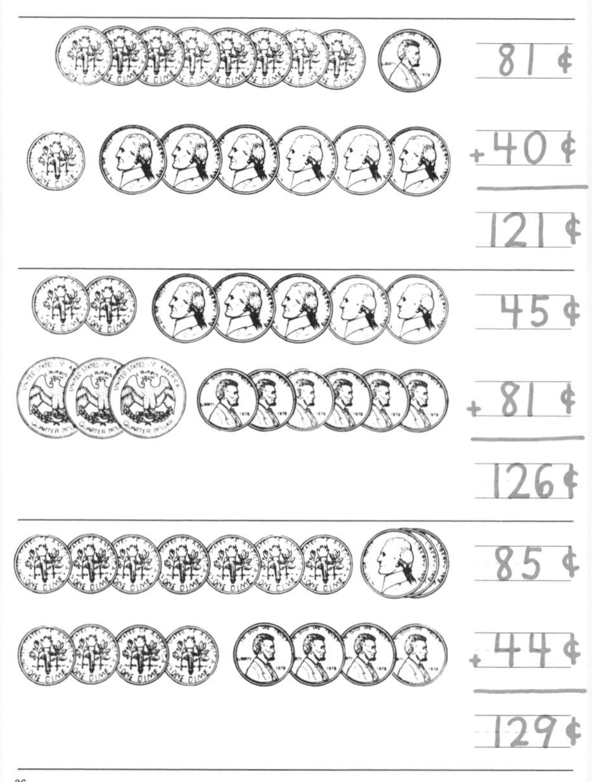

4. Point to Blossom 11 and 12 Charts.
   a. **Jump back and forth.**
      (11) 9 2
      (12) 9 3
      (11) 9 2 . . .
   b. **Jump back and forth.**
      (11) 8 3
      (12) 8 4
      (11) 8 3 . . .
5. a. **Can we say the 11 triplets by memory?**
      (11) 9 2
      (11) 8 3
      (11) 7 4
      (11) 6 5
   b. **Can we say the 12 triplets?**
      (12) 9 3; (12) 8 4 . . .
6. **Count and add the Money samples with me.**
7. Do the Speed Drill in Lesson 68.
8. Assign Lesson 68.

Answer these problems.
Carry *over* in every problem.

39 + 63	35 + 86	77 + 43	43 + 69	35 + 75	66 + 45
102	121	120	112	110	111

18 + 92	74 + 38	84 + 36	27 + 94	58 + 44	24 + 87
110	112	120	121	102	111

Write the numbers in the correct places.

	thousands	hundreds	tens	ones
1629	1,	6	2	9
1815	1,	8	1	5
600	_,	6	0	0
93	_,		9	3
1325	1,	3	2	5
1784	1,	7	8	4
1593	1,	5	9	3

	thousands	hundreds	tens	ones
39	_,		3	9
1298	1,	2	9	8
820	_,	8	2	0
1315	1,	3	1	5
290	_,	2	9	0
1324	1,	3	2	4
1976	1,	9	7	6

37

Blacklines

Fact Hives #10

Missing Whole or Parts #6

Number Facts #8

After Class

53 + 29	24 + 95	38 + 34	36 + 84	53 + 64	85 + 43	45 + 56

1. Call the children to the Addition samples.
   a. **3+9=__.** Write 2.
      Carry *over* 1. . . .
   b. **4+5=__.** Write 9.
      Do we have anything to carry *over*?
      2+9=__. Write 11.
   c. Have the children finish the samples. **Think. Do I have something to carry *over*?**
2. Review time.
   a. **60 minutes=__.** 1 hour
      30 minutes=__. ½ hour
   b. **1 hour has __.** 60 minutes
      1/2 hour has __. 30 minutes
   c. Set the clock at
      •6:30 **In ½ hour it will be __.**
      •9:30 **In ½ hour it will be __.**

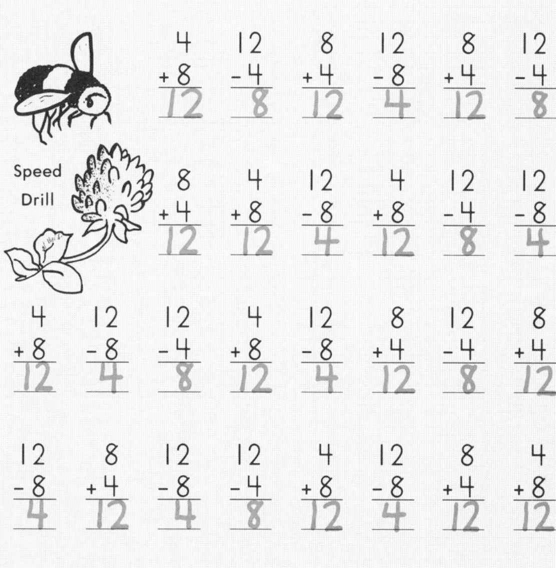
Speed Drill

4 + 8	12 − 4	8 + 4	12 − 8	8 + 4	12 − 4
12	8	12	4	12	8

8 + 4	4 + 8	12 − 8	4 + 8	12 − 4	12 − 8
12	12	4	12	8	4

4 + 8	12 − 8	12 − 4	4 + 8	12 − 8	8 + 4	12 − 4	8 + 4
12	4	8	12	4	12	8	12

12 − 8	8 + 4	12 − 8	12 − 4	4 + 8	12 − 8	8 + 4	4 + 8
4	12	4	8	12	4	12	12

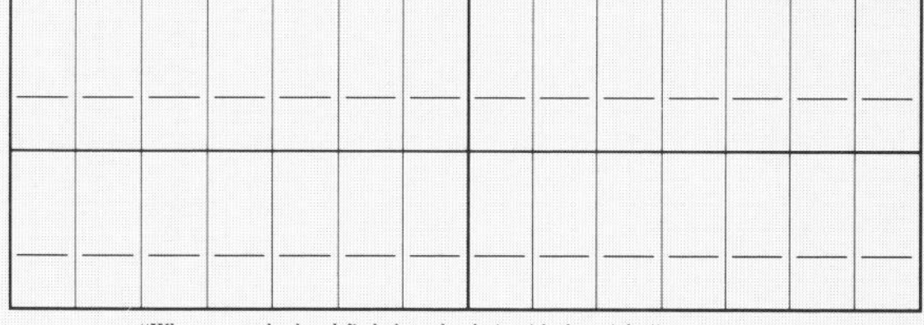

"Whatsoever thy hand findeth to do, do it with thy might." Ecclesiastes 9:10

38

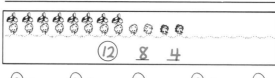

69

Fill in the whole and parts.

(12) 8 4

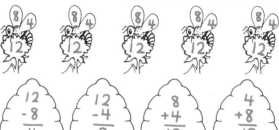

Write the facts.

12	12	8	4
−8	−4	+4	+8
4	8	12	12

Trace, answer, and write the facts.

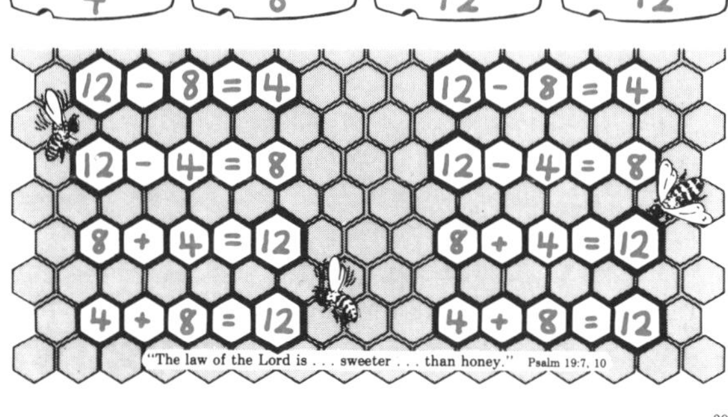

12 − 8 = 4
12 − 4 = 8
8 + 4 = 12
4 + 8 = 12
"The law of the Lord is . . . sweeter . . . than honey." Psalm 19:7, 10

39

Before Class

Materials

9's–12's flash cards

Chalkboard

43	59	24	35	56	42	76
+75	+43	+68	+94	+54	+87	+45

Class Time

1. Double Drill: 9's–12's flash cards.
2. Do the Addition samples. **Think. Do I have something to carry *over*?**
3. Stand near the clover patch.

   (12) 8 4

   Circle the clover with your finger.
   12 clovers in the patch;
   12 is the whole number.
   What part of the 12 has bees? 8
   What part of the 12 has no bees? 4
   12 is the whole number.
   Its parts are 8 and 4.
   a. **The triplet is (12) 8 4 . . .**
   b. **The facts are 12−8, 4; 12−4, 8; 8+4, 12; 4+8, 12 . . .**
4. **Begin with triplet (12) 9 3. Say the facts as I fill the beehive.**

69

Extra Activity

Fill in the missing whole or parts.

12 - 8 = 4	12 - 4 = 8	8 + 4 = 12
12 - 4 = 8	8 + 4 = 12	4 + 8 = 12
4 + 8 = 12	4 + 8 = 12	12 - 8 = 4
12 - 8 = 4	12 - 4 = 8	12 - 4 = 8
8 + 4 = 12	8 + 4 = 12	4 + 8 = 12
12 - 8 = 4	4 + 8 = 12	12 - 8 = 4

Answer these problems.

6	3	4	2	5	2	7	3
2	1	3	6	2	2	1	4
+4	+8	+4	+4	+4	+8	+4	+3
12	12	11	12	11	12	12	10

3	1	3	5	4	1	4	2
5	3	2	3	1	7	0	4
+4	+8	+6	+4	+6	+4	+8	+5
12	12	11	12	11	12	12	11

40

5. **Answer together. What number belongs on the blank?**
(Say *blank* for each blank.)

12, 9 __	**12 __ 4**	**__ 8, 4**
11, 9 __	**11 __ 3**	**__ 8, 3**
12, 8 __	**12 __ 3**	**__ 9, 2**
11, 8 __	**11 __ 2**	**__ 9, 3**

6. Assign Lesson 69.

Answer these problems.
Carry *over* in every problem.

84 + 36 = 120	35 + 86 = 121	39 + 63 = 102	74 + 38 = 112	27 + 94 = 121	77 + 43 = 120
18 + 92 = 110	66 + 45 = 111	43 + 69 = 112	58 + 44 = 102	24 + 87 = 111	35 + 75 = 110

Write the time.

Blacklines

Fact Hives #10

Missing Whole or Parts #6

Fact Form III

After Class

thousands	hundreds	tens	ones

Call the children to the grid on the board.

a. **When I call your name, come and write the number I say in the grid.** Use these numbers: **834; 1,265; 1,306; 1,529; 978; 1,150; 1,643; 781; 92; 1,417.**

b. **Find the number with 5 tens.** Have a child point to the number and read it. **Find the number with 2 hundreds . . .**

1 one — **9 ones**

0 tens — **4 hundreds . . .**

70

Fill in the whole and parts.

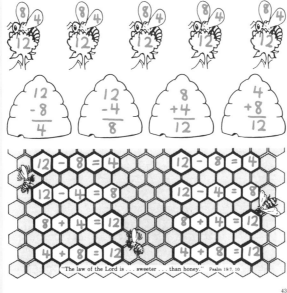

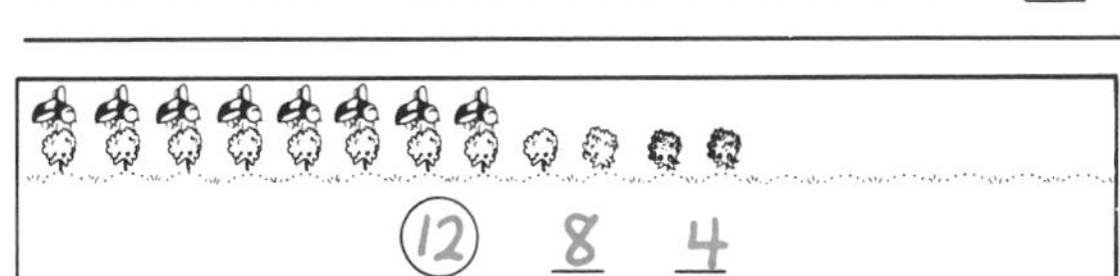

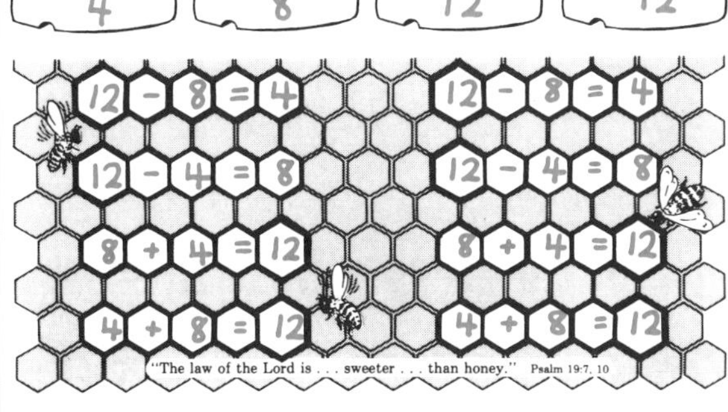

Write the facts.

12 − 8 = 4   12 − 4 = 8   8 + 4 = 12   4 + 8 = 12

Trace, answer, and write the facts.

12 − 8 = 4   12 − 8 = 4
12 − 4 = 8   12 − 4 = 8
8 + 4 = 12   8 + 4 = 12
4 + 8 = 12   4 + 8 = 12

"The law of the Lord is . . . sweeter . . . than honey." Psalm 19:7, 10

43

Before Class

Materials

11 blossoms
12 blossoms
11's and 12's flash cards

Chalkboard

63	17	83	89	76	34
+49	+94	+45	+32	+45	+85

Class Time

1. Call the children to the clover patch.

   God sent bread to the children of Israel. It was delicious! It tasted like wafers made with honey. Do you know what the children of Israel called it?

   Manna (Exodus 16:31)

2. Stand near the clover patch.

   (11) 9 2

   The whole number is __.
   Its parts are __ and __.
   The triplet is (11) 9 2 . . .

3. (11) 8 3

   The whole number is __.
   Its parts are __ and __.
   The triplet is (11) 8 3 . . .

4. (11) 7 4

   The whole number is __.
   Its parts are __ and __.
   The triplet is (11) 7 4 . . .

Read the story.
Write the numbers
in the beehive.
Write the label words
on the lines.
Answer the problem.

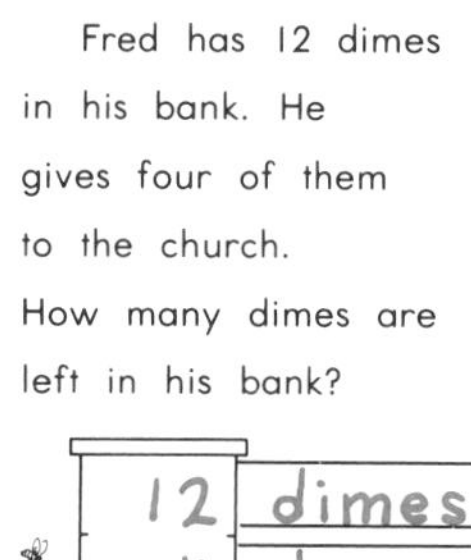

Fred has 12 dimes in his bank. He gives four of them to the church. How many dimes are left in his bank?

12 dimes
- 4 dimes
8 dimes

A mouse slips into a hive. 8 bees sting the mouse. Then four more bees sting it. How many bees is that in all?

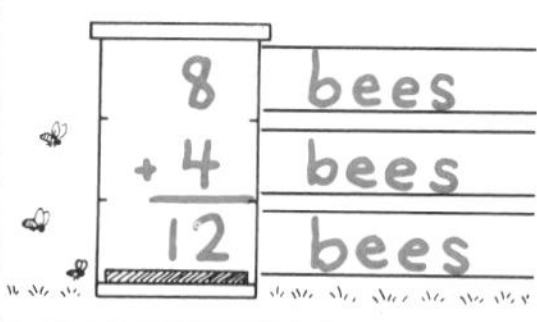

8 bees
+ 4 bees
12 bees

On the way to school Mark saw four trucks with pigs and 8 trucks with hens. How many trucks was that altogether?

4 trucks
+ 8 trucks
12 trucks

12 children ride in a van. The van stops at school, and 8 children get out. How many children are in the van now?

12 children
- 8 children
4 children

44

5. | (11) 6 5 |

The whole number is __.
Its parts are __ and __.
The triplet is (11) 6 5 . . .

6. | (12) 9 3 |

The whole number is __.
Its parts are __ and __.
The triplet is (12) 9 3 . . .

7. | (12) 8 4 |

The whole number is __.
Its parts are __ and __.
The triplet is (12) 8 4 . . .

8. Flash 11's and 12's cards.
Answer together.

9. Do the Addition samples.

10. Review time.
   a. **Father studied his Sunday school lesson from 7:00 to 8:00. How long was that?**
   1 hour or 60 minutes
   b. **Mervin studied his Sunday school lesson from 7:30 to 8:00. How long was that?**
   ½ hour or 30 minutes

11. Do the Speed Drill in Lesson 70.

12. Assign Lesson 70.

70

Answer these problems.
Carry *over* in some problems.

70					
68	35	84	39	78	96
+44	+83	+36	+63	+44	+33
112	118	120	102	122	129
83	32	88	44	76	52
+29	+97	+34	+58	+44	+66
112	129	122	102	120	118
54	44	85	53	95	42
63	30	43	32	32	75
+ 2	+ 2	+ 1	+ 1	+ 0	+ 2
119	76	129	86	127	119
32	82	33	44	23	88
93	42	51	82	51	40
+ 4	+ 3	+ 2	+ 3	+ 2	+ 1
129	127	86	129	76	129

45

Blacklines

Fact Hives #10

Missing Whole or Parts #6

After Class

1. **Count by 2's from 100–200.**
2. Chalkboard Drill: **Think. Write only the answer.**

37+1=	**40+1=**	**104+1=**
56+1=	**19+1=**	**125+1=**
93+1=	**68+1=**	**181+1=**

		4 +8 12	12 -4 8	12 -3 9	9 +3 12	12 -9 3	12 -8 4
		3 +9 12	12 -3 9	8 +4 12	12 -8 4	9 +3 12	4 +8 12
12 -4 8	4 +8 12	12 -8 4	12 -9 3	3 +9 12	12 -3 9	12 -4 8	8 +4 12
4 +8 12	12 -4 8	8 +4 12	3 +9 12	12 -8 4	4 +8 12	12 -3 9	9 +3 12

"Whatsoever thy hand findeth to do, do it with thy might." Ecclesiastes 9:10

46

Trace and fill in the whole and parts.

Trace, answer, and write the facts.

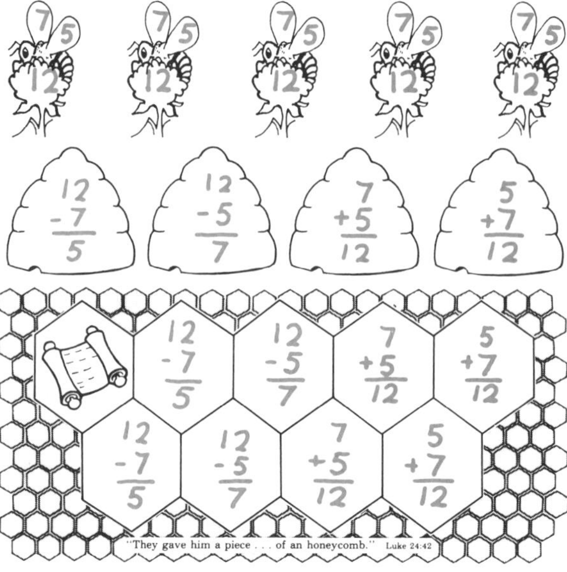
71
(12) 7 5
"They gave him a piece . . . of an honeycomb." Luke 24:42
47

Before Class

Make (12) 7 5 flash cards for each child.

Tack the (12) 7 5 flash cards above the clover patch in this order:

12 −7 = 5	12 −5 = 7	7 +5 = 12	5 +7 = 12

Materials

12 blossoms, 7 with bees

Chalkboard

73	44	28	93	46	65	19	64
+39	+83	+54	+36	+45	+43	+93	+38

Class Time

1. Call the children to the Blossom 11 and 12 Charts. **Say the triplets.**
2. Stand near the clover patch.

   (12) 7 5

   a. **How many pink clovers are in the patch?** 10
   We think—10 pink.
   2 more make __ altogether. 12
   We think—10 pink.
   3 less make __ clovers with bees. 7

   b. **12 clovers in the patch;**
   12 is the whole number.
   What part of the 12 has bees? 7
   What part of the 12 has no bees? 5
   12 is the whole number.
   Its parts are 7 and 5.

   c. **The triplet is (12) 7 5;**
   (12) 7 5 . . .

71

Answer these facts.

5 +7 12	12 -7 5	12 -5 7	7 +5 12	12 -7 5	5 +7 12	12 -5 7	12 -7 5
12 -5 7	7 +5 12	12 -7 5	5 +7 12	12 -5 7	7 +5 12	5 +7 12	12 -7 5
12 -7 5	12 -5 7	7 +5 12	12 -7 5	5 +7 12	12 -5 7	12 -7 5	7 +5 12
12 -5 7	5 +7 12	12 -7 5	7 +5 12	12 -7 5	12 -5 7	5 +7 12	12 -5 7
12 -7 5	12 -5 7	12 -7 5	12 -5 7	12 -7 5	5 +7 12	7 +5 12	12 -7 5
		12 -5 7	7 +5 12	12 -5 7	12 -7 5	5 +7 12	12 -7 5

48

d. Point to the flash cards. **The facts are 12−7, 5; 12−5, 7; 7+5, 12; 5+7, 12 . . .**

3. Ask a child to fill the clover and bees as everyone repeats: **(12) 7 5 . . .**
4. Point to the (12) 7 5 flash cards again. **Say the triplet; then say the answer.**
5. Fill the beehive. **Say the (12) 9 3 facts . . . (12) 8 4 facts . . . (12) 7 5 facts.**
6. Do the Addition samples. **Think. Do I have something to carry *over*?**
7. Assign Lesson 71.

71

Answer these problems.
Carry *over* in some problems.

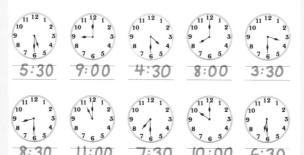

65 + 53 = 118	54 + 48 = 102	31 + 98 = 129	39 + 63 = 102	77 + 43 = 120	28 + 90 = 118
43 + 69 = 112	14 + 94 = 108	78 + 44 = 122	76 + 33 = 109	45 + 83 = 128	35 + 75 = 110
79 + 43 = 122	67 + 41 = 108	36 + 85 = 121	55 + 53 = 108	25 + 97 = 122	85 + 36 = 121

Write the time.

5:30	9:00	4:30	8:00	3:30
8:30	11:00	7:30	10:00	6:30

49

Blacklines

Fact Hives #11
Triplets With Facts #5
Form A: 600–699

After Class

1. Give each child his (12) 7 5 flash cards.
2. Have each child bring *My 1,000 Book* to the teaching corner.
   a. **Count by 10's to 200.**
   b. **Count on to 300 by 5's.**

Extra Activity
"His eye seeth every precious thing."
Job 28:10
12 − 7 = 5
12 − 5 = 7
7 + 5 = 12
5 + 7 = 12
12 − 8 = 4
12 − 4 = 8
8 + 4 = 12
4 + 8 = 12
12 − 9 = 3
12 − 3 = 9
9 + 3 = 12
3 + 9 = 12
12
50

Fill in the whole and parts.

Trace, answer, and write the facts.

"They gave him a piece . . . of an honeycomb." Luke 24:42
51

Before Class

Add bee (12) 7 5 to Blossom 12 Chart.

Materials

11's–12's flash cards
Large coins
Large clock
Addition and Subtraction 7–10 flash cards

Chalkboard

128	82	123	127	46	85	129
⊖85	⊕47	−43	−45	+83	+43	−82

Class Time

1. Stand near the clover patch.

   (12) 7 5

   12 clovers in the patch;
   12 is the whole number.
   What part of the 12 has bees? 7
   What part of the 12 has no bees? 5
   12 is the whole number.
   Its parts are 7 and 5.

   a. **The triplet is (12) 7 5 . . .**
   b. **The facts are 12−7, 5; 12−5, 7; 7+5, 12; 5+7, 12 . . .**

2. Point to the Blossom 11 and 12 Charts. **Say each triplet 3 times.**

3. Do the Computation samples.

   a. **Be careful to subtract in ones' place and in tens' place.**

   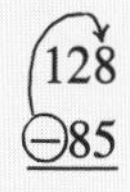

   b. **Be careful to add in ones' place and in tens' place.**

   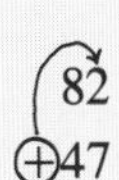

72

Answer these problems.

121	73	126	125	56	128
-70	+52	-54	-71	+72	-56
51	125	72	54	128	72
76	129	52	127	73	127
+53	-78	+75	-74	+55	-72
129	51	127	53	128	55
54	128	127	127	129	74
+71	-77	-73	-55	-57	+54
125	51	54	72	72	128
127	77	128	54	129	71
-76	+52	-75	+73	-74	+57
51	129	53	127	55	128
129	52	128	73	54	128
-55	+73	-72	+51	+75	-53
74	125	56	124	129	75
		52	126	129	74
		+77	-51	-73	+50
		129	75	56	124

52

4. Flash 11's and 12's cards.
   Answer together.
5. Have responsive counting. **Begin at 100. Count by 2's to 200.**
6. Flash the large coins.
   a. **Nickel, 5¢; dime, 10¢; penny, 1¢; quarter, 25¢ . . .**
   b. **We count pennies by __, nickels by __, dimes by __, and quarters by __.**
7. Do the Speed Drill in Lesson 72.
8. Assign Lesson 72.

72

Begin at 100. Count by 2's

Count by 2's

100	102	104	106	
108	110	112	114	
116	118	120	122	124
126	128	130	132	134
136	138	140	142	144
146	148	150	152	154
156	158	160	162	164

Answer these problems.
Carry *over* in some problems.

77	67	26	55	65	65
+45	+41	+85	+72	+57	+36
122	108	111	127	122	101

92	48	83	44	87	24
+36	+54	+34	+77	+34	+78
128	102	117	121	121	102

53

Blacklines

Fact Hives #11

Triplets With Facts #5

Number Facts #9

After Class

1. Flash Addition and Subtraction 7–10 cards.
2. Set the large clock at 2:00.
   a. **It is __.** 2:00
   In one hour it will be __. 3:00
   One hour ago it was __. 1:00
   In ½ hour it will be __. 2:30
   b. **One hour has __.** 60 minutes
   ½ **hour has __.** 30 minutes
   c. **How many minutes are between each number?** 5
   Count 5, 10, 15 minutes.
   It is 15 minutes after 2.
   It is 2:15. Write 2:15.
   d. Set the clock at
   •6:15 **15 minutes after 6 or 6:15**
   •8:15 **15 minutes after 8 or 8:15**
   •11:15 **15 minutes after 11 or 11:15**

Speed Drill

5	12	7	12	7	12
+7	-5	+5	-7	+5	-5
12	7	12	5	12	7

7	5	12	5	12	12
+5	+7	-7	+7	-5	-7
12	12	5	12	7	5

12	12	12	5	12	7	12	7
-5	-7	-5	+7	-7	+5	-5	+5
7	5	7	12	5	12	7	12

12	12	12	12	5	12	7	5
-7	-5	-7	-5	+7	-7	+5	+7
5	7	5	7	12	5	12	12

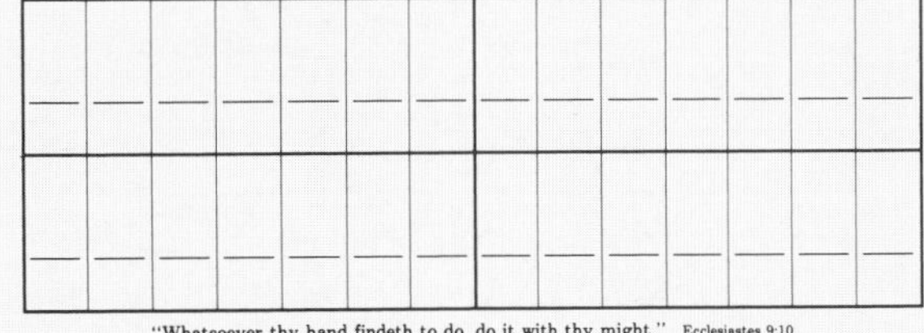

"Whatsoever thy hand findeth to do, do it with thy might." Ecclesiastes 9:10

54

73

Fill in the whole and parts.

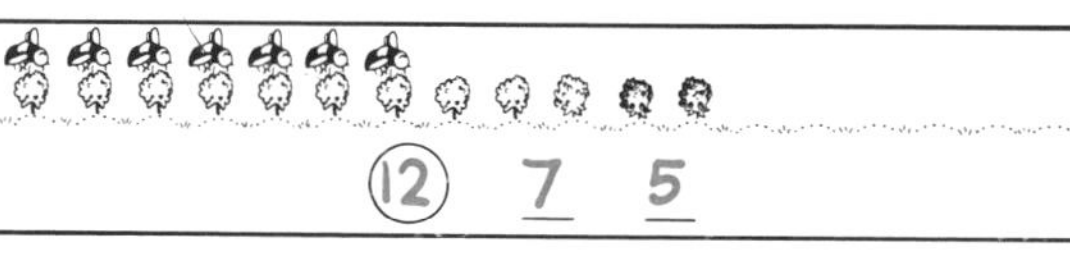

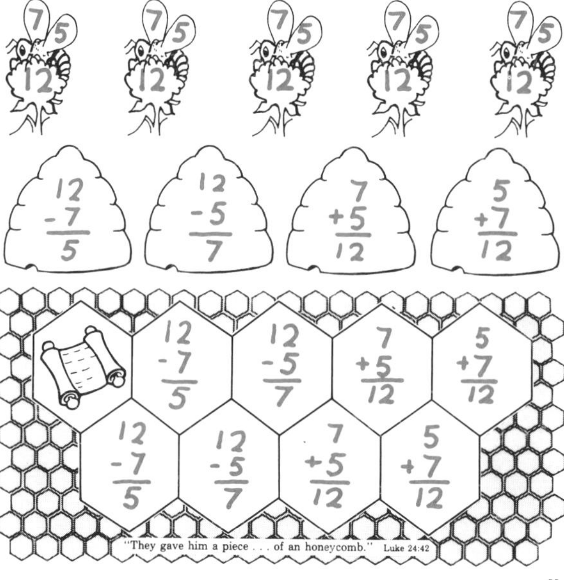

Trace, answer, and write the facts.

12 − 7 = 5 | 12 − 5 = 7 | 7 + 5 = 12 | 5 + 7 = 12

"They gave him a piece . . . of an honeycomb." Luke 24:42

55

Before Class

Materials

Large clock

12's flash cards

Chalkboard

8+__=12	__−7=5
12−9=__	3+9=__
__+7=12	5+__=12
4+__=12	12−__=4

(10¢)( )( )( ) (1¢)( )( ) ____

(25¢)( ) +____

(10¢)( )( )( )( ) (5¢)( )( ) ____

(10¢)( )( ) (1¢)( )( )( )( )( ) +____

Class Time

1. Stand near the clover patch.

   Jesus asked His disciples, "Have ye here any meat?" They gave Him a piece of fish and a—can you guess?
   honeycomb (Luke 24:41, 42)

2. | (12) 7 5 |

   12 clovers in the patch;
   12 is the whole number.
   What part of the 12 has bees? 7
   What part of the 12 has no bees? 5
   12 is the whole number.
   Its parts are 7 and 5.

   a. **The triplet is (12) 7 5 . . .**
   b. Point to the first flash card.
      Say each fact 3 times. 12−7, 5; 12−7, 5; 12−7, 5 . . .

73

Extra Activity

Count the first row.
Write the total.
Count the second row.
Write the total.
Add the two totals.

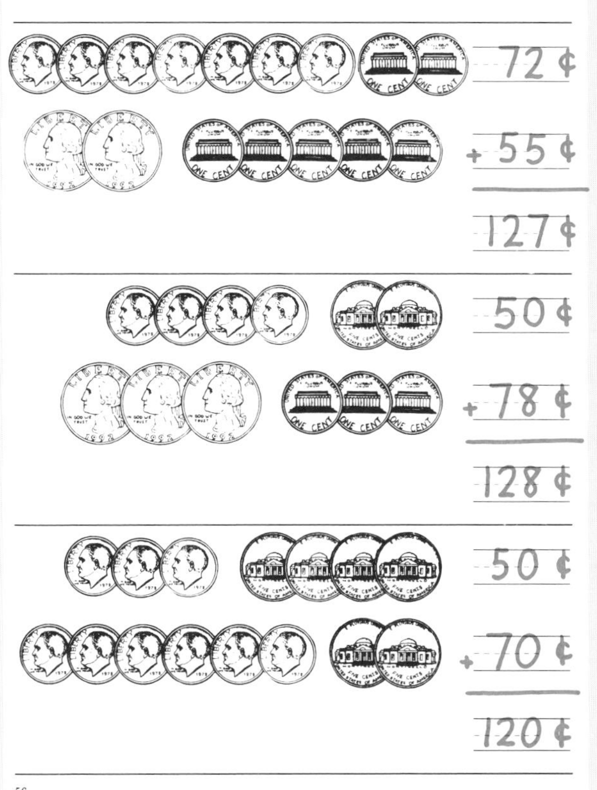

3. Point to Blossom 12 Chart.
   a. Drill the triplets 3 times.
      (12) 9 3
      (12) 8 4
      (12) 7 5 . . .
   b. **Can we say the 12 triplets by memory?**
4. Do the Missing Number samples.
5. Have individuals count aloud as they do the Money samples.
6. **Say the time together.**
   Set the clock at **1:15, 3:15, 5:15, 8:15, 10:15, 12:15 . . .**
7. Assign Lesson 73.

Answer these facts.

7 + 5 = 12	12 − 8 = 4	12 − 5 = 7	3 + 9 = 12	12 − 4 = 8	4 + 8 = 12	12 − 7 = 5	12 − 3 = 9
12 − 7 = 5	7 + 5 = 12	12 − 9 = 3	7 + 5 = 12	12 − 7 = 5	5 + 7 = 12	4 + 8 = 12	12 − 9 = 3
12 − 3 = 9	12 − 7 = 5	9 + 3 = 12	12 − 4 = 8	5 + 7 = 12	12 − 5 = 7	12 − 8 = 4	8 + 4 = 12

Read the story.
Write the numbers in the beehive.
Write the label words on the lines.
Answer the problem.

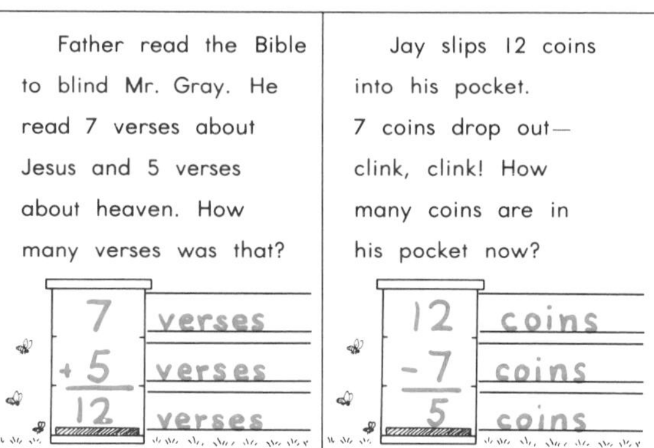

Father read the Bible to blind Mr. Gray. He read 7 verses about Jesus and 5 verses about heaven. How many verses was that?

7 verses
+5 verses
12 verses

Jay slips 12 coins into his pocket. 7 coins drop out— clink, clink! How many coins are in his pocket now?

12 coins
−7 coins
5 coins

57

Blacklines

Fact Hives #11

Missing Whole or Parts #7

Fact Form III

After Class

1. Drill each child with the 12's flash cards.
2. Chalkboard Drill: **Think. Write only the answer.**

76+1=	**134+1=**
99+1=	**187+1=**
45+2=	**151+2=**
63+2=	**120+2=**

58

Fill in the whole and parts.

Write the facts.

Trace, answer, and write the facts.

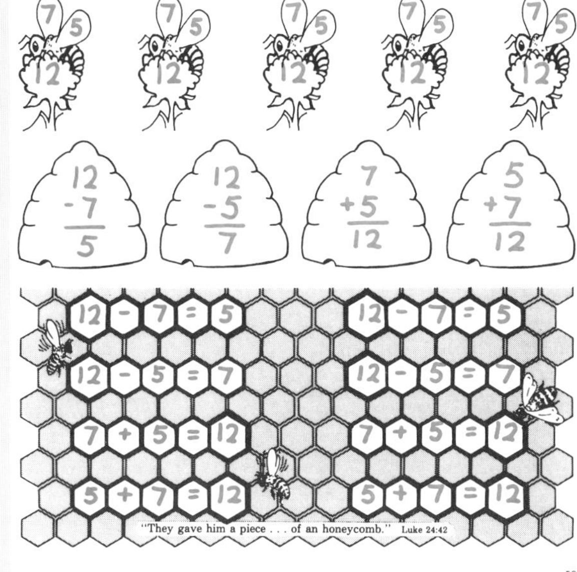

Before Class

Materials

9's–12's flash cards

Large clock

Make three 2″ × 2″ cards like this:

:00 :15 :30

Tape them near the 12, 3, and 6 on your classroom clock.

Class Time

1. Double Drill: Flash 9's–12's cards.
2. Stand near the clover patch.

   (12) 7 5

   12 clovers in the patch;
   12 is the whole number.
   What part of the 12 has bees? 7
   What part of the 12 has no bees? 5
   12 is the whole number.
   Its parts are 7 and 5.

   a. **The triplet is (12) 7 5 . . .**
   b. Point to the first flash card. **Close your eyes and say it 3 times.** Drill each fact.
3. Story Problems
   a. **Mother has 12 apples in a dish. 7 apples are red. How many apples are yellow? Who can give us the whole problem?**

      12 apples − 7 apples = 5 apples.

74

Fill in the missing whole or parts.

5 + 7 = 12	12 - 7 = 5	5 + 7 = 12
12 - 7 = 5	12 - 5 = 7	12 - 7 = 5
12 - 5 = 7	7 + 5 = 12	12 - 5 = 7
7 + 5 = 12	5 + 7 = 12	7 + 5 = 12
12 - 5 = 7	5 + 7 = 12	5 + 7 = 12
7 + 5 = 12	12 - 7 = 5	12 - 7 = 5

Speed Drill

Answer these problems.

6	3	1	4	1	3	5	1
1	2	6	3	4	2	1	4
+5	+5	+5	+5	+6	+7	+5	+7
12	10	12	12	11	12	11	12

5	1	2	1	5	3	5	4
2	3	5	6	0	4	4	1
+5	+7	+5	+4	+7	+5	+1	+7
12	11	12	11	12	12	10	12

60

b. **In Aunt Mary's fishbowl there are 7 goldfish and 5 spotted fish. How many is that altogether? Who . . . ?**
7 fish+5 fish=12 fish.

4. Review place value.
The number places are ones, tens, hundreds, (comma), thousands; ones, tens . . .

5. Hold the large clock. Ask a child to stand at the board and write the time that he hears his classmates say. Set the clock for each situation below.
   - **Father milks the cows at 15 minutes after 5 or __.** 5:15
   - **Mother makes breakfast at 15 minutes after 7 or __.** 7:15
   - **The mailman comes at 15 minutes after 11 or __.** 11:15
   - **Lunch is over at 15 minutes after 12 or __.** 12:15

6. Do the Speed Drill in Lesson 74.

7. Assign Lesson 74.

Write the time.

Blacklines

Fact Hives #12

Missing Whole or Parts #7

Number Facts #9

Write the numbers in the correct places.

	thousands	hundreds	tens	ones
1798	1,	7	9	8
1345	1,	3	4	5
1761	1,	7	6	1
817	__,	8	1	7
1590	1,	5	9	0
1614	1,	6	1	4
62	__,	__	6	2

	thousands	hundreds	tens	ones
89	__,	__	8	9
316	__,	3	1	6
1973	1,	9	7	3
1582	1,	5	8	2
1297	1,	2	9	7
86	__,	__	8	6
1308	1,	3	0	8

61

After Class

1. Drill each triplet 3 times.
2. You say a triplet from the Blossom Charts. Then ask a child to give four facts for that triplet.
3. Have responsive counting. **Count by 5's to 250. I will say the first number; you say the next number.**

Speed Drill
"Whatsoever thy hand findeth to do, do it with thy might." Ecclesiastes 9:10
62

75

Fill in the whole and parts.

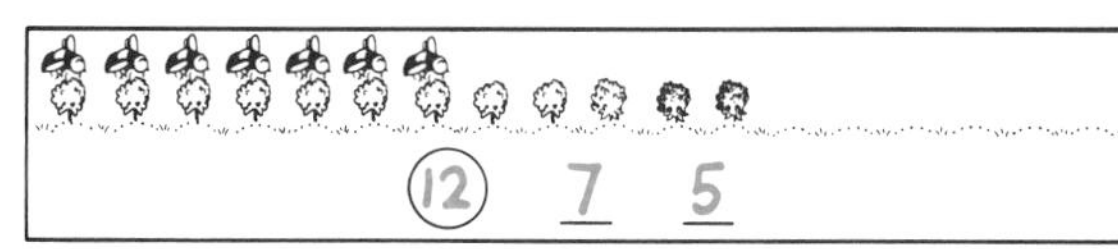

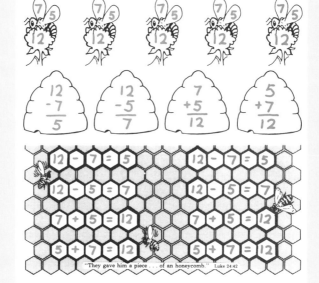

Write the facts.

Trace, answer, and write the facts.

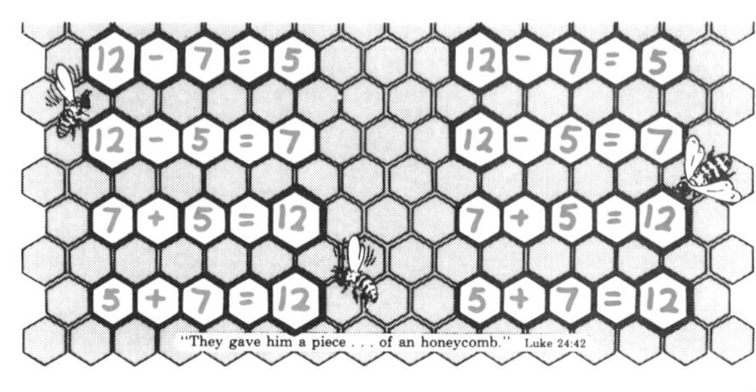

12 − 7 = 5
12 − 5 = 7
7 + 5 = 12
5 + 7 = 12
"They gave him a piece . . . of an honeycomb." Luke 24:42
63

Before Class

Materials

10's–12's flash cards
Form C
Large coins

Chalkboard

38	42	35	94	53	37	74
+84	+76	+46	+35	+57	+55	+43

Class Time

1. Stand near the clover patch.

(12) 9 3

   The whole number is __.
   Its parts are __ and __.
   The triplet is (12) 9 3 . . .

2. | (12) 8 4 |
   |---|

   The whole number is __.
   Its parts are __ and __.
   The triplet is (12) 8 4 . . .

3. | (12) 7 5 |
   |---|

   The whole number is __.
   Its parts are __ and __.
   The triplet is (12) 7 5 . . .

4. Point to the Blossom Charts.
   a. **Say the 11 triplets.**
   b. **Say the 12 triplets.**

75

Extra Activity

Read the story.
Write the numbers
in the beehive.
Write the label words
on the lines.
Answer the problem.

God sends rain. Splash, splash! Ray splashes in 7 puddles. Fred splashes in 5 puddles. How many puddles is that altogether?

Lee plays with his baby sister. He stacks up 12 blocks. 7 blocks fall down. How many blocks are left on the stack?

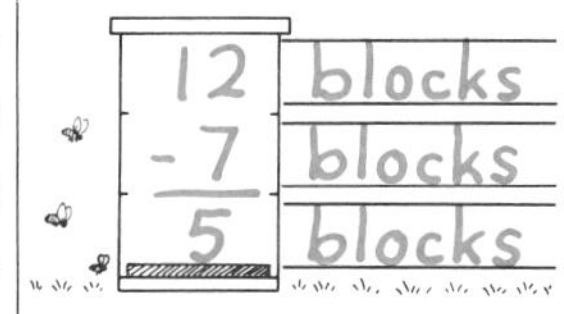

Mother had 12 eggs in a dish. She cooked 5 of them in a pan. How many eggs were left in the dish?

Five cows stand in the creek. 7 cows eat grass. How many cows is that?

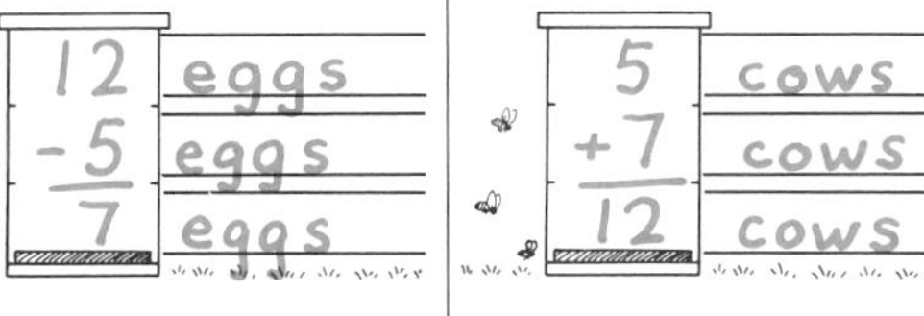

64

c. **Jump back and forth.** Drill
- **(11) 9 2** and **(12) 9 3**
- **(11) 8 3** and **(12) 8 4**
- **(11) 7 4** and **(12) 7 5**

5. Flash 10's–12's cards.
6. Flash Card Drill: 10's–12's flash cards.
   Use Form C. **Flower Row: Box 1 . . .**
7. Do the Addition samples.
8. Flash the coins.
   a. **Penny, quarter, dime, nickel . . .**
   b. **1¢, 25¢, 10¢, 5¢ . . .**
9. Assign Lesson 75.

Answer these facts.

8 + 4 = 12	12 − 7 = 5	12 − 3 = 9	6 + 5 = 11	11 − 5 = 6	7 + 5 = 12	12 − 8 = 4	12 − 5 = 7
12 − 4 = 8	6 + 5 = 11	12 − 7 = 5	5 + 6 = 11	12 − 4 = 8	5 + 7 = 12	9 + 3 = 12	12 − 7 = 5
12 − 5 = 7	12 − 8 = 4	5 + 7 = 12	11 − 5 = 6	5 + 6 = 11	12 − 3 = 9	12 − 7 = 5	4 + 8 = 12

Write the time.

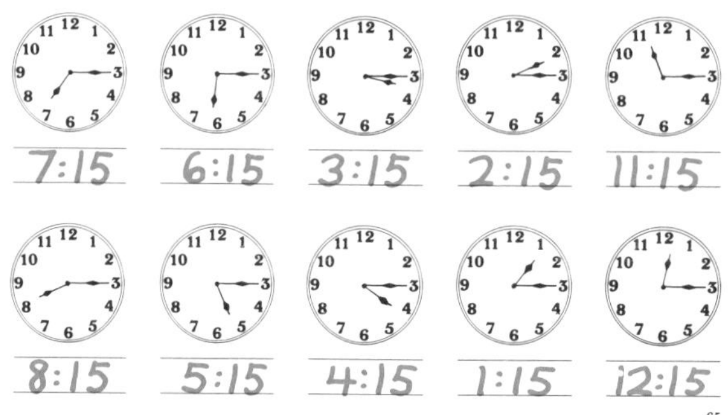

Blacklines

Fact Hives #12

Missing Whole or Parts #7

Fact Form IV

After Class

1. Drill each child with the 12's flash cards.
2. Chalkboard Drill: **Write the three numbers I say.**

   695 569 956

   Circle the largest number.

   743 437 374

   Circle the smallest number.

   809 908 890

   Circle the largest number.

   747 477 774

   Circle the smallest number.

   1,213 1,318 1,115

   Circle the largest number.

Extra Activity
"His eye seeth every precious thing."
Job 28:10
12 − 7 = 5
12 − 5 = 7
7 + 5 = 12
5 + 7 = 12
12 − 8 = 4
12 − 4 = 8
8 + 4 = 12
4 + 8 = 12
12 − 9 = 3
12 − 3 = 9
9 + 3 = 12
3 + 9 = 12
12
66

76

Trace and fill in the whole and parts.

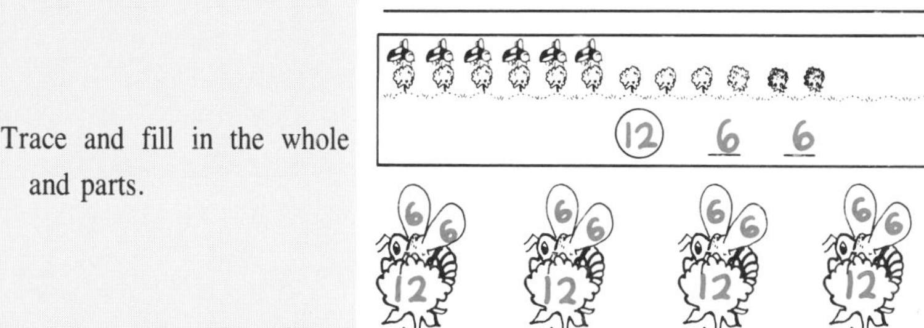

Trace, answer, and write the facts.

Before Class

Make (12) 6 6 flash cards for each child.

Tack the (12) 6 6 flash cards above the clover patch in this order:

12 −6 = 6	6 +6 = 12

12 −7	8 +4	12 −3	12 −5
12 −6	12 −5	3 +9	12 −8
12 −8	12 −7	7 +5	12 −9
12 −4	6 +6	12 −4	12 −6

Materials

12 blossoms, 6 with bees

Large clock

Chalkboard

76

Answer these facts.

6 + 6 = 12	11 − 5 = 6	12 − 6 = 6	6 + 5 = 11	11 − 6 = 5	5 + 6 = 11	12 − 6 = 6	11 − 6 = 5
12 − 6 = 6	6 + 6 = 12	11 − 6 = 5	6 + 6 = 12	12 − 6 = 6	6 + 5 = 11	5 + 6 = 11	11 − 6 = 5
11 − 6 = 5	12 − 6 = 6	6 + 5 = 11	11 − 6 = 5	5 + 6 = 11	11 − 5 = 6	12 − 6 = 6	6 + 6 = 12
12 − 6 = 6	6 + 6 = 12	12 − 6 = 6	5 + 6 = 11	12 − 6 = 6	11 − 6 = 5	6 + 6 = 12	11 − 5 = 6
12 − 6 = 6	11 − 6 = 5	11 − 5 = 6	12 − 6 = 6	11 − 5 = 6	6 + 6 = 12	6 + 6 = 12	11 − 5 = 6
		11 − 5 = 6	6 + 6 = 12	11 − 6 = 5	12 − 6 = 6	6 + 5 = 11	12 − 6 = 6

68

Class Time

1. Stand near the clover patch.

   God helps the bees know that the *best time* to sip nectar is when the blossoms are fresh, before the hot sun wilts them or the cold frost freezes them.

   Back and forth the worker bees fly, from the hive to the clover and from the clover to the hive. Each worker is as busy as a bee!

2. (12) 6 6

   a. **How many pink clovers are in the patch?** 10
   We think—10 pink.
   2 more make __ altogether. 12
   We think—10 pink.
   4 less make __ clovers with bees. 6

   b. **12 clovers in the patch;**
   12 is the whole number.
   What part of the 12 has bees? 6
   What part of the 12 has no bees? 6
   12 is the whole number.
   Its parts are 6 and 6.

   c. **The triplet is (12) 6 6 . . .**

   d. Point to the flash cards. **The facts are 12−6, 6; 6+6, 12 . . .**

3. **Say the triplet as I fill the clover and bees. (12) 6 6 . . .**

4. Stand near the beehive. **Begin with (12) 9 3. Say the 12's facts as I fill the beehive.**

5. Stand near the grid.

   a. **Answer together.** Drill the facts up and down, left and right.

   b. Have each child answer one row.

6. Review place value.
   The number places are ones, tens, hundreds, (comma), thousands; ones, tens . . .

7. Do the Speed Drill in Lesson 76.

8. Assign Lesson 76.

76

Answer these problems.
Carry *over* in some problems.

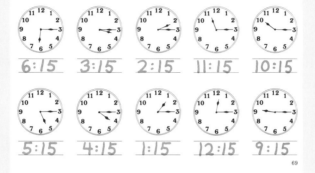

57 + 45 = 102	77 + 51 = 128	86 + 35 = 121	52 + 65 = 117	65 + 57 = 122	55 + 46 = 101
72 + 36 = 108	28 + 94 = 122	53 + 74 = 127	74 + 37 = 111	87 + 34 = 121	64 + 38 = 102
79 + 43 = 122	67 + 41 = 108	36 + 85 = 121	55 + 53 = 108	25 + 97 = 122	85 + 36 = 121

Write the time.

6:15	3:15	2:15	11:15	10:15
5:15	4:15	1:15	12:15	9:15

69

Blacklines

Fact Hives #13

Missing Whole or Parts #8

Number Facts #9

After Class

1. Give each child his (12) 6 6 flash cards.
2. Drill each child at the grid. Can he answer all the facts in 30 seconds?
3. Ask individuals to set the large clock at **2:15, 5:00, 7:15, 11:00, 12:15, 1:00, 3:15 . . .**

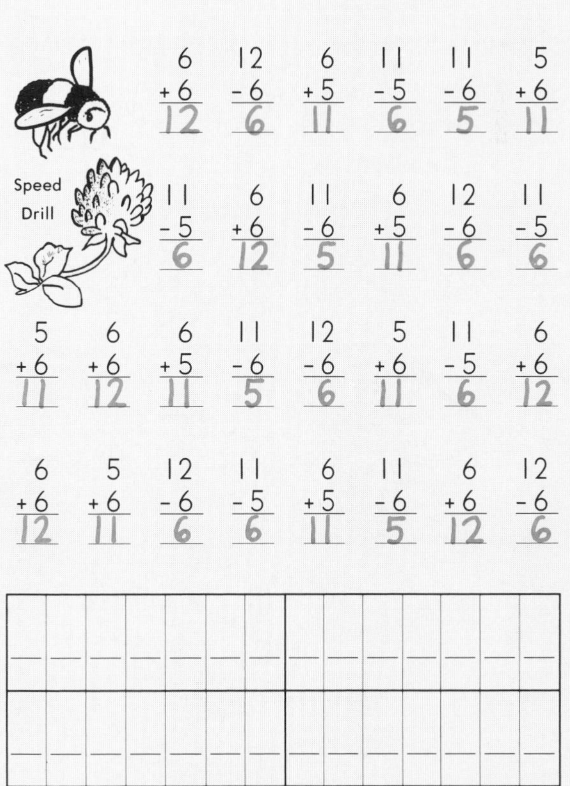

		6 + 6 = 12	12 - 6 = 6	6 + 5 = 11	11 - 5 = 6	11 - 6 = 5	5 + 6 = 11
		11 - 5 = 6	6 + 6 = 12	11 - 6 = 5	6 + 5 = 11	12 - 6 = 6	11 - 5 = 6
5 + 6 = 11	6 + 6 = 12	6 + 5 = 11	11 - 6 = 5	12 - 6 = 6	5 + 6 = 11	11 - 5 = 6	6 + 6 = 12
6 + 6 = 12	5 + 6 = 11	12 - 6 = 6	11 - 5 = 6	6 + 5 = 11	11 - 6 = 5	6 + 6 = 12	12 - 6 = 6

"Whatsoever thy hand findeth to do, do it with thy might." Ecclesiastes 9:10

70

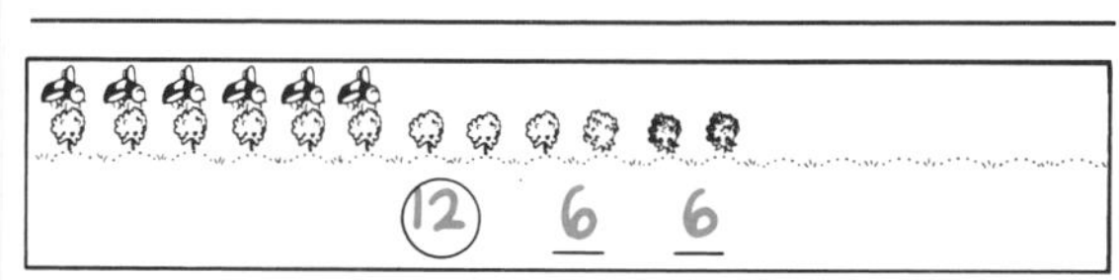

Fill in the whole and parts.

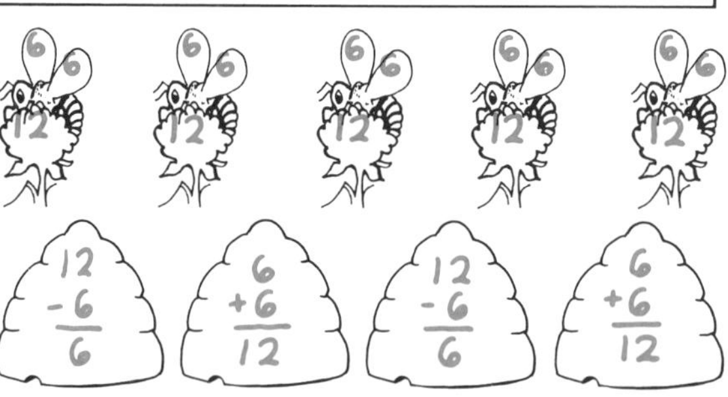

Trace, answer, and write the facts.

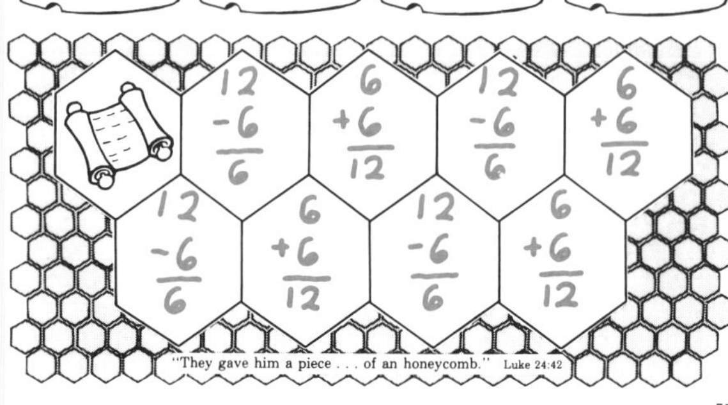

"They gave him a piece . . . of an honeycomb." Luke 24:42

71

Before Class

Add bee (12) 6 6 to Blossom 12 Chart.

Materials

12's flash cards

Large clock

Chalkboard

129	64	128	83	129	72	126
−83	+63	−63	+42	−65	+57	−94

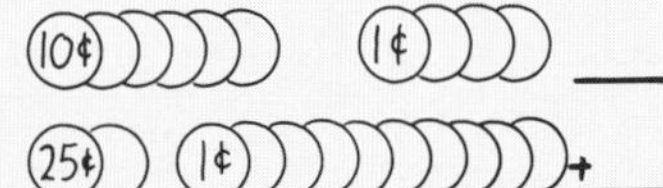

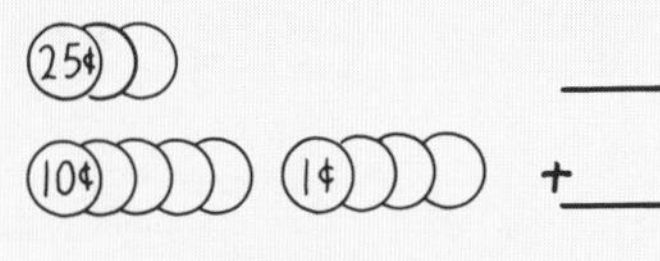

Class Time

1. a. **Count by 100's to 1,000.**
   b. **Count by 25's to 100.**
   c. **Count on to 300 by 10's.**
2. Stand near the clover patch.

   (12) 6 6

   12 clovers in the patch;
   12 is the whole number.
   What part of the 12 has bees? 6
   What part of the 12 has no bees? 6
   12 is the whole number.
   Its parts are 6 and 6.
   a. **The triplet is (12) 6 6 . . .**
   b. **The facts are 12−6, 6; 6+6, 12 . . .**
3. Ask a child to fill the beehive as everyone says the 12 facts.
4. Point to the Blossom Charts. Drill each triplet 3 times.
5. Double Drill: 12's flash cards.
6. Do the Computation samples.

77

Extra Activity

Answer these problems.

61 + 62 = 123	23 − 62 = 61	53 + 64 = 117	67 + 61 = 128	113 − 53 = 60	57 + 62 = 119
129 − 67 = 62	119 − 63 = 56	65 + 61 = 126	129 − 61 = 68	66 + 60 = 126	119 − 65 = 54
65 + 54 = 119	114 − 54 = 60	65 + 63 = 128	65 + 52 = 117	129 − 68 = 61	63 + 60 = 123
118 − 55 = 63	127 − 64 = 63	118 − 67 = 51	61 + 57 = 118	129 − 67 = 62	66 + 63 = 129
61 + 68 = 129	118 − 64 = 54	61 + 65 = 126	128 − 60 = 68	64 + 62 = 126	118 − 62 = 56
		127 − 65 = 62	62 + 56 = 118	118 − 67 = 51	125 − 62 = 63

72

7. Have individuals count aloud as they do the Money samples.
8. **Read the time as I set the clock. 11:00, 11:15, 12:00, 12:15, 2:00, 2:15 . . .**
9. Assign Lesson 77.

Answer these facts.

6 + 6 = 12	12 − 7 = 5	12 − 6 = 6	7 + 5 = 12	12 − 4 = 8	6 + 6 = 12	12 − 8 = 4	12 − 5 = 7
12 − 9 = 3	8 + 4 = 12	12 − 7 = 5	3 + 9 = 12	12 − 9 = 3	9 + 3 = 12	4 + 8 = 12	12 − 7 = 5
12 − 5 = 7	12 − 8 = 4	3 + 9 = 12	12 − 4 = 8	5 + 7 = 12	12 − 6 = 6	12 − 7 = 5	6 + 6 = 12

Blacklines

Fact Hives #13

Missing Whole or Parts #8

Number Triplets #2

Write the time.

73

After Class

1. Ask individuals to give by memory the 11's triplets . . . the 12's triplets.
2. Chalkboard Drill: **Write the number you hear.**
   - **The flood waters covered the earth for 150 days.** (Genesis 7:24)
   - **Samsom caught 300 foxes.** (Judges 15:4)
   - **The Gospel of John has 879 verses.**
   - **Adam lived 930 years.** (Genesis 5:5)
   - **God said that the cattle upon a thousand hills are His.** (Psalm 50:10)

78

Fill in the whole and parts.

Trace, answer, and write the facts.

78
"They gave him a piece . . . of an honeycomb." Luke 24:42
75

Before Class

Materials

11's and 12's flash cards

Addition and Subtraction 9 and 10 flash cards

Large clock

Chalkboard

12−__=6	__−3=9
6+6=__	12−__=7
12−__=5	12−4=__
8+__=12	__+3=12

Class Time

1. Stand near the clover patch.

   (12) 9 3

   The whole number is __.
   Its parts are __ and __.
   The facts are 12−9, 3; 12−3, 9; 9+3, 12; 3+9, 12.

2. (12) 8 4

   The whole number is __.
   Its parts are __ and __.
   The facts are 12−8, 4; 12−4, 8; 8+4, 12; 4+8, 12.

3. (12) 7 5

   The whole number is __.
   Its parts are __ and __.
   The facts are 12−7, 5; 12−5, 7; 7+5, 12; 5+7, 12.

78

Speed Drill

Read the story.
Write the numbers
in the beehive.
Write the label words
on the lines.
Answer the problem.

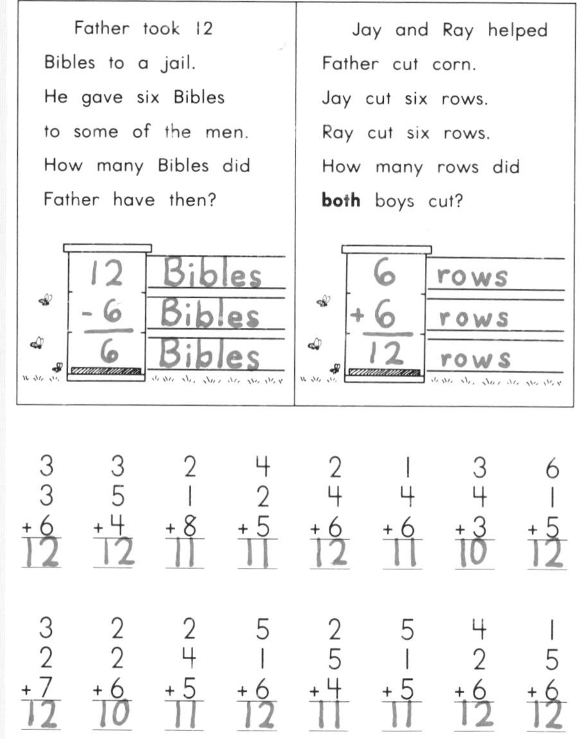

Father took 12 Bibles to a jail. He gave six Bibles to some of the men. How many Bibles did Father have then?

12	Bibles
− 6	Bibles
6	Bibles

Jay and Ray helped Father cut corn. Jay cut six rows. Ray cut six rows. How many rows did **both** boys cut?

6	rows
+ 6	rows
12	rows

Answer these problems.

3	3	2	4	2	1	3	6
3	5	1	2	4	4	4	1
+6	+4	+8	+5	+6	+6	+3	+5
12	12	11	11	12	11	10	12

3	2	2	5	2	5	4	1
2	2	4	1	5	1	2	5
+7	+6	+5	+6	+4	+5	+6	+6
12	10	11	12	11	11	12	12

76

4. (12) 6 6

   The whole number is __.
   Its parts are __ and __.
   The facts are 12−6, 6; 6+6, 12.

5. Point to the Blossom Charts.
   a. **Say the 11 triplets.**
   b. **Say the 12 triplets.**
   c. **Jump back and forth.** Drill
      - **(11) 9 2** and **(12) 9 3**
      - **(11) 8 3** and **(12) 8 4**
      - **(11) 7 4** and **(12) 7 5**
      - **(11) 6 5** and **(12) 6 6**
6. Flash the 11's and 12's cards. **Say the triplet; then say the answer.**
7. Do the Missing Number samples.
8. Do the Speed Drill in Lesson 78.
9. Assign Lesson 78.

78

Answer these problems.
Carry *over* in some problems.

78

82 + 43 = 125	86 + 26 = 112	92 + 36 = 128	54 + 48 = 102	55 + 57 = 112	74 + 32 = 106
77 + 45 = 122	21 + 94 = 115	63 + 59 = 122	78 + 30 = 108	83 + 33 = 116	68 + 34 = 102
96 + 32 = 128	84 + 43 = 127	36 + 86 = 122	55 + 73 = 128	25 + 97 = 122	42 + 85 = 127

Write the time.

10:15	1:00	9:15	12:00	8:15
1:15	3:00	12:15	2:00	11:15

77

Blacklines

Fact Hives #13

Missing Whole or Parts #8

Number Triplets #2

After Class

1. Drill Addition and Subtraction 9 and 10 flash cards.
2. **Add with me.**

10+5	**10+4**	**10+8**
10+3	**10+9**	**10+6**
10+1	**10+2**	**10+7**

3. Chalkboard Drill: Hold the large clock. **Write the time I show.**
4:00, 4:15, 6:00, 7:15, 9:15, 10:00, 11:15 . . .

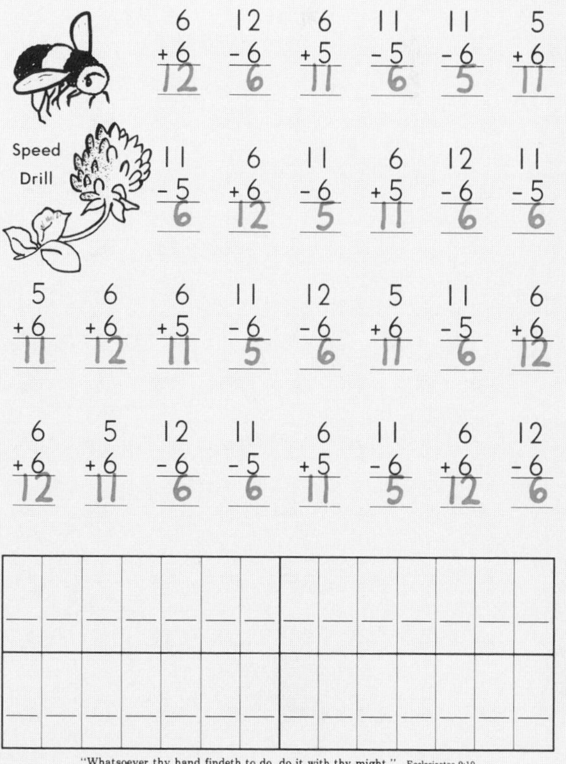
Speed Drill

6 + 6 = 12 | 12 − 6 = 6 | 6 + 5 = 11 | 11 − 5 = 6 | 11 − 6 = 5 | 5 + 6 = 11

11 − 5 = 6 | 6 + 6 = 12 | 11 − 6 = 5 | 6 + 5 = 11 | 12 − 6 = 6 | 11 − 5 = 6

5 + 6 = 11 | 6 + 6 = 12 | 6 + 5 = 11 | 11 − 6 = 5 | 12 − 6 = 6 | 5 + 6 = 11 | 11 − 5 = 6 | 6 + 6 = 12

6 + 6 = 12 | 5 + 6 = 11 | 12 − 6 = 6 | 11 − 5 = 6 | 6 + 5 = 11 | 11 − 6 = 5 | 6 + 6 = 12 | 12 − 6 = 6

"Whatsoever thy hand findeth to do, do it with thy might." Ecclesiastes 9:10

78

79

Trace and fill in the whole and parts.

Trace, answer, and write the facts.

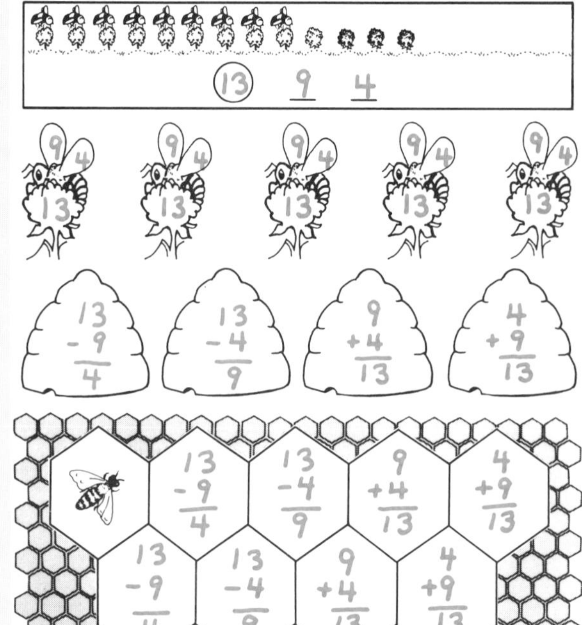

79
(13) 9 4
"Their father Israel said . . . carry down . . . a present . . . a little honey." Genesis 43:11
79

Before Class

Make (13) 9 4 flash cards for each child.

Tack (13) 9 4 flash cards above the clover patch in this order:

13	13	9	4
−9	−4	+4	+9
4	9	13	13

Materials

11's and 12's flash cards

13 blossoms, 9 with bees

Large coins

Large clock

Chalkboard

6 nickels + 2 pennies = __

1 quarter + 3 pennies = __

4 dimes + 4 pennies = __

3 quarters + 1 penny = __

2 dimes + 1 nickel = __

5 nickels + 2 pennies = __

79

Extra Activity

Answer these facts.

13 − 9 = 4	13 − 4 = 9	13 − 9 = 4	13 − 9 = 4	4 + 9 = 13	13 − 9 = 4	13 − 4 = 9	9 + 4 = 13
4 + 9 = 13	13 − 4 = 9	9 + 4 = 13	4 + 9 = 13	13 − 4 = 9	9 + 4 = 13	13 − 4 = 9	13 − 9 = 4
13 − 9 = 4	13 − 4 = 9	9 + 4 = 13	13 − 4 = 9	9 + 4 = 13	4 + 9 = 13	13 − 4 = 9	4 + 9 = 13
9 + 4 = 13	4 + 9 = 13	13 − 4 = 9	4 + 9 = 13	13 − 9 = 4	13 − 4 = 9	9 + 4 = 13	13 − 9 = 4
13 − 9 = 4	13 − 4 = 9	13 − 9 = 4	13 − 9 = 4	4 + 9 = 13	13 − 9 = 4	13 − 4 = 9	9 + 4 = 13
		4 + 9 = 13	13 − 4 = 9	9 + 4 = 13	13 − 4 = 9	4 + 9 = 13	13 − 9 = 4

80

Class Time

1. **Count by 2's from 100 to 200.**
2. Point to Blossom 11 and 12 Charts.
   Say each triplet 3 times.
3. **Say the 12's facts as I fill the beehive.**
   Begin with 12−9=3.
4. Double Drill: 11's and 12's flash cards.
5. Stand near the clover patch.

(13) 9 4

   a. **How many pink clovers are in the patch?** 10
      We think—10 pink.
      3 more make __ altogether. 13
      We think—10 pink.
      1 less makes __ clovers with bees. 9
   b. **13 clovers in the patch;**
      13 is the whole number.
      What part of the 13 has bees? 9
      What part of the 13 has no bees? 4
      13 is the whole number.
      Its parts are 9 and 4.
   c. **The triplet is (13) 9 4;**
      (13) 9 4 . . .
   d. Point to the flash cards. **The facts are 13−9, 4; 13−4, 9; 9+4, 13; 4+9, 13 . . .**
6. **Say the triplet as I fill the clover and bees. (13) 9 4 . . .**
7. Flash the large coins. **Nickel, 5¢; dime, 10¢; penny, 1¢; quarter, 25¢ . . .**
8. Do the Money samples.
9. Assign Lesson 79.

Note: Make Blossom 13 Chart for Lesson 80.

Count by 2's. Begin at 100.

79

Count by 2's

	100	102	104	106
	108	110	112	114
116	118	120	122	124
126	128	130	132	134
136	138	140	142	144
146	148	150	152	154

Write the time.

7:15	3:00	3:15	2:15	2:00
8:15	4:00	4:15	1:15	1:00

81

Blacklines

Fact Hives #14

Fact Form V

Form A: 700–799

After Class

1. Give each child his (13) 9 4 flash cards.
2. Set the large clock at 2:00.
   a. **Name the hands.**
   b. **How many minutes are between each number?** 5 **Count with me. 5, 10, 15 . . . 45 minutes**
   c. **Read the time together.** Set the clock at
      •2:00, 2:15, 2:30, 2:45
      •4:00, 4:15, 4:30, 4:45
      •6:00, 6:15, 6:30, 6:45
      •10:00, 10:15, 10:30, 10:45
   d. 10:45—**The hour hand is so close to 11 that we may think it is 11:45. No, it is not 11:00 yet. So it could not be 45 minutes past 11.**
   e. ***10*:45, *10*:45—The hour hand passed the 10. It is 45 minutes past 10.**

80

Fill in the whole and parts.

Trace, answer, and write the facts.

"Their father Israel said . . . carry down . . . a present . . . a little honey." Genesis 43:11

83

Before Class

Tack bee (13) 9 4 on Blossom 13 Chart. Mount it on the wall.

Materials

Large clock
11's–13's flash cards

Chalkboard

39	73	55	86	42	54	35
+94	+56	+67	+46	+96	+66	+94

Class Time

1. **Count by 100's to 1,000.**
   Count by 25's to 100.
   Count on to 200 by 5's.
2. Point to Blossom 11 and 12 Charts.
   a. **Say the 11 triplets.**
      (11) 9 2
      (11) 8 3
      (11) 7 4
      (11) 6 5
   b. **Say the 12 triplets.**
      (12) 9 3
      (12) 8 4
      (12) 7 5
      (12) 6 6
   c. **Say the 11 triplets by memory.**
   d. **Say the 12 triplets by memory.**

80

Answer these facts.

13 − 4 = 9	13 − 9 = 4	13 − 4 = 9	13 − 4 = 9	4 + 9 = 13	13 − 4 = 9	13 − 9 = 4	9 + 4 = 13
9 + 4 = 13	13 − 4 = 9	9 + 4 = 13	4 + 9 = 13	13 − 9 = 4	9 + 4 = 13	13 − 4 = 9	13 − 9 = 4
13 − 9 = 4	13 − 4 = 9	9 + 4 = 13	13 − 9 = 4	9 + 4 = 13	4 + 9 = 13	13 − 4 = 9	4 + 9 = 13
4 + 9 = 13	9 + 4 = 13	13 − 4 = 9	4 + 9 = 13	13 − 9 = 4	13 − 4 = 9	9 + 4 = 13	13 − 9 = 4
13 − 9 = 4	13 − 4 = 9	13 − 9 = 4	13 − 9 = 4	4 + 9 = 13	13 − 9 = 4	13 − 4 = 9	9 + 4 = 13
		9 + 4 = 13	13 − 4 = 9	4 + 9 = 13	13 − 4 = 9	4 + 9 = 13	13 − 4 = 9

84

Speed Drill

3. Stand near the clover patch.

(13) 9 4

   13 clovers in the patch;
   13 is the whole number.
   What part of the 13 has bees? 9
   What part of the 13 has no bees? 4
   13 is the whole number.
   Its parts are 9 and 4.
   a. **The triplet is (13) 9 4 . . .**
   b. **The facts are 13−9, 4; 13−4, 9; 9+4, 13; 4+9, 13 . . .**

4. Point to Blossom 13 Chart.
   (13) 9 4
   (13) 9 4
   (13) 9 4 . . .

5. Do the Addition samples.

6. Hold the large clock.
   Read the time together.
   Set the hands at
   •1:00, 1:15, 1:30, 1:45
   •5:00, 5:15, 5:30, 5:45
   •12:00, 12:15, 12:30, 12:45

7. Do the Speed Drill in Lesson 80.

8. Assign Lesson 80.

Note: Make a 2″ x 2″ card like this [:45]. Tape it near the 9 on your classroom clock.

80

Answer these problems.
Carry *over* in some problems.

92 +43 = 135	86 +26 = 112	89 +44 = 133	54 +48 = 102	55 +57 = 112	44 +94 = 138
42 +90 = 132	63 +52 = 115	33 +99 = 132	64 +39 = 103	83 +35 = 118	38 +94 = 132
74 +29 = 103	84 +43 = 127	66 +56 = 122	62 +41 = 103	25 +97 = 122	42 +85 = 127

Read the story.
Write the numbers in the beehive.
Write the label words on the lines.
Answer the problem.

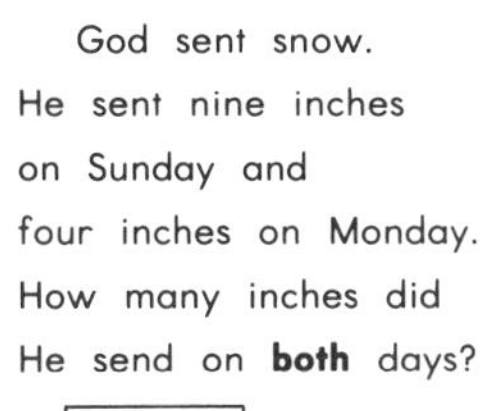
God sent snow. He sent nine inches on Sunday and four inches on Monday. How many inches did He send on **both** days?

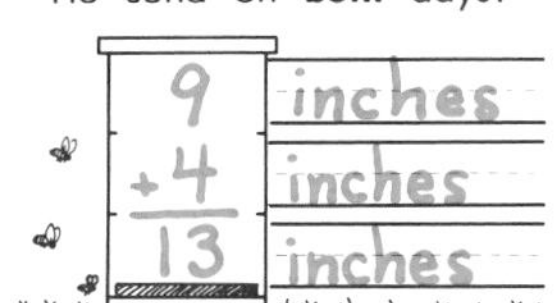
9 inches
+4 inches
13 inches

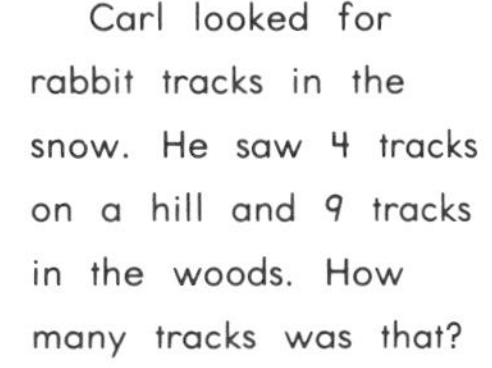
Carl looked for rabbit tracks in the snow. He saw 4 tracks on a hill and 9 tracks in the woods. How many tracks was that?

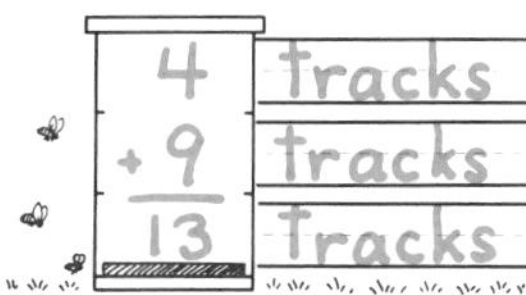
4 tracks
+9 tracks
13 tracks

85

Blacklines

Fact Hives #14

Fact Form III

Number Words #3

After Class

1. Flash 11's–13's cards. **Say the triplet; then say the answer.**
2. Story Problems
   a. **12, 8 __ The one *part* is missing. Shall we add or subtract?**
   b. **__ 9, 4 The *whole* number is missing. Shall we add or subtract?**
   c. **Father and Glen stacked firewood. Father stacked 9 pieces. Glen stacked 4 pieces. How many did they both stack? Who can give us the whole problem?**
      9 pieces + 4 pieces = 13 pieces.
   d. **Mother and Karen made 13 meatballs for supper. Karen made 4 of them. How many did Mother make? Who . . . ?**
      13 balls − 4 balls = 9 balls.

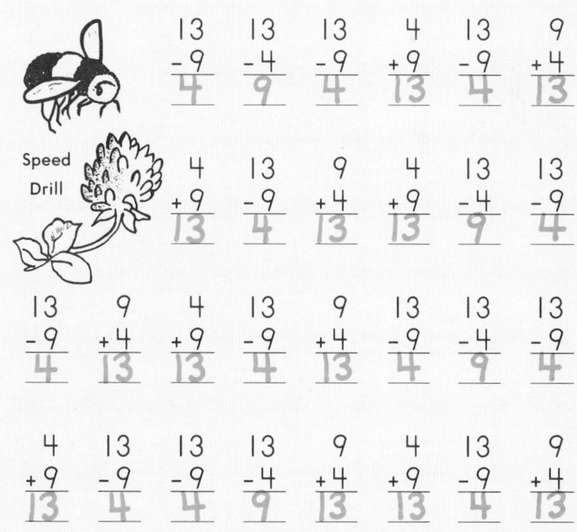

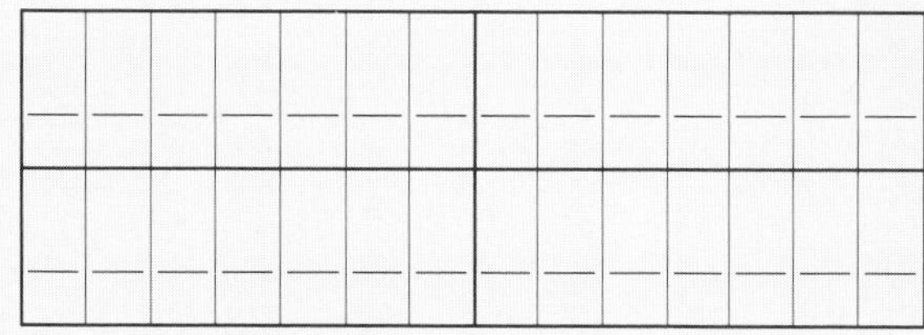

"Whatsoever thy hand findeth to do, do it with thy might." Ecclesiastes 9:10

86

81

Fill in the whole and parts.

Trace, answer, and write the facts.

"Their father Israel said . . . carry down . . . a present . . . a little honey." Genesis 43:11
87

Before Class

Materials

9's–13's flash cards
Large clock
11's–13's flash cards

Chalkboard

138	94	65	129
−93	+43	+63	−75

42	134	127	92	139
+97	−94	−53	+46	−97

Class Time

1. Double Drill: 9's–13's flash cards.
2. Point to the Blossom Charts.
   a. **Say each triplet 3 times.**
      (11) 9 2
      (11) 9 2
      (11) 9 2 . . .
   b. **Can we say the triplets in order without looking at the charts?**
      (11) 9 2
      (11) 8 3
      (11) 7 4
      (11) 6 5
      (12) 9 3
      (12) 8 4
      (12) 7 5
      (12) 6 6
      (13) 9 4

81

Answer these problems.
Carry *over* in some problems.

139 − 92 = 47	39 + 44 = 83	137 − 45 = 92	136 − 94 = 42	96 + 43 = 139	138 − 96 = 42
34 + 69 = 103	139 − 46 = 93	95 + 42 = 137	139 − 94 = 45	39 + 24 = 63	133 − 43 = 90
44 + 39 = 83	138 − 91 = 47	134 − 92 = 42	135 − 43 = 92	139 − 97 = 42	94 + 45 = 139
138 − 45 = 93	59 + 44 = 103	135 − 90 = 45	43 + 94 = 137	137 − 47 = 90	39 + 24 = 63
138 − 93 = 45	74 + 19 = 93	138 − 44 = 94	93 + 45 = 138	29 + 74 = 103	139 − 98 = 41
		44 + 94 = 138	137 − 43 = 94	29 + 64 = 93	137 − 92 = 45

88

3. Stand near the clover patch.

(13) 9 4

   13 clovers in the patch;
   13 is the whole number.
   What part of the 13 has bees? 9
   What part of the 13 has no bees? 4
   13 is the whole number.
   Its parts are 9 and 4.
   a. **The triplet is (13) 9 4 . . .**
   b. Point to the first flash card. **Close your eyes and say it 3 times. 13—9, 4; 13—9, 4 . . .**
   Drill each fact.

4. **Answer together. What number belongs on the blank?** (Say *blank* each time.)

12, 8 __	**11 __ 2**	**__ 6, 6**
13, 9, __	**13 __ 4**	**__ 7, 5**
11, 7 __	**12 __ 3**	**__ 9, 4**

5. Stand near the Addition and Subtraction samples.
   a. **Be careful to subtract in ones' place and in tens' place.**

   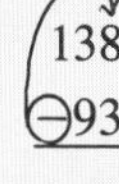

   b. **Be careful to add in ones' place and in tens' place.**

   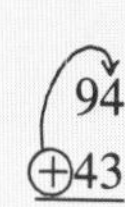

   c. Do the samples.

6. Hold the large clock. Ask a child to write the time on the board as his classmates read the time. Set the clock at **12:45, 3:45, 6:45, 10:45, 1:45, 4:45 . . .**

7. Assign Lesson 81.

Write the time.

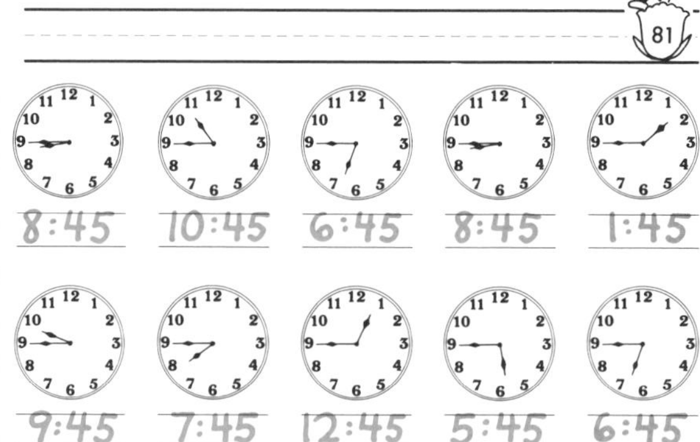

Write the numbers in the correct places.

	thousands	hundreds	tens	ones
1297	1,	2	9	7
1389	1,	3	8	9
1973	1,	9	7	3
798	,	7	9	8
1316	1,	3	1	6
1864	1,	8	6	4
62	,		6	2

	thousands	hundreds	tens	ones
45	,		4	5
590	,	5	9	0
1614	1,	6	1	4
1582	1,	5	8	2
1297	1,	2	9	7
761	,	7	6	1
1308	1,	3	0	8

89

Blacklines

Fact Hives #14

Missing Whole or Parts #9

Number Words #3

After Class

1. Drill individuals with the 11's–13's flash cards.
2. Chalkboard Drill: **Write the three numbers I say.**

   483 348 834

   Circle the number with 3 hundreds.

   506 605 650

   Circle the number with 0 ones.

   918 189 891

   Circle the number with 1 ten.

   1,432 1,243 1,324

   Circle the number with 4 hundreds.

   1,707 1,770 1,777

   Circle the greatest number.

   1,110 1,101 1,111

   Circle the smallest number.

Fill in the whole and parts.

Write the facts.

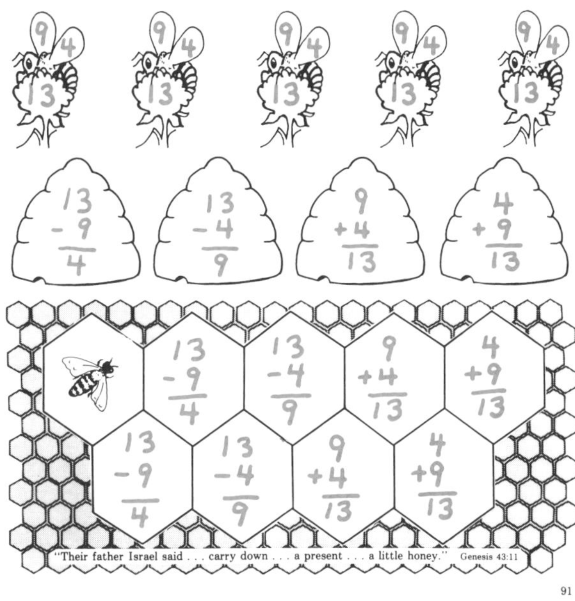

"Their father Israel said . . . carry down . . . a present . . . a little honey." Genesis 43:11
91

Before Class

Materials

Large coins

Chalkboard

25¢ 1¢ ___

10¢ 5¢ + ___

10¢ 5¢ ___

10¢ 1¢ + ___

Note: The Materials will no longer list how many blossoms you need. The boxed triplet (11) 9 2 and so forth, in the Class Time directives tell you. (11) is the number of blossoms. 9 is the number of blossoms with bees.

Class Time

1. Stand near the clover patch.

   A father bee is called a drone. A drone bee is very different from a worker bee. His tongue cannot sip nectar. He cannot make wax; he cannot make honey. He cannot fight a mouse because God did not give him a stinger.

   What can a drone do? He can crawl. He can fly. He can eat honey. He can be a father of the bees.

2. (11) 9 2

   The whole number is __.
   Its parts are __ and __.
   The facts are 11−9, 2; 11−2, 9; 9+2, 11; 2+9, 11.

3. (12) 9 3

   The whole number is __.
   Its parts are __ and __.
   The facts are 12−9, 3; 12−3, 9; 9+3, 12; 3+9, 12.

82

Count the first row.
Write the amount.
Count the second row.
Write the amount.
Add.

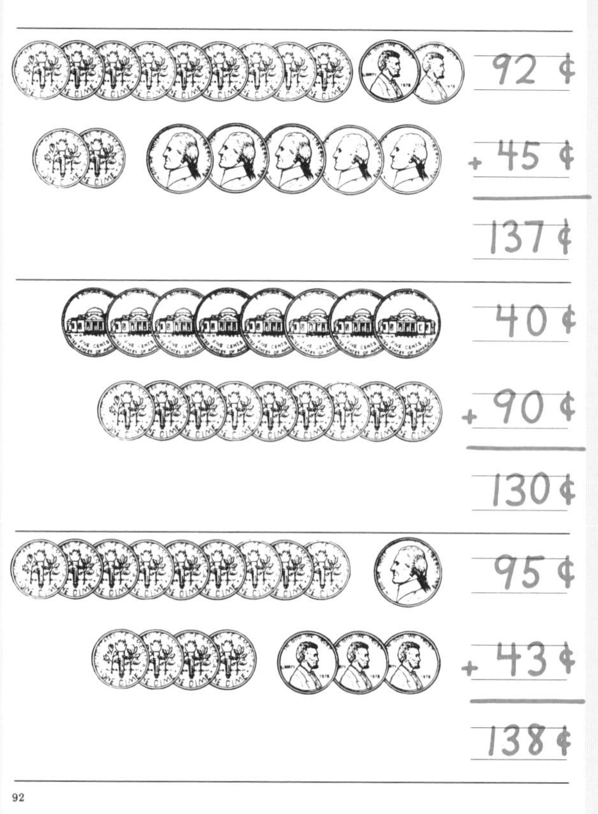

Speed Drill

4. (13) 9 4

   The whole number is __.
   Its parts are __ and __.
   The facts are 13−9, 4; 13−4, 9; 9+4, 13; 4+9, 13.

5. Point to the Blossom Charts. Drill
   (11) 9 2
   (12) 9 3
   (13) 9 4

6. Flash the large coins.
   a. **25¢, 1¢, 10¢, 5¢ . . .**
   b. **Quarter, penny, dime, nickel.**
   c. Have individuals count aloud as they do the Money samples.

7. Do the Speed Drill in Lesson 82.

8. Assign Lesson 82.

82

Answer these facts.

9	12	13	7	12	4	13	12
+4	-7	-9	+5	-6	+9	-4	-5
13	5	4	12	6	13	9	7

13	6	13	5	13	9	4	13
-9	+6	-4	+7	-9	+4	+9	-4
4	12	9	12	4	13	13	9

12	13	9	12	5	13	12	9
-5	-4	+4	-6	+7	-9	-7	+4
7	9	13	6	12	4	5	13

Blacklines

Number Facts #10

Missing Whole or Parts #9

2-Place Computation #5

Write the time.

5:45 1:45 7:45 10:45 9:45

12:45 6:45 2:45 8:45 11:45

After Class

1. Oral Drill: Speak slowly. **Raise your hand when you know the answer.**

3+9−4=	8	**4+9−4=**	9
2+8−6=	4	**3+7−2=**	8
5+6−7=	4	**5+7−9=**	3
4+5−2=	7	**8+4−5=**	7
6+6−6=	6	**2+7−4=**	5
3+8−5=	6	**9+3−8=**	4

2. Have individuals give the 11 and 12 triplets by memory.

Speed Drill
13 −4 = 9; 12 −3 = 9; 12 −9 = 3; 13 −9 = 4; 4 +9 = 13; 13 −9 = 4
9 +3 = 12; 12 −3 = 9; 9 +4 = 13; 3 +9 = 12; 13 −9 = 4; 12 −9 = 3
9 +4 = 13; 3 +9 = 12; 13 −9 = 4; 4 +9 = 13; 13 −9 = 4; 12 −9 = 3; 13 −4 = 9; 12 −3 = 9
9 +3 = 12; 4 +9 = 13; 12 −9 = 3; 13 −9 = 4; 3 +9 = 12; 9 +4 = 13; 13 −4 = 9; 9 +3 = 12

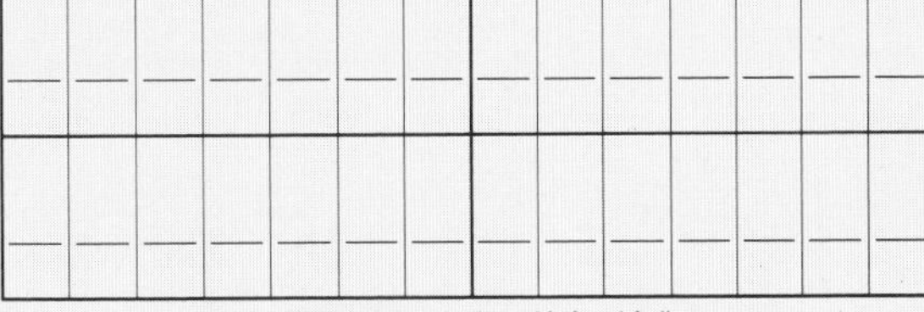

"Whatsoever thy hand findeth to do, do it with thy might." Ecclesiastes 9:10

83

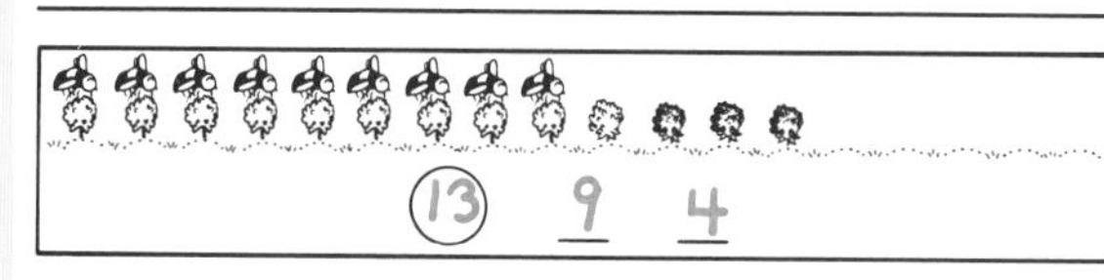

Fill in the whole and parts.

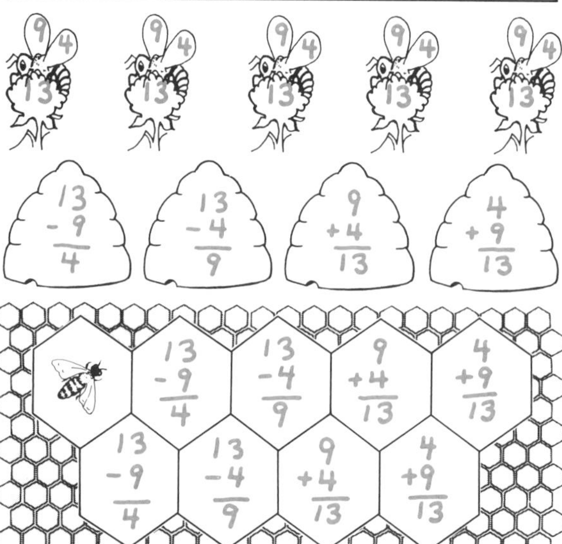

Write the facts.

Before Class

Materials

Large clock
9's–13's flash cards

Chalkboard

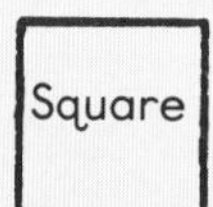

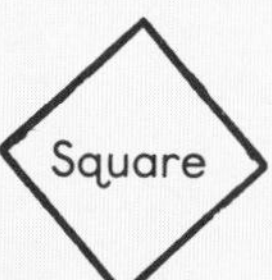

__+2=11	13−__=9
9+__=12	__−2=9
__−9=4	3+9=__
11−__=2	9+__=13

Class Time

1. Use the large clock.
   a. **60 minutes=__.** 1 hour
   30 minutes=__. ½ hour
   1 hour has __. 60 minutes
   ½ hour has __. 30 minutes
   b. Set the clock for the following situations.
   - 3:00 **Mother thought, "In 15 minutes the children will be home from school." What time will the children come?** 3:15
   - 6:00 **Father said, "We will leave for prayer meeting in 45 minutes." What time will that be?** 6:45
   - 8:00 **Grandmother took her Bible to the rocking chair and sat down. She read for 30 minutes. What time did she stop reading?** 8:30

83

Extra Activity

Fill in the missing whole or parts.

9 + 4 = 13	13 - 9 = 4	13 - 4 = 9
4 + 9 = 13	4 + 9 = 13	4 + 9 = 13
13 - 9 = 4	13 - 9 = 4	13 - 9 = 4
13 - 4 = 9	13 - 4 = 9	13 - 4 = 9
4 + 9 = 13	4 + 9 = 13	4 + 9 = 13
13 - 9 = 4	9 + 4 = 13	13 - 9 = 4

Answer these problems.

6	3	4	3	8	2	4	1
3	2	5	5	1	7	3	1
+4	+7	+4	+2	+4	+4	+5	+9
13	12	13	10	13	13	12	11

5	2	7	3	5	2	1	2
4	2	2	6	3	2	6	2
+2	+6	+4	+4	+2	+9	+3	+9
11	10	13	13	10	13	10	13

96

2. Stand near the clover patch.

   (13) 9 4

   13 clovers in the patch;
   13 is the whole number.
   What part of the 13 has bees? 9
   What part of the 13 has no bees? 4
   13 is the whole number.
   Its parts are 9 and 4.
   a. **The triplet is (13) 9 4 . . .**
   b. **The facts are 13−9, 4; 13−4, 9; 9+4, 13; 4+9, 13.**

3. Point to the Blossom Charts.
   a. Drill the triplets.
   (11) 9 2; (11) 8 3 . . .
   b. **Jump back and forth.**
   (11) 9 2
   (12) 9 3
   (13) 9 4 . . .

4. Fill in the Missing Whole or Parts samples.

5. Flash the 9's–13's cards.
   Answer together.

6. Shapes
   a. Trace *C* in the circle.
   This is a circle.
   b. Trace *S* in each square.
   This is a square.
   c. **Circle, square, square; circle, square . . .**

7. Assign Lesson 83.

Answer these problems.
Carry *over* in some problems.

34 + 69 = 103	139 − 46 = 93	95 + 42 = 137	139 − 94 = 45	49 + 54 = 103	138 − 45 = 93
139 − 97 = 42	74 + 49 = 123	138 − 44 = 94	93 + 45 = 138	29 + 74 = 103	139 − 98 = 41
136 − 95 = 41	74 + 29 = 103	46 + 92 = 138	137 − 43 = 94	69 + 54 = 123	137 − 95 = 42

Write the time.

9:45	12:45	6:45	4:45	8:45
8:45	3:45	5:45	12:45	9:45

97

Blacklines

- Fact Hives #14
- Missing Whole or Parts #9
- 2-Place Computation #5

After Class

____ ____ 120 122 ____ ____ ____

____ 55 ____ ____ ____ 75 ____

____ 310 ____ ____ 340 ____ ____

____ ____ 175 ____ 185 ____ ____

1. **Count by 5's from 100–200.**
   Count by 100's to 1,000.
2. Fill in the Missing Number samples.
   Decide if you should count by 2's, 5's, or 10's.

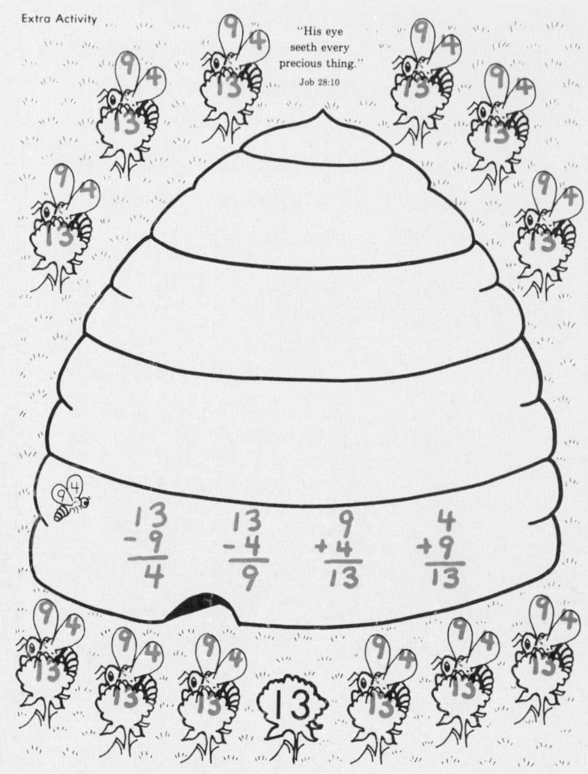

Fill in the whole and parts.

Write the facts.

"Their father Israel said . . . carry down . . . a present . . . a little honey." Genesis 43:11

99

Before Class

Materials

10's–13's flash cards

Form C

Large clock

Chalkboard

53	72	43	83	44	85
24	44	33	44	45	34
+44	+ 6	+54	+ 3	+42	+ 4

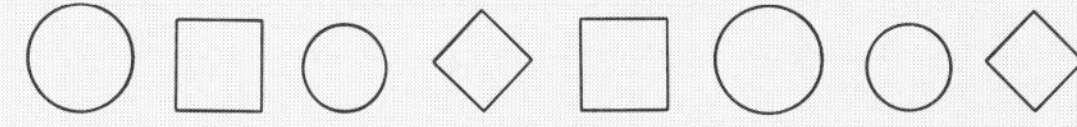

	thousands	hundreds	tens	ones
1598				
1246				
963				
1372				
1609				
1011				
25				
1437				

Class Time

1. Point to the Blossom Charts.
   Say each triplet 3 times.
2. Circle Drill: 10's–13's flash cards. **As soon as you have given ten answers, sit down.**
3. Flash Card Drill: 10's–13's flash cards. Use Form C. **Flower Row: Box 1 . . .**
4. Do the Column Addition samples.
5. Stand near the grid on the board.
   a. **Number places are ones, tens, hundreds, thousands . . .**
   b. Have the children fill the grid as everyone says **8 ones, 9 tens, 5 hundreds, (comma), 1 thousand.**
   c. **Read the numbers with me. 1,598; 1,246 . . .**
6. **Can you name the shapes?**
   Write *C* in each circle and *S* in each square as the children name them.

Read the story.
Write the numbers
in the beehive.
Write the label words
on the lines.
Answer the problem.

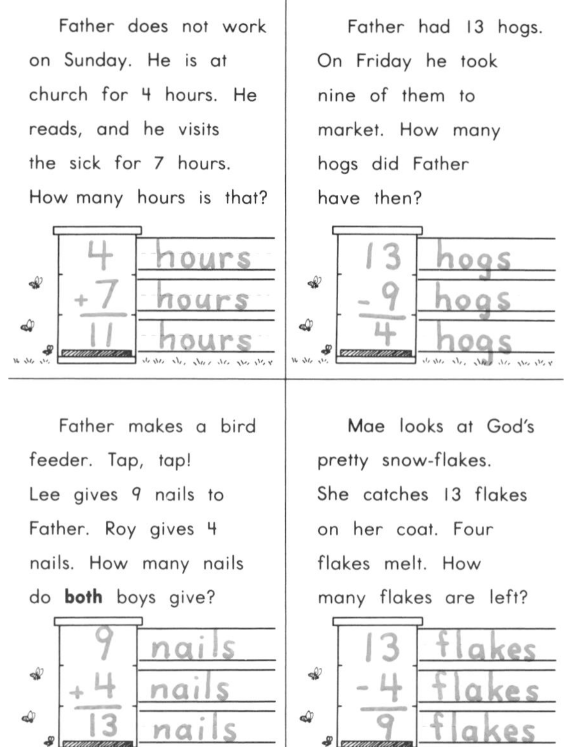

Father does not work on Sunday. He is at church for 4 hours. He reads, and he visits the sick for 7 hours. How many hours is that?

4 hours
+7 hours
11 hours

Father had 13 hogs. On Friday he took nine of them to market. How many hogs did Father have then?

13 hogs
-9 hogs
4 hogs

Father makes a bird feeder. Tap, tap! Lee gives 9 nails to Father. Roy gives 4 nails. How many nails do **both** boys give?

9 nails
+4 nails
13 nails

Mae looks at God's pretty snow-flakes. She catches 13 flakes on her coat. Four flakes melt. How many flakes are left?

13 flakes
-4 flakes
9 flakes

100

7. Do the Speed Drill in Lesson 84.
8. Assign Lesson 84.

84

Answer these problems.
Carry *over* in some problems.

45	52	35	55	44	61
23	37	43	32	42	25
+52	+42	+51	+25	+45	+42
120	131	129	112	131	128

92	32	63	44	23	45
43	17	61	92	26	80
+ 4	+ 3	+ 2	+ 3	+ 3	+ 1
139	52	126	139	52	126

14	44	35	56	24	74
23	34	43	12	14	15
+94	+42	+34	+61	+90	+42
131	120	112	129	128	131

Follow the directions.

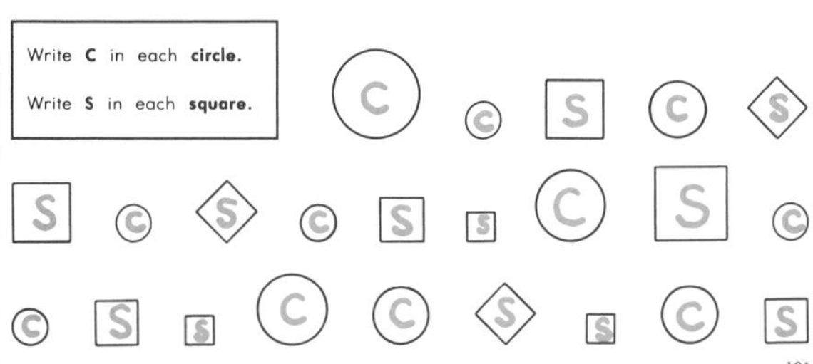

Write C in each circle.
Write S in each square.

101

Blacklines

Form C (Class Time)

Number Facts #10

Triplets With Facts #6

2-Place Computation (+) #6

After Class

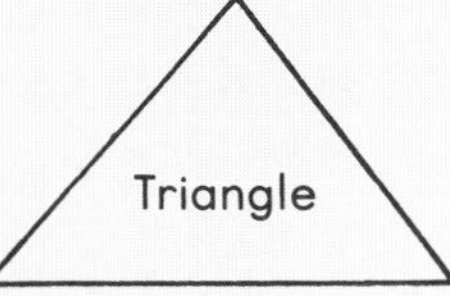

Triangle

1. Hold the large clock. Ask individuals to set the clock at
   •1:45, 3:45, 6:45, 9:45
   •11:15, 2:15, 4:15, 7:15
   •8:45, 10:15, 12:45, 1:15 . . .
2. Shapes
   a. **Name some fruits and vegetables that are round.** peaches, squash, watermelon, peas, cherries . . .
   b. **Name some things in your house that are square.** block, cake pan, hot pad, floor tile, book . . .
   c. Trace *T* in the triangle.
   This is a triangle.

Speed
Drill

13	12	12	12	13	12
-9	-6	-5	-8	-9	-3
4	6	7	4	4	9

11	12	11	12	13	11
-5	-8	-5	-5	-4	-2
6	4	6	7	9	9

11	13	12	11	12	11	12	13
-4	-4	-3	-7	-8	-4	-6	-9
7	9	9	4	4	7	6	4

13	12	11	13	12	12	13	11
-4	-5	-2	-4	-5	-6	-9	-5
9	7	9	9	7	6	4	6

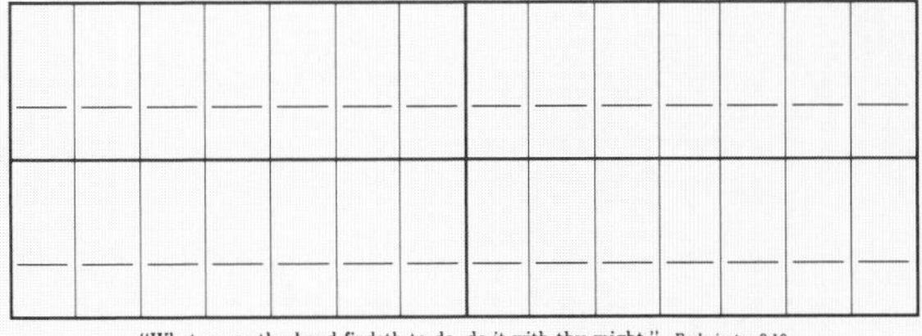

"Whatsoever thy hand findeth to do, do it with thy might." Ecclesiastes 9:10

102

Fill in the whole and parts.

(13) 9 4

Write the facts.

13	13	9	4
−9	−4	+4	+9
4	9	13	13

Trace, answer, and write the facts.

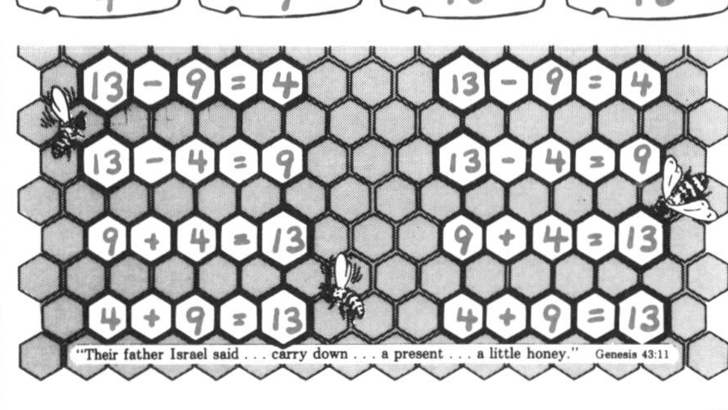

13 − 9 = 4
13 − 4 = 9
9 + 4 = 13
4 + 9 = 13
"Their father Israel said . . . carry down . . . a present . . . a little honey." Genesis 43:11

103

Before Class

Materials

Large clock

11's–13's flash cards

Chalkboard

Class Time

1. Stand near the clover patch.

   In the Book of Genesis a father helped his ten sons to prepare a gift. The sons were to take the gift to the ruler of Egypt.

   What was the gift? It was fruit, spices, nuts, and __. honey

   Who was the father? Jacob (Israel)

   Who was the ruler? Joseph

   (Genesis 43:11, 15)

2. | (13) 9 4 |
   |---|

   13 clovers in the patch;
   13 is the whole number.
   What part of the 13 has bees? 9
   What part of the 13 has no bees? 4
   13 is the whole number.
   Its parts are 9 and 4.

   a. **The triplet is (13) 9 4 . . .**

   b. **Girls, the facts are 13−9, 4 . . .**
      Boys, the facts are 13−9, 4 . . .

3. Drill the triplets on each Blossom Chart.

85

Extra Activity

Answer these facts.

13 -9 4	12 -3 9	13 -4 9	13 -9 4	9 +4 13	13 -4 9	12 -3 9	9 +4 13
4 +9 13	13 -4 9	3 +9 12	4 +9 13	13 -9 4	9 +3 12	13 -4 9	13 -9 4
12 -9 3	12 -3 9	4 +9 13	12 -9 3	9 +3 12	9 +4 13	12 -3 9	3 +9 12
9 +3 12	4 +9 13	13 -9 4	3 +9 12	12 -9 3	13 -9 4	9 +4 13	12 -9 3
13 -9 4	12 -3 9	13 -9 4	13 -4 9	12 -9 3	13 -9 4	12 -3 9	3 +9 12
		9 +3 12	12 -9 3	13 -4 9	12 -3 9	9 +3 12	13 -9 4

104

4. **Say the facts as I fill the beehives.** Begin with (11) 9 2.
5. Hold the large clock.
   The boys will answer the first time. The girls will answer the second time.
   Set the clock at
   •4:15, 4:45, 7:15, 7:45
   •10:15, 11:45, 1:15, 3:45 . . .
6. Review shapes.
   Have each child name a shape and then write *S* or *T* in it.
7. Assign Lesson 85.

Write the time.

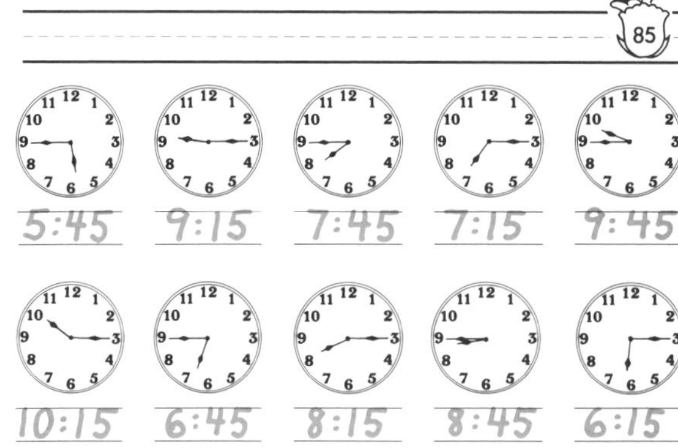

Follow the directions.

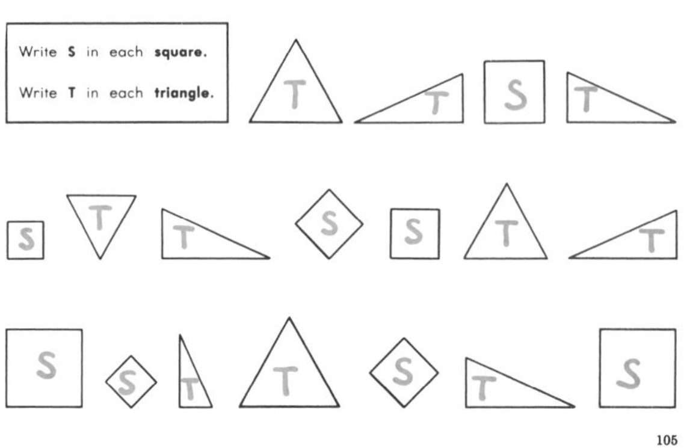

Blacklines

2-Place Computation (+) #6

Triplets With Facts #6

After Class

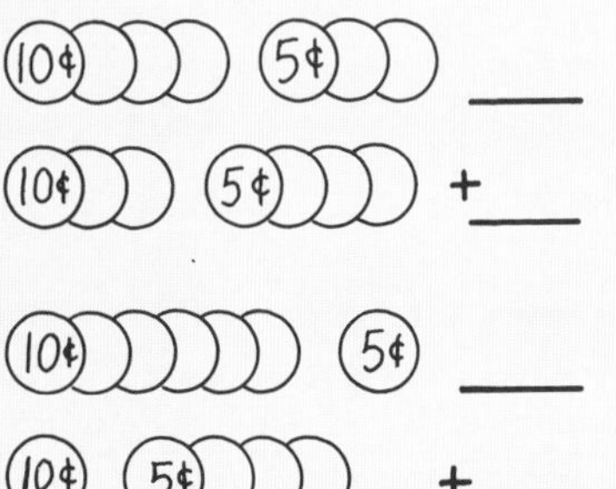

1. Drill 11's–13's flash cards. **Say the triplet; then say the answer.**
2. Stand near the Number Line.
   Count by 10's; then count by 5's.
   •10, 20, 25, 30, 35
   •10, 20, 30, 40, 45, 50, 55, 60
   •10, 20, 30, 40, 50, 60, 65, 70, 75
   •10, 15, 20, 25, 30, 35, 40
3. Have individuals count aloud as they do the Money samples.

Extra Activity
"His eye seeth every precious thing."
Job 28:10
106

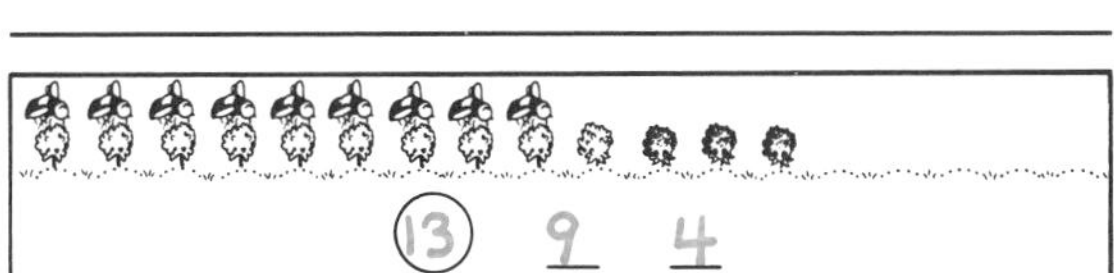

Fill in the whole and parts.

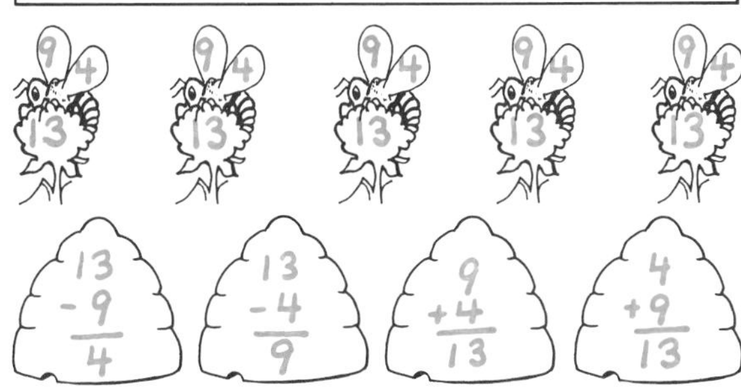

Write the facts.

Trace, answer, and write the facts.

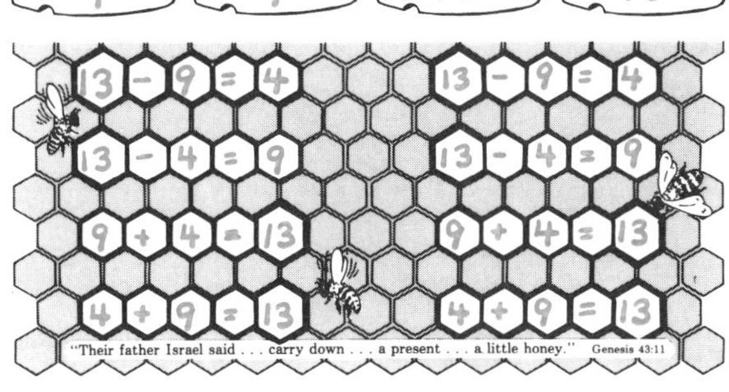

"Their father Israel said . . . carry down . . . a present . . . a little honey." Genesis 43:11
107

Before Class

Materials

9's–13's flash cards

Chalkboard

138	75	43	36	127	85	119	138
−96	+47	+94	+84	−63	+45	−67	−45

Class Time

1. Stand near the clover patch.

(12) 9 3

   The whole number is __.
   Its parts are __ and __.
   The facts are 12−9, 3; 12−3, 9; 9+3, 12; 3+9, 12.

2. | (12) 8 4 |
   |---|

   The whole number is __.
   Its parts are __ and __.
   The facts are 12−8, 4; 12−4, 8; 8+4, 12; 4+8, 12.

3. | (12) 7 5 |
   |---|

   The whole number is __.
   Its parts are __ and __.
   The facts are 12−7, 5; 12−5, 7; 7+5, 12; 5+7, 12.

86

Answer these facts.

Speed Drill

13	11	12	13	8	11	12	3
-9	-2	-8	-9	+4	-7	-3	+9
4	9	4	4	12	4	9	12
4	12	6	9	11	5	12	12
+9	-9	+5	+4	-7	+6	-9	-8
13	3	11	13	4	11	3	4
12	11	4	11	6	9	12	7
-6	-8	+9	-5	+6	+4	-9	+5
6	3	13	6	12	13	3	12
8	3	12	9	11	11	5	11
+3	+9	-7	+2	-9	-6	+7	-9
11	12	5	11	2	5	12	2
11	13	11	12	4	12	11	9
-3	-4	-4	-4	+9	-5	-2	+4
8	9	7	8	13	7	9	13
		3	13	7	12	4	11
		+8	-4	+4	-3	+9	-2
		11	9	11	9	13	9

108

4. (12) 6 6

The whole number is __.
Its parts are __ and __.
The facts are 12−6, 6; 6+6, 12.

5. (13) 9 4

The whole number is __.
Its parts are __ and __.
The facts are 13−9, 4; 13−4, 9; 9+4, 13; 4+9, 13.

6. Story Problems
   a. **Carl and Dale's family worship at a small church. There are 6 benches on the women's side and 6 benches on the men's side. How many is that altogether? Who can give us the whole problem?**

      6 benches + 6 benches = 12 benches.

   b. **Hold that answer in your mind as you listen again. When Carl and Dale's family cleaned the church, the boys helped to dust. Carl dusted 5 benches. How many did Dale dust? Who . . . ?**

      12 benches − 5 benches = 7 benches.

7. Do the Computation samples.
8. Do the Speed Drill in Lesson 86.
9. Assign Lesson 86.

After Class

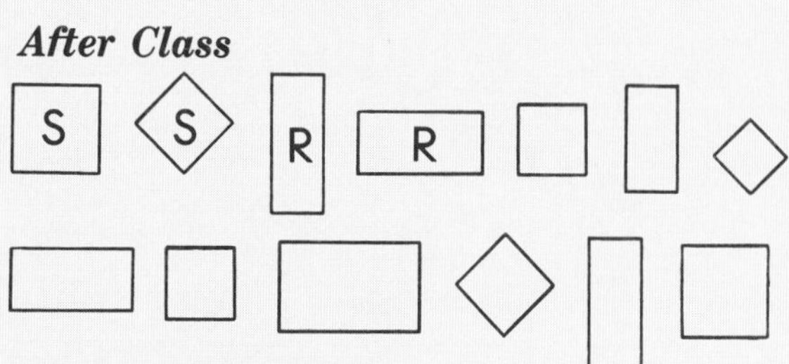

Write the time.

1:15 | 1:45 | 3:15 | 4:45 | 5:15

12:45 | 2:15 | 3:45 | 4:15 | 10:45

Follow the directions.

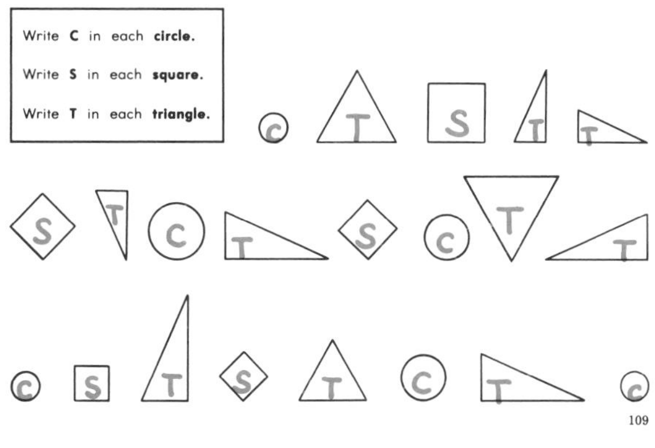

Blacklines

Number Facts #10

Triplets With Facts #6

2-Place Computation (+) #6

1. Circle Drill: 9's–13's flash cards.
2. Shapes
   a. Trace *S* in each square. **Square, square . . .**
   b. Trace *R* in each rectangle. **Rectangle, rectangle . . .**
   c. Have the children name and label the other shapes.
3. Chalkboard Drill: **Write the number you hear.**
   - **King Asa's priests offered 700 oxen to the Lord.** (2 Chronicles 15:11)
   - **A king gave Abraham 1,000 pieces of silver.** (Genesis 20:16)
   - **King Ahab counted 232 princes.** (1 Kings 20:15)
   - **A king took 832 people to his land.** (Jeremiah 52:29)
   - **King David had 1,700 officers.** (1 Chronicles 26:30)

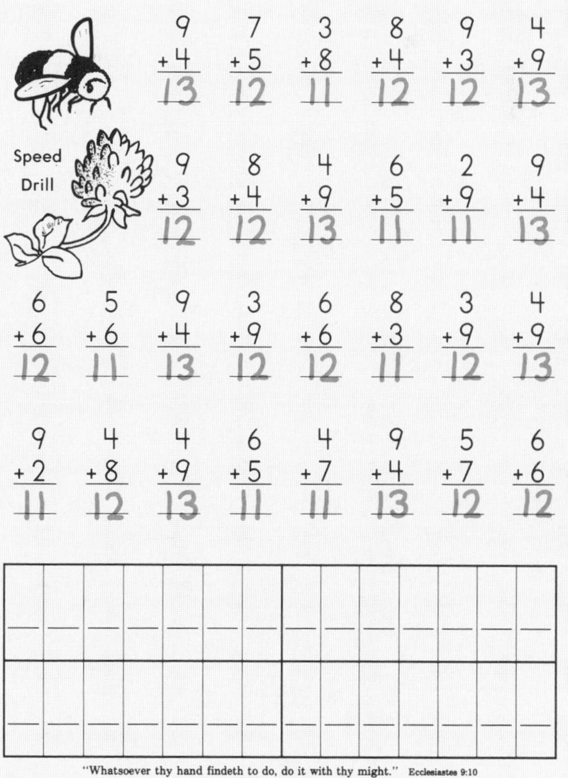
Speed Drill

9 + 4 = 13 | 7 + 5 = 12 | 3 + 8 = 11 | 8 + 4 = 12 | 9 + 3 = 12 | 4 + 9 = 13

9 + 3 = 12 | 8 + 4 = 12 | 4 + 9 = 13 | 6 + 5 = 11 | 2 + 9 = 11 | 9 + 4 = 13

6 + 6 = 12 | 5 + 6 = 11 | 9 + 4 = 13 | 3 + 9 = 12 | 6 + 6 = 12 | 8 + 3 = 11 | 3 + 9 = 12 | 4 + 9 = 13

9 + 2 = 11 | 4 + 8 = 12 | 4 + 9 = 13 | 6 + 5 = 11 | 4 + 7 = 11 | 9 + 4 = 13 | 5 + 7 = 12 | 6 + 6 = 12

"Whatsoever thy hand findeth to do, do it with thy might." Ecclesiastes 9:10

110

87

Trace and fill in the whole and parts.

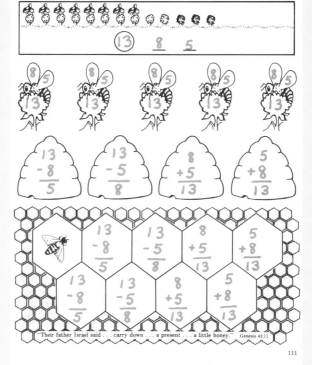

Trace, answer, and write the facts.

"Their father Israel said . . . carry down . . . a present . . . a little honey." Genesis 43:11

111

Before Class

Make (13) 8 5 flash cards for each child.

Tack (13) 8 5 flash cards above the clover patch in the order:

13	13	8	5
−8	−5	+5	+8
5	8	13	13

Materials

11's–13's flash cards

Chalkboard

Class Time

1. Have each child bring *My 1,000 Book* to the teaching corner.
   a. **Count by 10's to 400.**
   b. **Count on to 600 by 5's.**
2. Stand near the clover patch.

   (13) 8 5

   a. **How many pink clovers are in the patch?** 10
   We think—10 pink.
   3 more make __ altogether. 13
   We think—10 pink.
   2 less make __ clovers with bees. 8
   b. **13 clovers in the patch;**
   13 is the whole number.
   What part of the 13 has bees? 8
   What part of the 13 has no bees? 5
   13 is the whole number.
   Its parts are 8 and 5.

87

Extra Activity

Answer these facts.

13 − 8 = 5	13 − 8 = 5	13 − 5 = 8	13 − 8 = 5	5 + 8 = 13	13 − 5 = 8	13 − 8 = 5	8 + 5 = 13
5 + 8 = 13	13 − 5 = 8	8 + 5 = 13	5 + 8 = 13	13 − 5 = 8	8 + 5 = 13	13 − 5 = 8	13 − 5 = 8
13 − 8 = 5	13 − 5 = 8	5 + 8 = 13	13 − 5 = 8	8 + 5 = 13	5 + 8 = 13	13 − 5 = 8	5 + 8 = 13
8 + 5 = 13	5 + 8 = 13	13 − 8 = 5	5 + 8 = 13	13 − 5 = 8	13 − 8 = 5	8 + 5 = 13	13 − 5 = 8
13 − 8 = 5	13 − 5 = 8	13 − 8 = 5	13 − 5 = 8	8 + 5 = 13	13 − 8 = 5	13 − 5 = 8	5 + 8 = 13
		8 + 5 = 13	13 − 8 = 5	5 + 8 = 13	13 − 8 = 5	8 + 5 = 13	13 − 5 = 8

112

c. **The triplet is (13) 8 5; (13) 8 5 . . .**

d. **The facts are 13−8, 5; 13−5, 8; 8+5, 13; 5+8, 13 . . .**

3. Ask a child to write the triplet in the clover and bees as everyone says **(13) 8 5; (13) 8 5 . . .**
4. **Say the facts as I fill the beehive.** Begin with 13−9=4.
5. Have the children name and label the shapes.
6. **Answer together.**

10+2	**10+6**	**10+1**
10+5	**10+4**	**10+3**
10+9	**10+8**	**10+7**

7. Assign Lesson 87.

Write the time.

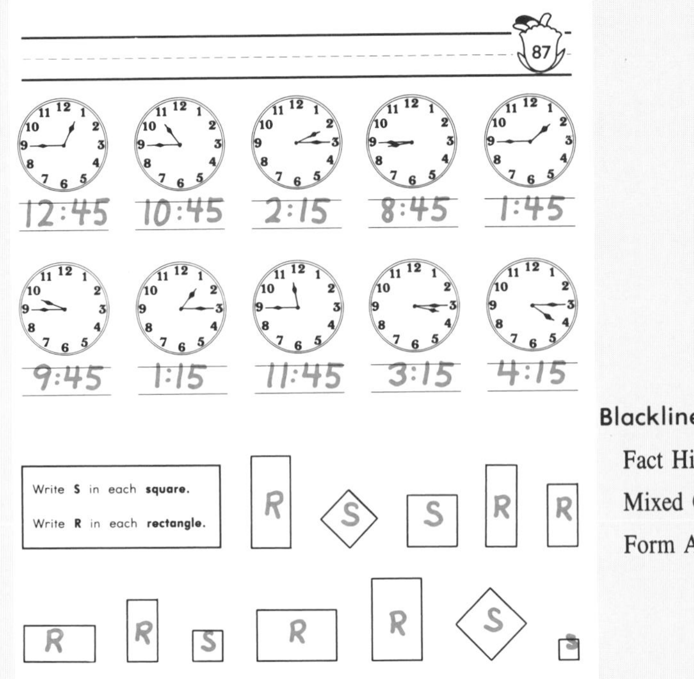

Blacklines

Fact Hives #15

Mixed Computation #1

Form A: 800–899

After Class

98	67	89	97	58	96
−75	−42	−68	−63	−33	−53

Use white chalk to write these problems on the board.

1. Give each child his (13) 8 5 flash cards.
2. Flash 11's–13's cards. **Answer together.**
3. Call the children to the Subtraction samples.
   a. **The sign says we should __.** subtract
   b. Point to ones' place. **We always do __.** ones' place first
   c. **Which number is greater, 8 or 5?** Circle 8 with colored chalk. ***The greater number is at the top.***
   d. Continue down the row. Point to ones' place. **Which number is greater?** Circle it. ***The greater number is at the top.***
   e. Have the children answer the problems.

Extra Activity
"His eye seeth every precious thing."
Job 28:10
13 − 8 = 5
13 − 5 = 8
8 + 5 = 13
5 + 8 = 13
13 − 9 = 4
13 − 4 = 9
9 + 4 = 13
4 + 9 = 13
13
114

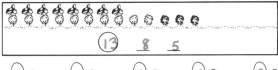

88

Fill in the whole and parts.

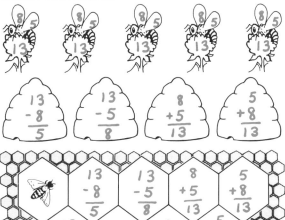

(13) 8 5

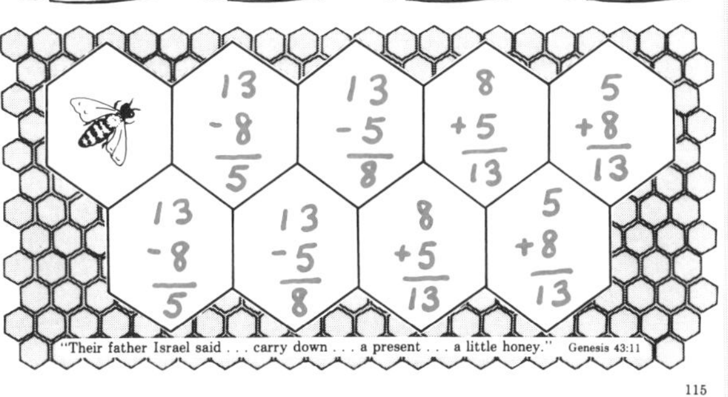

Trace, answer, and write the facts.

13	13	8	5
− 8	− 5	+ 5	+ 8
5	8	13	13

13	13	8	5
− 8	− 5	+ 5	+ 8
5	8	13	13

13	13	8	5
− 8	− 5	+ 5	+ 8
5	8	13	13

"Their father Israel said . . . carry down . . . a present . . . a little honey." Genesis 43:11

115

Before Class

Add bee (13) 8 5 to Blossom 13 Chart.

Materials

11's–13's flash cards

Large clock

Chalkboard

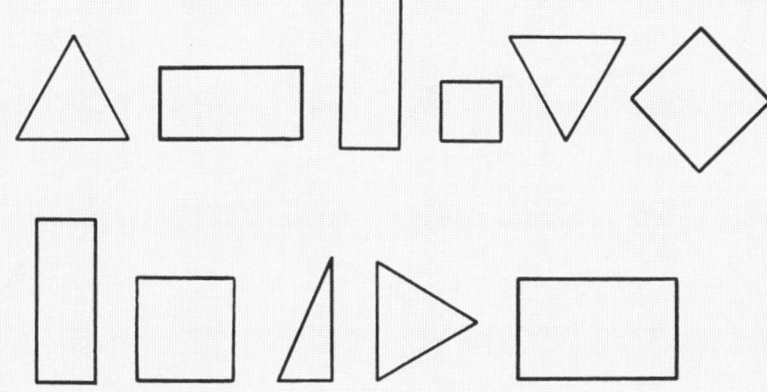

Class Time

1. Stand near the clover patch.

(13) 8 5

   13 clovers in the patch;
   13 is the whole number.
   What part of the 13 has bees? 8
   What part of the 13 has no bees? 5
   13 is the whole number.
   Its parts are 8 and 5.
   a. **The triplet is (13) 8 5;**
   (13) 8 5 . . .
   b. Point to the first flash card.
   Close your eyes and say it 3 times.
   13−8, 5; 13−8, 5 . . .
2. Drill the triplets on each Blossom Chart.
3. Flash 11's–13's cards.
   Boys, say the triplet.
   Girls, say the answer.

88

Answer these facts.

13 -5 8	13 -8 5	13 -5 8	13 -5 8	8 +5 13	13 -5 8	13 -8 5	5 +8 13
8 +5 13	13 -8 5	5 +8 13	8 +5 13	13 -5 8	5 +8 13	13 -8 5	13 -5 8
13 -8 5	13 -5 8	8 +5 13	13 -8 5	5 +8 13	8 +5 13	13 -5 8	5 +8 13
8 +5 13	5 +8 13	13 -8 5	8 +5 13	13 -5 8	13 -8 5	5 +8 13	13 -5 8
13 -8 5	13 -8 5	13 -5 8	13 -8 5	8 +5 13	13 -5 8	13 -8 5	5 +8 13
		8 +5 13	13 -5 8	5 +8 13	13 -5 8	8 +5 13	13 -8 5

116

4. Set the large clock at 5:00.
   a. **What time will it be in**
      30 minutes? **1 hour?**
      45 minutes? **2 hours?**
      15 minutes? **1½ hours?**
   b. **Read the time together.**
      6:45, 7:15, 8:00, 9:30, 10:15, 11:00, 12:45, 1:30, 2:15 . . .
5. Shapes
   a. **Name the first row of shapes.**
      Write *T, R, R, S* . . .
   b. Ask individuals to name and label the second row.
6. Do the Speed Drill in Lesson 88.
7. Assign Lesson 88.

Note on ***After Class:*** Today subtraction and place value converge into the borrowing process. The term "borrow *back*" will be used to help the child remember which way to go when he borrows. A tens' place number is borrowed back to ones' place when subtracting.

"Borrow *back*" is a directional term that guides the child through this complex step in subtraction. Saying "*back*" as he does the calculation will help the child establish the proper direction of transfer.

88

Answer these problems.
Carry *over* in some problems.

76 + 45 = 121	97 + 42 = 139	86 + 36 = 122	35 + 96 = 131	36 + 93 = 129	84 + 48 = 132
53 + 76 = 129	37 + 94 = 131	89 + 32 = 121	86 + 46 = 132	55 + 67 = 122	94 + 45 = 139
43 + 96 = 139	33 + 88 = 121	87 + 44 = 131	57 + 65 = 122	35 + 97 = 132	93 + 36 = 129

Write **S** in each **square.**

Write **T** in each **triangle.**

Write **R** in each **rectangle.**

117

Blacklines

Fact Hives #15

Number Facts #11

After Class

57	98	76	88
−43	−45	−45	−63
93	71	82	62
−74	−56	−66	−47

Use white chalk.

Stand near the Subtraction samples.

a. Do the first row. Have individuals circle the greater number in ones' place with colored chalk and then answer the problem.

b. Point to the second row. **Which number is greater, 3 or 4?** Circle 4. ***The greater number is not at the top.*** **What shall we do?**

c. **We will go to 9 and borrow *back*** (cross out 9) **one.**
Write a small 1.
1 less than 9 is __.
Write 8 above the 9.

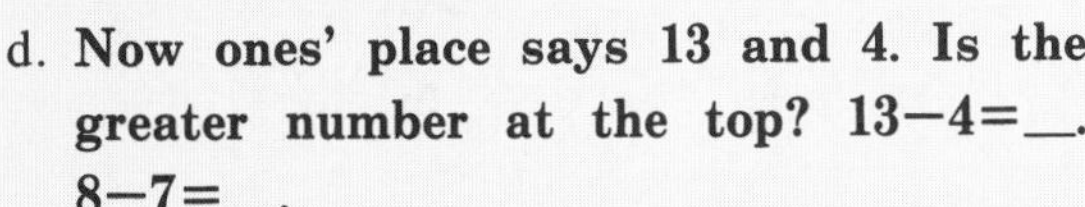

d. **Now ones' place says 13 and 4. Is the greater number at the top? 13−4=__. 8−7=__.**

e. Work each problem step by step for the children. Circle the greater number, borrow *back*, subtract.

Speed Drill
13 − 5 = 8, 5 + 8 = 13, 13 − 8 = 5, 13 − 5 = 8, 8 + 5 = 13, 8 + 5 = 13
13 − 8 = 5, 13 − 5 = 8, 13 − 8 = 5, 8 + 5 = 13, 13 − 5 = 8, 5 + 8 = 13
5 + 8 = 13, 13 − 5 = 8, 8 + 5 = 13, 5 + 8 = 13, 13 − 5 = 8, 13 − 8 = 5, 8 + 5 = 13, 13 − 5 = 8
13 − 5 = 8, 5 + 8 = 13, 8 + 5 = 13, 13 − 5 = 8, 5 + 8 = 13, 13 − 8 = 5, 13 − 5 = 8, 13 − 8 = 5
"Whatsoever thy hand findeth to do, do it with thy might." Ecclesiastes 9:10
118

89

Fill in the whole and parts.

Trace, answer, and write the facts.

89
(13) 8 5
"Their father Israel said ... carry down . . . a present ... a little honey." Genesis 43:11
119

Before Class

Materials

9's–13's flash cards

Large clock

Large coins

Chalkboard

82	73	91	82	72	93
−45	−34	−36	−43	−28	−48

Class Time

1. Circle Drill: 9's–13's flash cards.
2. Point to Blossom 11, 12, and 13 Charts.
   a. **Say each triplet 3 times.**
   b. **Jump from chart to chart.**
      (11) 9 2
      (12) 9 3
      (13) 9 4 . . .
3. Stand near the clover patch.

(13) 8 5

   13 clovers in the patch;
   13 is the whole number.
   What part of the 13 has bees? 8
   What part of the 13 has no bees? 5
   13 is the whole number.
   Its parts are 8 and 5.
   a. **The triplet is (13) 8 5 . . .**
   b. **The facts are 13−8, 5; 13−5, 8; 8+5, 13; 5+8, 13 . . .**

89

Extra Activity

Answer these problems.

136 − 86 = 50	38 + 45 = 83	137 − 55 = 82	136 − 84 = 52	56 + 83 = 139	138 − 56 = 82
35 + 68 = 103	139 − 86 = 53	75 + 55 = 130	139 − 54 = 85	38 + 25 = 63	139 − 81 = 58
55 + 28 = 83	138 − 88 = 50	134 − 82 = 52	135 − 53 = 82	139 − 57 = 82	84 + 55 = 139
138 − 85 = 53	58 + 45 = 103	137 − 52 = 85	46 + 84 = 130	138 − 80 = 58	35 + 28 = 63
138 − 83 = 55	82 + 52 = 134	138 − 54 = 84	78 + 25 = 103	74 + 56 = 130	139 − 88 = 51
		85 + 18 = 103	137 − 53 = 84	51 + 83 = 134	137 − 82 = 55

120

4. Story Problems
   a. **At recess the children rolled 8 huge snowballs and 5 tiny snowballs. How many was that? Who can give us the whole problem?**
      8 snowballs + 5 snowballs = 13 snowballs.
   b. **Hold that answer in your mind. By and by God sent warm sunshine. The 5 tiny snowballs melted. How many snowballs were left? Who . . . ?**
      13 snowballs − 5 snowballs = 8 snowballs.
5. Do the Borrow *back* samples.
   a. **Which number is greater, 2 or 5?** Circle 5. ***The greater number is not at the top.* We borrow *back*** (cross out 8) **one from** ___. Write a small 1. **1 less than 8 is** ___.
   b. Have the children finish the samples. Each child will say, **"The greater number is not at the top. Borrow *back* 1 . . ."**
6. Use the large clock.
   Read the time together.
   •3:00, 3:15, 3:30, 3:45
   •8:00, 8:15, 8:30, 8:45 . . .
7. Assign Lesson 89.

Note: Beginning in Lesson 90, you need one colored pencil for each child. He will use it to shade the greater number in ones' place. That will help him decide if he needs to borrow before he subtracts.

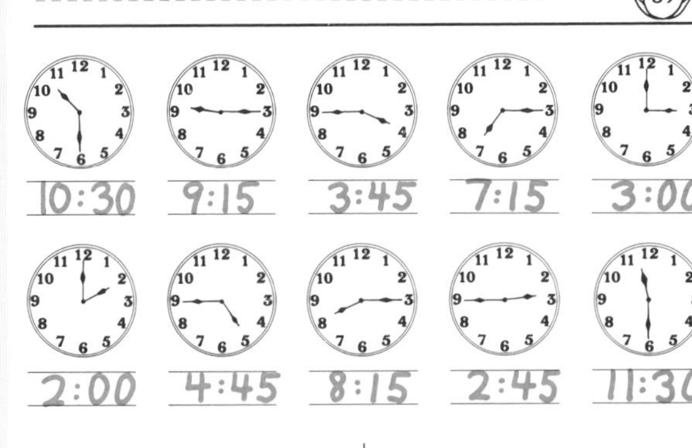

Write the time.

Read the story.
Write the numbers in the beehive.
Write the label words on the lines.
Answer the problem.

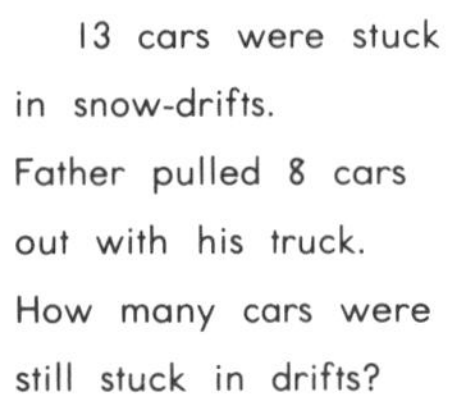

13 cars were stuck in snow-drifts. Father pulled 8 cars out with his truck. How many cars were still stuck in drifts?

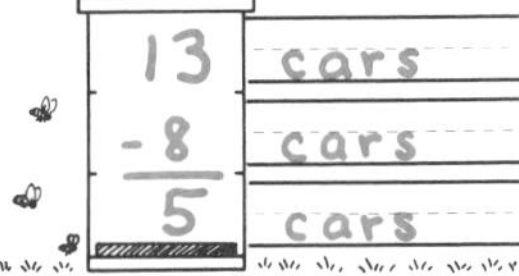

Joy sang eight songs as she swept snow from the porch and 5 songs as she helped make pies. How many songs was that altogether?

8	songs
+ 5	songs
13	songs

121

Blacklines

- Fact Hives #15
- Missing Whole or Parts #10
- Fact Form IV

After Class

1 dime + 1 nickel= __
3 dimes + 2 pennies= __
1 dime + 8 pennies= __
1 quarter + 5 pennies= __
4 dimes + 1 nickel= __
2 dimes + 4 nickels= __

1. Have individuals give the 11, 12, and 13 triplets by memory.
2. Flash the large coins.
   a. **Dime, 10¢; nickel, 5¢; penny, 1¢; quarter, 25¢ . . . .**
   b. **Which coin is worth the same as**
      5 pennies? nickel
      5 nickels? quarter
      2 nickels? dime
      10 pennies? dime
      2 dimes+1 nickel? quarter
   c. Do the Money samples.

Fill in the whole and parts.

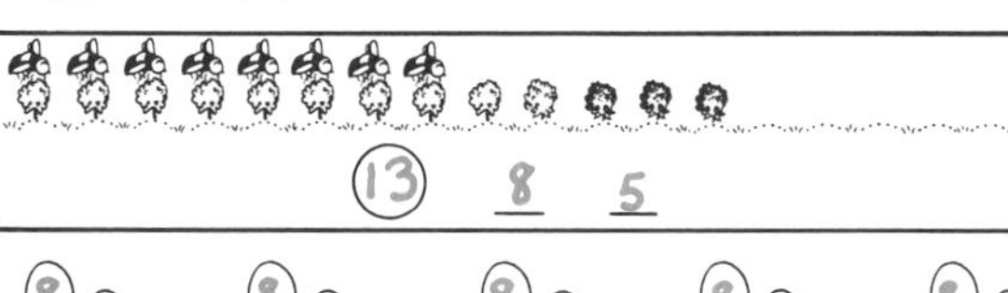

Write the facts.

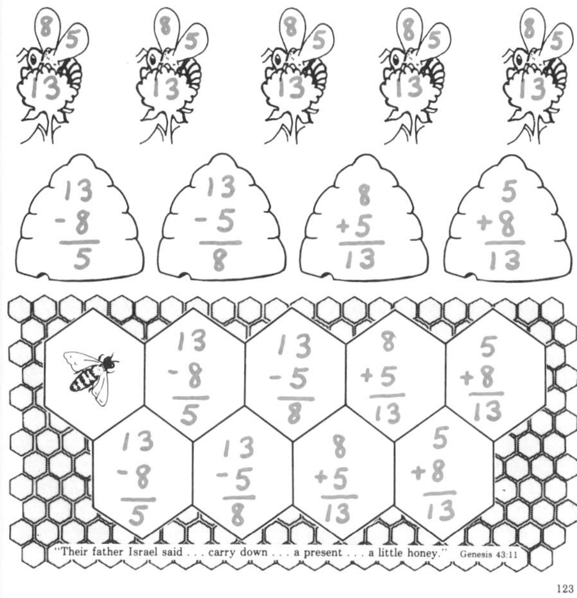

"Their father Israel said . . . carry down . . . a present . . . a little honey." Genesis 43:11
123

Before Class

Materials

1 colored pencil for each child

Chalkboard

63	83	92	82	73	91	72
−49	−35	−37	−26	−48	−55	−38

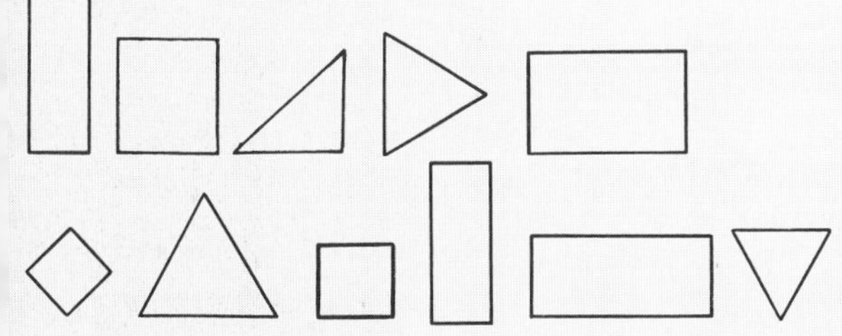

Class Time

1. Stand near the clover patch.

   When frosty nights freeze the blossoms, there is no more nectar. The worker bees swarm into the hive. They sting the drones. They chase and drag the drones out of the hive.

   The drones' work is done. They must die. When the drones are all gone, the worker bees eat honey and rest.

2. (11) 8 3

   The whole number is __.
   Its parts are __ and __.
   The facts are 11−8, 3; 11−3, 8; 8+3, 11; 3+8, 11.

3. (12) 8 4

   The whole number is __.
   Its parts are __ and __.
   The facts are 12−8, 4; 12−4, 8; 8+4, 12; 4+8, 12.

Count the first row.
Write the amount.
Count the second row.
Write the amount.
Add.

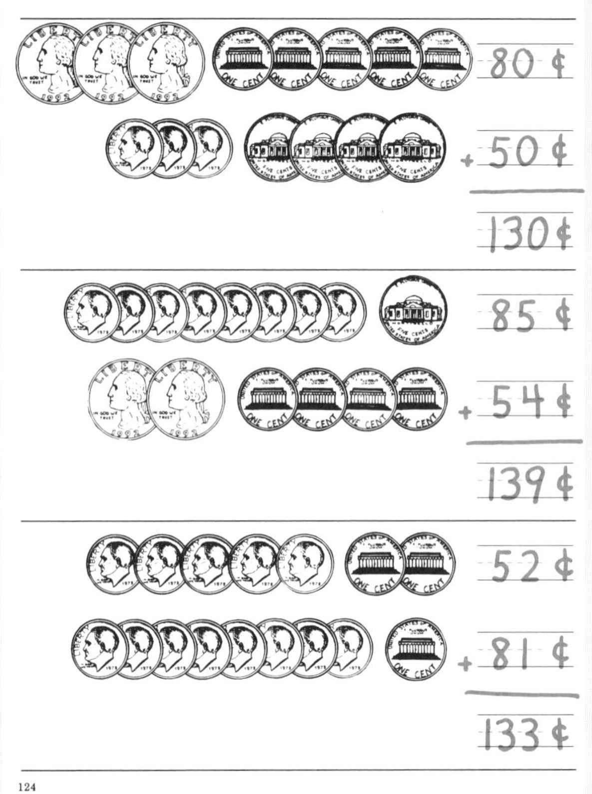

4. | (13) 8 5 |
   The whole number is __.
   Its parts are __ and __.
   The facts are 13−8, 5; 13−5, 8; 8+5, 13; 5+8, 13.

5. Point to the Blossom Charts. Drill
   (11) 8 3
   (12) 8 4
   (13) 8 5 . . .

6. Do the Borrow *back* samples.
   Where do we begin? ones' place
   Which number is greater? Circle it.
   Can you tell me what to do next?
   Borrow *back* 1 from . . .

7. **Name the shapes as I label them.**

8. Do the Speed Drill in Lesson 90.

9. Assign Lesson 90.

90

Shade the greater number in ones' place.
Borrow *back*.
Answer the problem.

93 − 65 = 28 | 52 − 16 = 36 | 81 − 32 = 49 | 52 − 28 = 24 | 71 − 46 = 25 | 93 − 49 = 44

83 − 49 = 34 | 91 − 66 = 25 | 73 − 49 = 24 | 83 − 34 = 49 | 61 − 15 = 46 | 93 − 65 = 28

Answer these facts.

8 + 5 = 13 | 12 − 7 = 5 | 13 − 9 = 4 | 7 + 5 = 12 | 12 − 6 = 6 | 4 + 9 = 13 | 13 − 8 = 5 | 12 − 5 = 7

13 − 5 = 8 | 6 + 6 = 12 | 13 − 4 = 9 | 5 + 7 = 12 | 13 − 5 = 8 | 8 + 5 = 13 | 5 + 8 = 13 | 13 − 4 = 9

12 − 5 = 7 | 13 − 8 = 5 | 5 + 8 = 13 | 12 − 6 = 6 | 5 + 7 = 12 | 13 − 9 = 4 | 12 − 7 = 5 | 9 + 4 = 13

125

Blacklines

Number Facts #11

Missing Whole or Parts #10

After Class

12	8	9	12	7	13	13	5
7	5	4	6	5	8	9	6
5	13	13	6	12	5	4	11

1. Have responsive counting. **Count by 10's to 300. I'll say the first number; you say the next number.**
2. Flash 9's–13's cards.
3. Complete the Computation samples.

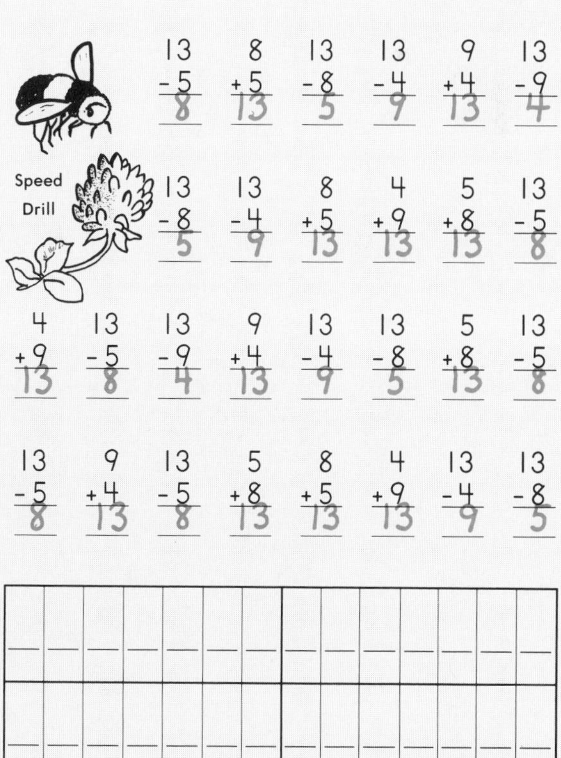

Speed Drill
"Whatsoever thy hand findeth to do, do it with thy might." Ecclesiastes 9:10
126

91

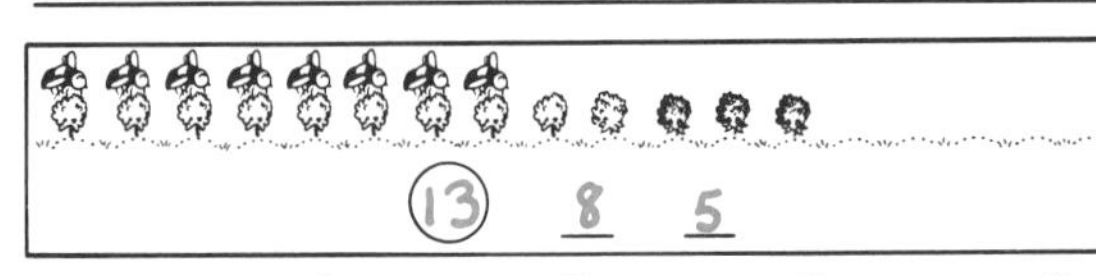

Fill in the whole and parts.

Write the facts.

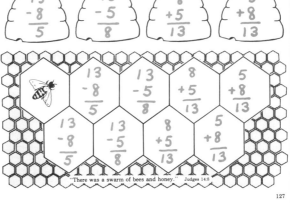

91
(13) 8 5
13 -8 5
13 -5 8
8 +5 13
5 +8 13
"There was a swarm of bees and honey." Judges 14:8
127

Before Class

Materials

Large clock

Chalkboard

52	45	43	42	75
64	43	24	46	54
+ 3	+43	+45	+51	+ 4

Class Time

1. Stand near the clover patch.

(13) 8 5

   13 clovers in the patch;
   13 is the whole number.
   What part of the 13 has bees? 8
   What part of the 13 has no bees? 5
   13 is the whole number.
   Its parts are 8 and 5.
   a. **The triplet is (13) 8 5 . . .**
   b. **The facts are 13−8, 5; 13−5, 8; 8+5, 13; 5+8, 13 . . .**

2. Point to the Blossom Charts.
   Say each triplet 3 times.

3. **Answer together. What number belongs on the blank?** (Say *blank* each time.)

12, 8 __	**11 __ 4**	**__ 8, 5**
11, 6 __	**13 __ 4**	**__ 8, 3**
13, 9 __	**12 __ 3**	**__ 7, 5**
13, 8 __	**13 __ 5**	**__ 9, 4**

91

Extra Activity

Fill in the missing whole or parts.

13 - 8 = 5	13 - 5 = 8	8 + 5 = 13
13 - 5 = 8	8 + 5 = 13	5 + 8 = 13
5 + 8 = 13	5 + 8 = 13	13 - 8 = 5
13 - 8 = 5	13 - 5 = 8	13 - 5 = 8
8 + 5 = 13	8 + 5 = 13	5 + 8 = 13
13 - 8 = 5	5 + 8 = 13	13 - 8 = 5

Answer these problems.

4	3	3	3	5	1	1	2
4	5	2	5	3	7	4	7
+5	+3	+8	+5	+2	+5	+8	+3
13	11	13	13	10	13	13	12

3	2	5	1	2	7	2	6
4	3	3	6	6	1	6	2
+5	+8	+5	+3	+5	+5	+3	+5
12	13	13	10	13	13	11	13

128

4. Do the Column Addition samples.
5. Use the large clock.
   a. **Name the hands.**
   b. Set the clock for the following situations.
      •2:00 **"The garage should be swept," Father said. "Will you boys please do it?" The boys were finished in 45 minutes. What time was that?**
      •3:00 **"Our work is finished until chore time," Father said. "You boys may sled for 1½ hours." What time will the boys stop?**
      •5:00 **"We should be finished with the chores in 60 minutes," said David and Daniel. What time will that be?**
   c. **Read the time together.**
      •6:00, 6:15, 6:30, 6:45
      •8:00, 9:30, 10:15, 12:45 . . .
6. **Count by 10's from 100–300.**
7. Assign Lesson 91.

Shade the greater number in ones' place.
Borrow *back*.
Answer the problem.

81	72	72	72	91	92
-69	-45	-29	-48	-36	-48
12	27	43	24	55	44

53	91	43	82	61	91
-29	-76	-19	-39	-14	-39
24	15	24	43	47	52

Count by 10's. Begin at 100.

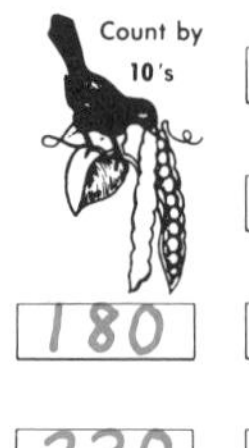

	100	110	120	130
	140	150	160	170
180	190	200	210	220
230	240	250	260	270
280	290	300	310	320
330	340	350	360	370

129

Blacklines

- Fact Hives #16
- Missing Whole or Parts #10
- Fact Form III

After Class

78	93	52	69	71	87
−25	−38	−37	−24	−46	−35

1. Ask individuals to give the 11, 12, and 13 triplets by memory.
2. Stand near the Subtraction samples.
   a. Ask a child to circle the greater number in the first problem. ***The greater number is at the top.*** **Do we need to borrow *back*?**
   b. Continue. Have each child circle the greater number, decide if he must borrow *back*, and then answer the problem.

Extra Activity
"His eye seeth every precious thing."
Job 28:10
13 −8 5
13 −5 8
8 +5 13
5 +8 13
13 −9 4
13 −4 9
9 +4 13
4 +9 13
13
130

Fill in the whole and parts.

Write the facts.

"There was a swarm of bees and honey." Judges 14:8
131

Before Class

Materials

11's–13's flash cards

Form C

9's–13's flash cards

Chalkboard

92	63	78	92	99	81	82	67
−56	−24	−64	−25	−53	−26	−37	−42

thousands	hundreds	tens	ones

Class Time

1. Point to the Blossom Charts.
   a. Drill each triplet.
   b. **Jump back and forth.**
      (11) 9 2
      (12) 9 3
      (13) 9 4
      (11) 8 3
      (12) 8 4
      (13) 8 5
      (11) 7 4
      (12) 7 5
      (11) 6 5
      (12) 6 6
   c. **Can we say the triplets in order without looking at the charts?**
2. Flash Card Drill: 11's–13's flash cards. Use Form C. **Flower Row: Box 1 . . .**
3. Do the Subtraction samples.

Read the story.
Write the numbers
in the beehive.
Write the label words
on the lines.
Answer the problem.

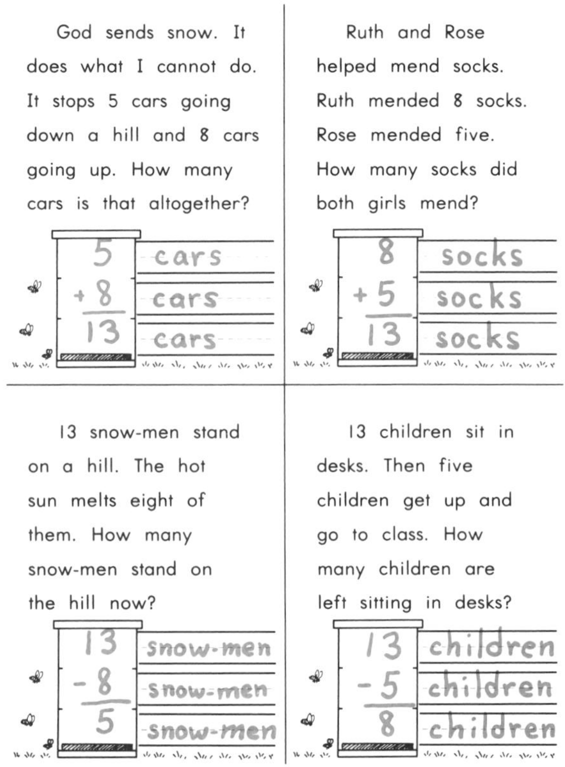

God sends snow. It does what I cannot do. It stops 5 cars going down a hill and 8 cars going up. How many cars is that altogether?

5 cars
+ 8 cars
13 cars

Ruth and Rose helped mend socks. Ruth mended 8 socks. Rose mended five. How many socks did both girls mend?

8 socks
+ 5 socks
13 socks

13 snow-men stand on a hill. The hot sun melts eight of them. How many snow-men stand on the hill now?

13 snow-men
− 8 snow-men
5 snow-men

13 children sit in desks. Then five children get up and go to class. How many children are left sitting in desks?

13 children
− 5 children
8 children

132

Speed Drill

4. Stand near the grid on the board.
   a. Have the children fill the grid as you say,
      1 one, 3 tens, 4 hundreds, 1 thousand
      0 ones, 2 tens, 5 hundreds
      8 ones, 6 tens, 3 hundreds, 1 thousand
      7 ones, 0 tens, 8 hundreds, 1 thousand
      6 ones, 7 tens
      2 ones, 4 tens, 6 hundreds, 1 thousand
      3 ones, 5 tens, 9 hundreds, 1 thousand
      5 ones, 9 tens, 6 hundreds
   b. **Read the numbers.**
5. Have responsive counting. **Begin at 100. Count by 10's to 400. I will say the first number; you say the next number.**
6. Do the Speed Drill in Lesson 92.
7. Assign Lesson 92.

Shade the greater number in ones' place.
Borrow *back*.
Answer the problem.

92

$72 - 48 = 24$	$82 - 69 = 13$	$83 - 34 = 49$	$73 - 49 = 24$	$71 - 46 = 25$	$83 - 59 = 24$
$73 - 59 = 14$	$51 - 26 = 25$	$52 - 28 = 24$	$81 - 32 = 49$	$52 - 29 = 23$	$93 - 69 = 24$

Count by 10's. Begin at 100.

Count by 10's

	100	110	120	130
	140	150	160	170
180	190	200	210	220
230	240	250	260	270
280	290	300	310	320
330	340	350	360	370

133

Blacklines

- Form C (Class Time)
- Fact Hives #16
- Triplets With Facts #7
- Mixed Computation #1

After Class

1. Circle Drill: 9's–13's flash cards.
2. Review shapes.
   a. **Which shapes have 4 corners?**
      square and rectangle
      Which shape has 3 corners? triangle
      Which shapes have 4 sides?
      square and rectangle
      Which shape has 3 sides? triangle
   b. **Name something in our classroom that is shaped like a rectangle.**

Speed Drill
13 - 5 = 8   13 - 8 = 5   5 + 8 = 13   12 - 8 = 4   8 + 4 = 12   13 - 5 = 8
8 + 4 = 12   5 + 8 = 13   12 - 4 = 8   4 + 8 = 12   12 - 8 = 4   13 - 8 = 5
12 - 4 = 8   5 + 8 = 13   13 - 5 = 8   4 + 8 = 12   12 - 8 = 4   8 + 5 = 13   13 - 8 = 5   13 - 5 = 8
8 + 5 = 13   13 - 5 = 8   13 - 8 = 5   12 - 8 = 4   8 + 4 = 12   12 - 4 = 8   5 + 8 = 13   4 + 8 = 12
"Whatsoever thy hand findeth to do, do it with thy might." Ecclesiastes 9:10
134

93

Fill in the whole and parts.

(13) 8 5

Write the facts.

Trace, answer, and write the facts.

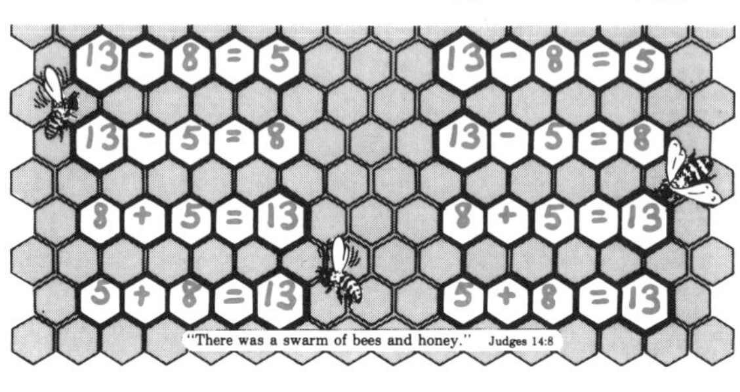

13 − 8 = 5
13 − 5 = 8
8 + 5 = 13
5 + 8 = 13
"There was a swarm of bees and honey." Judges 14:8

Before Class

Materials

10's–13's flash cards
Large coins
Large clock

Chalkboard

79	82	61	98	72	83	97
−24	−36	−17	−56	−47	−29	−65

7+5=__	13−5=__
__+8=13	6+__=12
13−__=4	__−8=5
9+4=__	__−9=4

Class Time

1. Stand near the clover patch.

   Moses told the children of Israel, "God does not want you to go up to that land." The people did not obey. They went up. Out came some men who chased the children of Israel back home like __ chase you. bees (Deuteronomy 1:44)

2. (13) 9 4

   The whole number is __.
   Its parts are __ and __.
   a. **The triplet is (13) 9 4 . . .**
   b. **The facts are 13−9, 4; 13−4, 9; 9+4, 13; 4+9, 13.**

3. (13) 8 5

   The whole number is __.
   Its parts are __ and __.
   a. **The triplet is (13) 8 5 . . .**
   b. **The facts are 13−8, 5; 13−5, 8; 8+5, 13; 5+8, 13.**

93

Extra Activity

Answer these facts.

$13 - 8 = 5$	$12 - 4 = 8$	$13 - 8 = 5$	$13 - 5 = 8$	$8 + 4 = 12$	$13 - 8 = 5$	$12 - 4 = 8$	$8 + 5 = 13$
$5 + 8 = 13$	$12 - 8 = 4$	$8 + 5 = 13$	$4 + 8 = 12$	$13 - 5 = 8$	$5 + 8 = 13$	$12 - 8 = 4$	$13 - 8 = 5$
$13 - 5 = 8$	$12 - 8 = 4$	$8 + 5 = 13$	$12 - 4 = 8$	$4 + 8 = 12$	$5 + 8 = 13$	$12 - 8 = 4$	$4 + 8 = 12$
$8 + 4 = 12$	$8 + 5 = 13$	$13 - 8 = 5$	$8 + 4 = 12$	$12 - 4 = 8$	$13 - 8 = 5$	$5 + 8 = 13$	$13 - 5 = 8$
$12 - 8 = 4$	$13 - 5 = 8$	$12 - 4 = 8$	$13 - 5 = 8$	$13 - 8 = 5$	$12 - 4 = 8$	$13 - 5 = 8$	$5 + 8 = 13$
		$8 + 5 = 13$	$13 - 8 = 5$	$13 - 5 = 8$	$13 - 5 = 8$	$8 + 5 = 13$	$12 - 8 = 4$

136

4. **Say the 13's facts as I fill the beehive.**
   Begin with 13−9=4.
5. Double Drill: 10's–13's flash cards.
6. Do the Missing Whole or Parts samples.
7. Do the Subtraction samples.
   Circle the greater number.
   Do you need to borrow *back*?
8. Flash the large coins.
   a. **Name the man on each coin.**
   b. **Dime, 10¢; nickel, 5¢; penny, 1¢; quarter, 25¢ . . .**
9. Assign Lesson 93.

Shade the greater number in ones' place.
Borrow *back* in some problems.
Answer the problem.

93 − 48 = 45	77 − 51 = 26	83 − 39 = 44	92 − 65 = 27	98 − 72 = 26	89 − 53 = 36
72 − 36 = 36	98 − 44 = 54	83 − 54 = 29	71 − 35 = 36	89 − 35 = 54	62 − 33 = 29
79 − 43 = 36	67 − 41 = 26	81 − 54 = 27	63 − 19 = 44	98 − 72 = 26	83 − 38 = 45

Blacklines

Fact Hives #16

Triplets With Facts #7

Fact Form V

Count by 10's. Begin at 200.

Count by 10's

	200	210	220	230
	240	250	260	270
280	290	300	310	320
330	340	350	360	370
380	390	400	410	420

137

After Class

1. a. **Count by 100's to 1,000.**
   b. **Count by 25's to 100.**
   c. **Count by 2's to 150.**
2. Hold the large clock. Ask individuals to set the clock at
   5:15, 6:45, 9:30, 11:15, 12:45, 2:30, 4:15 . . .

94

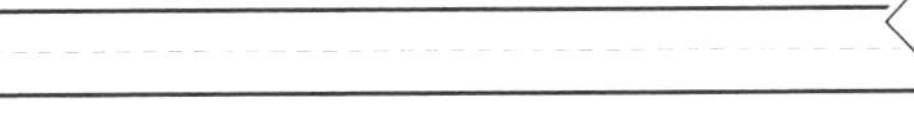

Fill in the whole and parts.

Write the facts.

Trace, answer, and write the facts.

"There was a swarm of bees and honey." Judges 14:8

139

Before Class

Materials

9's–13's flash cards

Chalkboard

88	75	93	52	39	81	78
−56	−23	−65	−39	−26	−36	−46

__ 140 __ 160 __ __ __

100 __ 300 __ __ __ __

__ __ 120 __ 124 __ __

__ 125 __ __ __ 145 __

Class Time

1. Have each child bring *My 1,000 Book* to the teaching corner.
   a. **Count to 200 by 5's.**
   b. **Count on to 400 by 10's.**
2. Fill in the Missing Number samples. **Decide if you should count by 2's, 5's, 10's, or 100's.**
3. Stand near the clover patch.

(12) 9 3

   The whole number is __.
   Its parts are __ and __.
   The facts are 12−9, 3; 12−3, 9; 9+3, 12; 3+9, 12.
4. | (13) 9 4 |
   |---|

   The whole number is __.
   Its parts are __ and __.
   The facts are 13−9, 4; 13−4, 9; 9+4, 13; 4+9, 13.

94

Answer these facts.

12 - 8 **4**	13 - 5 **8**	13 - 9 **4**	13 - 9 **4**	3 + 9 **12**	11 - 7 **4**	12 - 4 **8**	8 + 4 **12**
5 + 8 **13**	12 - 9 **3**	8 + 3 **11**	9 + 4 **13**	12 - 8 **4**	5 + 6 **11**	12 - 9 **3**	11 - 7 **4**
11 - 5 **6**	11 - 8 **3**	5 + 8 **13**	12 - 6 **6**	6 + 6 **12**	9 + 4 **13**	12 - 9 **3**	7 + 5 **12**
9 + 2 **11**	3 + 9 **12**	12 - 7 **5**	6 + 5 **11**	11 - 9 **2**	11 - 6 **5**	5 + 7 **12**	11 - 9 **2**
13 - 5 **8**	13 - 8 **5**	11 - 4 **7**	11 - 3 **8**	4 + 9 **13**	12 - 5 **7**	13 - 8 **5**	8 + 5 **13**
		7 + 4 **11**	13 - 4 **9**	3 + 8 **11**	12 - 3 **9**	4 + 9 **13**	13 - 8 **5**

140

Speed Drill

5. (12) 8 4

The whole number is __.
Its parts are __ and __.
The facts are 12−8, 4; 12−4, 8; 8+4, 12; 4+8, 12.

6. (13) 8 5

The whole number is __.
Its parts are __ and __.
The facts are 13−8, 5; 13−5, 8; 8+5, 13; 5+8, 13.

7. Drill the triplets on each Blossom Chart.

8. Do the Subtraction samples.

9. Story Problems

a. **Clair counted the shiny icicles on the roof. There were 5 short icicles and 8 long icicles. How many was that in all? Who can give us the whole problem?**

5 icicles+8 icicles=13 icicles.

b. **Carol's house is near the woods. Her father put out a block of salt for the deer. On Thursday 7 deer came to lick. On Friday 5 deer came. How many deer came on both days? Who . . . ?**

7 deer+5 deer=12 deer.

10. Do the Speed Drill in Lesson 94.

11. Assign Lesson 94.

94

Shade the greater number in ones' place.
Borrow *back* in some problems.
Answer the problems.

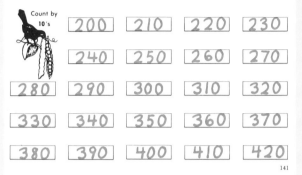

94

62 − 33 = 29	72 − 36 = 36	98 − 72 = 26	83 − 38 = 45	83 − 39 = 44	98 − 44 = 54
67 − 41 = 26	81 − 54 = 27	79 − 43 = 36	98 − 72 = 26	89 − 53 = 36	92 − 65 = 27
71 − 35 = 36	83 − 54 = 29	93 − 48 = 45	77 − 51 = 26	89 − 35 = 54	63 − 19 = 44

Count by 10's. Begin at 200.

Count by 10's

	200	210	220	230
	240	250	260	270
280	290	300	310	320
330	340	350	360	370
380	390	400	410	420

141

Blacklines

Fact Hives #16
Triplets With Facts #7
Mixed Computation #1

After Class

1. Drill individuals with 9's–13's flash cards.
2. Chalkboard Drill: **Write the number that comes next.**

270, 280, 290, __ 100, 105, 110, __
154, 156, 158, __ 100, 90, 80, __
500, 600, 700, __ 45, 40, 35, __
135, 140, 145, __ 86, 84, 82, __

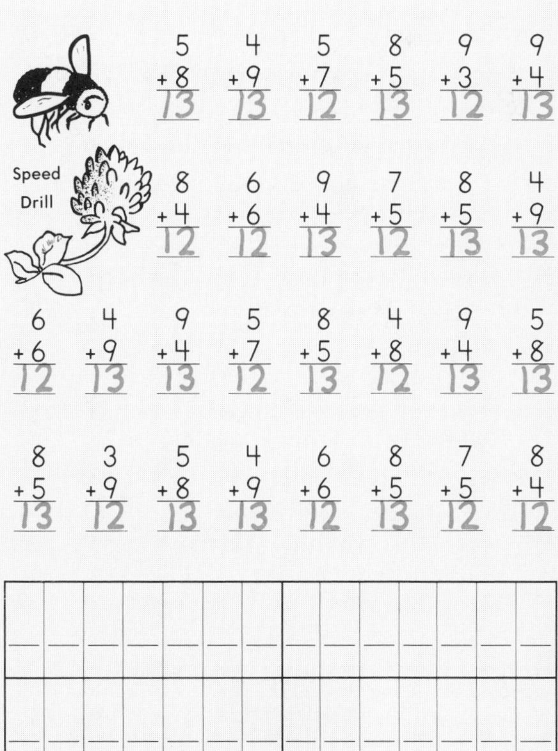
Speed Drill

		5 + 8 = 13	4 + 9 = 13	5 + 7 = 12	8 + 5 = 13	9 + 3 = 12	9 + 4 = 13
		8 + 4 = 12	6 + 6 = 12	9 + 4 = 13	7 + 5 = 12	8 + 5 = 13	4 + 9 = 13
6 + 6 = 12	4 + 9 = 13	9 + 4 = 13	5 + 7 = 12	8 + 5 = 13	4 + 8 = 12	9 + 4 = 13	5 + 8 = 13
8 + 5 = 13	3 + 9 = 12	5 + 8 = 13	4 + 9 = 13	6 + 6 = 12	8 + 5 = 13	7 + 5 = 12	8 + 4 = 12

"Whatsoever thy hand findeth to do, do it with thy might." Ecclesiastes 9:10

142

95

Trace and fill in the whole and parts.

Trace, answer, and write the facts.

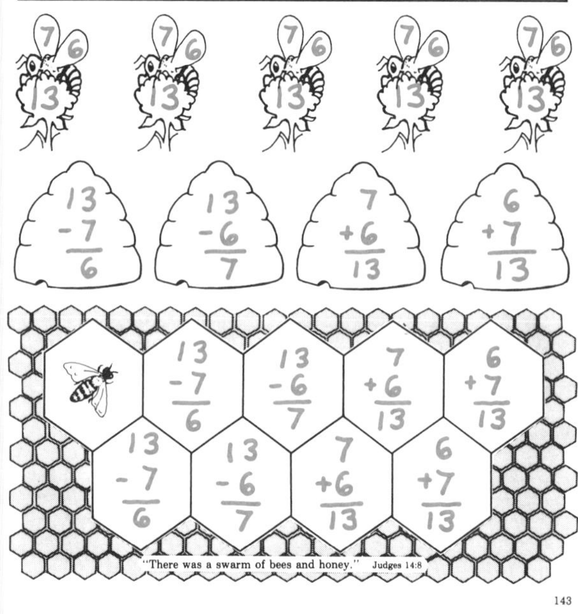

Before Class

Make (13) 7 6 flash cards for each child.

Tack (13) 7 6 flash cards above the clover patch in this order:

13	13	7	6
−7	−6	+6	+7
6	7	13	13

Materials

11's–13's flash cards

Large clock

9's–13's flash cards

Chalkboard

93	78	62	86	69	93	73	87
−58	−36	−35	−64	−43	−39	−45	−37

Class Time

1. Flash 11's–13's cards.
   Boys, say the triplet.
   Girls, say the answer.
2. Stand near the clover patch.

(13) 7 6

   a. **How many pink clovers are in the patch?** 10
   We think—10 pink.
   3 more make __ altogether. 13
   We think—10 pink.
   3 less make __ clovers with bees. 7

   b. **13 clovers in the patch;**
   13 is the whole number.
   What part of the 13 has bees? 7
   What part of the 13 has no bees? 6
   13 is the whole number.
   Its parts are 7 and 6.

   c. **The triplet is (13) 7 6;**
   (13) 7 6 . . .

   d. Point to the flash cards. **The facts are 13−7, 6; 13−6, 7; 7+6, 13; 6+7, 13 . . .**

95

Extra Activity

Answer these facts.

13	13	13	13	6	13	13	7
-7	-6	-7	-6	+7	-7	-6	+6
6	7	6	7	13	6	7	13
6	13	6	7	13	7	13	13
+7	-6	+7	+6	-6	+6	-6	-7
13	7	13	13	7	13	7	6
13	13	6	13	7	6	13	6
-6	-7	+7	-7	+6	+7	-7	+7
7	6	13	6	13	13	6	13
7	6	13	6	13	13	7	13
+6	+7	-6	+7	-7	-6	+6	-6
13	13	7	13	6	7	13	7
13	13	13	13	13	13	13	7
-7	-6	-7	-6	-7	-7	-6	+6
6	7	6	7	6	6	7	13

6	13	13	13	6	13
+7	-7	-6	-6	+7	-7
13	6	7	7	13	6

144

3. **Say the triplet as I fill the clover and bees.**
4. **Say the 13's facts as I fill the beehive.**
5. Drill the triplets on each Blossom Chart.
6. Point to the (13) 7 6 flash cards again. **Say the triplet; then say the answer.**
7. Do the Subtraction samples. Have each child circle the greater number, decide if he should borrow *back*, and then answer the problem.
8. Hold the large clock.
   Read the time together. 11:30, 1:45, 3:00, 5:15, 7:30, 9:45 . . .
9. Assign Lesson 95.

Shade the greater number in ones' place.
Borrow *back* in some problems.

93 − 25 = 68	69 − 57 = 12	93 − 69 = 24	99 − 65 = 34	83 − 64 = 19	83 − 38 = 45
82 − 46 = 36	67 − 24 = 43	92 − 57 = 35	68 − 32 = 36	98 − 63 = 35	92 − 49 = 43
91 − 46 = 45	92 − 73 = 19	68 − 34 = 34	82 − 58 = 24	58 − 46 = 12	82 − 14 = 68

Blacklines

Fact Hives #17
Number Words #4
Form A: 900-999

Write the time.

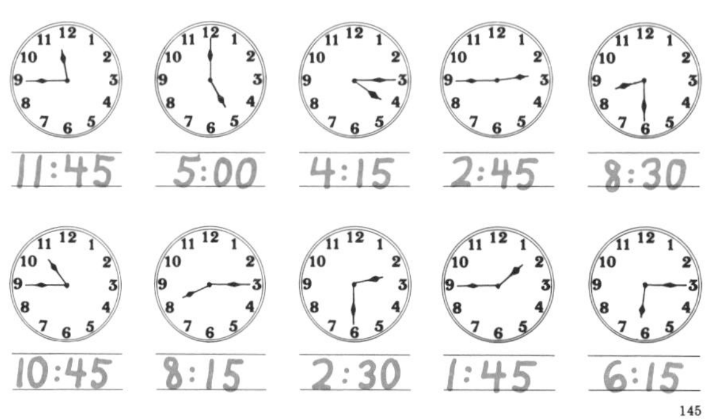

After Class

1. Give each child his (13) 7 6 flash cards.
2. Circle Drill: 9's–13's flash cards.
3. Point to the Number Line.
   a. **Count by 10's to 100.**
   b. **Answer together.**

30+10=	**10+10=**	**70−10=**
80+10=	**50+10=**	**40−10=**
60+10=	**90+10=**	**90−10=**

Extra Activity
"His eye seeth every precious thing." Job 28:10
13 − 7 = 6
13 − 6 = 7
7 + 6 = 13
6 + 7 = 13
13 − 8 = 5
13 − 5 = 8
8 + 5 = 13
5 + 8 = 13
13 − 9 = 4
13 − 4 = 9
9 + 4 = 13
4 + 9 = 13
13
146

Fill in the whole and parts.

Trace, answer, and write the facts.

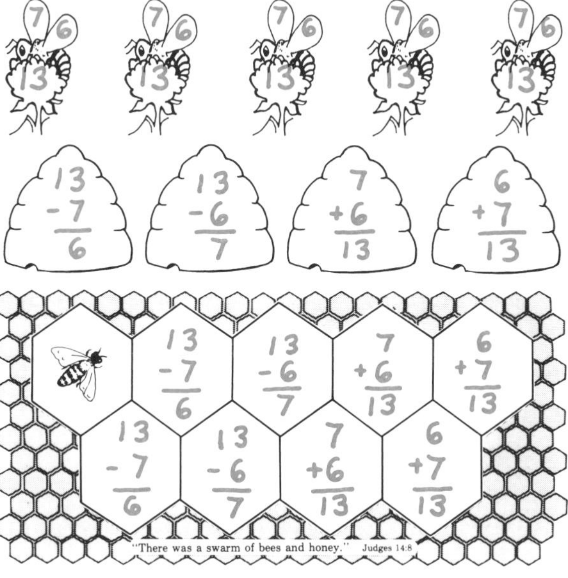
"There was a swarm of bees and honey." Judges 14:8

147

Before Class

Add bee (13) 7 6 to Blossom 13 Chart.

Materials

13's flash cards

Chalkboard

(ones)	76	1543	891	5	350	1158
(tens)	637	1284	19	402	7	1256
(hundreds)	88	1693	794	622	931	1505

64	63	43	22	32	74
55	25	42	25	41	42
+ 4	+45	+53	+86	+66	+ 7

Class Time

1. Stand near the Place Value samples.
   a. **The number places are ones, tens, hundreds, (comma), thousands; ones, tens . . .**
   b. **What is missing from some numbers?** Have the children add the commas and circle the correct numbers.
   c. **Read the numbers with me.**
2. Stand near the clover patch.

   (13) 7 6

   13 clovers in the patch;
   13 is the whole number.
   What part of the 13 has bees? 7
   What part of the 13 has no bees? 6
   13 is the whole number.
   Its parts are 7 and 6.
   a. **The triplet is (13) 7 6 . . .**

96

Answer these facts.

Speed Drill

13 - 6 7	13 - 7 6	13 - 6 7	13 - 6 7	6 + 7 13	13 - 6 7	13 - 7 6	7 + 6 13
7 + 6 13	13 - 6 7	6 + 7 13	7 + 6 13	13 - 6 7	6 + 7 13	13 - 6 7	13 - 6 7
13 - 7 6	13 - 7 6	6 + 7 13	13 - 6 7	7 + 6 13	6 + 7 13	13 - 7 6	6 + 7 13
7 + 6 13	6 + 7 13	13 - 6 7	6 + 7 13	13 - 6 7	13 - 6 7	7 + 6 13	13 - 7 6
13 - 6 7	13 - 6 7	13 - 7 6	13 - 6 7	13 - 7 6	13 - 7 6	13 - 6 7	7 + 6 13
		6 + 7 13	13 - 7 6	13 - 6 7	13 - 6 7	6 + 7 13	13 - 6 7

148

b. **The facts are 13−7, 6; 13−6, 7; 7+6, 13; 6+7, 13 . . .**

3. Point to the Blossom Charts.
   a. **Say each triplet 3 times.**
   b. **Jump from chart to chart.**
      (11) 9 2
      (12) 9 3
      (13) 9 4 . . .
4. Do the Addition samples.
5. **Raise your hand to give the answer.**

60+10=	**10+10=**	**90−10=**
50+10=	**70−10=**	**40−10=**
80+10=	**30−10=**	**20−10=**

6. Do the Speed Drill in Lesson 96.
7. Assign Lesson 96.

96

Answer these problems.
Carry *over* in some problems.

66	52	33	44	23	55
23	37	41	22	66	40
+44	+23	+52	+53	+44	+41
133	112	126	119	133	136

15	60	22	46	43	47
23	34	73	22	30	41
+94	+42	+24	+55	+43	+45
132	136	119	123	116	133

Read the story.
Write the numbers in the beehive.
Write the label words on the lines.
Answer the problem.

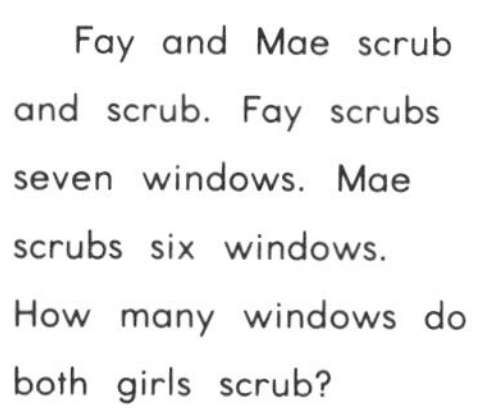

Fay and Mae scrub and scrub. Fay scrubs seven windows. Mae scrubs six windows. How many windows do both girls scrub?

Carl has twelve rabbits in a pen. 7 rabbits hop out of the pen. How many rabbits are left in the pen?

149

Blacklines

Fact Hives #17
Number Facts #12
Number Words #4

After Class

1. Drill individuals with the 13's flash cards.
2. Chalkboard Drill: **Write the number you hear.**

   Ze-rub-ba-bel led many of God's people to Jerusalem. (Ezra 2:65–67)
   - **The people had 736 horses.**
   - **They had 245 mules.**
   - **They had 435 camels.**
   - **There were 200 singing men and singing women.**
   - **At Jerusalem they offered 712 animal sacrifices.** (Ezra 6:17)

13 -6 = 7 | 7 +6 = 13 | 6 +7 = 13 | 13 -7 = 6 | 7 +6 = 13 | 13 -6 = 7
Speed Drill
13 -7 = 6 | 13 -6 = 7 | 6 +7 = 13 | 13 -6 = 7 | 7 +6 = 13 | 6 +7 = 13
13 -7 = 6 | 6 +7 = 13 | 13 -6 = 7 | 7 +6 = 13 | 13 -7 = 6 | 6 +7 = 13 | 7 +6 = 13 | 13 -6 = 7
6 +7 = 13 | 13 -7 = 6 | 7 +6 = 13 | 6 +7 = 13 | 13 -6 = 7 | 7 +6 = 13 | 13 -6 = 7 | 13 -7 = 6
"Whatsoever thy hand findeth to do, do it with thy might." Ecclesiastes 9:10

150

97

Fill in the whole and parts.

Trace, answer, and write the facts.

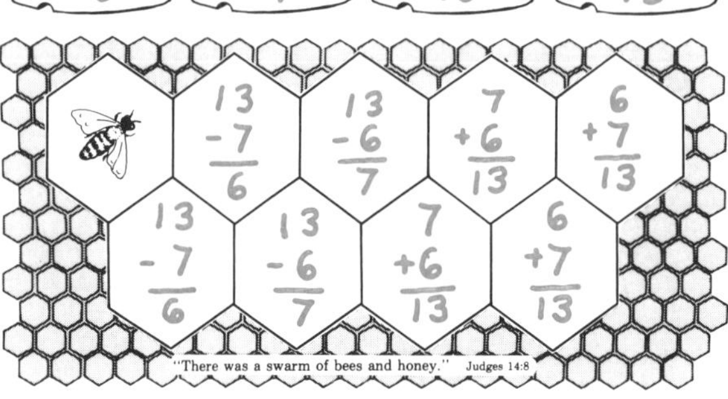

"There was a swarm of bees and honey." Judges 14:8
151

Before Class

Materials

8's–13's flash cards
Large coins
8's–13's flash cards

Chalkboard

47	79	138	129	46	136	58
+86	+44	−65	−74	+87	−84	+65

25¢

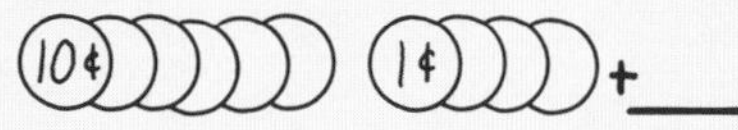

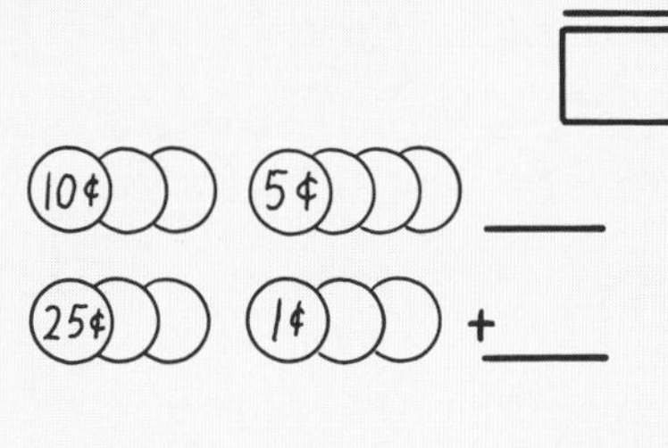

100¢
$1.00

Class Time

1. Flash 8's–13's flash cards.
   Boys, answer the addition facts.
   Girls, answer the subtraction facts.
2. Stand near the clover patch.
   (13) 7 6
   13 clovers in the patch;
   13 is the whole number.
   What part of the 13 has bees? 7
   What part of the 13 has no bees? 6
   13 is the whole number.
   Its parts are 7 and 6.
   a. **The triplet is (13) 7 6 . . .**
   b. **The facts are 13−7, 6; 13−6, 7; 7+6, 13; 6+7, 13 . . .**
3. Drill the triplets on Blossom 11, 12, and 13 Charts.
4. Do the Computation samples.
5. Flash the large coins.
   a. **Nickel, 5¢; quarter, 25¢; penny, 1¢; dime, 10¢ . . .**

97

Extra Activity

Answer these problems.
Carry *over* in some problems.

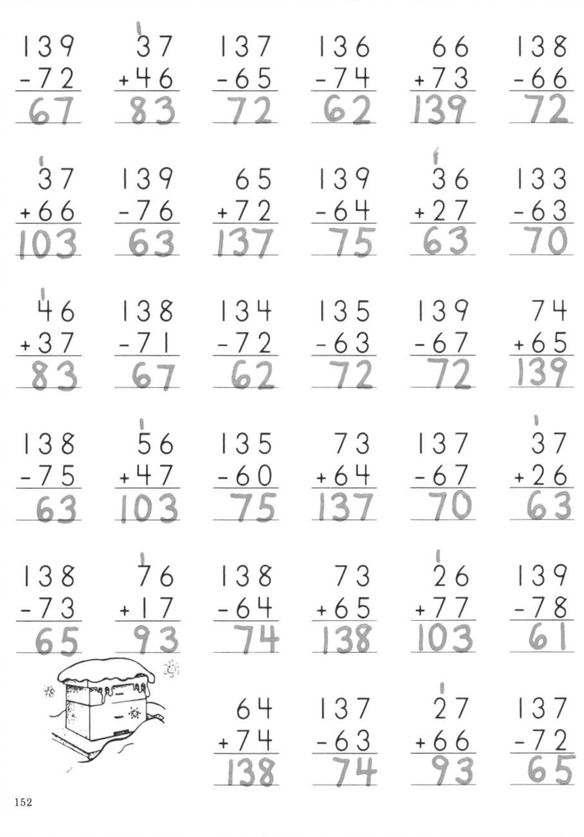

139 -72 67	37 +46 83	137 -65 72	136 -74 62	66 +73 139	138 -66 72
37 +66 103	139 -76 63	65 +72 137	139 -64 75	36 +27 63	133 -63 70
46 +37 83	138 -71 67	134 -72 62	135 -63 72	139 -67 72	74 +65 139
138 -75 63	56 +47 103	135 -60 75	73 +64 137	137 -67 70	37 +26 63
138 -73 65	76 +17 93	138 -64 74	73 +65 138	26 +77 103	139 -78 61
		64 +74 138	137 -63 74	27 +66 93	137 -72 65

152

b. ***How many quarters make 100¢?**
   How many pennies make 100¢?
   How many dimes make 100¢?
   How many nickels make 100¢?
   (*They may use the Number Line.)

6. Stand near the Money samples.
   a. **100¢ is the same as $1.00. 100¢=$1.00.**
   b. Have individuals count aloud as they do the Money samples.
   c. **The total is 139¢ or 1 dollar and 39 cents.** Write $1.39 in the box.
7. Assign Lesson 97.

Write the numbers in the correct places.

	thousands	hundreds	tens	ones
1784	1,	7	8	4
815	,	8	1	5
1945	1,	9	4	5
16	,		1	6
1325	1,	3	2	5
1784	1,	7	8	4
1406	1,	4	0	6

	thousands	hundreds	tens	ones
784	,	7	8	4
1623	1,	6	2	3
80	,		8	0
1315	1,	3	1	5
293	,	2	9	3
1324	1,	3	2	4
1583	1,	5	8	3

Write the time.

7:15 2:30 11:00 4:45 12:00

2:45 4:30 6:15 3:45 10:15

153

Blacklines

Fact Hives #17

Missing Whole or Parts #11

Number Facts #12

After Class

1. Circle Drill: 8's–13's flash cards.
2. Stand near the Number Line.
   Count by 10's.
   a. **Begin at 10. 10, 20 . . . 100.**
   b. **We can begin at 3. 3, 13 . . . 93.**
   c. **Begin at 7. 7, 17 . . . 97.**
   d. **Begin at 5. 5, 15 . . . 95.**

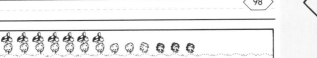

Fill in the whole and parts.

Write the facts.

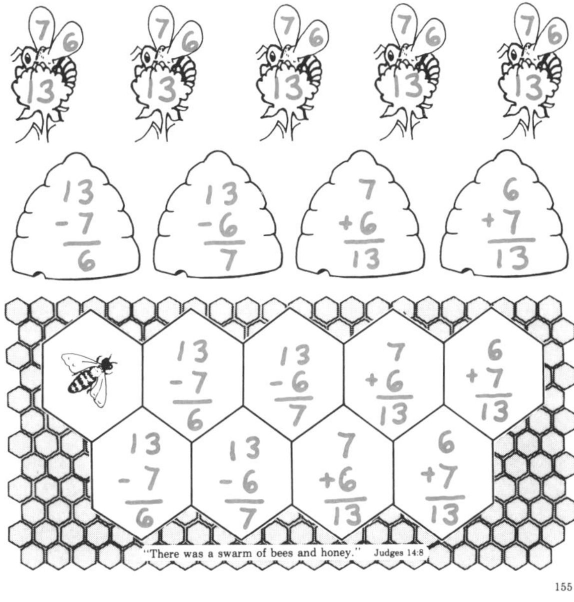

"There was a swarm of bees and honey." Judges 14:8
155

Before Class

Materials

8's–13's flash cards

Chalkboard

73	53	43	62	83	52	93
− 6	−37	− 8	− 7	− 9	−38	− 5

100¢	117¢
☐	☐
149¢	**186¢**
☐	☐

Class Time

1. Stand near the clover patch.

   How do honey bees stay warm in a beehive?

   Several bees sit on the honeycomb and eat honey. Then they wave their wings and buzz around. Up and down, back and forth; up and down, back and forth. This makes heat. The other bees cluster around the heat.

   Soon some bees are tired of buzzing. They change places with other bees. Yes, honeybees stay warm inside a snow-covered hive.

2. (13) 9 4

   The whole number is __.
   Its parts are __ and __.
   The facts are 13−9, 4; 13−4, 9; 9+4, 13; 4+9, 13.

Count the first row.
Write the amount.
Count the second row.
Write the amount.
Add.
Then copy the answer into the dollar box.

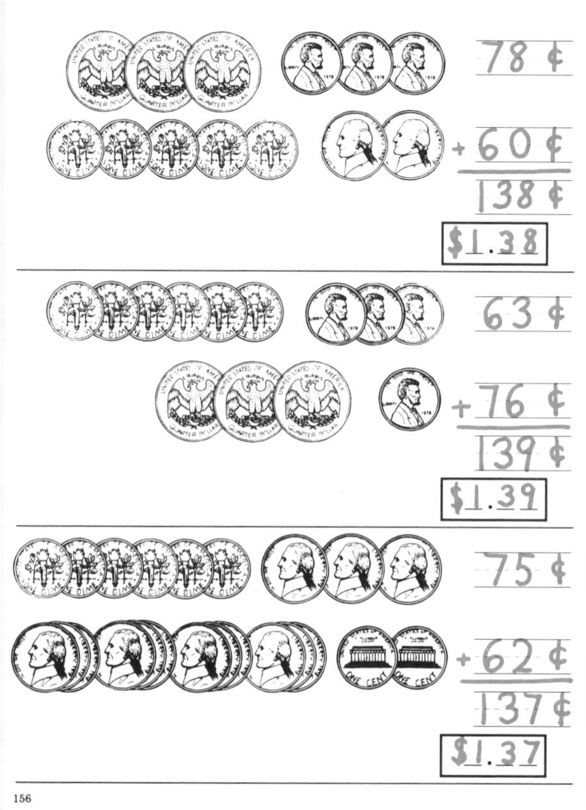

Speed Drill

3. | (13) 8 5 |

The whole number is __.
Its parts are __ and __.
The facts are 13−8, 5; 13−5, 8; 8+5, 13; 5+8, 13.

4. | (13) 7 6 |

The whole number is __.
Its parts are __ and __.
The facts are 13−7, 6; 13−6, 7; 7+6, 13; 6+7, 13.

5. **Jump from chart to chart.**
   (11) 9 2
   (12) 9 3
   (13) 9 4
   (11) 8 3
   (12) 8 4
   (13) 8 5
   (11) 7 4
   (12) 7 5
   (13) 7 6
   (11) 6 5
   (12) 6 6

6. Do the Borrow *back* samples.
7. **Read the money as I change it.**
   100¢ = $1.00
   149¢ = $1.49 (1 dollar and 49 cents)
8. Do the Speed Drill in Lesson 98.
9. Assign Lesson 98.

In the first two rows, shade the greater number in ones' place.
Borrow *back* in some problems.

In the following rows, answer the facts.

63 − 5 = 58	35 − 1 = 34	42 − 8 = 34	33 − 8 = 25	33 − 9 = 24	59 − 3 = 56
72 − 36 = 36	98 − 44 = 54	83 − 58 = 25	73 − 39 = 34	89 − 35 = 54	63 − 35 = 28

13 − 9 = 4	13 − 5 = 8	12 − 7 = 5	13 − 9 = 4	9 + 4 = 13	13 − 8 = 5	13 − 5 = 8	8 + 5 = 13
7 + 5 = 12	13 − 7 = 6	4 + 9 = 13	5 + 7 = 12	13 − 8 = 5	8 + 5 = 13	13 − 7 = 6	12 − 7 = 5
13 − 4 = 9	12 − 5 = 7	5 + 7 = 12	13 − 4 = 9	6 + 7 = 13	7 + 5 = 12	13 − 6 = 7	5 + 8 = 13
6 + 7 = 13	7 + 5 = 12	13 − 8 = 5	5 + 8 = 13	13 − 5 = 8	12 − 7 = 5	5 + 7 = 12	13 − 5 = 8

157

Blacklines

Fact Hives #18
Number Facts #12
Triplets With Facts #8

After Class

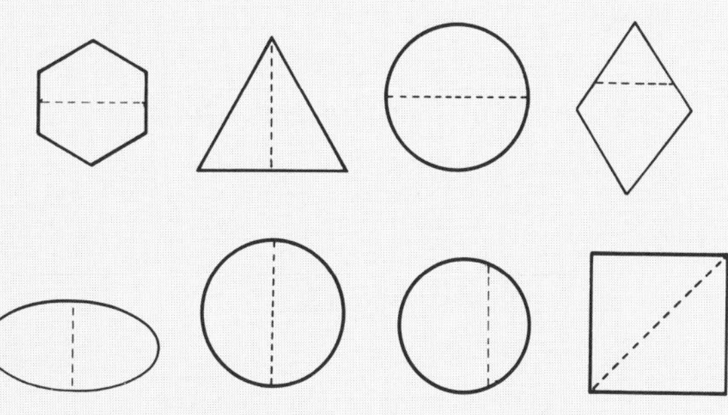

1. Flash 8's–13's cards. **Answer together.**
2. Ask individuals to give the 11, 12, and 13 triplets by memory.
3. Call the children to the shapes.
   a. Write ½ in the first piece. **1 whole cut into 2 *equal* parts.**
   b. **Say one-half as I write it in each piece.**

		7 + 6 = 13	6 + 7 = 13	13 − 6 = 7	8 + 5 = 13	13 − 5 = 8	13 − 7 = 6
		13 − 8 = 5	13 − 5 = 8	13 − 7 = 6	7 + 6 = 13	5 + 8 = 13	13 − 6 = 7
13 − 8 = 5	5 + 8 = 13	13 − 7 = 6	13 − 5 = 8	8 + 5 = 13	13 − 6 = 7	7 + 6 = 13	8 + 5 = 13
6 + 7 = 13	13 − 8 = 5	13 − 6 = 7	6 + 7 = 13	5 + 8 = 13	13 − 7 = 6	13 − 5 = 8	13 − 8 = 5

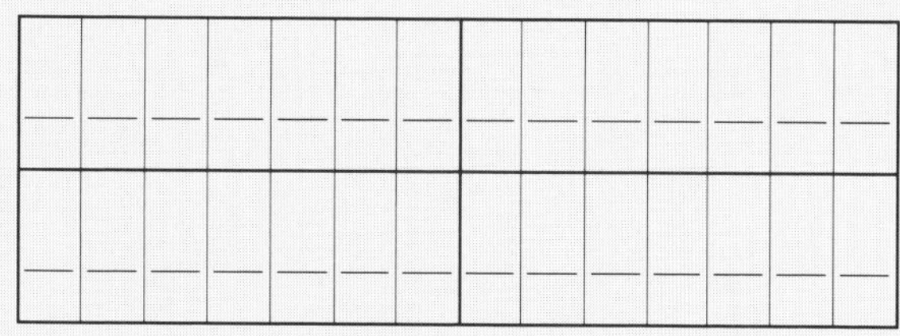

"Whatsoever thy hand findeth to do, do it with thy might." Ecclesiastes 9:10

158

99

Fill in the whole and parts.

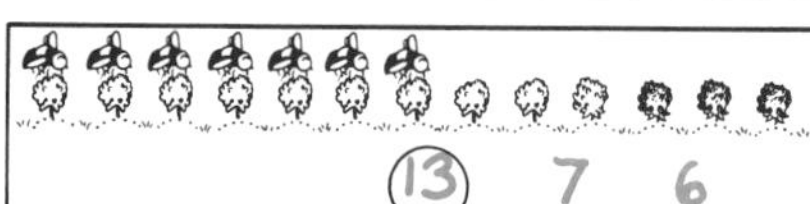

(13) 7 6

Write the facts.

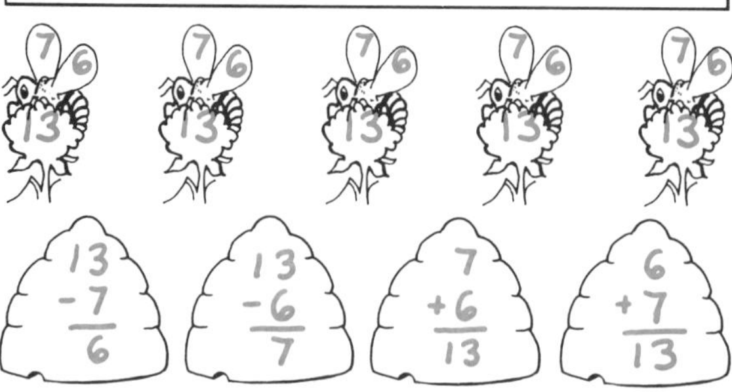

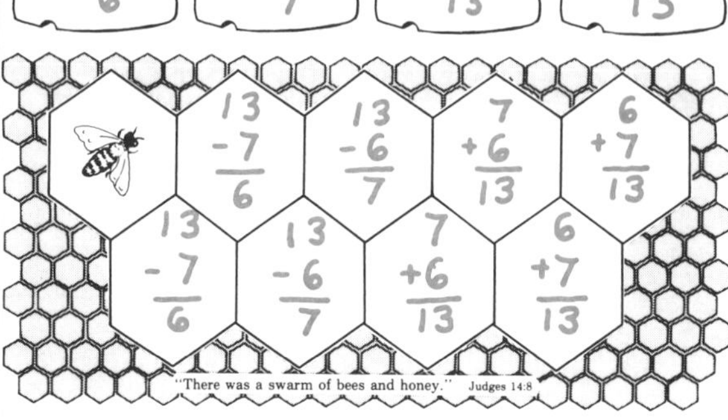

159

Before Class

Materials

8's–13's flash cards

Chalkboard

73	42	93	63	83	73	52
− 9	−28	− 4	−46	− 7	− 5	−36

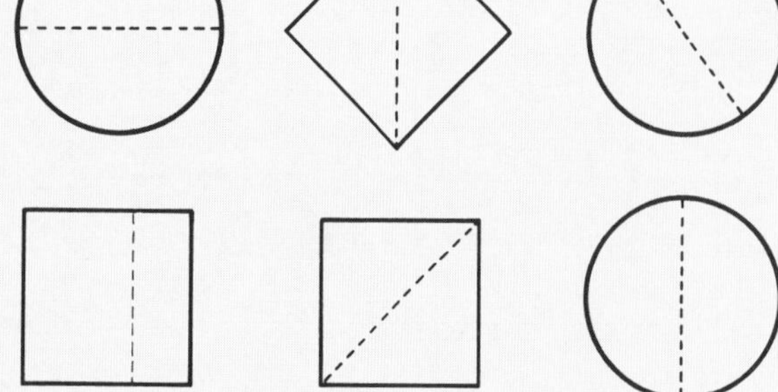

Class Time

1. Flash 8's–13's cards.
   Girls, answer the addition facts.
   Boys, answer the subtraction facts.
2. Stand near the clover patch.

   (13) 7 6

   13 clovers in the patch;
   13 is the whole number.
   What part of the 13 has bees? 7
   What part of the 13 has no bees? 6
   13 is the whole number.
   Its parts are 7 and 6.
   a. **The triplet is (13) 7 6 . . .**
   b. **The facts are 13−7, 6; 13−6, 7; 7+6, 13; 6+7, 13 . . .**
3. Point to the Blossom Charts.
   Say each triplet 3 times.

Fill in the missing whole or parts.

6 + 7 = 13	13 - 7 = 6	6 + 7 = 13
13 - 7 = 6	13 - 6 = 7	13 - 7 = 6
13 - 6 = 7	7 + 6 = 13	13 - 6 = 7
7 + 6 = 13	6 + 7 = 13	7 + 6 = 13
13 - 6 = 7	6 + 7 = 13	6 + 7 = 13
7 + 6 = 13	13 - 7 = 6	13 - 7 = 6

Answer these problems.

4	3	4	3	2	5	2	8
2	2	3	3	5	2	6	1
+7	+5	+4	+7	+6	+6	+4	+4
13	10	11	13	13	13	12	13

5	2	1	6	4	3	4	2
4	4	5	1	3	1	2	5
+4	+6	+7	+6	+6	+7	+4	+6
13	12	13	13	13	11	10	13

160

4. **Answer together. What number belongs on the blank?** (Say *blank* each time.)
   13, 7 __ 12 __ 6 __ 7, 5
   12, 8 __ 13 __ 5 __ 7, 6
   13, 9 __ 13 __ 6 __ 8, 3
   11, 6 __ 12 __ 3 __ 8, 5
5. Do the Borrow *back* samples.
6. Do the Fraction samples.
   a. **One-half is a fraction. 1 whole cut into 2 equal pieces.**
   b. Have the children say ½ as they fill each piece.
7. Stand near the Number Line. **Count by 10's.**
   a. **Begin at 1. 1, 11 . . . 91.**
   Begin at 4. 4, 14 . . . 94.
   Begin at 8. 8, 18 . . . 98.
   b. **18+10 64+10 48−10**
   48+10 61+10 54−10
   34+10 21+10 91−10
8. Assign Lesson 99.

Shade the greater number in ones' place.
Borrow *back* in some problems.

Count by 2's. Begin at 200.

93 − 37 = 56	72 − 35 = 37	93 − 68 = 25	89 − 17 = 72	93 − 76 = 17	89 − 58 = 31
88 − 57 = 31	81 − 24 = 57	98 − 26 = 72	82 − 57 = 25	93 − 56 = 37	82 − 66 = 16

Count by 2's

	200	202	204	206
	208	210	212	214
216	218	220	222	224
226	228	230	232	234
236	238	240	242	244
246	248	250	252	254
256	258	260	262	264

161

Blacklines

Fact Hives #18

Missing Whole or Parts #11

Mixed Computation #2

After Class

12 −8	6 +7	12 −6	13 −4	13 −8	4 +9
12 −7	13 −5	8 +4	5 +8	7 +5	12 −4
13 −9	4 +8	13 −6	6 +6	9 +4	13 −7
12 −9	5 +7	8 +5	12 −5	7 +6	12 −3

Note: You will use this grid in Lesson 100 too.

1. Drill individuals at the grid on the chalkboard. Can the facts be answered in 30 seconds?
2. Have each child bring *My 1,000 Book* to your teaching corner.
   a. **Count by 10's to 500.**
   b. **Count on to 600 by 5's.**

100

Fill in the whole and parts.

Write the facts.

100
13 7 6
"There was a swarm of bees and honey." Judges 14:8
163

Before Class

Chalkboard

thousands	hundreds	tens	ones

Class Time

1. Call the children to the Computation Grid on the board.
   a. **Say the triplet; then say the answer.**
   b. **Answer as quickly as you can!**
2. Drill the triplets on Blossom 11, 12, and 13 Charts.
3. **Can we say the triplets by memory?**
   (11) 9 2
   (11) 8 3
   (11) 7 4
   (11) 6 5
   (12) 9 3
   (12) 8 4 . . .
4. Stand near the Place Value Grid on the board.
   a. Have the children fill the grid as you say
   3 ones, 0 tens, 1 hundred, 1 thousand
   8 ones, 6 tens, 8 hundreds
   0 ones, 2 tens, 4 hundreds, 1 thousand

100

Read the story.
Write the numbers
in the beehive.
Write the label words
on the lines.
Answer the problem.

Fred found 13 eggs in the hen house. Six eggs were brown. The rest were white. How many eggs were white?

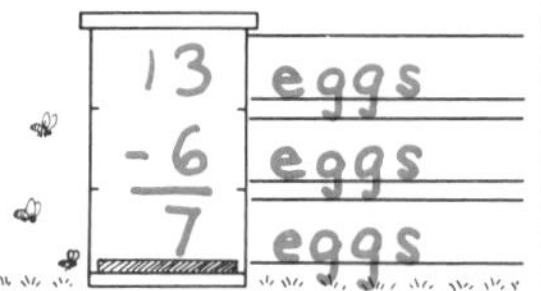

Glen and Fay helped Mother clean the church. Glen dusted 7 benches. Fay dusted six. How many benches did both children dust?

Mother hung twelve mittens on the line to dry. 8 mittens were blue. The rest were green. How many mittens were green?

12 mittens
- 8 mittens
4 mittens

Thirteen fish swim in a bowl. Seven fish are small. The rest are big. How many fish are big?

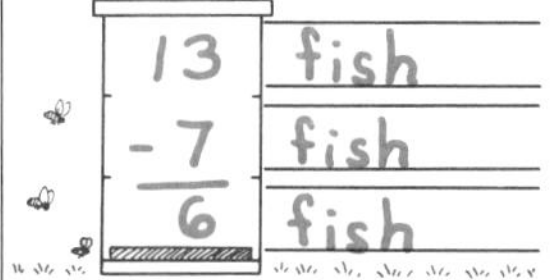

164

4 ones, 5 tens, 9 hundreds, 1 thousand
5 ones, 7 tens, 6 hundreds, 1 thousand
9 ones, 3 tens, 3 hundreds
1 one, 4 tens, 2 hundreds, 1 thousand
7 ones, 9 tens, 5 hundreds, 1 thousand
(Do the 4-digit numbers have a comma?)

b. **Read the numbers.**

5. **One-half is a __.** fraction
   1 whole cut __. into 2 equal parts
6. Do the Speed Drill in Lesson 100.
7. Assign Lesson 100.

Answer these problems.
Carry *over* in some problems.

77	86	44	88	94	66
+56	+36	+27	+50	+45	+72
133	122	71	138	139	138

76	65	65	62	79	87
+57	+70	+48	+53	+54	+46
133	135	113	115	133	133

77	88	53	33	54	63
+45	+45	+85	+38	+84	+76
122	133	138	71	138	139

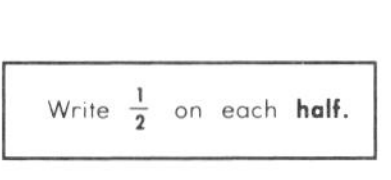

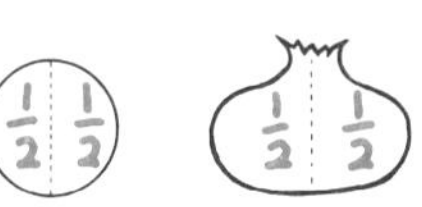

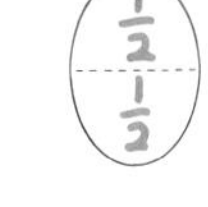

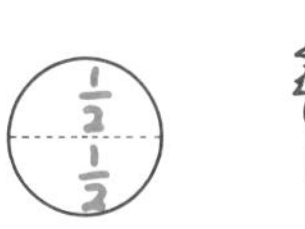

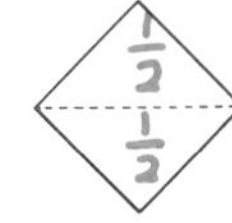

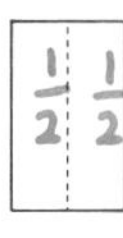

165

Blacklines

Fact Hives #18

Triplets With Facts #8

Fact Form VI

After Class

11 is how much more than 8?
13 is how much more than 7?
12 is how much more than 6?
12 is how much more than 9?
13 is how much more than 5?

Call the children to the chalkboard samples. **11 is how much more than 8?**

a. Circle 11 and 8. **Do we want to see how much these two numbers are in all? No, we will not add.**

b. **We want to see how much *more* 11 is than 8. We will subtract.** Write 11−8=3.

11 is 3 more than 8.

c. Have individuals read the question aloud and write the subtraction problem.

Speed Drill

5	13	7	12	12	13
+7	-6	+6	-7	-5	-7
12	7	13	5	7	6

6	13	12	7	7	12
+7	-7	-5	+6	+5	-7
13	6	7	13	12	5

13	5	13	12	12	6	13	5
-6	+7	-7	-5	-7	+7	-6	+7
7	12	6	7	5	13	7	12

7	12	12	5	6	13	13	7
+5	-5	-7	+7	+7	-6	-7	+6
12	7	5	12	13	7	6	13

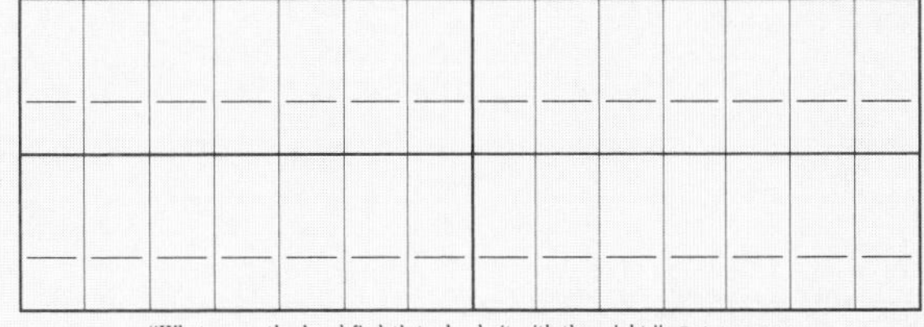

"Whatsoever thy hand findeth to do, do it with thy might." Ecclesiastes 9:10

166

101

Fill in the whole and parts.

Write the facts.

Trace, answer, and write the facts.

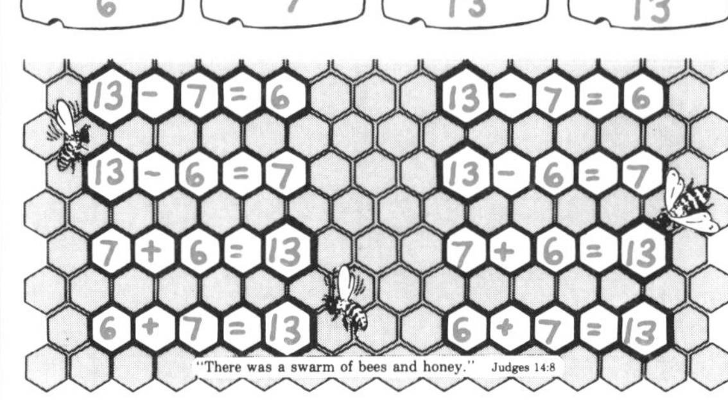

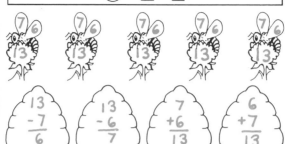

"There was a swarm of bees and honey." Judges 14:8

167

Before Class

Materials

Large coins

10's–13's flash cards

Chalkboard

Class Time

1. Stand near the clover patch.

   In the Bible a man and his parents were walking toward the Philistines' land. On the way the man found bees and honey. He ate some honey and gave honey to his parents. Who was the man?

   Samson (Judges 14:8, 9)

2. (13) 9 4

   The whole number is __.
   Its parts are __ and __.

   a. **The triplet is (13) 9 4 . . .**

   b. **The facts are 13−9, 4; 13−4, 9; 9+4, 13; 4+9, 13 . . .**

3. (13) 8 5

   The whole number is __.
   Its parts are __ and __.

   a. **The triplet is (13) 8 5 . . .**

   b. **The facts are 13−8, 5; 13−5, 8; 8+5, 13; 5+8, 13 . . .**

101

Extra Activity

Answer these facts.

13 - 7 = 6	13 - 6 = 7	12 - 5 = 7	13 - 6 = 7	6 + 7 = 13	12 - 5 = 7	13 - 6 = 7	7 + 6 = 13
6 + 7 = 13	13 - 6 = 7	5 + 7 = 12	7 + 6 = 13	13 - 6 = 7	7 + 5 = 12	13 - 6 = 7	13 - 7 = 6
12 - 7 = 5	13 - 7 = 6	6 + 7 = 13	13 - 7 = 6	5 + 7 = 12	6 + 7 = 13	13 - 7 = 6	6 + 7 = 13
7 + 6 = 13	6 + 7 = 13	13 - 6 = 7	7 + 5 = 12	13 - 7 = 6	13 - 6 = 7	7 + 6 = 13	12 - 7 = 5
7 + 5 = 12	13 - 6 = 7	12 - 7 = 5	13 - 6 = 7	13 - 7 = 6	12 - 7 = 5	12 - 5 = 7	7 + 6 = 13
		6 + 7 = 13	13 - 7 = 6	13 - 6 = 7	12 - 5 = 7	6 + 7 = 13	5 + 7 = 12

168

4. (13) 7 6

The whole number is __.

Its parts are __ and __.

a. **The triplet is (13) 7 6 . . .**

b. **The facts are 13−7, 6; 13−6, 7; 7+6, 13; 6+7, 13 . . .**

5. **Say the 13's facts as I fill the beehive.**

6. **Who can give the whole problem?**
   - **13 is how much more than 6?** 13−6=7
   - **9 is how much more than 3?** 9−3=6
   - **12 is how much more than 7?** 12−7=5
   - **10 is how much more than 2?** 10−2=8
   - **11 is how much more than 5?** 11−5=6
   - **13 is how much more than 8?** 13−8=5
   - **12 is how much more than 3?** 12−3=9

7. Flash the large coins.

   a. **Quarter, penny, dime, nickel.**

   b. **25¢, 1¢, 10¢, 5¢ . . .**

8. Assign Lesson 101.

Shade the greater number in ones' place.

Borrow *back* in some problems.

101

73 − 46 = 27	98 − 75 = 23	93 − 37 = 56	82 − 55 = 27	99 − 74 = 25	93 − 35 = 58
93 − 48 = 45	93 − 14 = 79	92 − 57 = 35	82 − 43 = 39	99 − 23 = 76	98 − 52 = 46
72 − 14 = 58	87 − 62 = 25	73 − 46 = 27	83 − 27 = 56	68 − 45 = 23	82 − 55 = 27

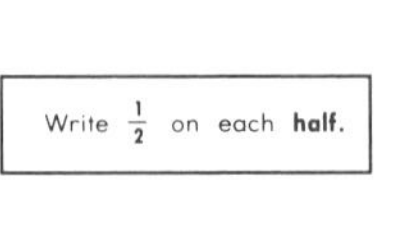

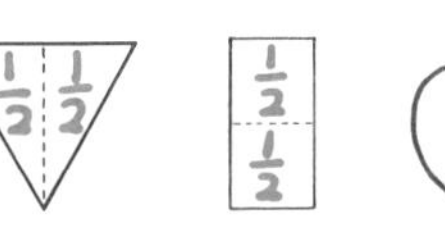

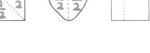

169

Blacklines

Fact Hives #18

Missing Whole or Parts #11

Number Triplets #3

After Class

__	21	31	__	__	__
__	__	65	__	__	95
38	__	__	__	78	__
__	37	__	__	__	77

1. Circle Drill: 10's–13's flash cards.
2. **Count by 10's.**
   a. **Begin at 4.** **4, 14 . . .**
      Begin at 9. **9, 19 . . .**
      Begin at 7. **7, 17 . . .**
   b. Fill in the Missing Number samples.

Extra Activity
"His eye seeth every precious thing."
Job 28:10
170

102

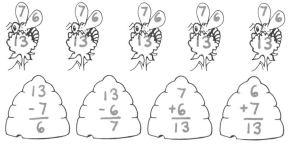

Fill in the whole and parts.

13
7
6

Write the facts.

Trace, answer, and write the facts.

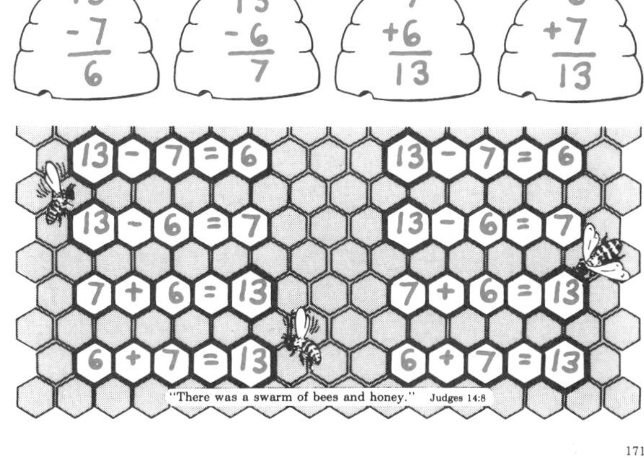
"There was a swarm of bees and honey." Judges 14:8

Before Class

Materials

11's–13's flash cards

11's–13's flash cards

Large clock

Class Time

1. Stand near the Number Line.
   a. **Count 2, 12 . . . 92**
   Answer together.

72+10	**82+10**	**22−10**
62+10	**32+10**	**92−10**
42+10	**72+10**	**52−10**

   b. **Count 6, 16 . . . 96**
   Answer together.

26+10	**36+10**	**86−10**
76+10	**66+10**	**56−10**
56+10	**46+10**	**96−10**

2. Stand near the Blossom Charts.
   a. **Say each triplet 3 times.**
   b. **Say the triplets by memory.**
   (11) 9 2
   (11) 8 3
   (11) 7 4 . . .

102

Answer these facts.

13 -7 6	11 -7 4	13 -8 5	11 -2 9	6 +7 13	12 -7 5	12 -8 4	3 +9 12
4 +8 12	12 -5 7	3 +8 11	7 +6 13	13 -4 9	2 +9 11	13 -6 7	11 -5 6
13 -5 8	13 -7 6	6 +7 13	13 -9 4	5 +8 13	4 +9 13	12 -6 6	6 +6 12
5 +7 12	6 +7 13	13 -4 9	9 +4 13	12 -8 4	12 -3 9	7 +6 13	11 -3 8
13 -5 8	13 -6 7	12 -9 3	11 -9 2	12 -7 5	11 -8 3	13 -6 7	7 +6 13
		8 +5 13	11 -6 5	11 -9 2	13 -6 7	6 +5 11	12 -4 8

172

c. **Jump from chart to chart.**

(11) 9 2

(12) 9 3

(13) 9 4 . . .

3. Flash the 11's–13's cards.
   Answer together.
4. **12 is how much more than 8?** 12−8=4
   13 . . . than 4? 13−4=9
   11 . . . than 7? 11−7=4
   12 . . . than 6? 12−6=6
   13 . . . than 5? 13−5=8
   11 . . . than 4? 11−4=7
5. **One-half is a __.** fraction
   1 whole cut __. into 2 equal parts
6. Do the Speed Drill in Lesson 102.
7. Assign Lesson 102.

Note: Beginning today, some Speed Drills have a row of Column Addition. If a child has a wrong answer for a Column Addition problem, he need not practice it below.

102

Answer these problems.
Carry *over* in some problems.

139	36	139	118	35	137
-76	+57	-64	-47	+17	-94
63	93	75	71	52	43
88	128	46	118	53	139
+45	-48	+77	-36	+85	-77
133	80	123	82	138	62
26	135	139	127	138	28
+17	-83	-68	-52	-45	+35
43	52	71	75	93	63

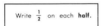

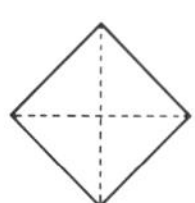

173

Blacklines

Number Triplets #3

Triplets With Facts #8

Mixed Computation #2

After Class

1. Drill individuals with the 11's–13's flash cards.
2. Hold the large clock.
   a. **60 minutes=__.** 1 hour
      30 minutes=__. ½ hour
   b. Set the clock at 3:00.
      In 15 minutes it will be __.
      In 30 minutes it will be __.
      In 45 minutes it will be __.
      In 1 hour it will be __.
   c. Set the clock at 7:00 and ask the same questions.

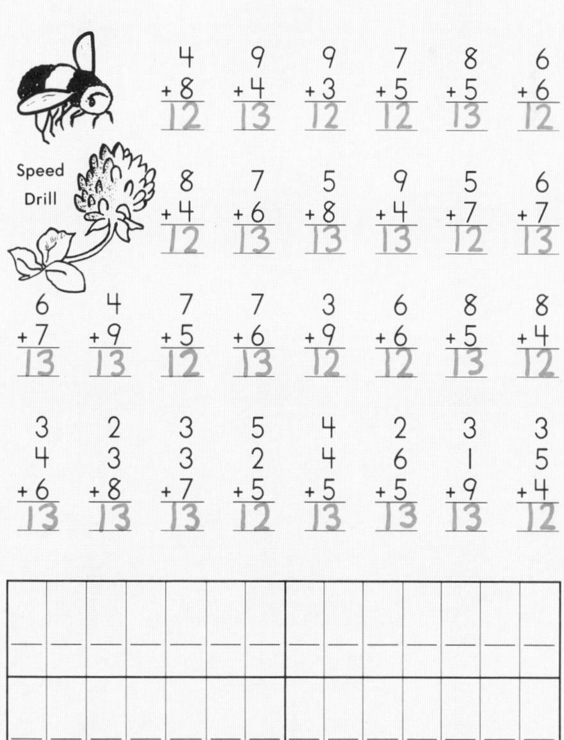

"Whatsoever thy hand findeth to do, do it with thy might." Ecclesiastes 9:10

174

Unit 4

Lessons 103–137

103

Trace and fill in the whole and parts.

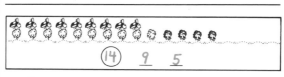

(14) 9 5

Trace, answer, and write the facts.

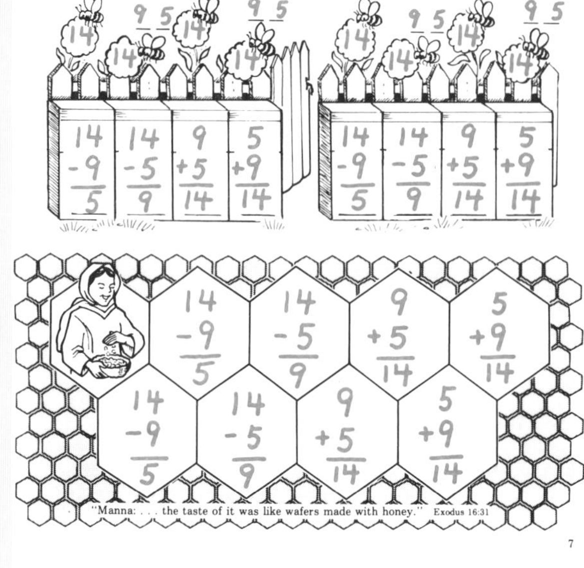
"Manna: . . . the taste of it was like wafers made with honey." Exodus 16:31

Before Class

Make (14) 9 5 flash cards for each child.

Tack (14) 9 5 flash cards above the clover patch in this order:

14	14	9	5
−9	−5	+5	+9
5	9	14	14

Materials

8's–13's flash cards

Chalkboard

83	89	62	93	68	83	75
− 6	−24	− 7	−59	−26	− 8	−35

Class Time

1. **Count by 5's from 100–300.**
   Have responsive counting. **I'll say the first number; you say the next number.**
2. Double Drill: Flash 8's–13's cards.
3. Stand near the clover patch.

   (14) 9 5

   a. **How many pink clovers are in the patch?** 10
   We think—10 pink.
   4 more make __ altogether. 14
   We think—10 pink.
   1 less makes __ clovers with bees. 9

   b. **14 clovers in the patch;**
   14 is the whole number.
   What part of the 14 has bees? 9
   What part of the 14 has no bees? 5
   14 is the whole number.
   Its parts are 9 and 5.

103

Extra Activity

Answer these facts.

14 − 9 = 5 | 14 − 5 = 9 | 14 − 9 = 5 | 14 − 5 = 9 | 9 + 5 = 14 | 14 − 9 = 5 | 14 − 5 = 9 | 9 + 5 = 14

5 + 9 = 14 | 14 − 9 = 5 | 9 + 5 = 14 | 5 + 9 = 14 | 14 − 5 = 9 | 5 + 9 = 14 | 14 − 9 = 5 | 14 − 9 = 5

14 − 5 = 9 | 14 − 9 = 5 | 5 + 9 = 14 | 14 − 9 = 5 | 5 + 9 = 14 | 9 + 5 = 14 | 14 − 9 = 5 | 9 + 5 = 14

5 + 9 = 14 | 9 + 5 = 14 | 14 − 5 = 9 | 5 + 9 = 14 | 14 − 9 = 5 | 14 − 5 = 9 | 9 + 5 = 14 | 14 − 5 = 9

14 − 9 = 5 | 14 − 5 = 9 | 14 − 9 = 5 | 14 − 5 = 9 | 14 − 9 = 5 | 14 − 9 = 5 | 14 − 5 = 9 | 5 + 9 = 14

9 + 5 = 14 | 14 − 9 = 5 | 14 − 5 = 9 | 14 − 5 = 9 | 5 + 9 = 14 | 14 − 9 = 5

8

c. **The triplet is (14) 9 5 . . .**

d. **The facts are 14−9, 5; 14−5, 9; 9+5, 14; 5+9, 14 . . .**

4. **Say the triplets as I fill the clover and bees.**
5. **Say the facts as I fill the beehive.**
6. Drill the triplets.
   Girls, say the 11 triplets.
   Boys, say the 12 triplets.
   Everyone say the 13 triplets.
7. Do the Subtraction samples.
8. a. **One half is a __.** fraction
   1 whole cut __. into 2 equal parts
   b. **2 halves of a sandwich make __.** 1 whole sandwich
   2 halves of a pie make __. 1 whole pie
   2 halves of an apple make __. 1 whole apple
   2 halves make 1 whole.
9. Assign Lesson 103.

Note: Make Blossom 14 Chart for Lesson 104.

Shade the greater number in ones' place.
Borrow *back* in some problems.
Answer the problems.

93 − 77 = 16	99 − 76 = 23	93 − 36 = 57	92 − 65 = 27	77 − 47 = 30	93 − 55 = 38
98 − 20 = 78	89 − 37 = 52	73 − 34 = 39	99 − 78 = 21	72 − 46 = 26	63 − 39 = 24
62 − 24 = 38	83 − 26 = 57	57 − 34 = 23	95 − 65 = 30	62 − 35 = 27	53 − 37 = 16

Blacklines

Fact Hives #19

Fact Form III

9

After Class

1. Give each child his (14) 9 5 flash cards.
2. Chalkboard Drill: **Write only the answer.**

12−5	**6+6**	**13−8**	**6+7**
11−8	**7+6**	**9+4**	**12−7**
13−6	**5+7**	**12−4**	**2+9**
13−4	**3+9**	**8+5**	**13−7**

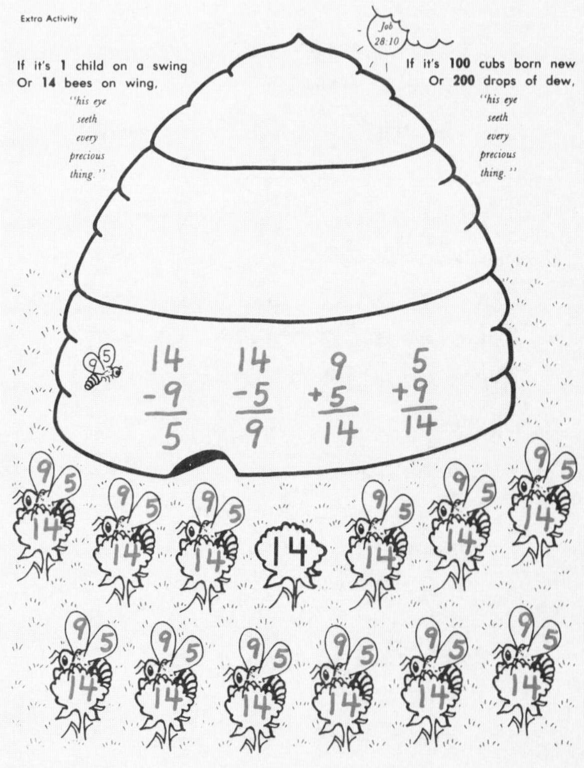

10

Fill in the whole and parts.

Trace, answer, and write the facts.

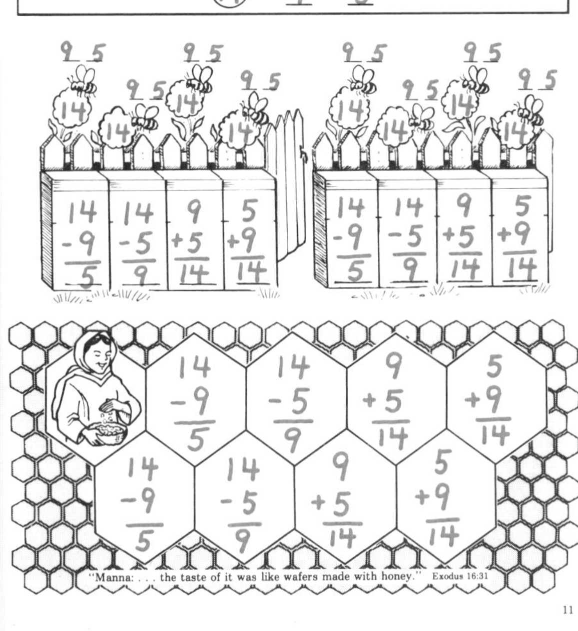
104
14 9 5
"Manna: . . . the taste of it was like wafers made with honey." Exodus 16:31
11

Before Class

Tack bee (14) 9 5 on Blossom 14 Chart.
Mount it on the wall.

Materials

9's–14's flash cards
Large clock
13's and 14's flash cards

Chalkboard

23	16	25	46	38	53
54	50	63	33	41	27
+26	+45	+34	+54	+44	+50

Class Time

1. Stand near the clover patch.
   God's Word was dear to King David's heart. He said that it was sweeter than __.
   honey (Psalm 19:10)

2. (14) 9 5
   14 clovers in the patch;
   14 is the whole number.
   What part of the 14 has bees? 9
   What part of the 14 has no bees? 5
   14 is the whole number.
   Its parts are 9 and 5.
   a. **The triplet is (14) 9 5 . . .**
   b. Point to the first flash card.
      Close your eyes and say it 3 times.
      14−9, 5; 14−9, 5 . . . Drill each fact.

3. Drill the 11, 12, 13, and 14 triplets on the Blossom Charts.

4. Flash 9's–14's cards.

5. Do the Column Addition samples.

104

Answer these facts.

14 - 5 = 9	14 - 9 = 5	14 - 5 = 9	14 - 5 = 9	9 + 5 = 14	14 - 5 = 9	14 - 9 = 5	5 + 9 = 14
9 + 5 = 14	14 - 9 = 5	5 + 9 = 14	5 + 9 = 14	14 - 5 = 9	9 + 5 = 14	14 - 9 = 5	14 - 5 = 9
14 - 9 = 5	14 - 5 = 9	5 + 9 = 14	14 - 9 = 5	5 + 9 = 14	9 + 5 = 14	14 - 5 = 9	9 + 5 = 14
9 + 5 = 14	5 + 9 = 14	14 - 5 = 9	5 + 9 = 14	14 - 9 = 5	14 - 5 = 9	9 + 5 = 14	14 - 9 = 5
14 - 5 = 9	14 - 5 = 9	14 - 9 = 5	14 - 5 = 9	9 + 5 = 14	14 - 9 = 5	14 - 5 = 9	5 + 9 = 14
		9 + 5 = 14	5 + 9 = 14	14 - 5 = 9	14 - 5 = 9	5 + 9 = 14	14 - 5 = 9

12

6. **One half is a __.** fraction
   1 whole cut __. into 2 equal parts
   2 halves make __. 1 whole
7. Stand near the Number Line.
   Count by 10's. Begin at
   •4 4, 14 . . . 94
   •7 7, 17 . . . 97
   •1 1, 11 . . . 91
   •9 9, 19 . . . 99
8. Hold the large clock.
   a. **Name the hands.**
   b. **Read the time together.**
   4:15, 5:45, 8:15, 9:45, 11:15, 1:45 . . .
9. Do the Speed Drill in Lesson 104.
10. Assign Lesson 104.

Answer these problems.
Carry *over* in some problems.

43	14	56	24	74	35
34	23	12	14	15	43
+62	+94	+61	+95	+42	+34
139	131	129	133	131	112

55	34	61	35	52	44
32	42	25	43	37	23
+25	+55	+47	+51	+42	+72
112	131	133	129	131	139

Write the time.

Blacklines

Fact Hives #19

Fact Form VI

Number Words #5

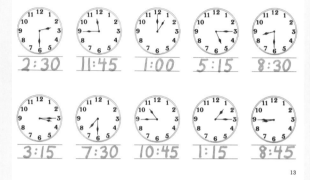

After Class

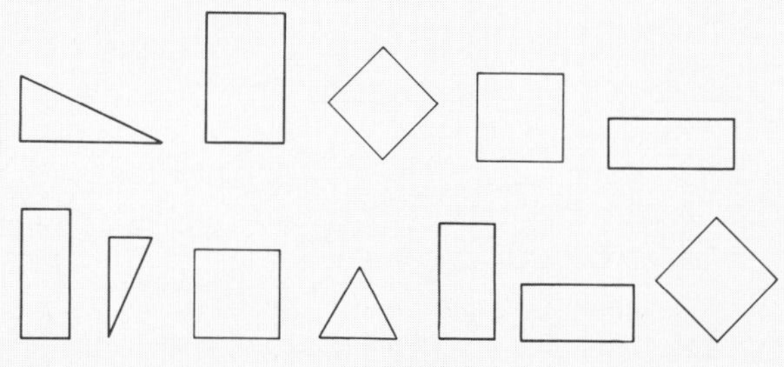

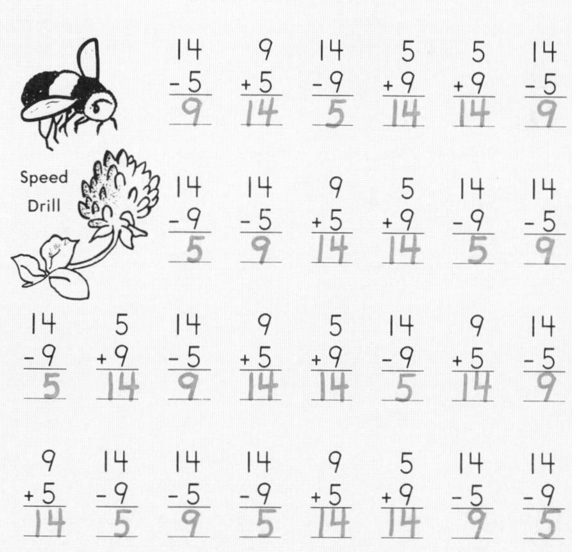

Speed Drill
14 − 5 = 9; 9 + 5 = 14; 14 − 9 = 5; 5 + 9 = 14; 5 + 9 = 14; 14 − 5 = 9
14 − 9 = 5; 14 − 5 = 9; 9 + 5 = 14; 5 + 9 = 14; 14 − 9 = 5; 14 − 5 = 9
14 − 9 = 5; 5 + 9 = 14; 14 − 5 = 9; 9 + 5 = 14; 5 + 9 = 14; 14 − 9 = 5; 9 + 5 = 14; 14 − 5 = 9
9 + 5 = 14; 14 − 9 = 5; 14 − 5 = 9; 14 − 9 = 5; 9 + 5 = 14; 5 + 9 = 14; 14 − 5 = 9; 14 − 9 = 5

1. Flash the 13's and 14's cards. **Say the triplet; then say the answer.**

13
−7
6

   (13) 7 6
   The answer is 6.

2. Ask individuals to name the shapes and write *T*, *R*, or *S* inside.

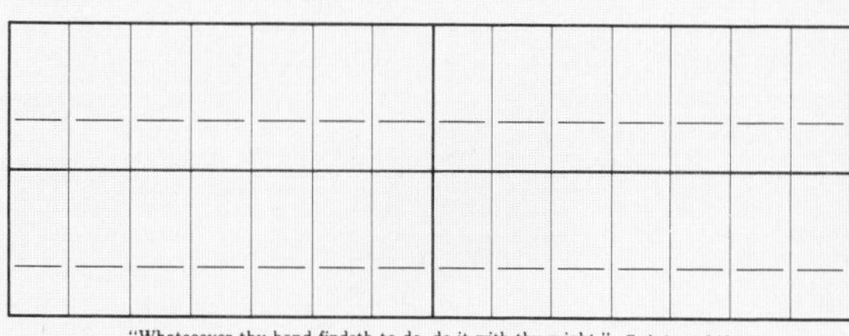

"Whatsoever thy hand findeth to do, do it with thy might." Ecclesiastes 9:10

105

Fill in the whole and parts.

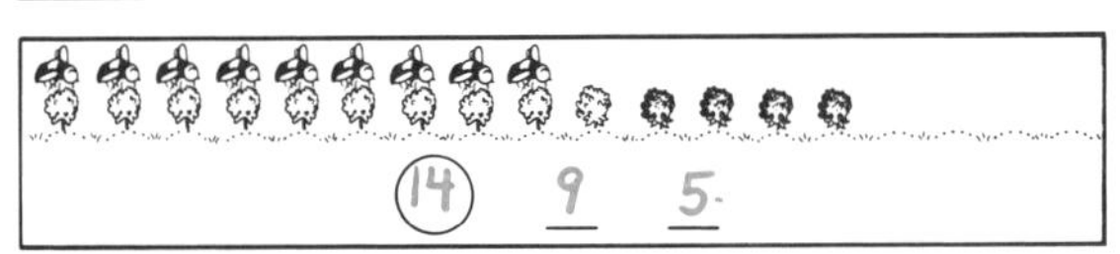

Trace, answer, and write the facts.

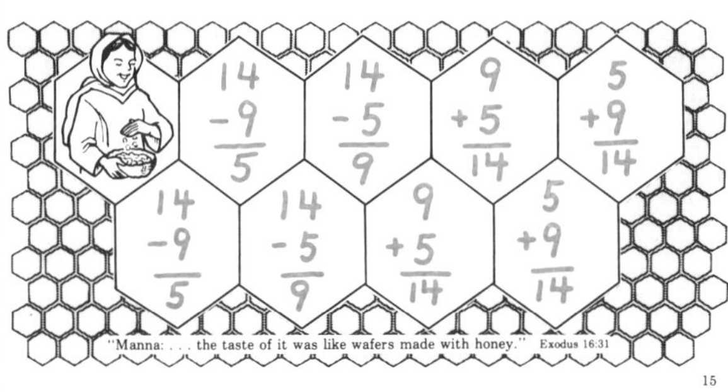

"Manna: . . . the taste of it was like wafers made with honey." Exodus 16:31
15

Before Class

Materials

11's–14's flash cards

6's–10's flash cards

Chalkboard

82	148	88	149
+57	−93	+55	−58
69	137	65	138
+45	−93	+69	−76

Class Time

1. Double Drill: 11's–14's flash cards.
2. Stand near the clover patch.

(14) 9 5

   14 clovers in the patch;
   14 is the whole number.
   What part of the 14 has bees? 9
   What part of the 14 has no bees? 5
   14 is the whole number.
   Its parts are 9 and 5.

   a. **The triplet is (14) 9 5 . . .**
   b. **The facts are 14−9, 5; 14−5, 9; 9+5, 14; 5+9, 14 . . .**
3. Point to the Blossom Charts.

   a. **Say each triplet 3 times.**
   b. **Jump from chart to chart.**

   (11) 9 2
   (12) 9 3
   (13) 9 4
   (14) 9 5 . . .

105

Extra Activity

Answer these problems.
Carry *over* in some problems.

144 -93 51	35 +49 84	147 -55 92	146 -94 52	96 +53 149	148 -56 92
35 +69 104	149 -56 93	85 +55 140	149 -94 55	35 +29 64	147 -54 93
59 +25 84	149 -98 51	144 -92 52	145 -53 92	149 -57 92	94 +55 149
148 -55 93	59 +45 104	147 -92 55	90 +50 140	146 -53 93	39 +25 64
145 -95 50	52 +92 144	148 -54 94	75 +29 104	84 +56 140	149 -58 91
		89 +15 104	147 -53 94	91 +53 144	147 -97 50

16

4. Do the Computation samples.
5. **Number places are ones, tens, hundreds, (comma), thousands; ones, tens . . .**
6. **One-half is a __.** fraction
   1 whole cut __. into 2 equal parts
   2 halves make __. 1 whole
7. Assign Lesson 105.

105

Write the numbers in the correct places.
Add a comma where needed.

	thousands	hundreds	tens	ones
1970	1,	9	7	0
37			3	7
1315	1,	3	1	5
582		5	8	2
603		6	0	3
1986	1,	9	8	6

	thousands	hundreds	tens	ones
1815	1,	8	1	5
380		3	8	0
1973	1,	9	7	3
1325	1,	3	2	5
1784	1,	7	8	4
1999	1,	9	9	9

Read the story.
Write the numbers in the beehive.
Write the label words on the lines.
Answer the problem.

14 deer made tracks in the snow. Five deer were big, but the rest were small. How many deer were small?

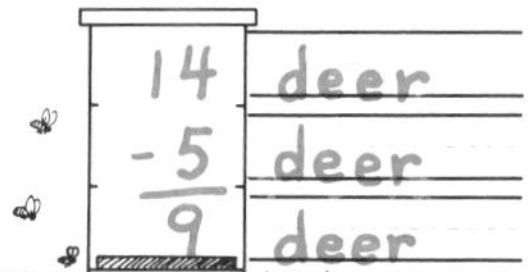

13 birds eat at a bird feeder. Six birds are red, and the rest are brown. How many birds are brown?

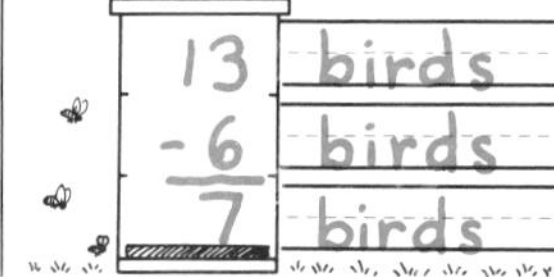

17

Blacklines

Fact Hives #19

Missing Whole or Parts #12

Number Words #5

After Class

1. Ask individuals to give the triplets by memory.
2. Flash the 6's–10's flash cards.
   Answer as quickly as you can!
3. Chalkboard Drill: **Write the number you hear.**
   - **Peter preached to 120 people in an upstairs room.** (Acts 1:15)
   - **The Book of Jeremiah has 1,364 verses.**
   - **Methuselah lived 969 years.** (Genesis 5:27)
   - **Nabal had 1,000 goats.** (1 Samuel 25:2)
   - **The Book of Genesis has 1,533 verses.**

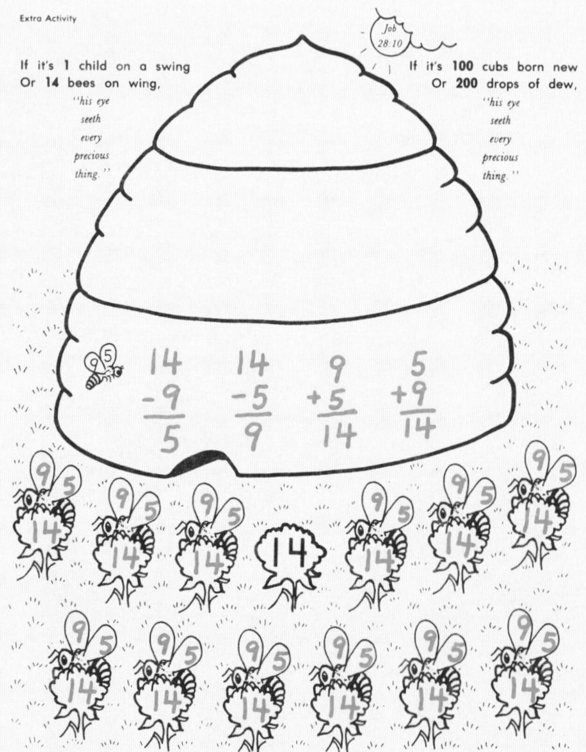

18

106

106
(14) 9 5

Fill in the whole and parts.

Write the facts.

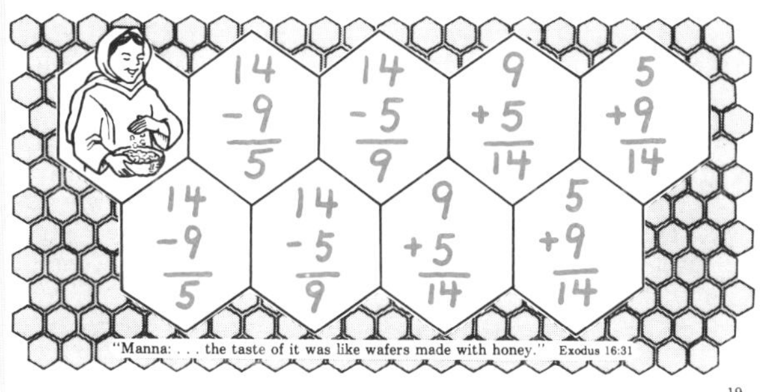
"Manna: . . . the taste of it was like wafers made with honey." Exodus 16:31

19

Before Class

Materials

9's–14's flash cards

Chalkboard

$1.50
$2.38
$1.94
$3.66

7 dimes + 3 pennies = __

2 quarters + 1 nickel = __

1 dime + 3 nickels = __

5 dimes + 9 pennies = __

8 nickels + 1 penny = __

Class Time

1. Stand near the clover patch.

(12) 9 3

   The whole number is __.
   Its parts are __ and __.
   The facts are 12−9, 3; 12−3, 9; 9+3, 12; 3+9, 12 . . .

2. | (13) 9 4 |
   |---|

   The whole number is __.
   Its parts are __ and __.
   The facts are 13−9, 4; 13−4, 9; 9+4, 13; 4+9, 13 . . .

3. | (14) 9 5 |
   |---|

   The whole number is __.
   Its parts are __ and __.
   The facts are 14−9, 5; 14−5, 9; 9+5, 14; 5+9, 14 . . .

106

Count the first row.
Write the amount.
Count the second row.
Write the amount.
Add.
Then copy the answer into the dollar box.

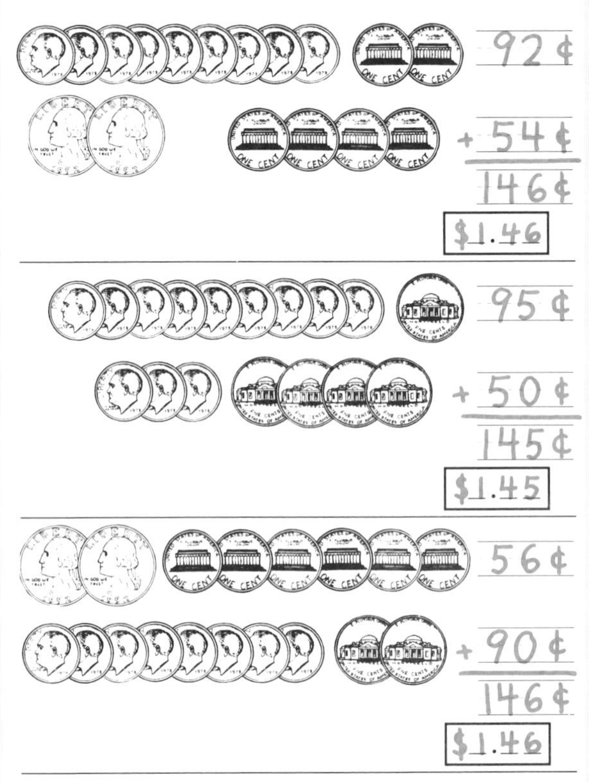

Speed Drill

4. Point to the Blossom Charts.
   Jump from chart to chart.
   (11) 9 2
   (12) 9 3
   (13) 9 4 . . .
5. Review money.
   a. **We count pennies by __, nickels by __, dimes by __, and quarters by __.**
   b. **100¢ is the same as __.** $1.00
      How many pennies are in $1.00?
      Continue with dimes, quarters, and nickels.
   c. Read the money in the box together.
      1 dollar and 50 cents . . .
   d. Do the Money samples.
6. Do the Speed Drill in Lesson 106.
7. Assign Lesson 106.

106

Answer these problems. Borrow *back* in some problems.

94 − 55 = 39	55 + 94 = 149	83 − 47 = 36	53 − 29 = 24	83 + 55 = 138	94 − 29 = 65
53 − 18 = 35	96 + 52 = 148	73 − 39 = 34	93 − 67 = 26	76 + 63 = 139	83 − 14 = 69
94 + 44 = 138	83 − 35 = 48	93 − 36 = 57	94 − 19 = 75	74 − 25 = 49	67 + 72 = 139

Blacklines

Triplets With Facts #9

Reading Problems #4

2-Place Computation (−) #7

Answer these facts.

14 − 9 = 5	13 − 9 = 4	14 − 5 = 9	13 − 8 = 5	9 + 5 = 14	13 − 4 = 9	13 − 9 = 4	5 + 9 = 14
7 + 6 = 13	13 − 7 = 6	8 + 5 = 13	9 + 4 = 13	14 − 5 = 9	6 + 7 = 13	13 − 7 = 6	14 − 5 = 9

21

After Class

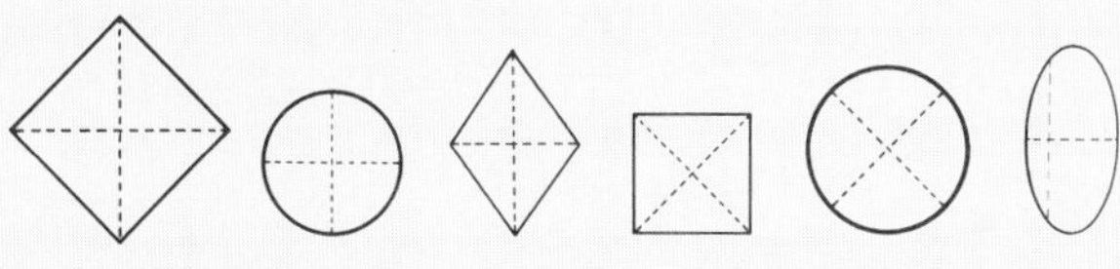

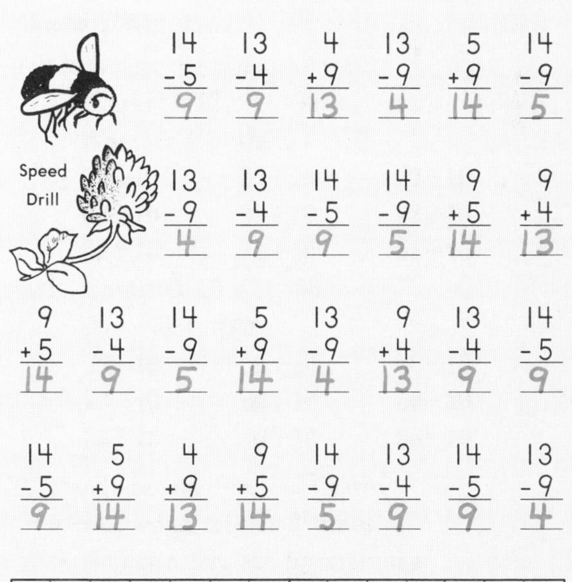

Speed
Drill
14 − 5 = 9, 13 − 4 = 9, 4 + 9 = 13, 13 − 9 = 4, 5 + 9 = 14, 14 − 9 = 5
13 − 9 = 4, 13 − 4 = 9, 14 − 5 = 9, 14 − 9 = 5, 9 + 5 = 14, 9 + 4 = 13
9 + 5 = 14, 13 − 4 = 9, 14 − 9 = 5, 5 + 9 = 14, 13 − 9 = 4, 9 + 4 = 13, 13 − 4 = 9, 14 − 5 = 9
14 − 5 = 9, 5 + 9 = 14, 4 + 9 = 13, 9 + 5 = 14, 14 − 9 = 5, 13 − 4 = 9, 14 − 5 = 9, 13 − 9 = 4

1. Circle Drill: 9's–14's flash cards.
2. Review one-half.
   One-half is a __. fraction
   1 whole cut __. into 2 equal parts
   2 halves make __. 1 whole
3. Introduce one-fourth.
   a. **One-fourth is a fraction.**
      1 whole cut into 4 *equal* parts.
      The 4 parts must be the same size.
   b. Fill in the shapes. ¼, ¼, ¼ . . .

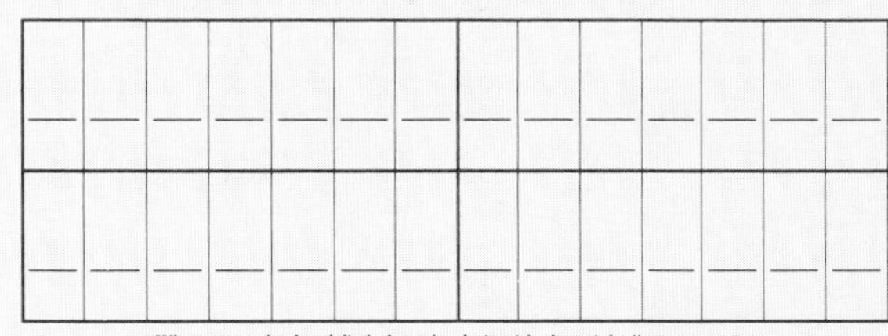

"Whatsoever thy hand findeth to do, do it with thy might." Ecclesiastes 9:10

22

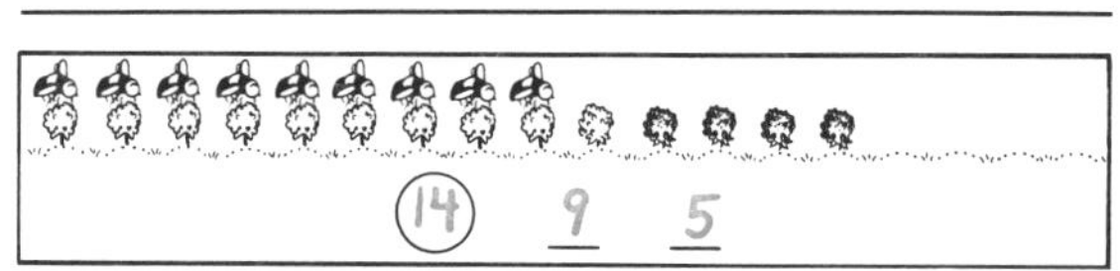

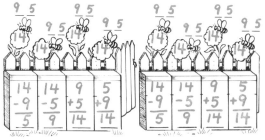

Fill in the whole and parts.

Write the facts.

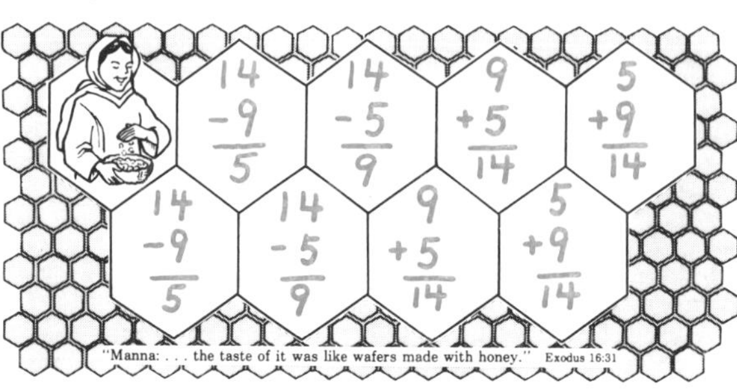

"Manna: . . . the taste of it was like wafers made with honey." Exodus 16:31
23

Before Class

Materials

11's–14's flash cards
Form C

Chalkboard

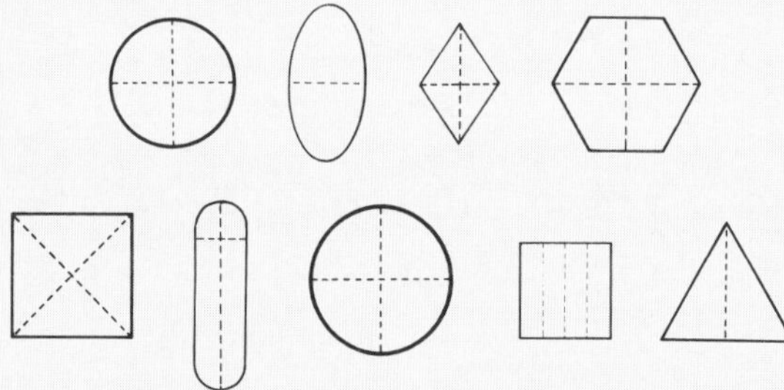

Class Time

1. Stand near the clover patch.

(14) 9 5

   14 clovers in the patch;
   14 is the whole number.
   What part of the 14 has bees? 9
   What part of the 14 has no bees? 5
   14 is the whole number.
   Its parts are 9 and 5.

   a. **The triplet is (14) 9 5 . . .**
   b. **The facts are 14−9, 5; 14−5, 9; 9+5, 14; 5+9, 14 . . .**

2. Point to the Blossom Charts. Drill these two triplets.

   (13) 9 4
   (14) 9 5
   (13) 9 4
   (14) 9 5 . . .

3. Flash 11's–14's flash cards.
   Answer together.

107

Extra Activity

Fill in the missing whole or parts.

9 + 5 = 14	14 - 9 = 5	14 - 5 = 9
5 + 9 = 14	5 + 9 = 14	5 + 9 = 14
14 - 9 = 5	14 - 9 = 5	14 - 9 = 5
14 - 5 = 9	14 - 5 = 9	14 - 5 = 9
5 + 9 = 14	5 + 9 = 14	5 + 9 = 14
14 - 9 = 5	9 + 5 = 14	14 - 9 = 5

Answer these problems.

6	3	6	4	8	5	7	3
3	2	2	5	1	2	2	2
+5	+9	+4	+2	+5	+6	+5	+9
14	14	12	11	14	13	14	14

5	2	2	4	6	1	1	5
4	3	7	1	3	8	4	0
+5	+9	+4	+9	+2	+3	+9	+9
14	14	13	14	11	12	14	14

24

4. Flash Card Drill: 11's–14's flash cards. Use Form C. **Flower Row: Box 1 . . .**
5. **Raise your hand to answer.**
   (Say *blank* each time.)

12, 7 __	**13 __ 6**	**__ 9, 5**
14, 9 __	**14 __ 5**	**__ 8, 5**
13, 8 __	**12 __ 6**	**__ 9, 4**

6. Fractions
   a. **One-half is a __.** fraction
      1 whole cut __. into 2 equal parts
      2 halves make __. 1 whole
   b. **One-fourth is a __.** fraction
      1 whole cut __. into 4 equal parts
      4 fourths make __. 1 whole
   c. Do the samples.
7. Assign Lesson 107.

107

Write the numbers in the correct places.
Add a comma where needed.

	thousands	hundreds	tens	ones		thousands	hundreds	tens	ones
1893	1,	8	9	3	897		8	9	7
306		3	0	6	1582	1,	5	8	2
1929	1,	9	2	9	607		6	0	7
93			9	3	1315	1,	3	1	5
1945	1,	9	4	5	1290	1,	2	9	0
1784	1,	7	8	4	324		3	2	4
623		6	2	3	1918	1,	9	1	8

Write the time.

25

Blacklines

Form C (Class Time)
Missing Whole or Parts #12
Mixed Computation #3

After Class

1. Ask individuals to give the triplets by memory.
2. **Count by 10's. Begin at**
   •2 2, 12 . . .
   •8 8, 18 . . .
   •4 4, 14 . . .
3. Chalkboard Drill: **Write the problem.**
   a. **Lester has 49¢ in his bank. Grandfather gives him a quarter. How much money does he have now?**
   49¢ + 25¢ = 74¢
   b. **Mother bought a tablet with 2 quarters. She bought a ruler with 3 dimes. How much did Mother pay in all?**
   50¢ + 30¢ = 80¢
   c. **Susan had 80¢ in her bank. She took 2 dimes out for the church offering. How many cents is in her bank now?**
   80¢ − 20¢ = 60¢
   d. **Father has 69¢. He buys a stamp for 25¢. How much money does he have left?**
   69¢ − 25¢ = 44¢

26

108

Fill in the whole and parts.

Write the facts.

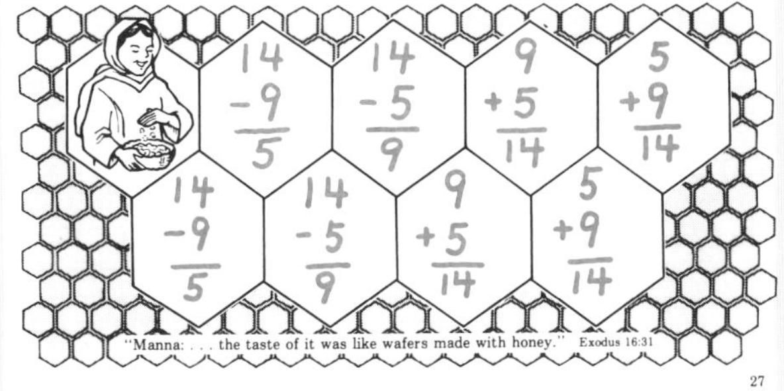

"Manna: . . . the taste of it was like wafers made with honey." Exodus 16:31
27

Before Class

Materials

8's–14's flash cards

Chalkboard

__ __ 260 __ __ 290 __

__ __ 32 __ __ 62 __

132 __ __ __ 140 __ __

__ 205 210 __ __ __ __

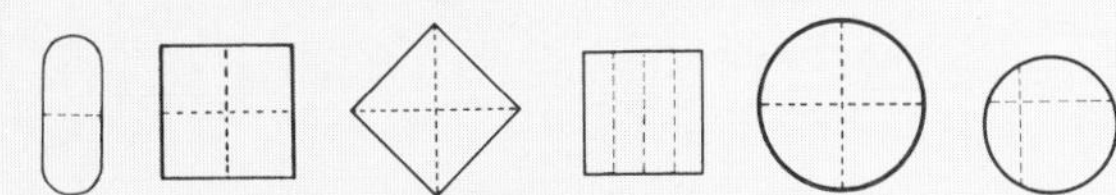

Class Time

1. Have each child bring *My 1,000 Book* to the teaching corner.
   a. **Begin at 100. Count by 10's to 300.**
   b. **Count on to 500 by 5's.**
2. Fill in the Missing Number samples.
   Decide if you should count by 10's, 5's, or 2's.
3. Stand near the Blossom Charts.
   a. Drill: **(13) 9 4; (14) 9 5 . . .**
   b. Begin with (11) 9 2.
   Say each triplet 3 times.
   c. **Jump from chart to chart.**
      (11) 9 2
      (12) 9 3
      (13) 9 4
      (14) 9 5
      (11) 8 3
      (12) 8 4 . . .

Read the story.
Write the numbers
in the beehive.
Write the label words
on the lines.
Answer the problem.

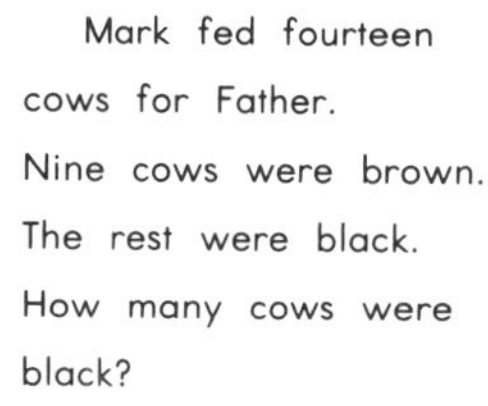

Mark fed fourteen cows for Father. Nine cows were brown. The rest were black. How many cows were black?

Father went to visit a new church. He drove five days to get to the church. He stayed 9 days to preach. How many days was that altogether?

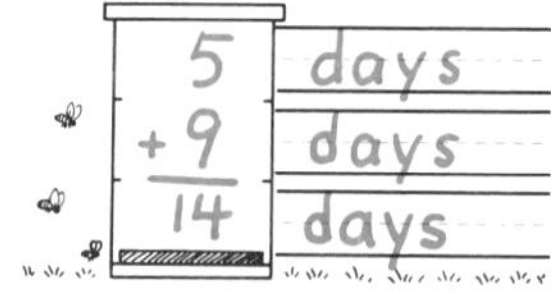

Lois peels thirteen apples for Mother. 7 apples are red, and the rest are yellow. How many apples are yellow?

Father has fourteen hives for bees. A bear opens 5 hives. How many hives does the bear not open?

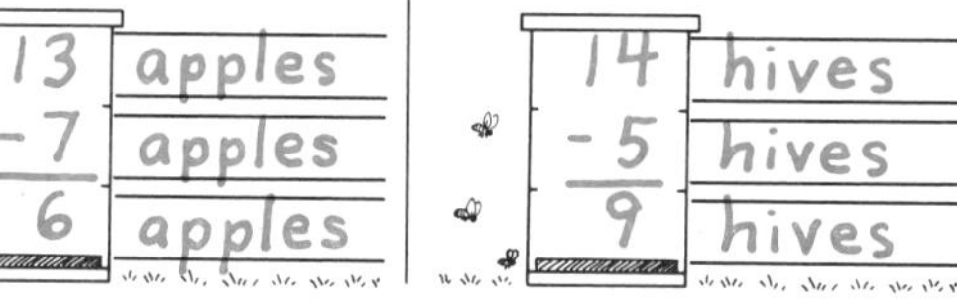

28

4. **Who can give the whole problem?**
   14 is how much more than 9? 14−9=5
   12 . . . than 8? 12−8=4
   13 . . . than 6? 13−6=7
   11 . . . than 5? 11−5=6
   10 . . . than 7? 10−7=3
   13 . . . than 9? 13−9=4
5. Review one-fourth.
   a. **One-fourth is a __.** fraction
      1 whole cut __. into 4 parts
      4 fourths make __. 1 whole
   b. Fill in the correct shapes.
6. Do the Speed Drill in Lesson 108.
7. Assign Lesson 108.

108

Answer these problems.
Borrow *back* in some problems.

94	73	99	74	94	93
-59	-57	+50	+63	-45	-69
35	16	149	137	49	24

53	94	92	83	53	73
+90	-69	+52	-57	+92	-46
143	25	144	26	145	27

82	93	53	55	82	83
-46	-78	+94	+84	-38	-54
36	15	147	139	44	29

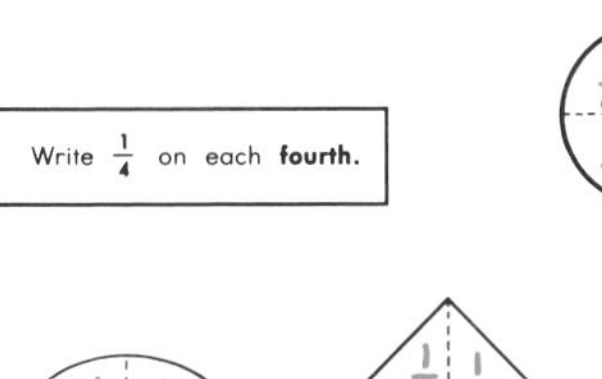
Write $\frac{1}{4}$ on each **fourth.**

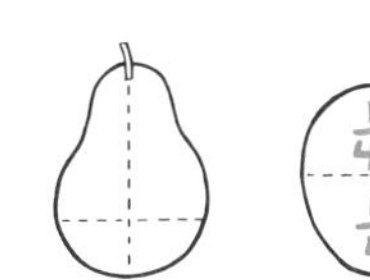
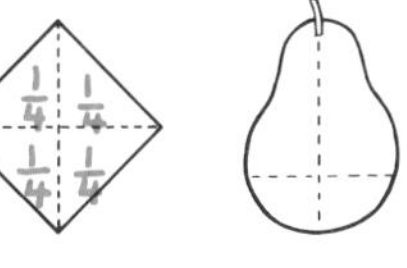
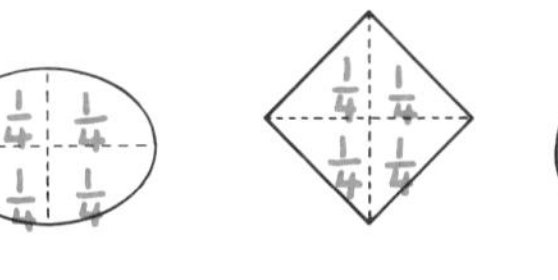

29

Blacklines

Triplets With Facts #9

Fact Form VI

2-Place Computation (−) #7

After Class

1. Double Drill: 8's–14's flash cards.
   Whoever gives the correct answer first may have the card. Collect the cards at the end of the drill.
2. **We can divide numbers into 2 equal parts.**
   a. **You have 2 apples. You give half of them to your brother.**
   You have __ apple left.
   Half of 2 is 1.
   b. **Your sister has 4 oranges. She gives half of them to you.**
   You have __ oranges.
   Half of 4 is 2.
   c. Give similar examples with
   •6 roses. **Half of 6 is 3.**
   •8 balloons. **Half of 8 is 4.**
   •10 peppermints. **Half of 10 is 5.**
   •12 pencils. **Half of 12 is 6.**

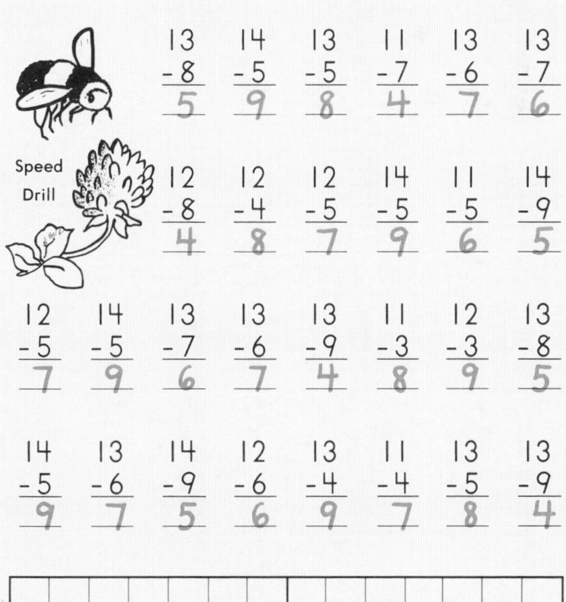

Speed Drill

13	14	13	11	13	13
-8	-5	-5	-7	-6	-7
5	9	8	4	7	6

12	12	12	14	11	14
-8	-4	-5	-5	-5	-9
4	8	7	9	6	5

12	14	13	13	13	11	12	13
-5	-5	-7	-6	-9	-3	-3	-8
7	9	6	7	4	8	9	5

14	13	14	12	13	11	13	13
-5	-6	-9	-6	-4	-4	-5	-9
9	7	5	6	9	7	8	4

"Whatsoever thy hand findeth to do, do it with thy might." Ecclesiastes 9:10

30

109

Fill in the whole and parts.

(14) 9 5

Write the facts.

Trace, answer, and write the facts.

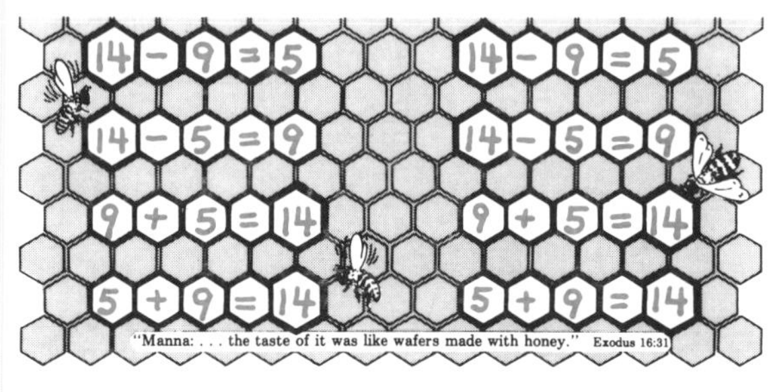

"Manna: . . . the taste of it was like wafers made with honey." Exodus 16:31

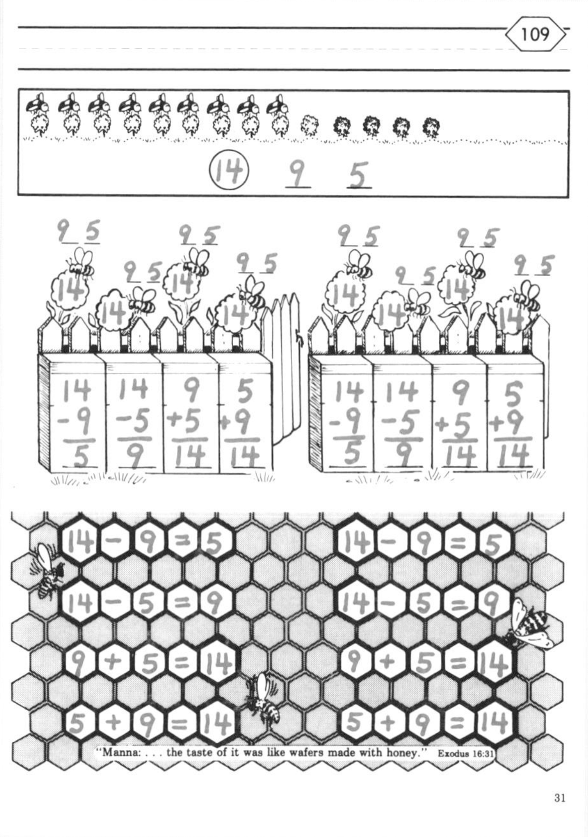

31

Before Class

Materials

9's–14's flash cards

Chalkboard

thousands	hundreds	tens	ones

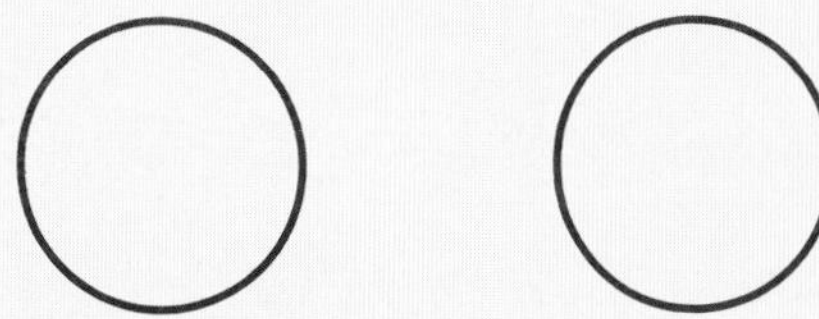

Class Time

1. Call the children to the clover patch.

   When a bear smells honey, he feels hungry. He sniffs his way to the beehive.

   The bear knocks the lid from the hive. Angry bees buzz out to sting his eyes and nose. The bear dabs his paw into the hive and scoops out a dripping chunk of honeycomb.

   Yes, a bear is the bees' enemy. In one minute he can spoil the work of 1,000 bees.

2. (14) 9 5

   The whole number is __.

   Its parts are __ and __.

   a. **The triplet is (14) 9 5 . . .**

   b. **Boys, say the facts.**

      Girls, say the facts.

109

Extra Activity

Answer these facts.

14 -5 9	13 -4 9	14 -9 5	14 -5 9	9 +4 13	14 -9 5	13 -4 9	4 +9 13
9 +4 13	13 -9 4	9 +5 14	4 +9 13	14 -5 9	5 +9 14	13 -9 4	14 -5 9
13 -9 4	14 -9 5	4 +9 13	13 -9 4	5 +9 14	9 +4 13	14 -9 5	9 +4 13
4 +9 13	9 +5 14	13 -4 9	5 +9 14	13 -9 4	13 -4 9	9 +5 14	13 -9 4
13 -4 9	14 -5 9	14 -9 5	14 -5 9	14 -9 5	14 -9 5	14 -5 9	5 +9 14
		9 +5 14	14 -9 5	14 -5 9	14 -5 9	5 +9 14	13 -4 9

32

3. Point to the Blossom Charts.
   a. Drill the 11, 12, 13, and 14 triplets.
   b. **Say the triplets by memory.**
4. Stand near the Place Value Grid.
   a. Have the children fill the grid.
      6 ones, 9 tens, 9 hundreds
      2 ones, 4 tens, 3 hundreds, 1 thousand
      0 ones, 0 tens, 8 hundreds, 1 thousand
      3 ones, 7 tens, 5 hundreds
      1 one, 6 tens, 4 hundreds, 1 thousand
      4 ones, 3 tens, 7 hundreds, 1 thousand
      5 ones, 8 tens, 6 hundreds, 1 thousand
      9 ones, 5 tens, 2 hundreds
      (Do the 4-digit numbers have a comma?)
   b. **Read the numbers.**
5. Review one-fourth.
   a. **One fourth is a __.** fraction
      1 whole cut __. into 4 equal parts
      4 fourths make __. 1 whole
   b. Divide the large circles and write the fractions as you say, **Mother cut one pie into halves. She cut the other pie into fourths. Which pie has smaller pieces?**
6. Assign Lesson 109.

Answer these problems. Borrow *back* in some problems.

109

94 − 79 = 15	73 − 26 = 47	74 + 63 = 137	53 + 96 = 149	94 − 69 = 25	93 − 27 = 66
90 + 52 = 142	73 − 15 = 58	50 + 90 = 140	83 − 27 = 56	62 + 76 = 138	83 − 29 = 54
82 − 65 = 17	84 − 39 = 45	54 + 85 = 139	93 + 54 = 147	82 − 56 = 26	84 − 19 = 65

Write $\frac{1}{4}$ on each **fourth.**

$\frac{1}{4}$ $\frac{1}{4}$ $\frac{1}{4}$ $\frac{1}{4}$

33

Blacklines

Missing Whole or Parts #12

Mixed Computation #3

Fact Form III

After Class

1. Drill 9's–14's flash cards.
2. Review one-half.
   Half of 2 is __.
   Half of 12 is __.
   Half of 8 is __.
   Half of 20 is __.
   Half of 6 is __.

Extra Activity
If it's 1 child on a swing
Or 14 bees on wing,
"his eye seeth every precious thing."
Job 28:10
If it's 100 cubs born new
Or 200 drops of dew,
"his eye seeth every precious thing."
14 − 9 = 5
14 − 5 = 9
9 + 5 = 14
5 + 9 = 14
14
34

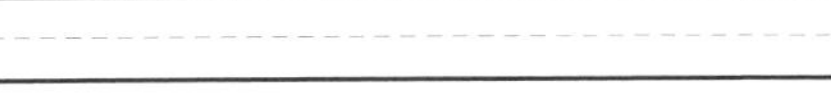

Fill in the whole and parts.

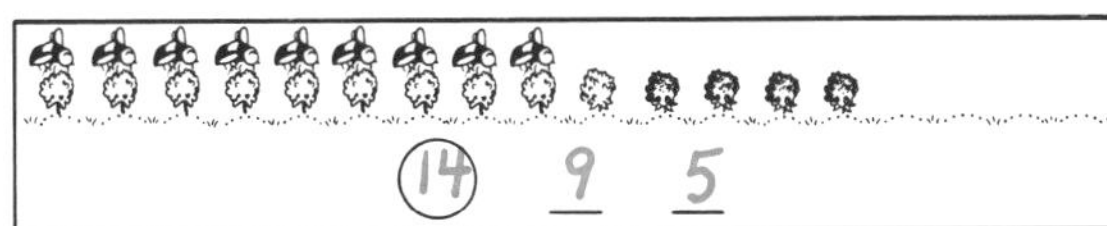

Write the facts.

Trace, answer, and write the facts.

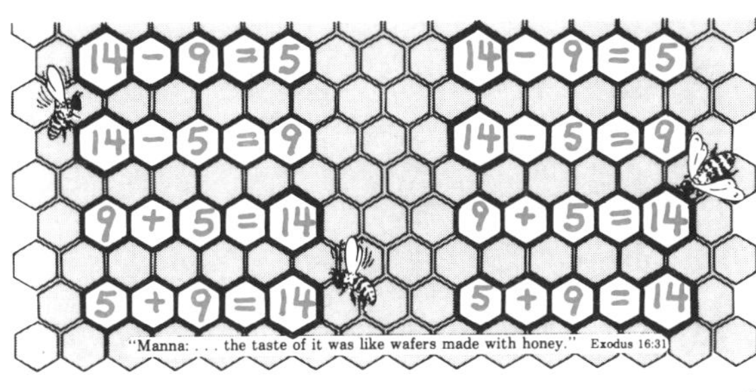
"Manna: . . . the taste of it was like wafers made with honey." Exodus 16:31

35

Before Class

Chalkboard

73	47	25	36	23
56	92	54	32	64
+ 5	+ 3	+44	+65	+56

4 nickels + 3 pennies = __
5 dimes + 2 nickels = __
2 quarters + 5 pennies = __
6 dimes + 1 nickel = __
3 quarters + 2 pennies = __
3 nickels + 3 pennies = __

Class Time

1. Stand near the clover patch.

   (13) 9 4

   The whole number is __.
   Its parts are __ and __.
   The triplet is (13) 9 4 . . .

2. (13) 8 5

   The whole number is __.
   Its parts are __ and __.
   The triplet is (13) 8 5 . . .

3. (13) 7 6

   The whole number is __.
   Its parts are __ and __.
   The triplet is (13) 7 6 . . .

4. (14) 9 5

   The whole number is __.
   Its parts are __ and __.
   The triplet is (14) 9 5 . . .

5. Begin at Blossom 11 Chart.
   Say each triplet 3 times.

110

Answer these facts.

14 -9 5	13 -7 6	12 -8 4	14 -5 9	7 +6 13	11 -7 4	12 -6 6	6 +5 11
4 +7 11	13 -8 5	9 +5 14	9 +4 13	14 -5 9	5 +9 14	11 -6 5	14 -9 5
12 -9 3	14 -9 5	5 +6 11	13 -5 8	8 +4 12	3 +8 11	14 -9 5	5 +7 12
4 +8 12	7 +5 12	13 -9 4	3 +9 12	12 -4 8	13 -9 4	6 +6 12	11 -8 3
13 -6 7	13 -8 5	12 -3 9	14 -5 9	11 -5 6	13 -4 9	12 -7 5	5 +8 13
		4 +9 13	13 -7 6	14 -5 9	12 -5 7	6 +7 13	11 -4 7

36

6. Do the Column Addition samples.
7. Review money.
   a. **We count pennies by __, nickels by __, dimes by __, and quarters by __.**
   b. Do the Money samples.
8. Do the Speed Drill in Lesson 110.
9. Assign Lesson 110.

110

Answer these problems.
Carry *over* in some problems.

89 + 55 = 144	96 − 73 = 23	47 + 96 = 143	53 + 76 = 129	96 − 54 = 42	99 − 38 = 61
53 + 79 = 132	89 − 21 = 68	69 + 65 = 134	80 − 10 = 70	62 + 74 = 136	98 − 26 = 72
46 + 97 = 143	88 − 64 = 24	94 + 55 = 149	35 + 88 = 123	78 − 37 = 41	87 − 25 = 62

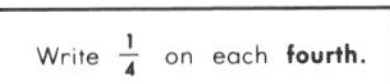

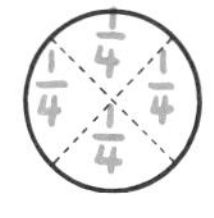

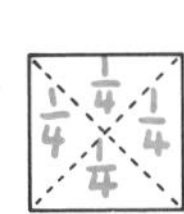

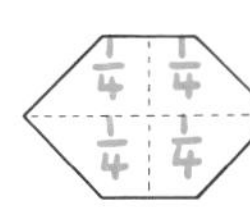

Blacklines

- Triplets With Facts #9
- Reading Problems #5
- 2-Place Computation (−) #7

After Class

1. Double Drill: **Whoever gives the correct answer first may go to the back of his line.**

8+5	**14−9**	**12−8**	**12−3**
5+9	**3+9**	**7+6**	**9+5**
13−6	**7+5**	**5+6**	**12−7**
11−5	**6+6**	**13−8**	**4+9**

2. Chalkboard Drill: **Write the three numbers I say.**

680 860 608
Circle the number with 8 tens.

574 745 457
Circle . . . 5 hundreds.

314 431 143
Circle . . . 1 one.

952 295 529
Circle . . . 2 tens.

1,670 1,607 1,760
Circle . . . 7 hundreds.

1,312 1,424 1,121
Circle . . . 3 hundreds.

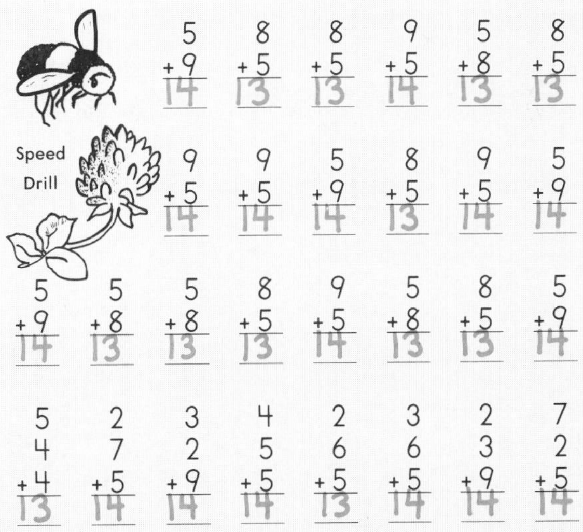

Speed Drill
5 + 9 = 14, 8 + 5 = 13, 8 + 5 = 13, 9 + 5 = 14, 5 + 8 = 13, 8 + 5 = 13
9 + 5 = 14, 9 + 5 = 14, 5 + 9 = 14, 8 + 5 = 13, 9 + 5 = 14, 5 + 9 = 14
5 + 9 = 14, 5 + 8 = 13, 5 + 8 = 13, 8 + 5 = 13, 9 + 5 = 14, 5 + 8 = 13, 8 + 5 = 13, 5 + 9 = 14
5 + 4 + 4 = 13, 2 + 7 + 5 = 14, 3 + 2 + 9 = 14, 4 + 5 + 5 = 14, 2 + 6 + 5 = 13, 3 + 6 + 5 = 14, 2 + 3 + 9 = 14, 7 + 2 + 5 = 14

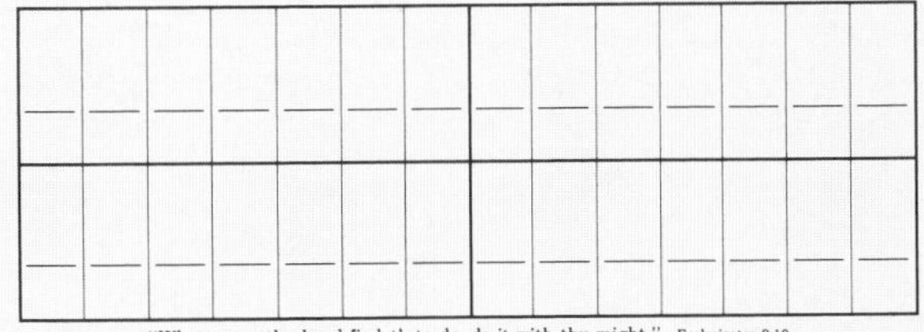

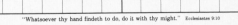

"Whatsoever thy hand findeth to do, do it with thy might." Ecclesiastes 9:10

111

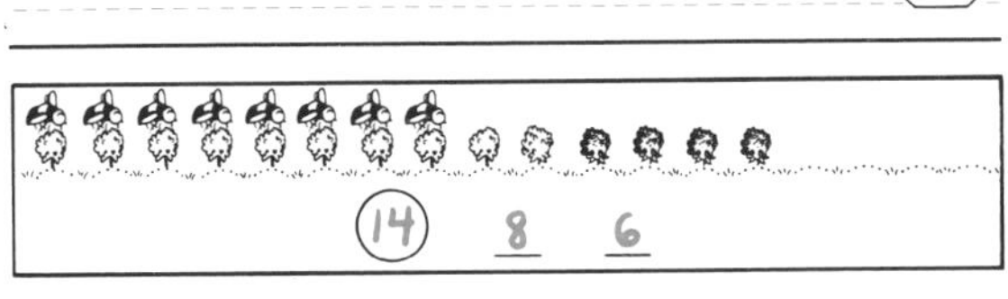

Trace and fill in the whole and parts.

Trace, answer, and write the facts.

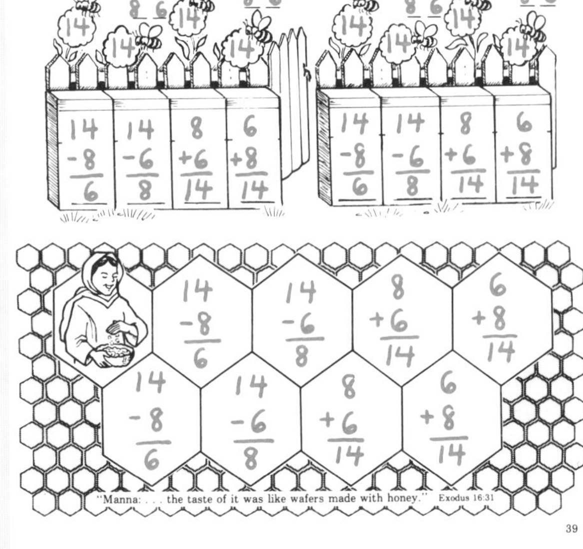

"Manna: . . . the taste of it was like wafers made with honey." Exodus 16:31
39

Before Class

Make (14) 8 6 flash cards for each child.

Tack (14) 8 6 flash cards above the clover patch in this order:

14	14	8	6
−8	−6	+6	+8
6	8	14	14

Materials

14's flash cards

Chalkboard

83	39	74	58	93	47	75	64
−65	+95	−25	+75	−57	+76	+59	−39

Class Time

1. Stand near the clover patch.

   (14) 8 6

   a. **How many pink clovers are in the patch?** 10
      We think—10 pink.
      4 more make __ altogether. 14
      We think—10 pink.
      2 less make __ clovers with bees. 8
   b. **14 clovers in the patch;**
      14 is the whole number.
      What part of the 14 has bees? 8
      What part of the 14 has no bees? 6
      14 is the whole number.
      Its parts are 8 and 6.
   c. **The triplet is (14) 8 6 . . .**
   d. **The facts are 14−8, 6; 14−6, 8; 8+6, 14; 6+8, 14 . . .**
2. **Say the triplet as I fill the clover and bees.**
3. Ask a child to write the 14's facts in the beehive as you say them together.

111

Extra Activity

Answer these facts.

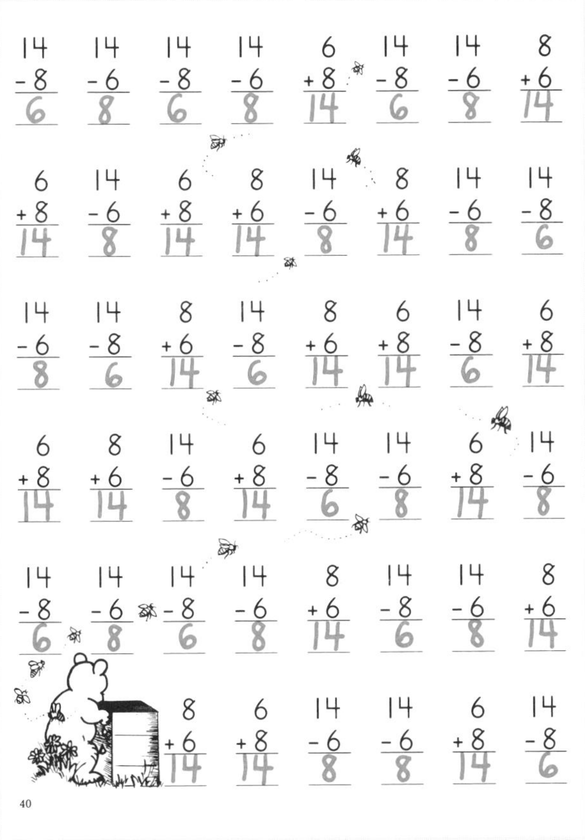

14 − 8 = 6	14 − 6 = 8	14 − 8 = 6	14 − 6 = 8	6 + 8 = 14	14 − 8 = 6	14 − 6 = 8	8 + 6 = 14
6 + 8 = 14	14 − 6 = 8	6 + 8 = 14	8 + 6 = 14	14 − 6 = 8	8 + 6 = 14	14 − 6 = 8	14 − 8 = 6
14 − 6 = 8	14 − 8 = 6	8 + 6 = 14	14 − 8 = 6	8 + 6 = 14	6 + 8 = 14	14 − 8 = 6	6 + 8 = 14
6 + 8 = 14	8 + 6 = 14	14 − 6 = 8	6 + 8 = 14	14 − 8 = 6	14 − 6 = 8	6 + 8 = 14	14 − 6 = 8
14 − 8 = 6	14 − 6 = 8	14 − 8 = 6	14 − 6 = 8	8 + 6 = 14	14 − 8 = 6	14 − 6 = 8	8 + 6 = 14
		8 + 6 = 14	6 + 8 = 14	14 − 6 = 8	14 − 6 = 8	6 + 8 = 14	14 − 8 = 6

40

4. Drill the triplets at the Blossom Charts.
5. Do the Computation samples.
6. **Answer together.**
   Half of 4 is __.
   Continue with half of 6, 14, 10, 8, 20, 12, 40.
7. Review one-fourth.
   One-fourth is a __. fraction
   1 whole cut __. into 4 parts
   4 fourths make __. 1 whole
8. Assign Lesson 111.

Answer these problems; carry *over* or borrow *back*.

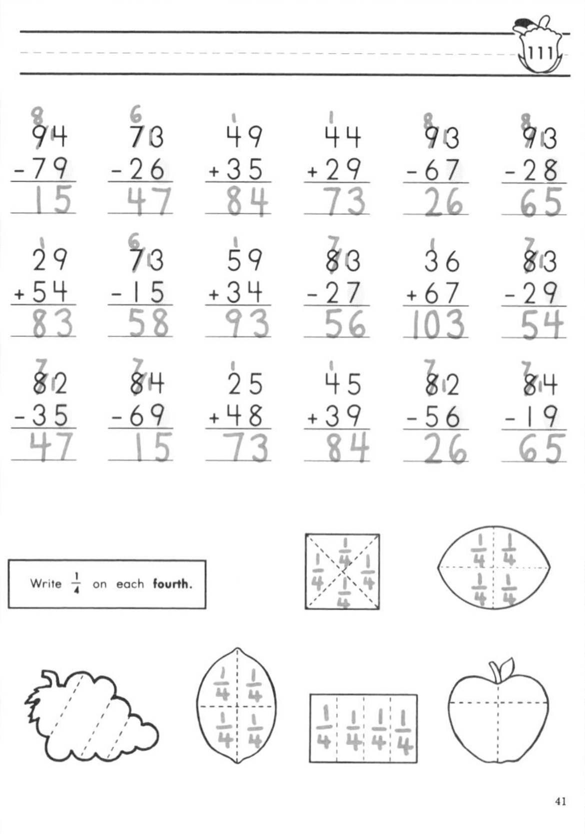

94 − 79 = 15	73 − 26 = 47	49 + 35 = 84	44 + 29 = 73	93 − 67 = 26	93 − 28 = 65
29 + 54 = 83	73 − 15 = 58	59 + 34 = 93	83 − 27 = 56	36 + 67 = 103	83 − 29 = 54
82 − 35 = 47	84 − 69 = 15	25 + 48 = 73	45 + 39 = 84	82 − 56 = 26	84 − 19 = 65

Blacklines

Fact Hives #20

Number Words #6

Fact Form III

Write $\frac{1}{4}$ on each **fourth.**

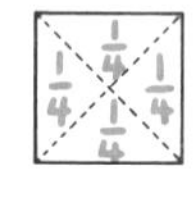

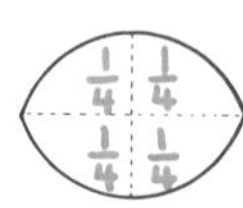

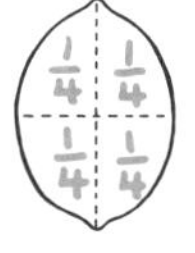

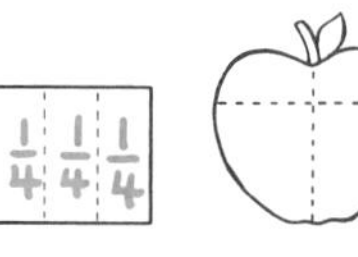

41

After Class

1. Give each child his (14) 8 6 flash cards.
2. Flash the 14's cards. **Say the triplet; then say the answer.**
3. **Count by 10's. Begin at**
   - •6 6, 16 . . .
   - •3 3, 13 . . .
   - •8 8, 18 . . .
   - •1 1, 11 . . .

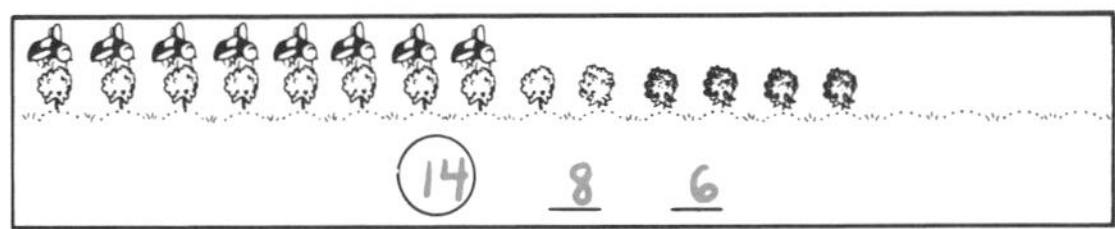

Fill in the whole and parts.

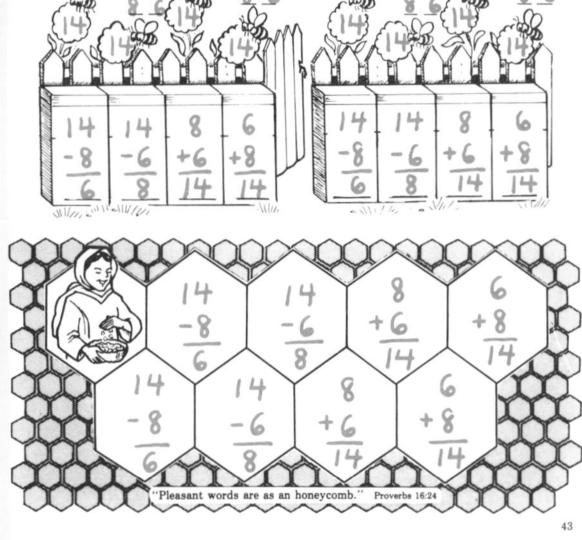

"Pleasant words are as an honeycomb." Proverbs 16:24
43

Trace, answer, and write the facts.

Before Class

Add bee (14) 8 6 to Blossom 14 Chart.

Materials

11's–14's flash cards

Large clock

14's flash cards

Chalkboard

64	94	73	83	94	62	83
– 5	– 9	– 6	– 8	–58	–36	–57

Class Time

1. Call the children to the clover patch.
   Please, thank you, and I forgive you are pleasant, heartwarming words. They are like __ to the heart. honey

2. (14) 8 6
   14 clovers in the patch;
   14 is the whole number.
   What part of the 14 has bees? 8
   What part of the 14 has no bees? 6
   14 is the whole number.
   Its parts are 8 and 6.
   a. **The triplet is (14) 8 6 . . .**
   b. Point to the first flash card.
      Close your eyes and say it 3 times. Drill each fact.

3. Point to the Blossom Charts.
   Say each triplet 3 times.

4. Flash the 11's–14's cards.
   Boys, answer the addition facts.
   Girls, answer the subtraction facts.

112

Answer these facts.

14 - 6 8	14 - 8 6	14 - 6 8	14 - 6 8	6 + 8 14	14 - 6 8	14 - 8 6	6 + 8 14
8 + 6 14	14 - 8 6	6 + 8 14	8 + 6 14	14 - 6 8	8 + 6 14	14 - 8 6	14 - 6 8
14 - 6 8	14 - 8 6	8 + 6 14	14 - 8 6	8 + 6 14	6 + 8 14	14 - 8 6	6 + 8 14
6 + 8 14	8 + 6 14	14 - 6 8	6 + 8 14	14 - 8 6	14 - 6 8	6 + 8 14	14 - 6 8
14 - 8 6	14 - 6 8	14 - 8 6	14 - 6 8	8 + 6 14	14 - 8 6	14 - 6 8	8 + 6 14
		8 + 6 14	6 + 8 14	14 - 6 8	14 - 6 8	6 + 8 14	14 - 8 6

44

5. Chalkboard Drill: **Write the problem you hear.**
   a. **Father bought 85 chicks. 43 chicks were in one box. How many chicks were in the other box?**

      85 chicks − 43 chicks = 42 chicks.
   b. **Mother made 56 sweet buns and 48 dinner buns. How many is that altogether?**

      56 buns + 48 buns = 104 buns.
6. Do the Subtraction samples.
7. Do the Speed Drill in Lesson 112.
8. Assign Lesson 112.

112

Answer these problems.

Read the story.
Write the numbers in the beehive.
Write the label words on the lines.
Answer the problem.

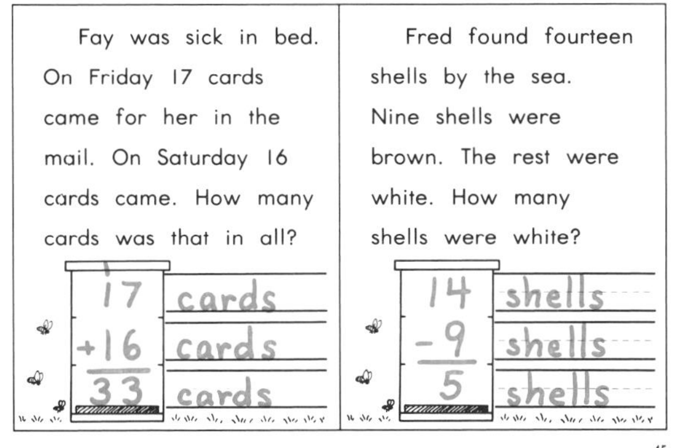

112
74 15 +42 131
52 37 +42 131
56 12 +61 129
24 14 +95 133
43 34 +62 139
55 32 +25 112
35 43 +4 82
44 23 +2 69
61 25 +7 93
35 43 +1 79
14 23 +4 41
34 42 +5 81
Fay was sick in bed. On Friday 17 cards came for her in the mail. On Saturday 16 cards came. How many cards was that in all?
17 cards
+16 cards
33 cards
Fred found fourteen shells by the sea. Nine shells were brown. The rest were white. How many shells were white?
14 shells
-9 shells
5 shells
45

Blacklines

Fact Hives #20

Number Facts #13

Fact Form IV

After Class

1. Ask individuals to say the triplets by memory.
2. Drill individuals with the 14's flash cards.
3. Hold the large clock. **Read the time together. 8:00, 10:15, 12:30, 2:45, 4:00, 6:15 . . .**

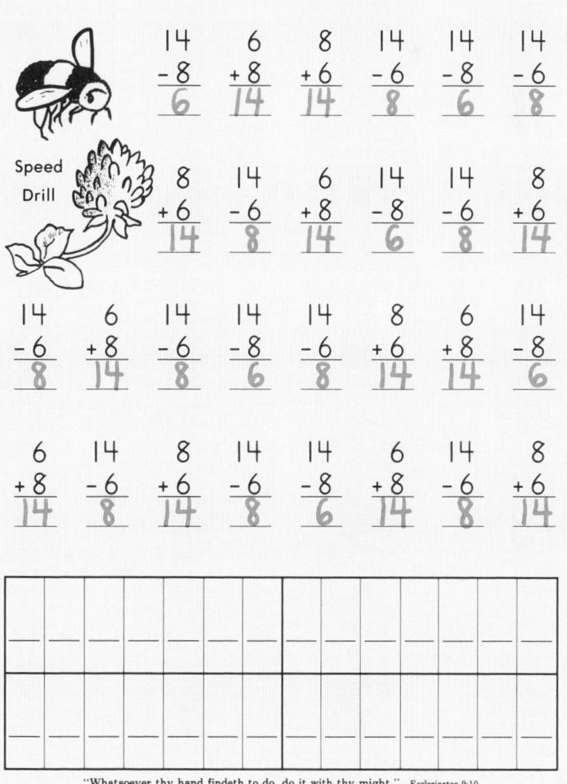

113

113

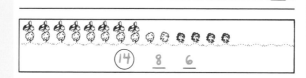

Fill in the whole and parts.

(14) 8 6

Trace, answer, and write the facts.

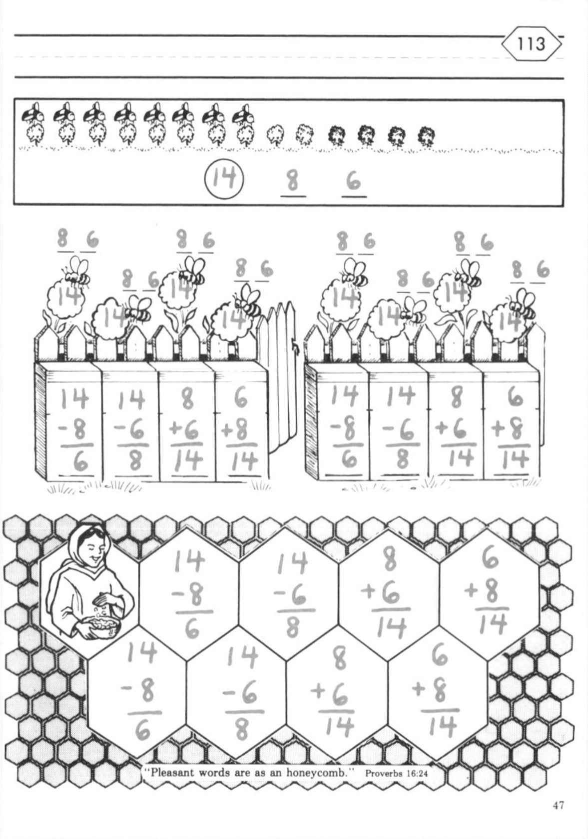

14	14	8	6
-8	-6	+6	+8
6	8	14	14

14	14	8	6
-8	-6	+6	+8
6	8	14	14

"Pleasant words are as an honeycomb." Proverbs 16:24

47

Before Class

Materials

Large coins
9's–14's flash cards

Chalkboard

9	13	14	8	14	5	4	12	13
5	7	8	5	9	7	9	6	5
14	6	6	13	5	12	13	6	8

100¢ =	157¢ =
265¢ =	180¢ =
133¢ =	342¢ =

Class Time

1. Have each child bring *My 1,000 Book* to the teaching corner.
   a. **Count by 10's to 500.**
   b. **Count on to 600 by 2's. I'll say the first number; you say the next number.**
2. **Raise your hand to answer.**

60+10	**34+10**	**67+10**
50−10	**74−10**	**57−10**
30+10	**84+10**	**27+10**
90−10	**44−10**	**97−10**

3. Stand near the clover patch.

   (14) 8 6

   14 clovers in the patch;
   14 is the whole number.
   What part of the 14 has bees? 8
   What part of the 14 has no bees? 6
   14 is the whole number.
   Its parts are 8 and 6.
   a. **The triplet is (14) 8 6 . . .**
   b. **The facts are 14−8, 6 . . .**

113

Extra Activity

Answer these problems.
Carry *over* in some problems.

148 -84 64	58 +26 84	147 -64 83	146 -84 62	66 +82 148	148 -66 82
76 +18 94	149 -86 63	75 +65 140	149 -64 85	28 +76 104	147 -84 63
36 +48 84	146 -82 64	144 -82 62	148 -65 83	149 -67 82	83 +65 148
148 -85 63	58 +36 94	147 -62 85	60 +80 140	146 -83 63	56 +48 104
149 -82 67	83 +66 149	148 -64 84	78 +26 104	74 +66 140	148 -65 83
		46 +58 104	147 -63 84	64 +85 149	148 -81 67

48

4. Drill all the triplets.
   Jump from chart to chart.
   (11) 9 2
   (12) 9 3
   (13) 9 4 . . .
5. Fill in the missing sign at the Computation samples.
6. Review money.
   a. Flash the large coins. **Quarter, 25¢; nickel, 5¢ . . .**
   b. Do the Money samples.
   100¢=__. You write each answer as the children respond.
   c. **How many dimes are in $1.00?**
   Continue with quarters, nickels, and pennies.
7. **The number places are ones, tens, hundreds, (comma), thousands.**
8. Assign Lesson 113.

Write the numbers in the correct places.
Add a comma where needed.

	thousands	hundreds	tens	ones
1984	1,	9	8	4
815		8	1	5
1945	1,	9	4	5
16			1	6
1625	1,	6	2	5
1784	1,	7	8	4
1315	1,	3	1	5

	thousands	hundreds	tens	ones
584		5	8	4
1623	1,	6	2	3
80			8	0
1415	1,	4	1	5
293		2	9	3
1324	1,	3	2	4
1583	1,	5	8	3

Blacklines

Fact Hives #21

Missing Whole or Parts #13

Number Facts #13

Write the time.

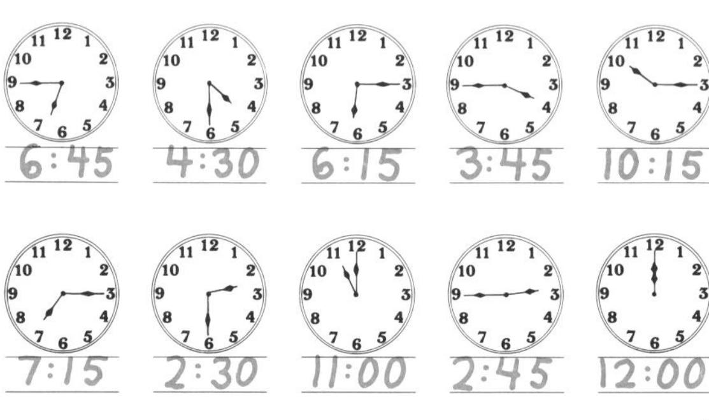

49

After Class

8 is how much less than 12? 6 is how much less than 13? 9 is how much less than 14? 7 is how much less than 11? 8 is how much less than 14?

1. Flash the 9's–14's cards. **How many can we answer in a minute?**
2. Stand near the questions on the board.
   a. **8 is how much less than 12? 8 *is* less, but how much less? Shall we add or subtract?**
   b. Write 12−8=4. **8 is 4 less than 12.**
   c. Have the children read the questions and write the problems.

Extra Activity
Job 28:10
If it's 1 child on a swing
Or 14 bees on wing,
"his eye seeth every precious thing."
If it's 100 cubs born new
Or 200 drops of dew,
"his eye seeth every precious thing."
14 − 8 = 6
14 − 6 = 8
8 + 6 = 14
6 + 8 = 14
14 − 9 = 5
14 − 5 = 9
9 + 5 = 14
5 + 9 = 14
14

50

114

Fill in the whole and parts.

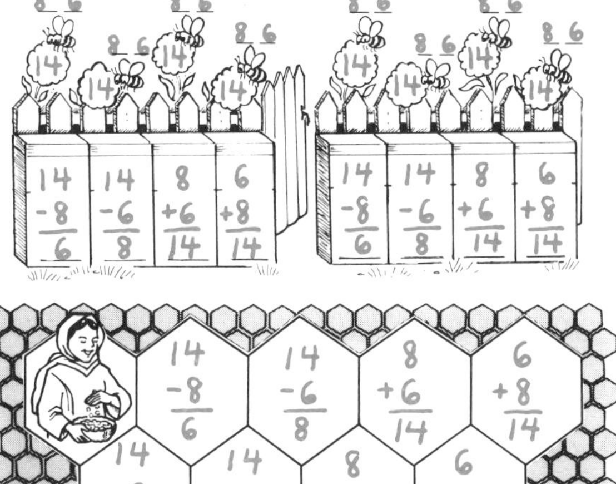

Write the facts.

14 − 8 = 6   14 − 6 = 8   8 + 6 = 14   6 + 8 = 14

"Pleasant words are as an honeycomb." Proverbs 16:24

51

Before Class

Materials

9's–14's flash cards

Chalkboard

83	88	79	84	63	75	94
−38	+46	+65	−56	−27	+57	−68

1 quarter + 6 pennies =
5 dimes + 3 nickels =
7 nickels + 4 pennies =
3 quarters + 2 pennies =
8 dimes + 5 pennies =

Class Time

1. Stand near the clover patch.

   (12) 8 4

   The whole number is __.
   Its parts are __ and __.
   The facts are 12−8, 4; 12−4, 8 . . .

2. (13) 8 5

   The whole number is __.
   Its parts are __ and __.
   The facts are 13−8, 5; 13−5, 8 . . .

3. (14) 8 6

   The whole number is __.
   Its parts are __ and __.
   The facts are 14−8, 6; 14−6, 8 . . .

4. Double Drill: 9's–14's flash cards.
   Whoever gives the correct answer first may have the card.

5. Do the Computation samples.

Count the first row.
Write the amount.
Count the second row.
Write the amount.
Add.
Then copy the answer into the dollar box.

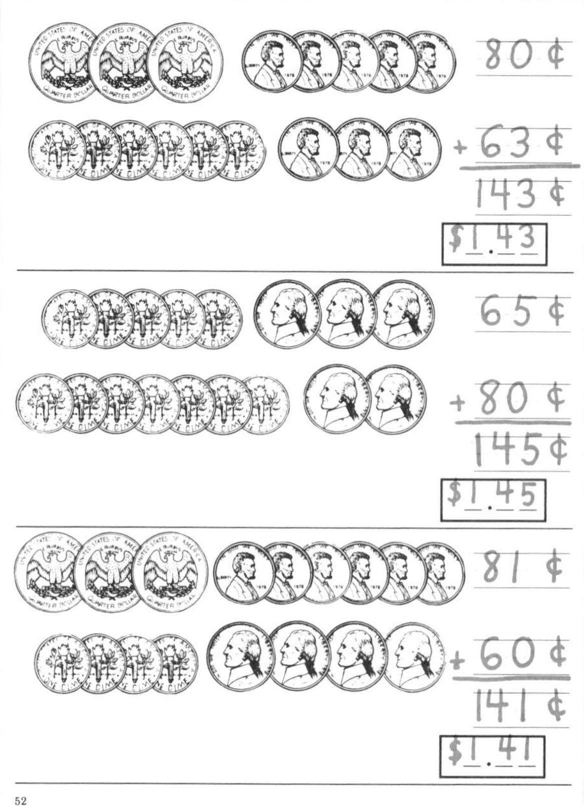

6. a. **We count pennies by __, nickels by __, dimes by __, and quarters by __.**
   b. Do the Money samples.
7. **Name two fractions.** ½ and ¼
   Which is larger, ½ of a pie or ¼ of a pie? ½ of a pie
   2 halves make __. 1 whole
   4 fourths make __. 1 whole
8. Do the Speed Drill in Lesson 114.
9. Assign Lesson 114.

114

Answer these problems; carry *over* or borrow *back*.

89 +55 = 144	94 −78 = 16	47 +96 = 143	56 +78 = 134	94 −56 = 38	84 −26 = 58
53 +79 = 132	35 +88 = 123	69 +55 = 124	93 +36 = 129	84 −16 = 68	94 −29 = 65
46 +97 = 143	84 −65 = 19	46 +87 = 133	68 +66 = 134	74 −36 = 38	82 −24 = 58

Read the story.
Write the numbers in the beehive.
Write the label words on the lines.
Answer the problem.

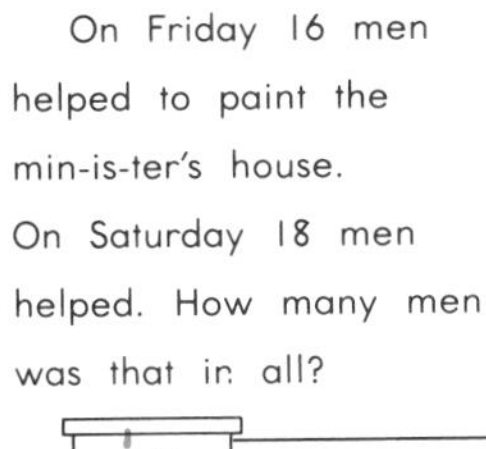

On Friday 16 men helped to paint the min-is-ter's house. On Saturday 18 men helped. How many men was that in all?

16 men
+18 men
34 men

Father has 89 nails in a bag. He hammers 57 of the nails into a roof he is mending. How many nails are left in his bag?

89 nails
−57 nails
32 nails

53

Blacklines

Fact Hives #21

Triplets With Facts #10

Fact Form V

After Class

144 +257	368 +234	189 +152	276 +268	167 +263

1. Call the children to the Carry *over* samples.
   a. **4+7=__. Carry *over* 1.**
      1+4=__+5=__. Carry *over* 1 . . .
   b. Have the children add aloud as they work the problems.
2. **Who can give the whole problem?**
   6 is how much less than 14? 14−6=8
   6 . . . than 12? 12−6=6
   4 . . . than 13? 13−4=9
   9 . . . than 14? 14−9=5
   8 . . . than 11? 11−8=3
   7 . . . than 13? 13−7=6

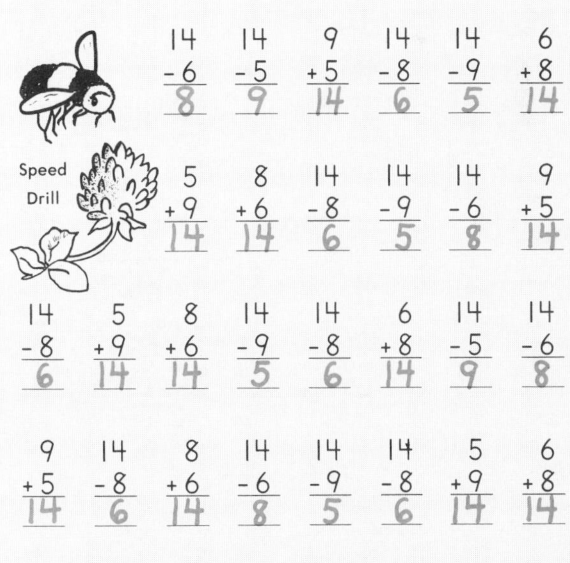

		14 −6 = 8	14 −5 = 9	9 +5 = 14	14 −8 = 6	14 −9 = 5	6 +8 = 14
		5 +9 = 14	8 +6 = 14	14 −8 = 6	14 −9 = 5	14 −6 = 8	9 +5 = 14
14 −8 = 6	5 +9 = 14	8 +6 = 14	14 −9 = 5	14 −8 = 6	6 +8 = 14	14 −5 = 9	14 −6 = 8
9 +5 = 14	14 −8 = 6	8 +6 = 14	14 −6 = 8	14 −9 = 5	14 −8 = 6	5 +9 = 14	6 +8 = 14

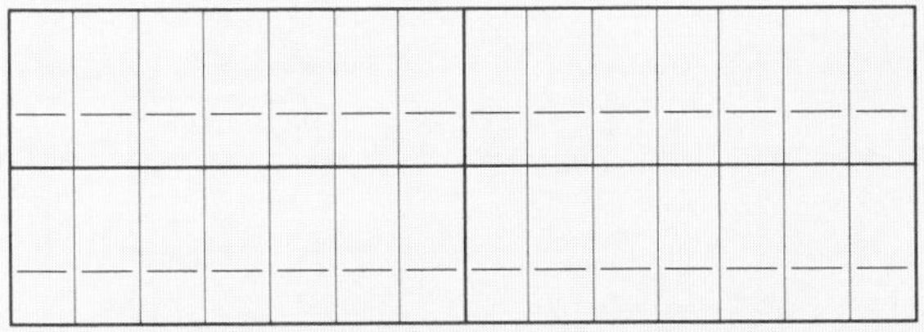

"Whatsoever thy hand findeth to do, do it with thy might." Ecclesiastes 9:10

54

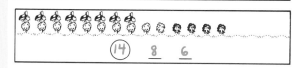

115

115

Fill in the whole and parts.

14 8 6

Write the facts.

14	14	8	6
-8	-6	+6	+8
6	8	14	14

14	14	8	6
-8	-6	+6	+8
6	8	14	14

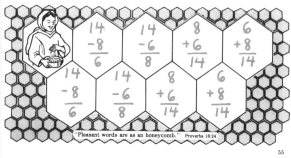

"Pleasant words are as an honeycomb." Proverbs 16:24

55

Before Class

Materials

11's–14's flash cards

Form C

Chalkboard

453	678	565	355	484	585
+268	+246	+268	+279	+439	+357

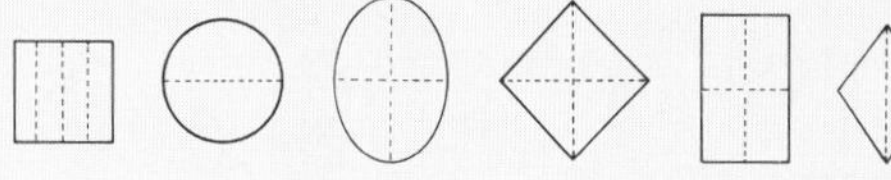

Class Time

1. Call the children to the Blossom Charts.
   a. **Girls, say each triplet once.**
   b. **Boys, say each triplet once.**
   c. **Say the 13 and 14 triplets together.**
2. **What belongs on the blank?**
   (Say *blank* each time.)

14, 9 __	**13 __ 6**	**__ 9, 5**
13, 8 __	**13 __ 4**	**__ 9, 3**
14, 8 __	**14 __ 6**	**__ 8, 6**
12, 7 __	**12 __ 4**	**__ 7, 6**

3. **Say the 14's facts as I fill the beehive.**
4. Flash the 11's–14's cards.
   Answer together.
5. Flash Card Drill: 11's–14's flash cards. Use Form C. **Flower Row: Box 1 . . .**
6. Do the Carry *over* samples. Have each child add aloud as he works.
7. Do the Fraction samples.

115

Extra Activity

Fill in the missing whole or parts.

14 - 8 = 6	14 - 6 = 8	8 + 6 = 14
14 - 6 = 8	8 + 6 = 14	6 + 8 = 14
6 + 8 = 14	6 + 8 = 14	14 - 8 = 6
14 - 8 = 6	14 - 6 = 8	14 - 6 = 8
8 + 6 = 14	8 + 6 = 14	6 + 8 = 14
14 - 8 = 6	6 + 8 = 14	14 - 8 = 6

Answer these problems.

6	3	3	4	6	2	1	4
2	5	2	2	3	7	6	4
+6	+6	+8	+8	+4	+3	+3	+6
14	14	13	14	13	12	10	14

6	2	5	6	4	7	3	5
2	4	3	3	5	1	3	3
+5	+8	+6	+3	+4	+6	+8	+2
13	14	14	12	13	14	14	10

56

8. **Who can give us the whole problem?**
   5 is how much less than 14? 14−5=9
   9 is how much less than 13? 13−9=4
   3 . . . than 12? 12−3=9
   7 . . . than 13? 13−7=6
   8 . . . than 14? 14−8=6
9. Assign Lesson 115.

Answer these problems.
Carry *over* in two places.

583 + 257 = 840	328 + 596 = 924	256 + 178 = 434	489 + 354 = 843	168 + 653 = 821	458 + 184 = 642
433 + 268 = 701	476 + 164 = 640	286 + 248 = 534	307 + 394 = 701	154 + 486 = 640	158 + 376 = 534
259 + 383 = 642	223 + 598 = 821	578 + 265 = 843	145 + 289 = 434	266 + 658 = 924	456 + 384 = 840

Write $\frac{1}{2}$ on each **half.**

Write $\frac{1}{4}$ on each **fourth.**

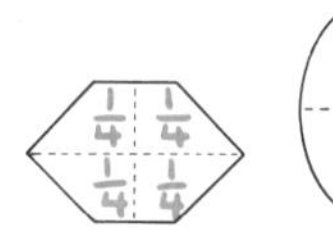

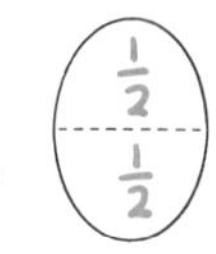

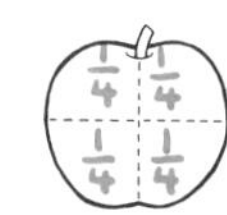

57

Blacklines

Fact Hives #21

Missing Whole or Parts #13

Form C (Class Time)

2-Place Computation (+) #8

After Class

1. Ask individuals to say the triplets by memory.
2. Introduce dozen and one-half dozen.
   a. **Count the first row of eggs.**
   1, 2 . . . Write
   (1)(2)(e)(g)(g)(s) = (1)(d)(o)(z)(e)(n)
   b. **What is half of 12?** Write
   6 e g g s = (½)(d)(o)(z)(e)(n)
   c. **Read each equation 3 times.**

Extra Activity
Job 28:10
If it's 1 child on a swing
Or 14 bees on wing,
"his eye seeth every precious thing."
If it's 100 cubs born new
Or 200 drops of dew,
"his eye seeth every precious thing."
14 − 8 = 6
14 − 6 = 8
8 + 6 = 14
6 + 8 = 14
14 − 9 = 5
14 − 5 = 9
9 + 5 = 14
5 + 9 = 14
14
58

116

Fill in the whole and parts.

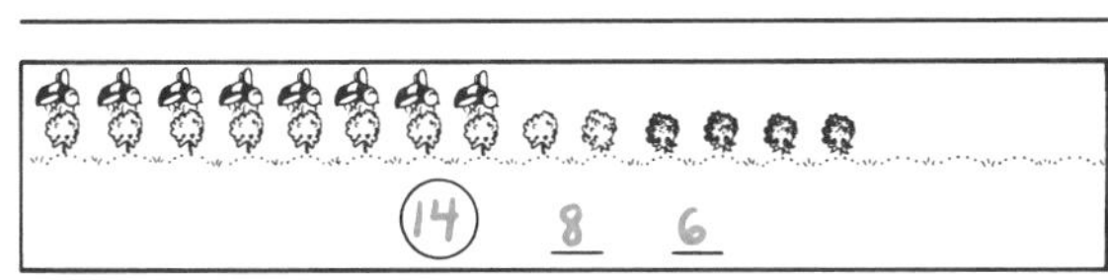

Write the facts.

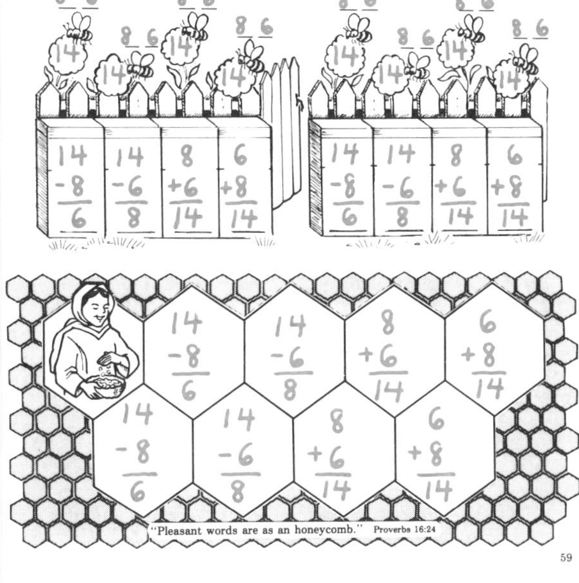

"Pleasant words are as an honeycomb." Proverbs 16:24
59

Before Class

Materials

13's and 14's flash cards

10's–14's flash cards

Chalkboard

535	627	359	338	788	174
+396	+276	+275	+376	+135	+569

12 things =

6 things =

Class Time

1. Call the children to the Number Line.
   a. **Count by 10's. Begin at**
      - **1** **1, 11 . . .**
      - **9** **9, 19 . . .**
      - **2** **2, 12 . . .**
      - **8** **8, 18 . . .**

   b. **Raise your hand to give the answer.**

59+10	**68−10**	**29+10**	**82+10**
32+10	**71−10**	**62+10**	**29−10**
88+10	**99−10**	**38+10**	**41−10**
41+10	**52−10**	**71+10**	**58+10**

2. Stand near the Blossom Charts.
   Jump from chart to chart.
   (11) 9 2; (12) 9 3 . . .
3. Flash 13's and 14's cards.
   Say the triplet; then say the answer.
4. Do the Carry *over* samples.

Read the story.
Write the numbers
in the beehive.
Write the label words
on the lines.
Answer the problem.

Father planted 14 trees. Six trees were pine. The rest were oak. How many trees were oak?

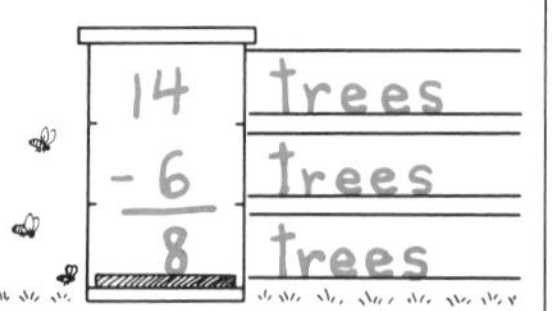

Fred gave 83¢ to the Lord's work. Lois gave 64¢. How many cents did both children give?

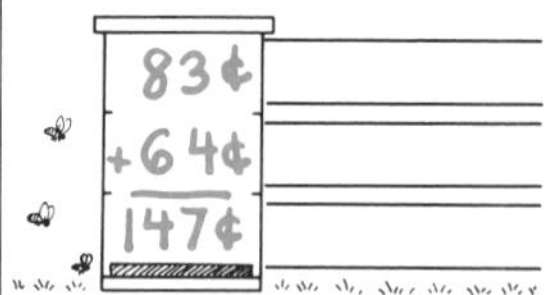

A flock of 89 geese swim on the lake. 57 geese fly up and away. How many geese are on the lake now?

Fourteen goats eat grass. Eight goats have bells around their necks. How many goats do not have bells?

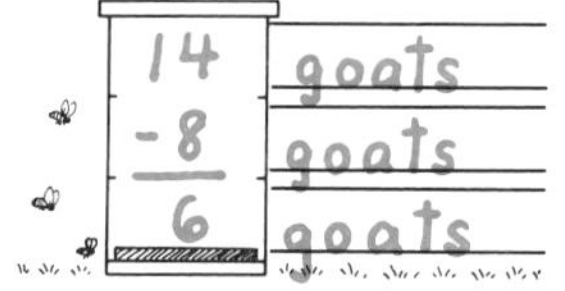

60

5. **Who can give the whole problem?**
   6 is how much less than 14? 14−6=8
   6 is how much less than 11? 11−6=5
   8 . . . than 12? 12−8=4
   7 . . . than 13? 13−7=6
6. Review dozen and one-half dozen.
   a. **12 eggs=__.** 1 dozen
      12 pencils=__. 1 dozen
      12 ears of corn=__. 1 dozen
      Complete **12 things=1 dozen.**
   b. **6 eggs=__.** ½ dozen
      6 cupcakes=__. ½ dozen
      6 crayons=__. ½ dozen
      Complete **6 things=½ dozen.**
7. Do the Speed Drill in Lesson 116.
8. Assign Lesson 116.

Answer these problems.
Carry *over* in two places.

287	528	256	489	168	658
+654	+296	+578	+354	+553	+284
941	824	834	843	721	942

483	376	286	357	354	158
+258	+564	+248	+384	+586	+376
741	940	534	741	940	534

456	523	558	345	366	755
+486	+198	+285	+489	+458	+186
942	721	843	834	824	941

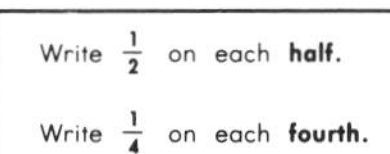

Write $\frac{1}{2}$ on each **half.**
Write $\frac{1}{4}$ on each **fourth.**

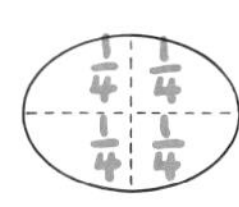

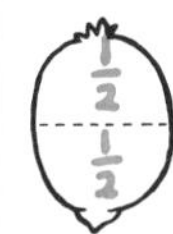

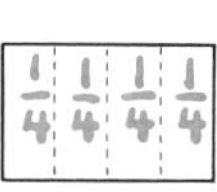

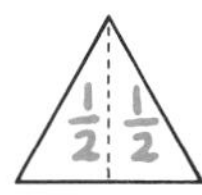

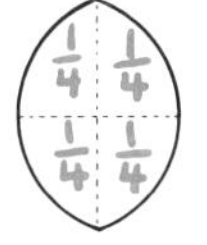

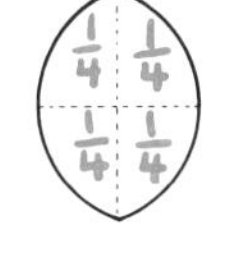

61

Blacklines

Reading Problems #6

Triplets With Facts #10

Fact Form VI

After Class

1. Double Drill: 10's–14's flash cards.
2. Chalkboard Drill: **Change what I say to cents.**

3 nickels (pause)	15¢
1 quarter	25¢
4 dimes	40¢
Add to find the total.	80¢
2 dimes	20¢
16 pennies	16¢
2 quarters	50¢
Add to find the total.	86¢
4 nickels	20¢
3 quarters	75¢
23 pennies	23¢
Add to find the total.	118¢

Speed Drill

8	8	14	13	6	13
+6	+5	-6	-5	+8	-8
14	13	8	8	14	5

13	14	8	13	8	14
-8	-6	+6	-5	+5	-8
5	8	14	8	13	6

14	8	13	6	14	13	8	8
-6	+5	-8	+8	-6	-5	+5	+6
8	13	5	14	8	8	13	14

8	13	14	5	13	8	14	13
+5	-5	-8	+8	-5	+6	-6	-8
13	8	6	13	8	14	8	5

"Whatsoever thy hand findeth to do, do it with thy might." Ecclesiastes 9:10

62

Fill in the whole and parts.

Write the facts.

Trace, answer, and write the facts.

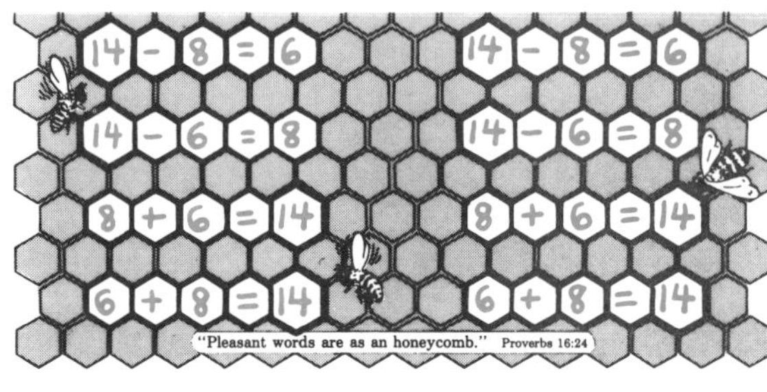

63

Before Class

Materials

10's–14's flash cards
Large classroom calendar
13's and 14's flash cards

Chalkboard

(ones)	156	1719	4	301	1802	1240
(tens)	1164	25	903	1358	6	1515
(hundreds)	998	1477	1686	1010	731	1094

Class Time

1. Call the children to the clover patch.

   One bee in the beehive is longer than all the other bees. This is the mother bee. She is the queen—a busy, busy queen.

   Worker bees feed her. They keep her clean. They protect her from enemies.

   What does the queen do? She lays eggs. During the summer she lays about 1,500 eggs every day!

2. | (14) 8 6 |
   |---|

   14 clovers in the patch;
   14 is the whole number.
   What part of the 14 has bees? 8
   What part of the 14 has no bees? 6
   14 is the whole number.
   Its parts are 8 and 6.

   a. **The triplet is (14) 8 6 . . .**
   b. **The facts are 14−8, 6 . . .**

117

Extra Activity

Answer these facts.

14 -8 6	14 -6 8	13 -5 8	13 -8 5	8 +6 14	13 -5 8	14 -6 8	8 +5 13
5 +8 13	14 -6 8	6 +8 14	8 +6 14	13 -8 5	8 +6 14	14 -6 8	14 -8 6
14 -8 6	13 -8 5	8 +5 13	14 -6 8	6 +8 14	8 +5 13	13 -8 5	5 +8 13
8 +5 13	6 +8 14	13 -5 8	8 +6 14	14 -6 8	13 -5 8	8 +6 14	14 -8 6
14 -8 6	13 -5 8	14 -8 6	14 -6 8	13 -8 5	14 -8 6	13 -5 8	8 +5 13
		5 +8 13	13 -8 5	14 -6 8	13 -5 8	8 +5 13	14 -8 6

64

3. Stand near the Blossom Charts.
   Say each triplet 3 times.
4. Flash the 10's–14's cards. **Can we answer these in one minute?**
5. Stand near the Place Value samples.
   a. Add the missing commas.
   b. Circle the correct number.
   c. **Read the numbers with me.**
6. **Name two fractions.** ½ and ¼
   2 halves make __. 1 whole
   4 fourths make __. 1 whole
7. **Answer together.**
   Half of 12 is __.
   Continue with half of 8, 6, 10, 20, 40.
8. Assign Lesson 117.

Answer these problems.
Carry *over* in two places.

573 + 267 = 840	328 + 596 = 924	356 + 378 = 734	488 + 356 = 844	165 + 658 = 823	458 + 184 = 642
433 + 268 = 701	276 + 564 = 840	286 + 248 = 534	307 + 394 = 701	354 + 486 = 840	158 + 376 = 534
259 + 383 = 642	228 + 595 = 823	576 + 268 = 844	445 + 289 = 734	266 + 658 = 924	486 + 354 = 840

Trace and copy.

12 things = 1 dozen

12 things = 1 dozen

6 things = ½ dozen

6 things = ½ dozen

65

Blacklines

Missing Whole or Parts #13

Mixed Computation #4

Number Facts #13

After Class

> Kenneth has 1 dozen ears of corn in his pail. He gives 9 of them to the pigs. How many ears are left?

1. Drill individuals with the 13's and 14's flash cards.
2. Story Problem: Ask a child to read the problem.
   a. **How shall I write the problem?** Change 1 dozen to 12.
      12 ears−9 ears=3 ears.
   b. **12 things=__.** 1 dozen
      6 things=__. ½ dozen
3. Stand near your classroom calendar.
   a. **Today is __.**
      Name the days of the week.
   b. **7 days make 1 week.**
      7 days=1 week.

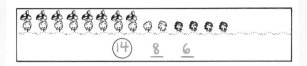

118

118

Fill in the whole and parts.

(14) 8 6

Write the facts.

Trace, answer, and write the facts.

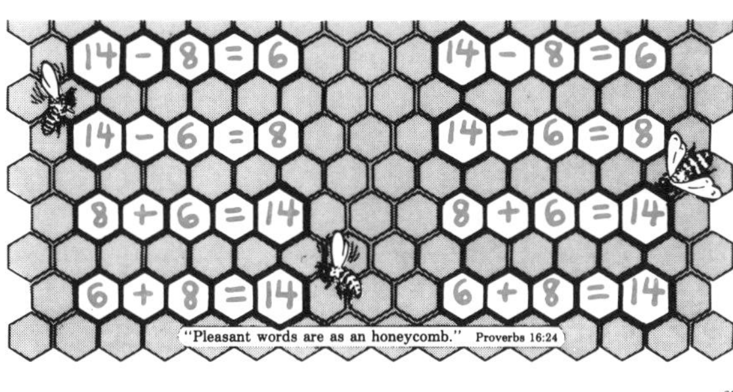

14 - 8 = 6
14 - 6 = 8
8 + 6 = 14
6 + 8 = 14
"Pleasant words are as an honeycomb." Proverbs 16:24

67

Before Class

Materials

11's–14's flash cards

Chalkboard

78	93	64	95	82	74	89
−42	−57	− 8	−73	−56	− 9	−76

Class Time

1. Stand near the clover patch.

   (14) 9 5

   The whole number is __.
   Its parts are __ and __.
   a. **The triplet is (14) 9 5 . . .**
   b. **The facts are 14−9, 5 . . .**

2. (14) 8 6

   The whole number is __.
   Its parts are __ and __.
   a. **The triplet is (14) 8 6 . . .**
   b. **The facts are 14−8, 6 . . .**

3. Drill the triplets.
   a. **Boys, say the 11 triplets.**
   Girls, say the 12 triplets.
   b. **Everyone say the 13 and 14 triplets.**

4. Do the Subtraction samples.

5. **12 things=__.** 1 dozen
   6 things=__. ½ dozen

118

Answer these facts.

14	14	13	12	8	14	13	9
-8	-5	-5	-8	+6	-6	-4	+3
6	9	8	4	14	8	9	12
8	14	6	9	11	7	13	13
+4	-9	+5	+5	-7	+4	-8	-7
12	5	11	14	4	11	5	6
12	12	9	12	6	6	11	4
-4	-3	+4	-5	+8	+7	-2	+9
8	9	13	7	14	13	9	13
8	7	11	5	13	12	6	11
+5	+5	-4	+9	-6	-5	+6	-3
13	12	7	14	7	7	12	8
12	11	12	13	9	11	12	8
-7	-8	-6	-9	+2	-5	-9	+6
5	3	6	4	11	6	3	14
		6	8	12	12	5	11
		+8	+3	-8	-9	+9	-6
		14	11	4	3	14	5

68

Speed Drill

6. Review the week.
   a. **7 days=__.** 1 week
   b. **What comes after Friday?**
      . . . Wednesday? . . . Sunday?
   c. **What comes before Tuesday?**
      . . . Saturday? . . . Thursday?
   d. **This month began on a __. It will end on a __.**
   e. Ask a child to begin at Thursday and name the days of the week.
7. Do the Speed Drill in Lesson 118.
8. Assign Lesson 118.

118

Answer these problems. Borrow *back* in some problems.

94 − 76 = 18	94 − 78 = 16	93 − 36 = 57	94 − 68 = 26	74 − 42 = 32	93 − 55 = 38
93 − 27 = 66	89 − 37 = 52	73 − 34 = 39	99 − 78 = 21	74 − 46 = 28	63 − 39 = 24
62 − 24 = 38	83 − 26 = 57	54 − 38 = 16	99 − 67 = 32	64 − 38 = 26	54 − 36 = 18

Trace and copy.

12 things = 1 dozen

12 things = 1 dozen

6 things = ½ dozen

6 things = ½ dozen

69

Blacklines

Triplets With Facts #10

2-Place Computation (+) #8

Form III

After Class

1. Circle Drill: 11's–14's flash cards.
2. Chalkboard Drill: **Write the number you hear.**
   - **200 soldiers helped to protect Paul at night.** (Acts 23:23)
   - **Noah lived 950 years.** (Genesis 9:29)
   - **The Book of Acts has 1,007 verses.**
   - **A servant brought David and his men 200 loaves of bread.** (2 Samuel 16:1)
   - **The Book of Exodus has 1,213 verses.**

Speed Drill

		4 + 9 = 13	6 + 8 = 14	4 + 9 = 13	8 + 5 = 13	8 + 6 = 14	6 + 6 = 12
		7 + 5 = 12	6 + 7 = 13	9 + 5 = 14	9 + 4 = 13	8 + 6 = 14	8 + 5 = 13
9 + 5 = 14	5 + 8 = 13	4 + 8 = 12	6 + 8 = 14	7 + 6 = 13	9 + 4 = 13	5 + 9 = 14	6 + 7 = 13
5 + 3 + 5 = 13	4 + 2 + 8 = 14	3 + 6 + 4 = 13	4 + 5 + 5 = 14	3 + 4 + 6 = 13	6 + 2 + 6 = 14	3 + 2 + 8 = 13	3 + 4 + 5 = 12

"Whatsoever thy hand findeth to do, do it with thy might." Ecclesiastes 9:10

70

119

119

Trace and write the whole and parts.

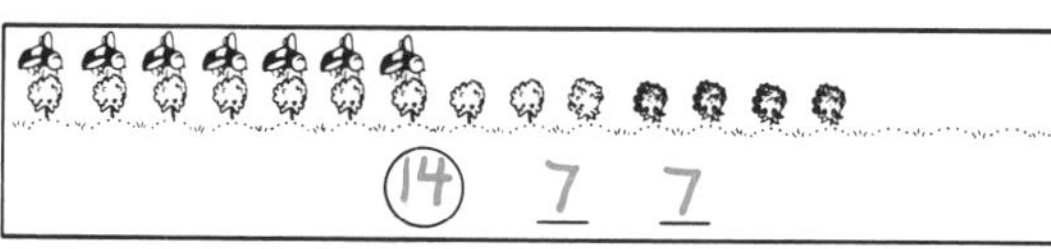

Trace, answer, and write the facts.

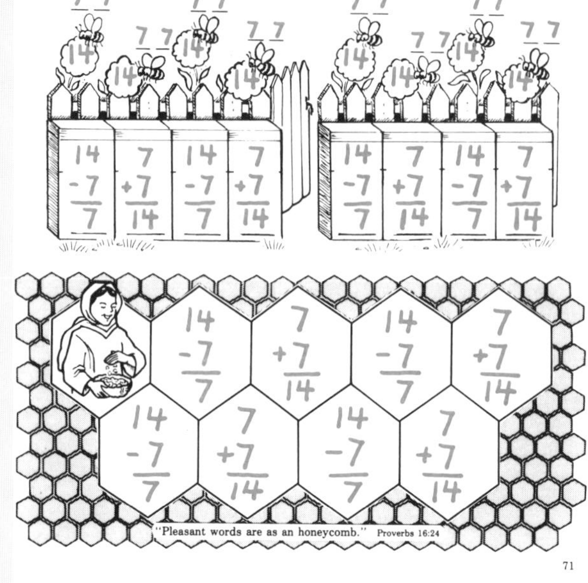

"Pleasant words are as an honeycomb." Proverbs 16:24

71

Before Class

Make (14) 7 7 flash cards for each child.

Tack (14) 7 7 flash cards above the clover patch in this order:

14	7
−7	+7
7	14

Materials

10's–14's flash cards

Chalkboard

75	94	76	84	93	86	74
+49	−68	+58	−59	−38	+57	−26

32	__	__	__	72	__	__
__	705	__	__	__	__	710
__	__	185	__	195	__	__
6	__	__	36	__	__	__

Class Time

1. a. **Count by 100's to 1,000.**
   b. **Count by 10's. Begin at**
      - •2 2, 12 . . .
      - •6 6, 16 . . .
2. Fill in the Missing Number samples.
3. Circle Drill: 10's–14's flash cards.
4. Stand near the clover patch.

   (14) 7 7

   a. **How many pink clovers are in the patch?** 10
      We think—10 pink.
      4 more makes __ altogether. 14
      We think—10 pink.
      3 less makes __ clovers with bees. 7

   b. **14 clovers in the patch;**
      14 is the whole number.
      What part of the 14 has bees? 7
      What part of the 14 has no bees? 7
      14 is the whole number.
      Its parts are 7 and 7.

119

Extra Activity

Answer these facts.

14 − 7 = 7	13 − 7 = 6	13 − 6 = 7	14 − 7 = 7	7 + 7 = 14	14 − 7 = 7	13 − 7 = 6	7 + 7 = 14
7 + 7 = 14	14 − 7 = 7	6 + 7 = 13	7 + 7 = 14	13 − 6 = 7	7 + 6 = 13	14 − 7 = 7	13 − 6 = 7
14 − 7 = 7	13 − 6 = 7	7 + 7 = 14	13 − 7 = 6	7 + 6 = 13	7 + 7 = 14	14 − 7 = 7	6 + 7 = 13
7 + 6 = 13	7 + 7 = 14	14 − 7 = 7	6 + 7 = 13	13 − 7 = 6	14 − 7 = 7	7 + 7 = 14	13 − 6 = 7
14 − 7 = 7	13 − 6 = 7	13 − 7 = 6	14 − 7 = 7	7 + 6 = 13	13 − 7 = 6	14 − 7 = 7	7 + 7 = 14
		7 + 7 = 14	6 + 7 = 13	13 − 6 = 7	14 − 7 = 7	7 + 7 = 14	14 − 7 = 7

72

c. **The triplet is (14) 7 7 . . .**
d. **The facts are 14−7, 7; 7+7, 14.**

5. **Say the triplet as I fill the clover and bees.**
6. **Say the 14's facts as I fill the beehive.**
7. Do the Computation samples.
8. Story Problem

   The white hen laid 1 dozen eggs in her nest. Last night an opossum ate 3 of them. How many eggs does she have now?

   12 eggs − 3 eggs = 9 eggs.
9. Assign Lesson 119.

Answer these problems; carry *over* or borrow *back*.

94 − 78 = 16	56 + 87 = 143	84 − 66 = 18	84 − 45 = 39	38 + 66 = 104	64 − 29 = 35
88 + 45 = 133	93 − 49 = 44	46 + 77 = 123	94 − 38 = 56	58 + 84 = 142	93 − 54 = 39
76 + 67 = 143	92 − 38 = 54	94 − 48 = 46	93 − 68 = 25	72 − 24 = 48	78 + 65 = 143

Trace and copy.

12 things = 1 dozen

12 things = 1 dozen

6 things = ½ dozen

6 things = ½ dozen

73

Blacklines

Fact Hives #22

Mixed Computation #4

Fact Form VII

After Class

1. Give each child his (14) 7 7 flash cards.
2. Review
   60 minutes=__. 1 hour
   30 minutes=__. ½ hour
   12 things=__. 1 dozen
   6 things=__. ½ dozen
   7 days=__. 1 week
3. Stand near the calendar.
   a. **This is the month of __.**
   Last month was __.
   Next month will be __.
   b. **Name the months of the year.**
   January . . . December.
   c. **12 months=1 year.**
   12 months . . .

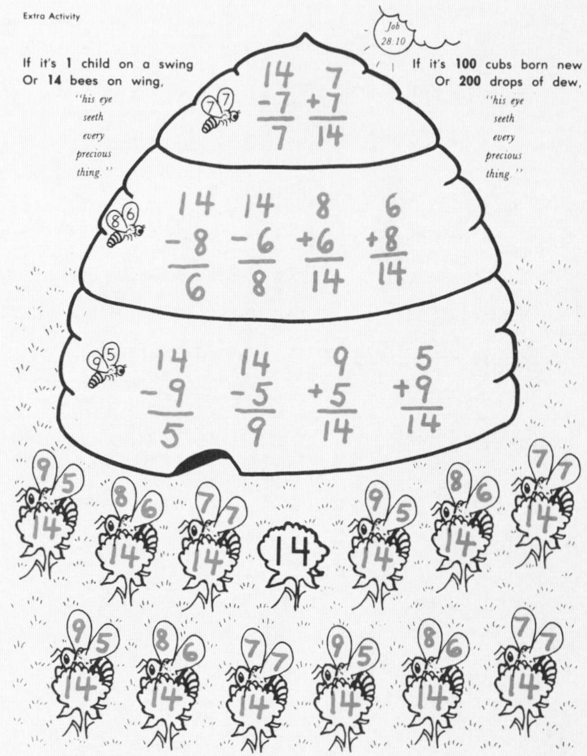

120

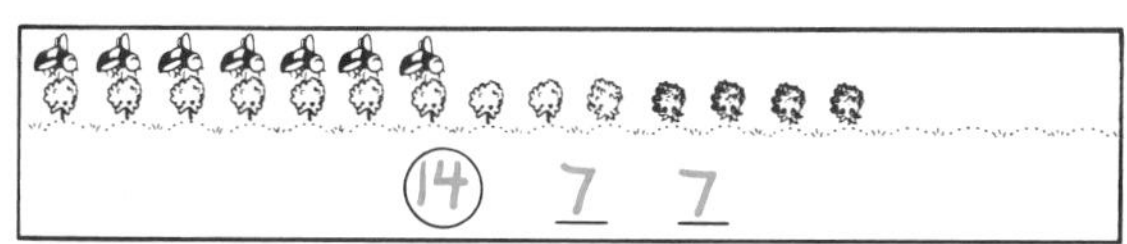

Fill in the whole and parts.

Trace, answer, and write the facts.

"Pleasant words are as an honeycomb." Proverbs 16:24

75

Before Class

Add bee (14) 7 7 to Blossom 14 Chart.

Materials

11's–14's flash cards

Large clock

14's flash cards

Chalkboard

115¢
173¢
248¢
364¢

Class Time

1. Have each child bring *My 1,000 Book* to your teaching corner. Begin at 5. **Count by 5's to 200.**
2. Stand near the clover patch.

   (14) 7 7

   14 clovers in the patch;
   14 is the whole number.
   What part of the 14 has bees? 7
   What part of the 14 has no bees? 7
   14 is the whole number.
   Its parts are 7 and 7.

   a. **The triplet is (14) 7 7 . . .**
   b. **The facts are 14−7, 7 . . .**
3. Drill each triplet on the Blossom Chart 3 times.
4. Ask a child to fill the beehive as you say the 14's facts together.
5. Flash the 11's–14's cards. **How many can we say in 1 minute?**

120

Answer these problems.
Carry *over* in some problems.

144 -73 = 71	37 +47 = 84	137 -77 = 60	148 -74 = 74	76 +63 = 139	148 -76 = 72
37 +67 = 104	139 -66 = 73	65 +75 = 140	149 -74 = 75	67 +37 = 104	137 -64 = 73
139 -79 = 60	149 -78 = 71	137 -62 = 75	149 -75 = 74	46 +57 = 103	74 +75 = 149
138 -65 = 73	57 +47 = 104	147 -72 = 75	70 +70 = 140	136 -63 = 73	77 +27 = 104
149 -77 = 72	63 +76 = 139	147 -73 = 74	135 -75 = 60	27 +57 = 84	149 -78 = 71
		148 -74 = 74	138 -63 = 75	148 -77 = 71	137 -77 = 60

76

6. **How many quarters are in $1.00?** Continue with dimes, nickels, and pennies.
7. Do the Money samples. Have the children change 115¢ to $1.15 and then read their answer.
8. Hold the large clock. **Read the time. 11:45, 1:30, 3:15, 5:45, 6:30, 7:15, 8:45 . . .**
9. Do the Speed Drill in Lesson 120.
10. Assign Lesson 120.

120

Count by 5's. Begin at 100.

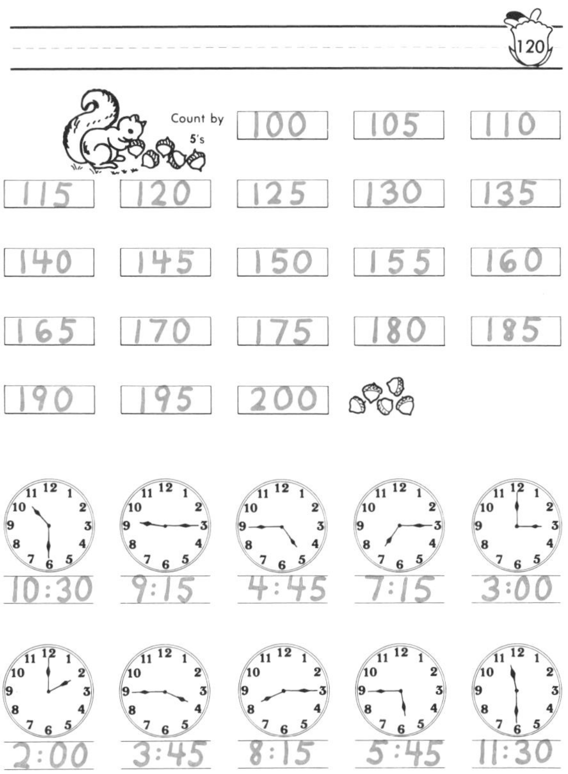

Count by 5's

100	105	110		
115	120	125	130	135
140	145	150	155	160
165	170	175	180	185
190	195	200		

Blacklines

Fact Hives #22

2-Place Computation (+) #8

Number Triplets #4

Write the time.

10:30 9:15 4:45 7:15 3:00

2:00 3:45 8:15 5:45 11:30

77

After Class

1. Drill individuals with the 14's flash cards.
2. Ask individuals to say the triplets by memory.
3. Fill in the shapes with *T, R, S,* or *C.*

14 − 7 = 7	14 − 6 = 8	6 + 8 = 14	14 − 9 = 5	5 + 9 = 14	14 − 7 = 7		
14 − 8 = 6	14 − 5 = 9	8 + 6 = 14	7 + 7 = 14	14 − 6 = 8	14 − 7 = 7		
6 + 8 = 14	14 − 9 = 5	14 − 7 = 7	8 + 6 = 14	14 − 9 = 5	6 + 8 = 14	14 − 6 = 8	14 − 7 = 7
14 − 9 = 5	7 + 7 = 14	14 − 7 = 7	14 − 6 = 8	9 + 5 = 14	7 + 7 = 14	14 − 5 = 9	14 − 8 = 6

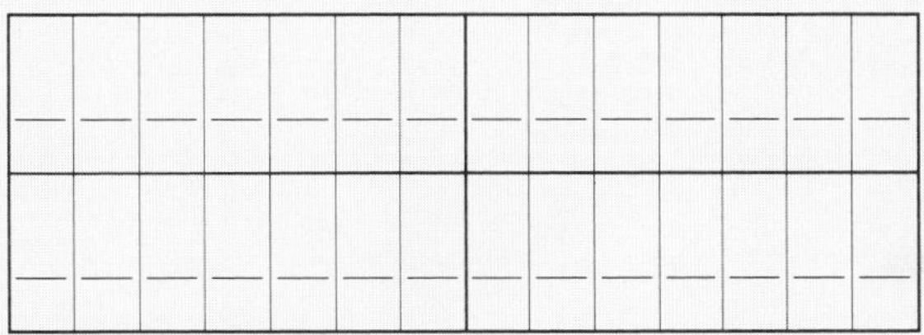

"Whatsoever thy hand findeth to do, do it with thy might." Ecclesiastes 9:10

78

121

Fill in the whole and parts.

Trace, answer, and write the facts.

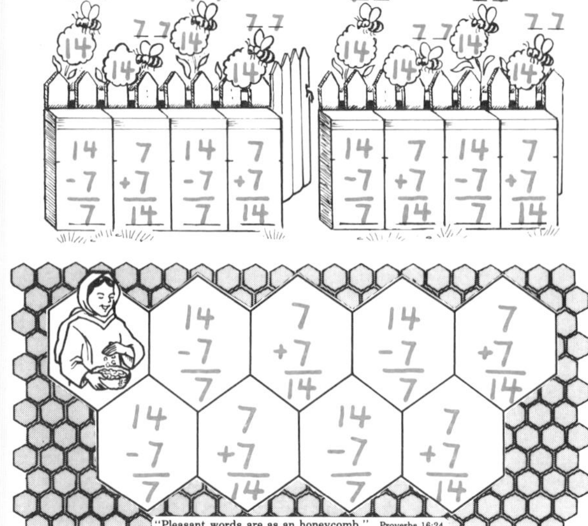
"Pleasant words are as an honeycomb." Proverbs 16:24

Before Class

Materials

10's–14's flash cards

Class Time

1. Stand near the clover patch.

(14) 9 5

   The whole number is __.
   Its parts are __ and __.
   a. **The triplet is (14) 9 5 . . .**
   b. **The facts are 14−9, 5 . . .**

2. | (14) 8 6 |
   |---|

   The whole number is __.
   Its parts are __ and __.
   a. **The triplet is (14) 8 6 . . .**
   b. **The facts are 14−8, 6 . . .**

3. | (14) 7 7 |
   |---|

   The whole number is __.
   Its parts are __ and __.
   a. **The triplet is (14) 7 7 . . .**
   b. **The facts are 14−7, 7 . . .**

Read the story.
Write the numbers in the beehive.
Write the label words on the lines.
Answer the problem.

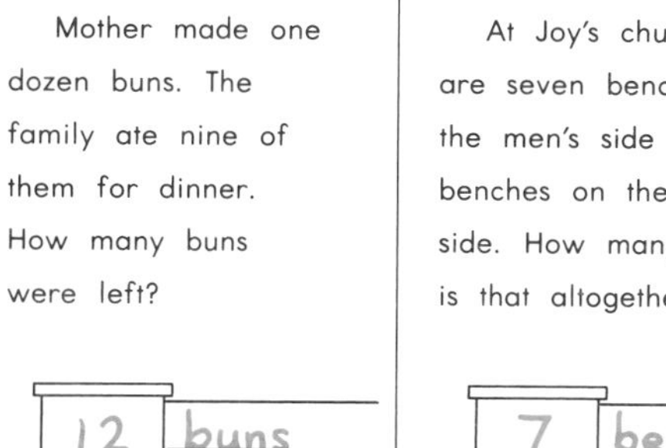

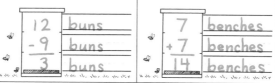

Mother made one dozen buns. The family ate nine of them for dinner. How many buns were left?	At Joy's church there are seven benches on the men's side and 7 benches on the women's side. How many benches is that altogether?
12 buns − 9 buns 3 buns	7 benches + 7 benches 14 benches

Answer these problems.

6	2	3	3	8	5	3	3
1	2	6	4	1	2	6	2
+7	+6	+4	+7	+5	+7	+4	+9
14	10	13	14	14	14	13	14

1	7	5	2	4	5	4	7
6	2	3	5	3	3	4	0
+7	+2	+4	+7	+7	+5	+5	+7
14	11	12	14	14	13	13	14

80

4. Point to the Blossom Charts.
   Jump from chart to chart.
   - **(11) 9 2**
   - **(12) 9 3**
   - **(13) 9 4**
   - **(14) 9 5 . . .**
5. **Who can give the whole problem?**
   a. **1 dozen cupcakes are on a plate. 8 of them are brown. The rest are white. How many are white?**
      12 cupcakes − 8 cupcakes = 4 cupcakes.
   b. **6 is how much less than 14?** 14−6=8
      9 . . . than 14? 14−9=5
      8 . . . than 13? 13−8=5
      5 . . . than 12? 12−5=7
      7 . . . than 13? 13−7=6
6. Review
   60 minutes=__. 1 hour
   30 minutes=__. ½ hour
   12 things=__. 1 dozen
   6 things=__. ½ dozen
   7 days=__. 1 week
   12 months=__. 1 year
7. Assign Lesson 121.

121

Answer these facts.

7 + 7 = 14	14 − 6 = 8	14 − 8 = 6	7 + 5 = 12	14 − 7 = 7	4 + 9 = 13	13 − 7 = 6	14 − 5 = 9
13 − 9 = 4	7 + 7 = 14	14 − 8 = 6	6 + 8 = 14	13 − 9 = 4	5 + 9 = 14	8 + 6 = 14	14 − 8 = 6
14 − 5 = 9	13 − 7 = 6	9 + 4 = 13	14 − 7 = 7	5 + 7 = 12	14 − 8 = 6	14 − 6 = 8	6 + 8 = 14

Count by 5's. Begin at 100.

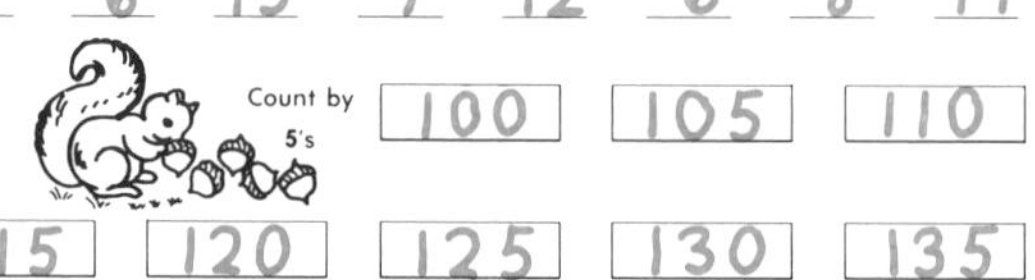

Count by 5's

		100	105	110
115	120	125	130	135
140	145	150	155	160
165	170	175	180	185
190	195	200		

81

Blacklines

Fact Hives #22

Reading Problems #7

Fact Form VII

After Class

1. Double Drill: 10's–14's flash cards. **Whoever says the correct answer first may have the card.**
2. Ask individuals to name the 12 months of the year.
3. **Answer together.**

10+7	**10+5**	**10+3**
10+4	**10+9**	**10+6**
10+1	**10+5**	**10+2**

Extra Activity

82

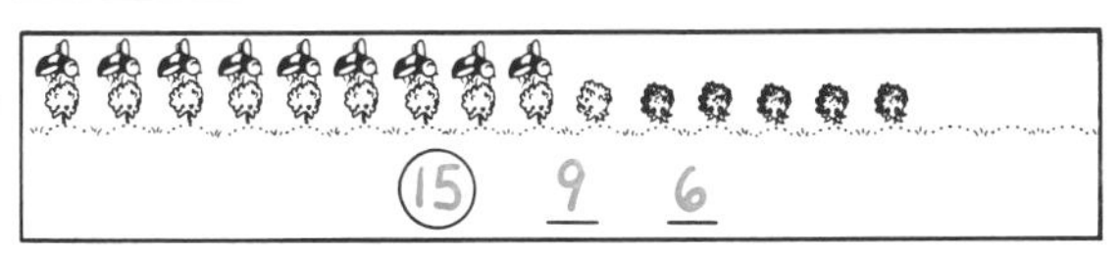

Trace and write the whole and parts.

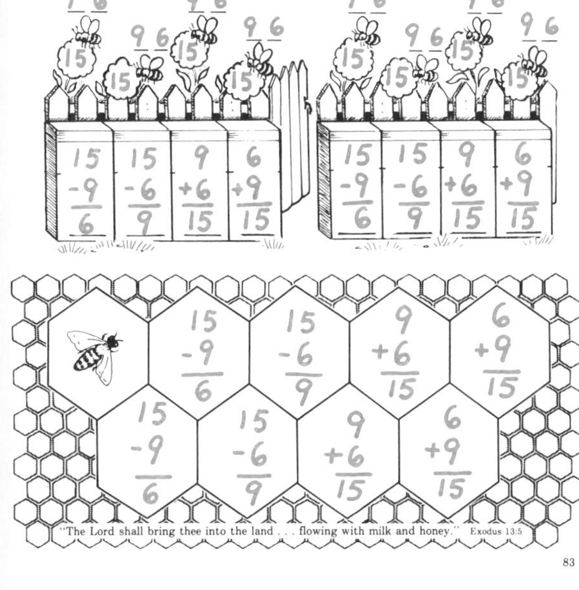

Trace, answer, and write the facts.

"The Lord shall bring thee into the land . . . flowing with milk and honey." Exodus 13:5

83

Before Class

Make (15) 9 6 flash cards for each child.

Tack (15) 9 6 flash cards above the clover patch in this order:

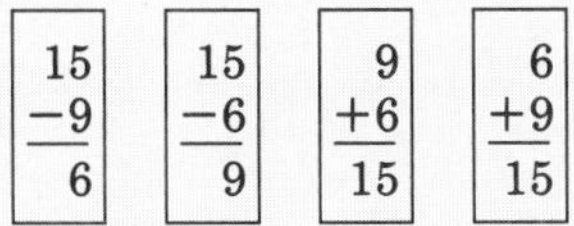

15	15	9	6
−9	−6	+6	+9
6	9	15	15

Materials

11's–14's flash cards

Chalkboard

269	327	365	158	537	476	458
+475	+566	+269	+485	+277	+514	+266

Class Time

1. Have each child bring *My 1,000 Book* to the teaching corner. **Begin at 5. Count by 5's to 300.**
2. Flash the 11's–14's cards.
3. Stand near the clover patch.

(15) 9 6

a. **How many pink clovers are in the patch?** 10
We think—10 pink.
5 more make __ altogether. 15
We think—10 pink.
1 less makes __ clovers with bees. 9

b. **15 clovers in the patch;**
15 is the whole number.
What part of the 15 has bees? 9
What part of the 15 has no bees? 6
15 is the whole number.
Its parts are 9 and 6.

Answer these facts.

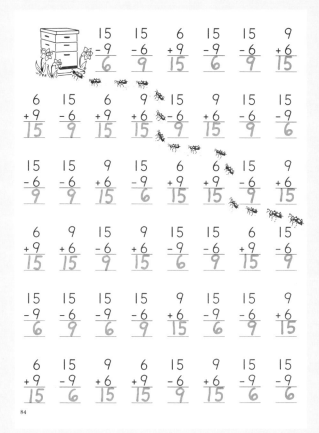

		15 − 9 = 6	15 − 6 = 9	6 + 9 = 15	15 − 9 = 6	15 − 6 = 9	9 + 6 = 15
6 + 9 = 15	15 − 6 = 9	6 + 9 = 15	9 + 6 = 15	15 − 6 = 9	9 + 6 = 15	15 − 6 = 9	15 − 9 = 6
15 − 6 = 9	15 − 6 = 9	9 + 6 = 15	15 − 9 = 6	6 + 9 = 15	6 + 9 = 15	15 − 6 = 9	9 + 6 = 15
6 + 9 = 15	9 + 6 = 15	15 − 6 = 9	9 + 6 = 15	15 − 9 = 6	15 − 6 = 9	6 + 9 = 15	15 − 6 = 9
15 − 9 = 6	15 − 6 = 9	15 − 9 = 6	15 − 6 = 9	9 + 6 = 15	15 − 9 = 6	15 − 6 = 9	9 + 6 = 15
6 + 9 = 15	15 − 9 = 6	9 + 6 = 15	6 + 9 = 15	15 − 6 = 9	9 + 6 = 15	15 − 9 = 6	15 − 9 = 6

84

c. **The triplet is (15) 9 6 . . .**

d. **The facts are 15−9, 6; 15−6, 9; 9+6, 15; 6+9, 15 . . .**

4. **Say the triplet as I fill the clover and bees.**
5. **Say the facts as I fill the beehive.**
6. Point to the flash cards again. **Say the triplet; then say the answer. (15) 9 6; the answer is 6. . . .**
7. Do the Carry *over* samples.
8. Do the Speed Drill in Lesson 122.
9. Assign Lesson 122.

Note: Make Blossom 15 Chart for Lesson 123.

Count by 5's. Begin at 100.

		100	105	110
115	120	125	130	135
140	145	150	155	160
165	170	175	180	185
190	195	200		

Blacklines

Fact Hives #23

Number Words #6

Fact Form VII

Trace and copy.

12 things = 1 dozen

12 things = 1 dozen

6 things = ½ dozen

6 things = ½ dozen

85

After Class

1. Give each child his (15) 9 6 flash cards.
2. **Say the 12 months of the year.**
3. **Answer together.**
   60 minutes=__. 1 hour
   30 minutes=__. ½ hour
   12 things=__. 1 dozen
   6 things=__. ½ dozen
   7 days=__. 1 week
   12 months=__. 1 year

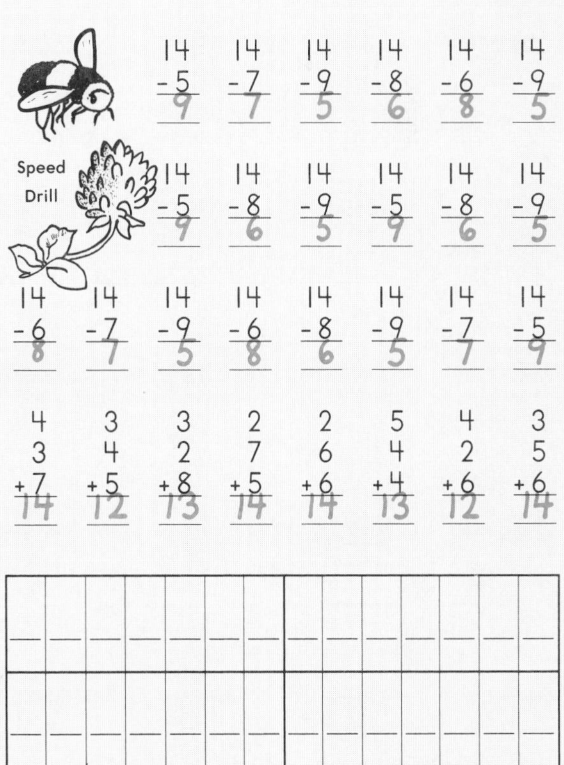

86

123

123

Fill in the whole and parts

(15) 9 6

Trace, answer, and write the facts.

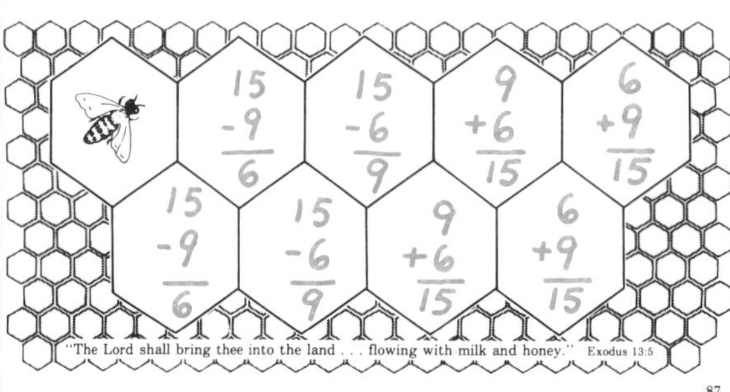

87

Before Class

Tack bee (15) 9 6 to Blossom 15 Chart.
Mount it on the wall.

Materials

12's–15's flash cards

Chalkboard

647	567	276	469	368	248	527
+225	+377	+467	+225	+275	+746	+256

Class Time

1. Call the children to the clover patch.

   (15) 9 6

   15 clovers in the patch;
   15 is the whole number.
   What part of the 15 has bees? 9
   What part of the 15 has no bees? 6
   15 is the whole number.
   Its parts are 9 and 6.
   a. **The triplet is (15) 9 6 . . .**
   b. **The facts are 15−9, 6 . . .**
2. Drill each triplet on the Blossom Charts.
3. **Can we say the triplets by memory?**
   (11) 9 2; (11) 8 3 . . .
4. Do the Carry *over* samples.
5. **12 things=__.** 1 dozen
   6 things=__. ½ dozen

123

Extra Activity

Answer these facts.

		15 − 6 = 9	15 − 9 = 6	6 + 9 = 15	15 − 9 = 6	15 − 6 = 9	6 + 9 = 15
9 + 6 = 15	15 − 9 = 6	9 + 6 = 15	6 + 9 = 15	15 − 9 = 6	9 + 6 = 15	15 − 9 = 6	15 − 6 = 9
15 − 9 = 6	15 − 6 = 9	6 + 9 = 15	15 − 9 = 6	9 + 6 = 15	6 + 9 = 15	15 − 6 = 9	6 + 9 = 15
9 + 6 = 15	9 + 6 = 15	15 − 6 = 9	9 + 6 = 15	15 − 9 = 6	15 − 6 = 9	9 + 6 = 15	15 − 9 = 6
15 − 9 = 6	15 − 6 = 9	15 − 9 = 6	15 − 6 = 9	6 + 9 = 15	15 − 9 = 6	15 − 6 = 9	9 + 6 = 15
9 + 6 = 15	15 − 9 = 6	9 + 6 = 15	6 + 9 = 15	15 − 6 = 9	9 + 6 = 15	15 − 9 = 6	15 − 9 = 6

88

6. Story Problems

   Who can give the whole problem?

   a. **The storekeeper put ½ dozen loaves of white bread and ½ dozen loaves of brown bread on a shelf. How many loaves is that?**

      6 loaves + 6 loaves = 12 loaves.

   b. **Hold that answer in your mind. That evening there were only 3 loaves left. How many loaves had been sold?**

      12 loaves − 3 loaves = 9 loaves.

7. **Answer together.**

   Half of 4 is __. Continue with half of 10, 6, 16, 20, 18.

8. Assign Lesson 123.

Note: If you plan to begin Multiplication Table 2 in Lesson 124, you will want to prepare Key 1 for each child.

Answer these problems.

Carry *over* in one or two places.

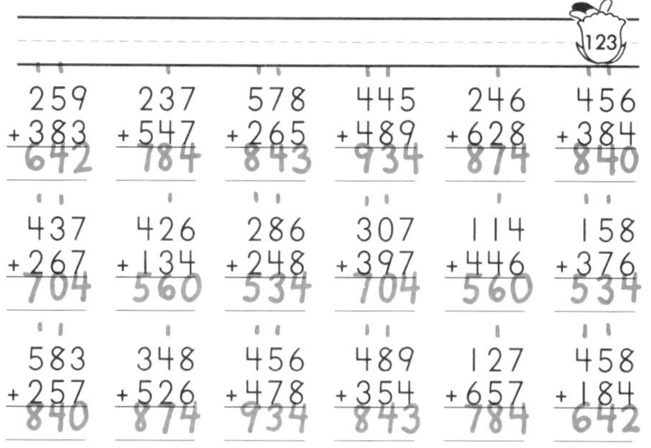

123
259 +383 642
237 +547 784
578 +265 843
445 +489 934
246 +628 874
456 +384 840
437 +267 704
426 +134 560
286 +248 534
307 +397 704
114 +446 560
158 +376 534
583 +257 840
348 +526 874
456 +478 934
489 +354 843
127 +657 784
458 +184 642

Read the story.

Write the numbers in the beehive.

Write the label words on the lines.

Answer the problem.

Mother made 98 cookies. She gave 65 cookies to a family in need. How many cookies did she have left?

98 cookies
-65 cookies
33 cookies

Carl's teacher had one dozen pencils. She gave 8 pencils to the boys and girls. How many pencils did she have left?

89

Blacklines

Fact Hives #23

Number Facts #14

Fact Form III

After Class

1. Double Drill: 12's–15's flash cards.
2. Chalkboard Drill: **Write**

1,215	**Circle the numeral in ones' place.**
1,700	**. . . hundreds' place.**
1,610	**. . . tens' place.**
1,508	**. . . tens' place.**
1,101	**. . . hundreds' place.**
1,390	**. . . ones' place.**
1,046	**. . . thousands' place.**

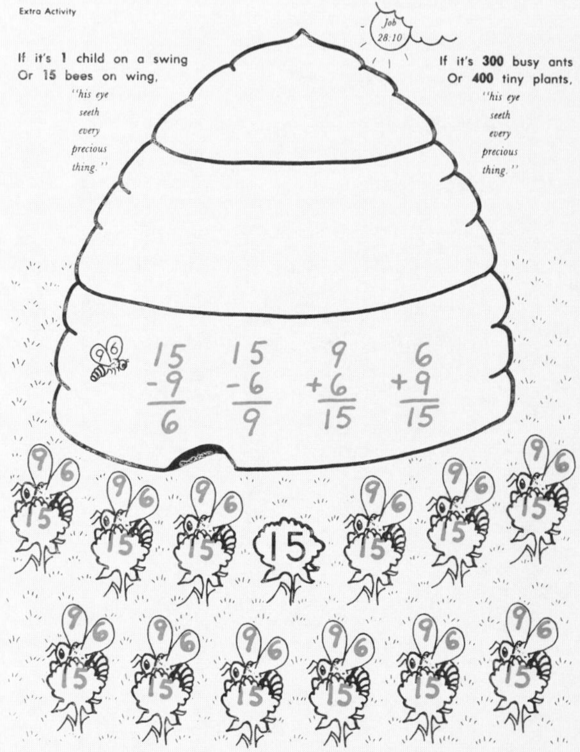

Extra Activity
Job 28:10
If it's 1 child on a swing
Or 15 bees on wing,
"his eye seeth every precious thing."
If it's 300 busy ants
Or 400 tiny plants,
"his eye seeth every precious thing."
15 -9 6
15 -6 9
9 +6 15
6 +9 15
15

90

Fill in the whole and parts.

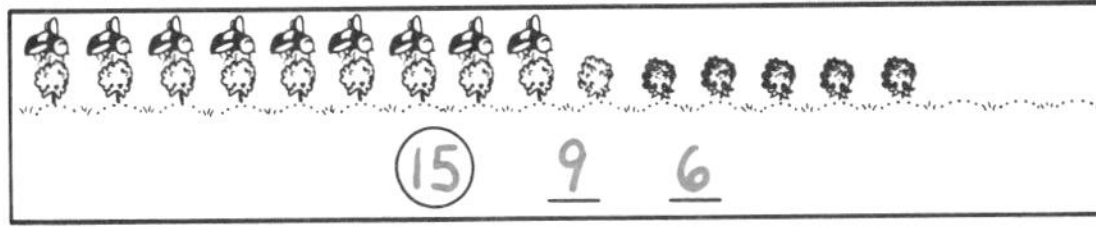

Trace, answer, and write the facts.

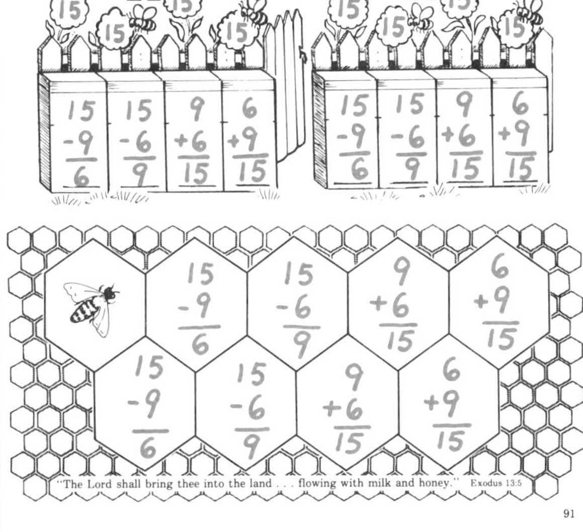

"The Lord shall bring thee into the land . . . flowing with milk and honey." Exodus 13:5

91

Before Class

Materials

12's–15's flash cards

Large clock

Chalkboard

35	73	60	25	40	94	70
−26	−69	−52	−19	−33	−89	−64

Class Time

1. Call the children to the Number Line.
   Count by 10's. Begin at
   - **5** 5, 15 . . .
   - **7** 7, 17 . . .
   - **8** 8, 18 . . .
2. **Answer together.**

35+10	**67+10**	**53+10**
65−10	**27−10**	**73−10**
95−10	**87−10**	**43−10**
45+10	**37+10**	**83+10**

3. Stand near the clover patch.

   (15) 9 6

   15 clovers in the patch;
   15 is the whole number.
   What part of the 15 has bees? 9
   What part of the 15 has no bees? 6
   15 is the whole number.
   Its parts are 9 and 6.
   a. **The triplet is (15) 9 6 . . .**
   b. **The facts are 15−9, 6 . . .**

Answer these problems.
Carry *over* in some problems.

		159 -97 62	158 -63 95	95 +63 158	159 -92 67
66 +29 95	158 -96 62	94 +63 157	159 -64 95	60 +90 150	156 -95 61
83 +67 150	155 -62 93	157 -93 64	158 -67 91	157 -94 63	52 +98 150
159 -98 61	54 +96 150	157 -62 95	95 +62 157	157 -95 62	79 +16 95
155 -93 62	56 +49 105	157 -90 67	60 +98 158	159 -64 95	158 -96 62
86 +64 150	156 -93 63	155 -64 91	156 -92 64	158 -65 93	54 +96 150

92

4. Flash the 12's–15's cards.
   Girls, answer the addition facts.
   Boys, answer the subtraction facts.
5. Stand near the Borrow *back* samples.
   a. Point to the first problem.
      What must I do before I subtract?
      Borrow *back*. **15−6=__.** Write 9.
      2−2=__. Write 0.
   b. **Is the answer 09?**
      No, it is 9. Erase the 0.
   c. Have the children finish the samples.
6. Hold the large clock. **Read the time.**
   6:45, 8:15, 9:30, 11:00 . . .
7. Do the Speed Drill in Lesson 124.
8. Assign Lesson 124.

Note: Multiplication may be introduced in Grade 2, beginning in this lesson. (See "Outline of Multiplication and Division" in the Overview, page 11.) In each lesson the points dealing with multiplication and division are marked by a star.

You will continue to spend **all** your Grade 2 Class Time with addition and subtraction. Multiplication and division are **optional.** Some classes may be ready for it. Many will not be ready. Do not introduce multiplication and division unless your children are able to say the triplets by memory and can answer 35 flash cards in 30 seconds.

Multiplication and division are taught as new concepts in Grade 3. The work in Grade 2 is limited to copying facts from the keys.

124

Answer these facts.

9 + 6 = 15	14 − 7 = 7	15 − 9 = 6	6 + 9 = 15	14 − 8 = 6	6 + 8 = 14	13 − 7 = 6	14 − 6 = 8
14 − 5 = 9	5 + 9 = 14	13 − 6 = 7	6 + 7 = 13	14 − 5 = 9	8 + 6 = 14	13 − 6 = 7	7 + 6 = 13
14 − 6 = 8	13 − 7 = 6	7 + 7 = 14	14 − 8 = 6	9 + 6 = 15	15 − 9 = 6	14 − 7 = 7	6 + 9 = 15

Blacklines

Fact Hives #23

Missing Whole or Parts #14

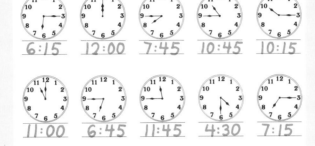

Multiply Form

Write the time.

6:15 12:00 7:45 10:45 10:15

11:00 6:45 11:45 4:30 7:15

93

After Class

9+5=	9+2=	13−9=	9+6=
12−3=	6+9=	5+9=	12−9=
14−5=	9+4=	11−9=	15−9=
11−2=	15−6=	9+3=	2+9=
4+9=	3+9=	14−9=	13−4=

1. Drill individuals at the grid on the chalkboard. You will need the grid in Lesson 125 too.
2. Ask a child to begin with April and name the months of the year.
   April, May . . . March

*3. Give each child Multiplication Key 1.
   Follow as I read the 2 times table.
   2 times 0=0
   2 times 1=2 . . .

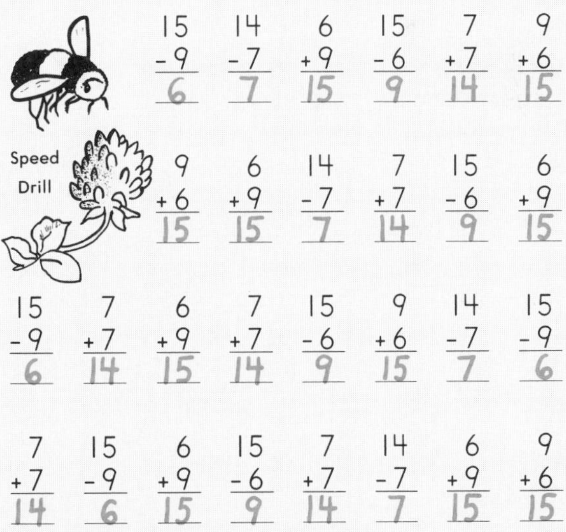

15 − 9 = 6	14 − 7 = 7	6 + 9 = 15	15 − 6 = 9	7 + 7 = 14	9 + 6 = 15		
9 + 6 = 15	6 + 9 = 15	14 − 7 = 7	7 + 7 = 14	15 − 6 = 9	6 + 9 = 15		
15 − 9 = 6	7 + 7 = 14	6 + 9 = 15	7 + 7 = 14	15 − 6 = 9	9 + 6 = 15	14 − 7 = 7	15 − 9 = 6
7 + 7 = 14	15 − 9 = 6	6 + 9 = 15	15 − 6 = 9	7 + 7 = 14	14 − 7 = 7	6 + 9 = 15	9 + 6 = 15

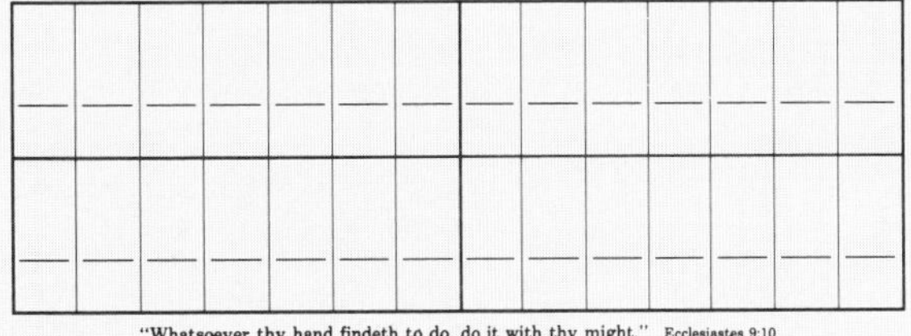

"Whatsoever thy hand findeth to do, do it with thy might." Ecclesiastes 9:10

94

125

Fill in the whole and parts.

Write the facts.

15 − 9 = 6 | 15 − 6 = 9 | 9 + 6 = 15 | 6 + 9 = 15

15 − 9 = 6 | 15 − 6 = 9 | 9 + 6 = 15 | 6 + 9 = 15

"The Lord shall bring thee into the land . . . flowing with milk and honey." Exodus 13:5

95

Before Class

Materials

Large coins

12" ruler

Chalkboard

42	80	35	64	50	53	90
−35	−72	−29	−57	−46	−46	−87

104¢
137¢
245¢
189¢

Class Time

1. Stand near the clover patch.

   (13) 9 4

   The whole number is __.
   Its parts are __ and __.
   The triplet is (13) 9 4 . . .

2. (14) 9 5

   The whole number is __.
   Its parts are __ and __.
   The triplet is (14) 9 5 . . .

3. (15) 9 6

   The whole number is __.
   Its parts are __ and __.
   The triplet is (15) 9 6 . . .

125

Extra Activity

Count the first row.
Write the amount.
Count the second row.
Write the amount.
Add.
Then copy the answer into the dollar box.

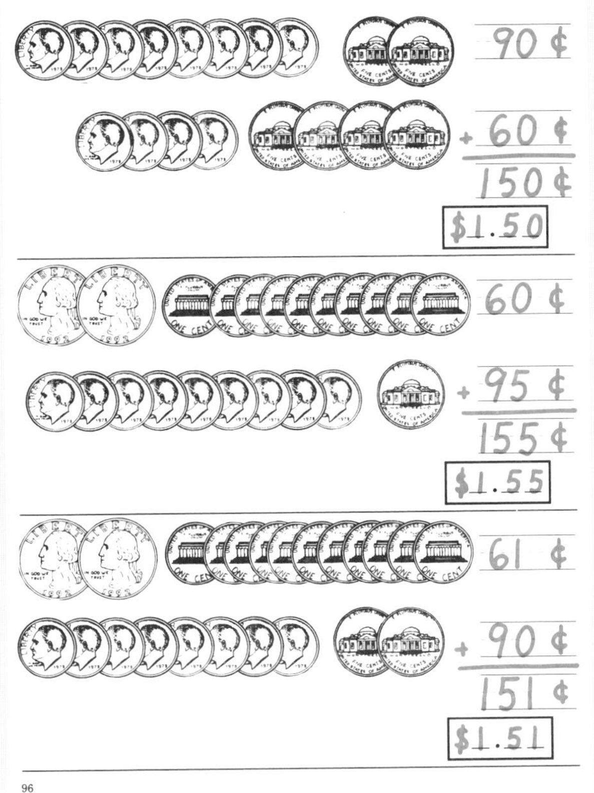

4. Point to the Blossom Charts. Drill all the triplets that have a 9.
   (11) 9 2
   (12) 9 3
   (13) 9 4
   (14) 9 5
   (15) 9 6 . . .
5. Stand near the grid on the board.
   Answer together. Drill the facts right and left, up and down.
6. Do the Borrow *back* samples.
7. Flash the large coins.
   a. **Name the man on the coin.**
   b. **We count pennies by __, nickels by __, dimes by __, and quarters by __.**
   c. **How many pennies are in $1.00?** Continue with nickels, dimes, and quarters.
   d. Do the money samples. Have a child change 104¢ to $1.04 and then read his answer.
8. Assign Lesson 125.

Answer these problems; carry *over* or borrow *back*.

79 + 66 = 145	85 − 76 = 9	95 − 49 = 46	93 − 68 = 25	62 − 54 = 8	78 + 65 = 143
94 − 78 = 16	56 + 87 = 143	84 − 67 = 17	84 − 45 = 39	38 + 66 = 104	94 − 89 = 5
88 + 45 = 133	74 − 67 = 7	46 + 77 = 123	94 − 38 = 56	58 + 84 = 142	94 − 56 = 38

Count by 5's. Begin at 100.

Blacklines

Triplets With Facts #11

2-Place Computation (−) #9

Multiply Form

After Class

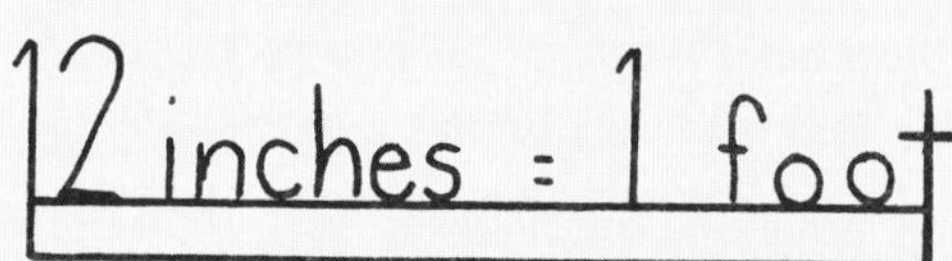

Make this diagram 12″ long.

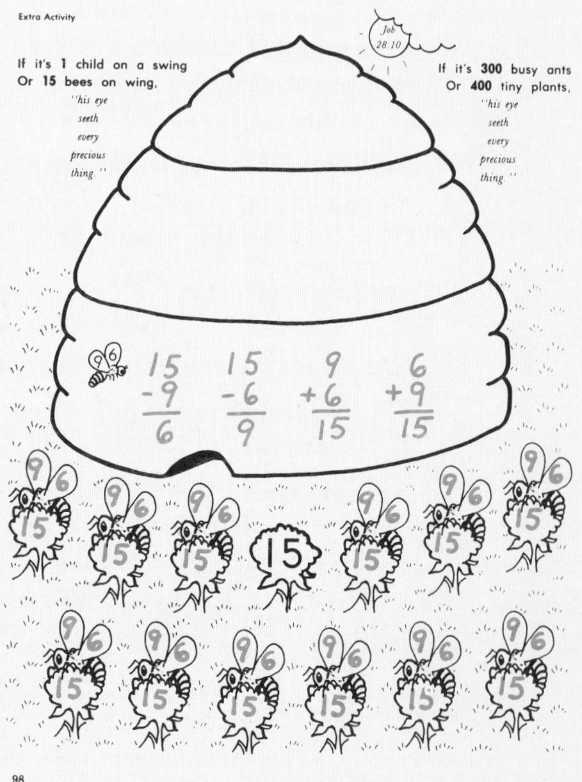

Extra Activity
If it's 1 child on a swing
Or 15 bees on wing,
"his eye seeth every precious thing"
Job 28:10
If it's 300 busy ants
Or 400 tiny plants,
"his eye seeth every precious thing"
15 − 9 = 6
15 − 6 = 9
9 + 6 = 15
6 + 9 = 15
15
98

1. Ask individuals to say the triplets by memory.
2. Hold the 12″ ruler.
   a. **The numbers on this ruler help us to measure things by __.** inches
   Count with me. 1 inch, 2 inches . . .
   b. Point to the chalkboard.
   12 inches=1 foot.
   12 inches . . .

*3. Have each child bring Key 1 to the teaching corner. **Say the 2 times table with me. 2 times 0=0 . . .**

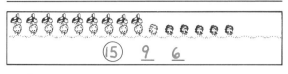

126

Fill in the whole or parts.

Write the facts.

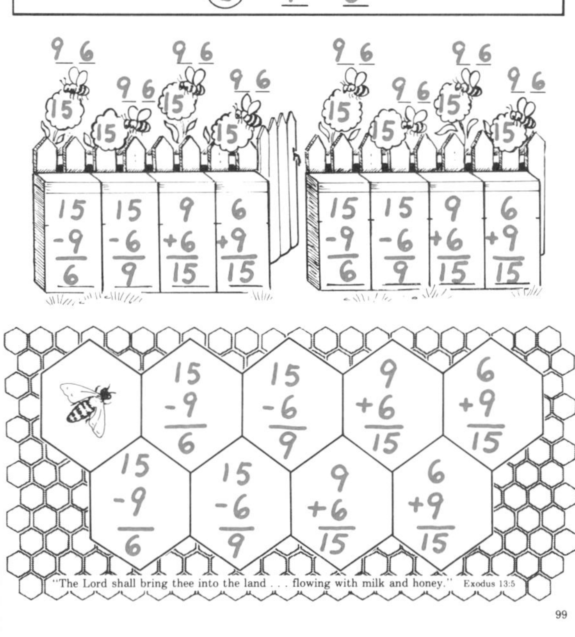
126
15 9 6
"The Lord shall bring thee into the land . . . flowing with milk and honey." Exodus 13:5
99

Before Class

Materials

11's–15's flash cards

11's–15's flash cards

Chalkboard

55	73	80	64	95	44	84
− 6	−37	−59	− 8	−89	−26	−47

Class Time

1. **Father planted one dozen apple trees. He planted half of them in one row and half of them in another row.**
   a. **How many trees are in one row?**
   ½ dozen or 6
   b. **How many trees are in both rows?**
   1 dozen or 12
2. **Answer together.**
   12 things=__. 1 dozen
   6 things=__. ½ dozen
   7 days=__. 1 week
   12 months=__. 1 year
   12 inches=__. 1 foot
3. Stand near the Blossom Charts.
   Say the 11 triplets 1 time.
   . . . 12 triplets 2 times.
   . . . 13 triplets 3 times.
   . . . 14 triplets 4 times.
   . . . 15 triplet 5 times.

Fill in the missing whole or parts.

9 + 6 = 15	15 − 9 = 6	15 − 6 = 9
6 + 9 = 15	6 + 9 = 15	6 + 9 = 15
15 − 9 = 6	15 − 9 = 6	15 − 9 = 6
15 − 6 = 9	15 − 6 = 9	15 − 6 = 9
6 + 9 = 15	6 + 9 = 15	6 + 9 = 15
15 − 9 = 6	9 + 6 = 15	15 − 9 = 6

Speed Drill

Answer these problems.

6	7	6	4	8	5	4	1
3	2	3	5	1	2	2	5
+6	+5	+4	+6	+6	+6	+8	+9
15	14	13	15	15	13	14	15

5	7	2	4	3	3	3	5
4	2	7	2	3	3	6	1
+6	+3	+6	+8	+8	+9	+3	+9
15	12	15	14	14	15	12	15

100

4. Flash the 11's–15's cards for 1 minute.
   Answer together.
5. Do the Borrow *back* samples.
6. **Who can give the whole problem?**
   6 is how much less than 15? 15−6=9
   7 . . . than 14? 14−7=7
   8 . . . than 13? 13−8=5
   5 . . . than 14? 14−5=9
   9 . . . than 15? 15−9=6
7. Do the Speed Drill in Lesson 126.
8. Assign Lesson 126.

126

Answer these problems. Borrow *back* in some problems.

95 − 9 = 86	94 − 8 = 86	74 − 2 = 72	93 − 7 = 86	94 − 7 = 87	93 − 5 = 88
89 − 37 = 52	94 − 88 = 6	94 − 89 = 5	99 − 78 = 21	74 − 48 = 26	83 − 74 = 9
62 − 24 = 38	55 − 39 = 16	85 − 29 = 56	99 − 67 = 32	64 − 38 = 26	45 − 36 = 9

Trace and copy.

12 inches = 1 foot

12 inches = 1 foot

12 inches = 1 foot

12 inches = 1 foot

101

Blacklines

Missing Whole or Parts #14

Number Facts #14

Multiply Form

After Class

1. Double Drill: 11's–15's flash cards.
   Whoever says the correct answer first may have the card.
2. a. **Name something that is about 1 inch long.** Cricket, safety pin, eraser, barrette . . .
   b. **Name something that is about 1 foot long.** Cake pan, loaf of bread, paper, shoe string . . .

*3. Have the children bring Key 1 to the teaching corner.
   a. **Read the answers to the 2 times table.**
   b. **Say the facts together.**

Speed Drill

14 − 8 = 6	15 − 9 = 6	15 − 6 = 9	6 + 8 = 14	14 − 6 = 8	9 + 6 = 15		
15 − 6 = 9	9 + 6 = 15	6 + 9 = 15	14 − 6 = 8	15 − 9 = 6	8 + 6 = 14		
15 − 9 = 6	6 + 9 = 15	9 + 6 = 15	14 − 6 = 8	6 + 8 = 14	15 − 6 = 9	15 − 9 = 6	14 − 8 = 6
6 + 9 = 15	14 − 8 = 6	8 + 6 = 14	15 − 9 = 6	14 − 6 = 8	9 + 6 = 15	6 + 9 = 15	15 − 6 = 9

"Whatsoever thy hand findeth to do, do it with thy might." Ecclesiastes 9:10

102

127

Fill in the whole or parts.

Write the facts.

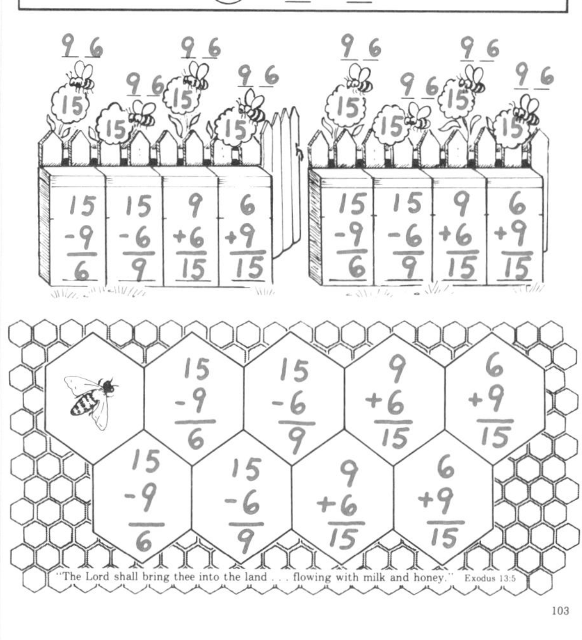

Before Class

Materials

12's–15's flash cards
Form C

Class Time

1. Call the children to the clover patch.

   Why do tiny ants crawl toward a large beehive? Are the ants enemies or friends of the bees?

   The ants will crawl up on the hive and chew holes in the wood. Then they will crawl through the holes and steal wax, honey, or baby bees from the hive.

   Sometimes the bees are so busy that they do not notice their tiny enemies until much damage is done.

2. | (15) 9 6 |
   |---|

   15 clovers in the patch;
   15 is the whole number.
   What part of the 15 has bees? 9
   What part of the 15 has no bees? 6
   15 is the whole number.
   Its parts are 9 and 6.

127

Extra Activity

Read the story.
Write the numbers
in the beehive.
Write the label words
on the lines.
Answer the problem.

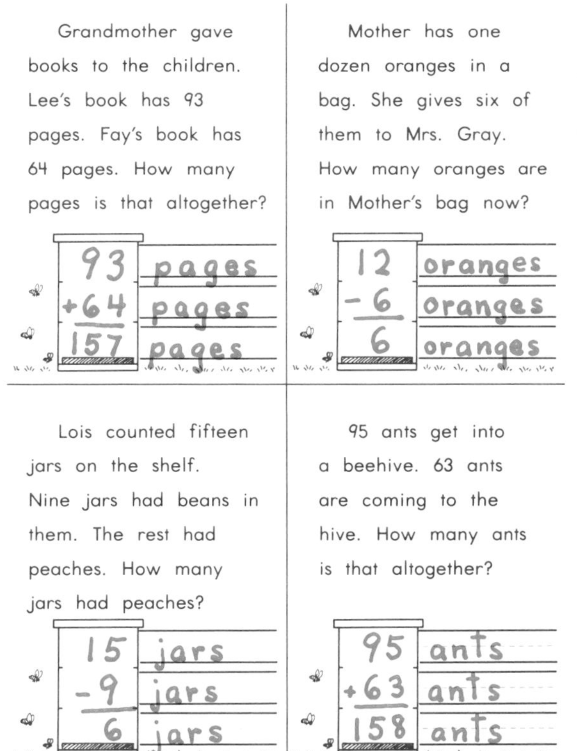

Grandmother gave books to the children. Lee's book has 93 pages. Fay's book has 64 pages. How many pages is that altogether?

93 pages
+64 pages
157 pages

Mother has one dozen oranges in a bag. She gives six of them to Mrs. Gray. How many oranges are in Mother's bag now?

12 oranges
−6 oranges
6 oranges

Lois counted fifteen jars on the shelf. Nine jars had beans in them. The rest had peaches. How many jars had peaches?

15 jars
−9 jars
6 jars

95 ants get into a beehive. 63 ants are coming to the hive. How many ants is that altogether?

95 ants
+63 ants
158 ants

104

a. **The triplet is (15) 9 6 . . .**
b. **Boys, say the facts.**
Girls, say the facts.

3. Drill the triplets on each Blossom Chart.
4. **What belongs on the blank?**
(Say *blank* each time.)

15 __ 6	**13, 7 __**	**__ 9, 3**
14 __ 6	**15, 9 __**	**__ 9, 5**
13 __ 5	**14, 7 __**	**__ 7, 6**
14 __ 5	**13, 9 __**	**__ 9, 6**

5. Flash the 12's–15's cards.
Answer together.
6. Flash Card Drill: 12's–15's flash cards. Use Form C. **Flower Row: Box 1 . . .**
7. Assign Lesson 127.

127

Answer these problems; carry *over* or borrow *back*.

65 + 78 = 143	94 − 78 = 16	47 + 96 = 143	56 + 78 = 134	94 − 55 = 39	93 − 36 = 57
56 + 99 = 155	65 − 56 = 9	68 + 76 = 144	85 − 76 = 9	69 + 55 = 124	94 − 29 = 65
46 + 97 = 143	84 − 65 = 19	89 + 56 = 145	49 + 86 = 135	75 − 36 = 39	84 − 27 = 57

Trace and copy.

12 inches = 1 foot

12 inches = 1 foot

12 inches = 1 foot

12 inches = 1 foot

105

Blacklines

Form C (Class Time)

Triplets With Facts #11

Number Facts #14

Multiply/Divide #1

After Class

2 quarters + 4 nickels =	____
6 dimes + 3 nickels =	+ ____
8 nickels + 6 pennies =	____
1 quarter + 4 pennies =	+ ____

1. Do the Money samples.
2. Ask a child to begin with September and name the months of the year.

*3. Ask the children to bring their Multiplication Keys to the teaching corner.

   a. **Say the 2 times table.**
      2 times 0=0
      2 times 1=2 . . .

   b. **Can we say them again without using our keys?**

Extra Activity
Job 28:10
If it's 1 child on a swing
Or 15 bees on wing,
"his eye seeth every precious thing."
If it's 300 busy ants
Or 400 tiny plants,
"his eye seeth every precious thing."
15 − 9 = 6
15 − 6 = 9
9 + 6 = 15
6 + 9 = 15
15
106

128

Fill in the whole and parts.

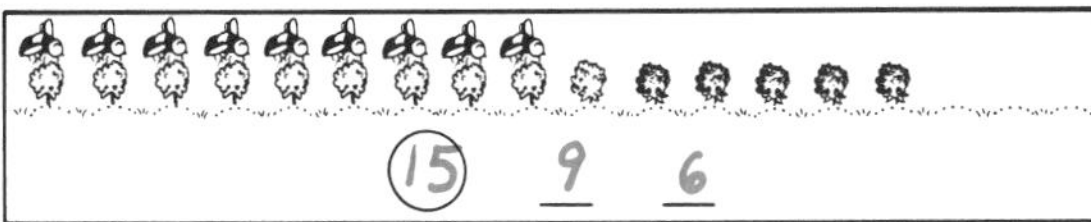

Write the facts.

Trace, answer, and write the facts.

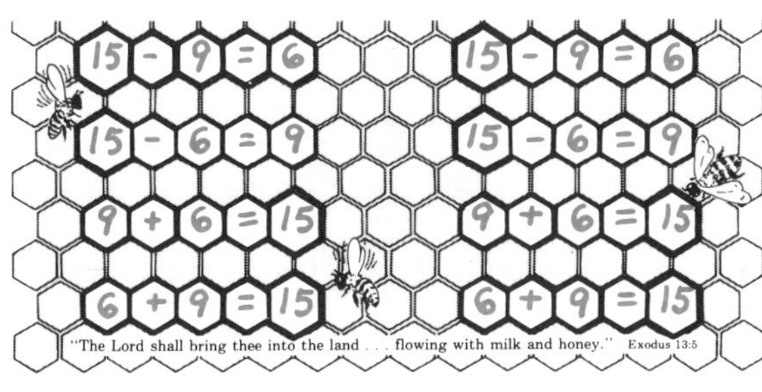

15 - 9 = 6
15 - 6 = 9
9 + 6 = 15
6 + 9 = 15
"The Lord shall bring thee into the land . . . flowing with milk and honey." Exodus 13:5

107

Before Class

Materials

13's–15's flash cards

1 yardstick, three 12" rulers

Chalkboard

56	14	43	51	24	23
20	25	36	35	64	34
+58	+36	+26	+48	+52	+57

__	__	500	__	700	__	__
__	13	15	__	__	21	__
__	410	__	__	425	__	__
73	__	__	__	81	__	__

Class Time

1. Circle Drill: 13's–15's flash cards.
2. Stand near the Blossom Charts.
   Jump from chart to chart.
   (11) 9 2; (12) 9 3 . . .
   Drill all the triplets.
3. Do the Column Addition samples.
4. **Count by 10's. Begin at**
   •1 1, 11 . . .
   •2 2, 12 . . .
   •3 3, 13 . . .
   •4 4, 14 . . .
   •5 5, 15 . . .
5. Introduce even and odd numbers.
   a. **2, 4, 6, 8 . . . are *even* numbers. We can easily divide them into two equal groups.**
   b. **Half of 2 is __.** Continue with half of 4, 6, 8, 10.

128

Answer these facts.

Speed Drill

		15 -6 9	15 -9 6	9 +5 14	14 -5 9	15 -9 6	9 +6 15
6 +9 15	14 -9 5	9 +6 15	5 +9 14	15 -9 6	6 +9 15	14 -9 5	15 -6 9
15 -9 6	14 -5 9	6 +9 15	14 -9 5	6 +9 15	9 +6 15	14 -5 9	5 +9 14
9 +5 14	9 +6 15	15 -6 9	9 +6 15	14 -9 5	15 -6 9	6 +9 15	15 -9 6
15 -6 9	14 -9 5	15 -6 9	15 -9 6	9 +5 14	15 -6 9	14 -9 5	5 +9 14
9 +5 14	15 -6 9	9 +6 15	5 +9 14	15 -9 6	6 +9 15	15 -6 9	15 -6 9

108

c. **1, 3, 5, 7 . . . are *odd* numbers. How could you divide 3 apples into two equal groups?** (Accept answers.) You would have to cut one apple in half.

d. **Odd numbers are hard to divide. Say the odd numbers to 99. 1, 3, 5, 7 . . .**

6. Fill in the Missing Numbers.
7. Do the Speed Drill in Lesson 128.
8. Assign Lesson 128.

128

Answer these problems; carry *over* or borrow *back*.

56 + 99 = 155	94 − 55 = 39	68 + 75 = 143	85 − 76 = 9	84 − 27 = 57	65 + 78 = 143
56 + 78 = 134	84 − 65 = 19	49 + 86 = 135	94 − 78 = 16	69 + 55 = 124	94 − 29 = 65
75 − 36 = 39	89 + 66 = 155	65 − 56 = 9	47 + 96 = 143	46 + 97 = 143	93 − 36 = 57

Trace and copy.

12 inches = 1 foot
12 inches = 1 foot
12 inches = 1 foot
12 inches = 1 foot

109

Blacklines

Missing Whole or Parts #14

2-Place Computation (−) #9

Multiply/Divide #1

After Class

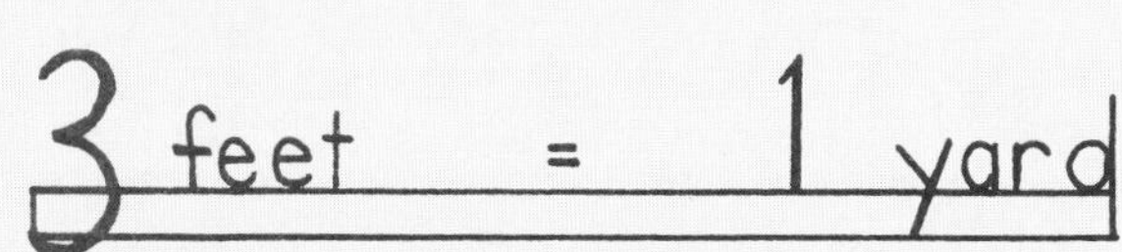

Make this diagram 36″ long.

1. Drill individuals with 13's–15's flash cards.
2. Introduce 3 feet=1 yard.
   a. Hold up each 12-inch ruler.
   12 inches=1 foot. . . .
   Three rulers make 1, 2, 3 feet.
   b. Lay the three rulers on the yardstick. **Three rulers are as long as one yardstick.**
   c. Point to the chalkboard.
   3 feet=1 yard; 3 feet . . .

*3. **Can we say the 2 times table by memory?**
2 times 0=0
2 times 1=2 . . .

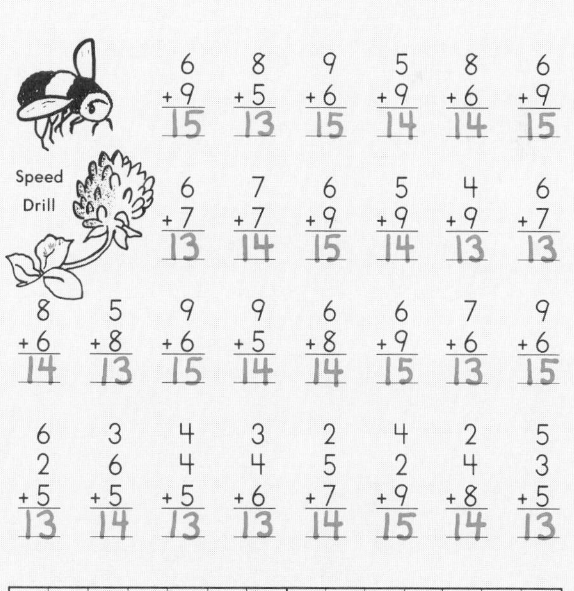

Speed Drill
6 + 9 = 15, 8 + 5 = 13, 9 + 6 = 15, 5 + 9 = 14, 8 + 6 = 14, 6 + 9 = 15
6 + 7 = 13, 7 + 7 = 14, 6 + 9 = 15, 5 + 9 = 14, 4 + 9 = 13, 6 + 7 = 13
8 + 6 = 14, 5 + 8 = 13, 9 + 6 = 15, 9 + 5 = 14, 6 + 8 = 14, 6 + 9 = 15, 7 + 6 = 13, 9 + 6 = 15
6 + 2 + 5 = 13, 3 + 6 + 5 = 14, 4 + 4 + 5 = 13, 3 + 4 + 6 = 13, 2 + 5 + 7 = 14, 4 + 2 + 9 = 15, 2 + 4 + 8 = 14, 5 + 3 + 5 = 13

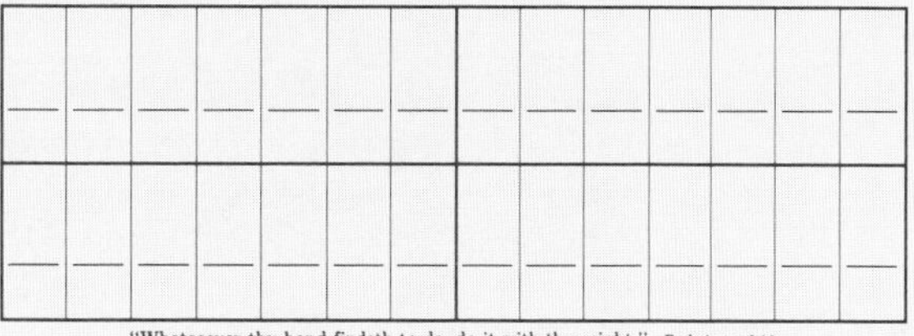

"Whatsoever thy hand findeth to do, do it with thy might." Ecclesiastes 9:10

110

129

129

Fill in the whole and parts.

(15) 9 6

Write the facts.

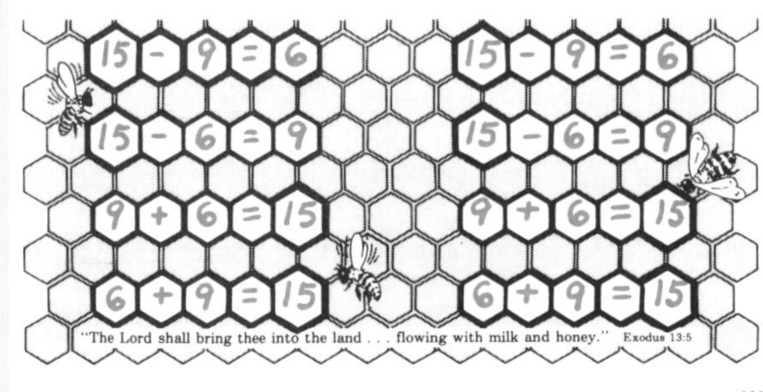

Trace, answer, and write the facts.

15 − 9 = 6 15 − 9 = 6

15 − 6 = 9 15 − 6 = 9

9 + 6 = 15 9 + 6 = 15

6 + 9 = 15 6 + 9 = 15

"The Lord shall bring thee into the land . . . flowing with milk and honey." Exodus 13:5

111

Before Class

Materials

10's–15's flash cards

Chalkboard

thousands	hundreds	tens	ones

Class Time

1. Call the children to the clover patch.

   God promised to bring the children of Israel to the good land of Canaan. It would be a land with brooks and fountains, wheat and barley, vines and fig trees and __.

   honey (Deuteronomy 8:7, 8)

2. (14) 9 5

   The whole number is __.
   Its parts are __ and __.

   a. **The triplet is (14) 9 5 . . .**
   b. **The facts are 14−9, 5 . . .**

3. (14) 8 6

   The whole number is __.
   Its parts are __ and __.

   a. **The triplet is (14) 8 6 . . .**
   b. **The facts are 14−8, 6 . . .**

129

Extra Activity

Answer these facts.

		15 -9 6	12 -4 8	6 +9 15	14 -5 9	12 -6 6	7 +7 14
6 +8 14	14 -9 5	6 +6 12	9 +6 15	13 -5 8	5 +7 12	13 -8 5	13 -7 6
13 -6 7	13 -9 4	6 +7 13	14 -7 7	9 +5 14	5 +8 13	12 -8 4	6 +9 15
9 +6 15	3 +9 12	13 -4 9	5 +9 14	14 -7 7	15 -6 9	4 +8 12	12 -5 7
12 -7 5	15 -6 9	14 -8 6	12 -4 8	4 +9 13	15 -9 6	12 -3 9	5 +9 14
8 +6 14	12 -9 3	7 +6 13	8 +5 13	14 -6 8	6 +7 13	12 -9 3	14 -9 5

112

4. (14) 7 7

The whole number is __.
Its parts are __ and __.
a. **The triplet is (14) 7 7 . . .**
b. **The facts are 14−7, 7 . . .**

5. (15) 9 6

The whole number is __.
Its parts are __ and __.
a. **The triplet is (15) 9 6 . . .**
b. **The facts are 15−9, 6 . . .**

6. Point to the Blossom Charts.
Say each triplet 3 times.

7. Review
12 things=__. 1 dozen
6 things=__. ½ dozen
7 days=__. 1 week
12 months=__. 1 year
12 inches=__. 1 foot
3 feet=__. 1 yard

8. **Count the odd numbers to 99.**

9. Stand near the grid.
a. **When there are thousands but no hundreds, then 0 fills hundreds' place.**
b. Have individuals write these numbers in the grid:
1,034; 1,065; 1,050; 1,090
1,017; 1,078; 1,021; 1,040

10. Assign Lesson 129.

Answer these problems.

15	63	22	62	36	47
23	34	37	23	22	41
+94	+42	+85	+54	+55	+45
132	139	144	139	113	133

66	54	33	44	23	55
23	32	44	22	66	33
+46	+63	+57	+53	+44	+46
135	149	134	119	133	134

Trace and copy.

3 feet = 1 yard

3 feet = 1 yard

3 feet = 1 yard

3 feet = 1 yard

113

Blacklines

Triplets With Facts #11

Fact Form VII

Multiply/Divide #1

After Class

1. Double Drill: 10's–15's flash cards.
2. Chalkboard Drill

   Write only the answer.

50+10	**89+10**	**32+10**
40−10	**64+10**	**41−10**
60+10	**35−10**	**73+10**
10+10	**97−10**	**25−10**

*3. Ask each child to bring his key to the teaching corner.
   Review the 2 times table.

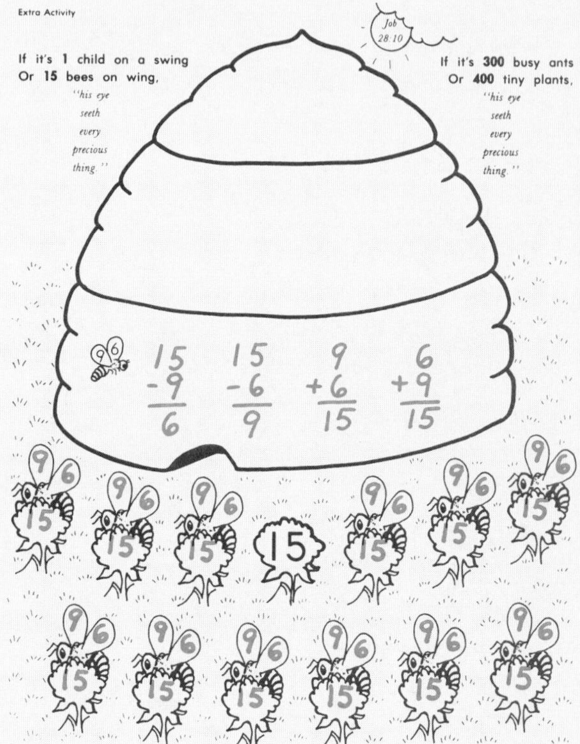

Extra Activity
Job 28:10
If it's 1 child on a swing
Or 15 bees on wing,
"his eye seeth every precious thing."
If it's 300 busy ants
Or 400 tiny plants,
"his eye seeth every precious thing."
15 −9 = 6
15 −6 = 9
9 +6 = 15
6 +9 = 15
15
114

Note: If you are teaching multiplication and division, prepare Key #2 for Lesson 130.

130

Trace and fill in the whole and parts.

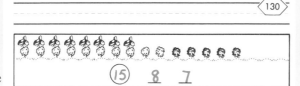

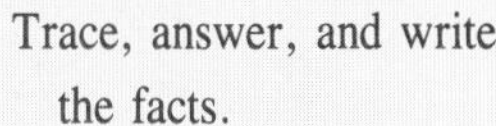

Trace, answer, and write the facts.

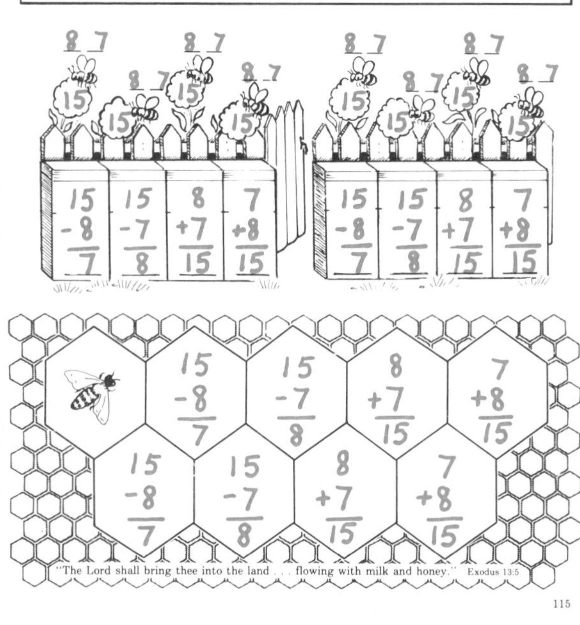
130
(15) 8 7
"The Lord shall bring thee into the land . . . flowing with milk and honey." Exodus 13:5
115

Before Class

Make (15) 8 7 flash cards for each child.

Tack (15) 8 7 flash cards above the clover patch in this order:

15	15	8	7
−8	−7	+7	+8
7	8	15	15

Materials

13's–15's flash cards

Large clock

Chalkboard

1,728	1,200
1,531	1,017
1,460	1,093
1,350	1,006
1,800	1,002

Class Time

1. Flash the 13's–15's cards.
   Answer together.
2. Stand near the clover patch.

   (15) 8 7

   a. **How many pink clovers are in the patch?** 10
   We think—10 pink.
   5 more makes __ altogether. 15
   We think—10 pink.
   2 less makes __ clovers with bees. 8

   b. **15 clovers in the patch;**
   15 is the whole number.
   What part of the 15 has bees? 8
   What part of the 15 has no bees? 7
   15 is the whole number.
   Its parts are 8 and 7.

   c. **The triplet is (15) 8 7 . . .**

   d. **The facts are 15−8, 7; 15−7, 8; 8+7, 15; 7+8, 15 . . .**

130

Answer these facts.

		15 -8 7	15 -7 8	7 +8 15	15 -8 7	15 -7 8	8 +7 15
7 +8 15	15 -8 7	8 +7 15	7 +8 15	15 -7 8	7 +8 15	15 -8 7	15 -8 7
15 -7 8	15 -7 8	7 +8 15	15 -8 7	8 +7 15	7 +8 15	15 -7 8	7 +8 15
8 +7 15	7 +8 15	15 -8 7	7 +8 15	15 -8 7	15 -8 7	8 +7 15	15 -7 8
15 -8 7	15 -7 8	15 -8 7	15 -7 8	8 +7 15	15 -8 7	15 -7 8	15 -8 7
15 -8 7	15 -7 8	8 +7 15	7 +8 15	15 -7 8	7 +8 15	15 -7 8	15 -8 7

116

3. **Say the triplet as I fill the clover and bees.**
4. Point to the flash cards again. **Say the triplet and then the answer.**
5. Ask a child to fill the beehive as you say the 15's facts. Begin with (15) 9 6.
6. a. **Give me some even numbers. . . . some odd numbers.**
   b. **Count the odd numbers to 99.**
7. Stand near the numbers on the board.
   a. **Read the numbers together.**
   b. Point to the numbers at random. Ask individuals to read them.
8. Do the Speed Drill in Lesson 130.
9. Assign Lesson 130.

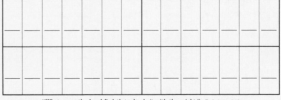

Shade the greater number in ones' place.
Borrow *back* in some problems.

130

95 − 79 = 16	99 − 69 = 30	83 − 44 = 39	99 − 35 = 64	83 − 37 = 46	95 − 66 = 29
94 − 27 = 67	73 − 48 = 25	99 − 56 = 43	83 − 16 = 67	64 − 39 = 25	78 − 35 = 43
84 − 55 = 29	95 − 49 = 46	88 − 24 = 64	95 − 56 = 39	87 − 57 = 30	84 − 68 = 16

Trace and copy.

3 feet = 1 yard

3 feet = 1 yard

3 feet = 1 yard

3 feet = 1 yard

117

Blacklines

Fact Hives #24

Fact Form VII

Number Words #7

Divide Form

After Class

1. Give each child his (15) 8 7 flash cards.
2. Hold the large clock.
   a. Set the hands at 8:00.
      •In 15 minutes it will be __.
      •In 30 minutes it will be __.
      •In 45 minutes it will be __.
      •In 60 minutes it will be __.
   b. Ask individuals to read the time as you set the clock at
      10:00, 10:15, 10:30, 10:45
      11:15, 12:30 . . .

*3. Call the children to the teaching corner.
   a. **I'll say the 2 times table; you say the answer.**
   b. Give each child Key #2.
      Follow as I read the facts.
      0 divided into 2=0
      2 divided into 2=1 . . .

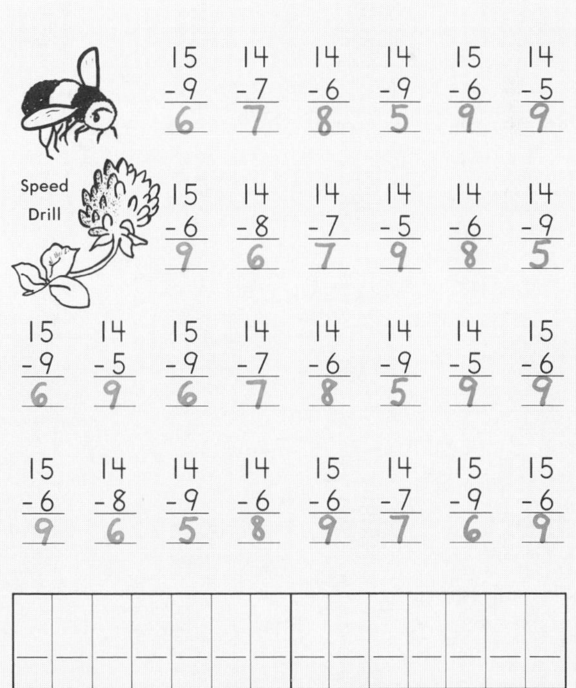
Speed Drill

		15 − 9 = 6	14 − 7 = 7	14 − 6 = 8	14 − 9 = 5	15 − 6 = 9	14 − 5 = 9
		15 − 6 = 9	14 − 8 = 6	14 − 7 = 7	14 − 5 = 9	14 − 6 = 8	14 − 9 = 5
15 − 9 = 6	14 − 5 = 9	15 − 9 = 6	14 − 7 = 7	14 − 6 = 8	14 − 9 = 5	14 − 5 = 9	15 − 6 = 9
15 − 6 = 9	14 − 8 = 6	14 − 9 = 5	14 − 6 = 8	15 − 6 = 9	14 − 7 = 7	15 − 9 = 6	15 − 6 = 9

"Whatsoever thy hand findeth to do, do it with thy might." Ecclesiastes 9:10

118

131

131

Fill in the whole and parts.

(15) 8 7

Trace, answer, and write the facts.

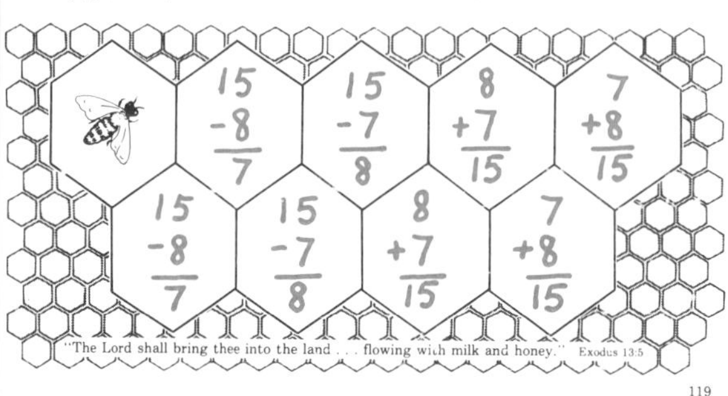

15 -8 7
15 -7 8
8 +7 15
7 +8 15
"The Lord shall bring thee into the land . . . flowing with milk and honey." Exodus 13:5

119

Before Class

Add bee (15) 8 7 to Blossom 15 Chart.

Materials

14's and 15's flash cards

15's flash cards

Chalkboard

546	348	745	376	157	454
+447	+297	+237	+347	+588	+239

Class Time

1. Have each child bring *My 1,000 Book* to the teaching corner.
   a. **Count by 10's to 400.**
   b. **Count on to 600 by 5's.**
2. Stand near the clover patch.

   (15) 8 7

   15 clovers in the patch;
   15 is the whole number.
   What part of the 15 has bees? 8
   What part of the 15 has no bees? 7
   15 is the whole number.
   Its parts are 8 and 7.
   a. **The triplet is (15) 8 7 . . .**
   b. **The facts are 15−8, 7 . . .**
3. Drill the 12, 13, 14, and 15 triplets at the Blossom Charts.
4. Flash the 14's and 15's cards. **Say the triplet; then say the answer.**
5. Do the Computation samples.

131

Extra Activity

Answer these facts.

		15 −7 8	15 −8 7	8 +7 15	15 −8 7	15 −7 8	15 −7 8
15 −7 8	15 −8 7	8 +7 15	7 +8 15	15 −8 7	7 +8 15	15 −8 7	15 −7 8
15 −8 7	15 −7 8	8 +7 15	15 −7 8	7 +8 15	7 +8 15	15 −7 8	8 +7 15
7 +8 15	8 +7 15	15 −8 7	8 +7 15	15 −7 8	15 −8 7	7 +8 15	15 −8 7
15 −7 8	15 −8 7	15 −7 8	15 −8 7	7 +8 15	15 −7 8	15 −8 7	8 +7 15
7 +8 15	15 −8 7	7 +8 15	8 +7 15	15 −8 7	8 +7 15	15 −8 7	15 −7 8

120

6. Review
   60 minutes=__. 1 hour
   30 minutes=__. ½ hour
   12 things=__. 1 dozen
   6 things=__. ½ dozen
   7 days=__. 1 week
   12 months=__. 1 year
   12 inches=__. 1 foot
   3 feet=__. 1 yard
7. Assign Lesson 131.

Answer these problems.

Carry *over* in one or two places.

579 +366 945	337 +367 704	266 +529 795	436 +358 794	355 +449 804	387 +366 753
485 +269 754	576 +369 945	349 +355 704	257 +497 754	179 +766 945	118 +586 704
268 +436 704	266 +679 945	525 +269 794	359 +436 795	454 +299 753	126 +678 804

Trace and copy.

3 feet = 1 yard

3 feet = 1 yard

3 feet = 1 yard

3 feet = 1 yard

121

Blacklines

Fact Hives #24

Fact Form III

Divide Form

Multiply/Divide #2

After Class

1. Drill individuals with the 15's flash cards.
2. Ask individuals to name the months of the year.

*3. Have the children bring their keys to the teaching corner.
Read Key #2 together.

132

Fill in the whole and parts.

(15) 8 7

Trace, answer, and write the facts.

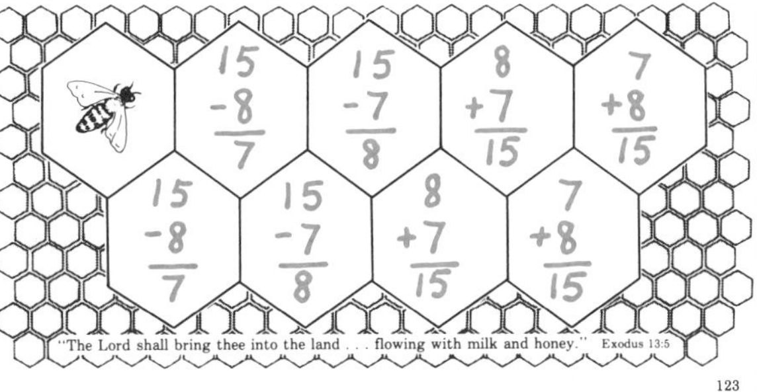

"The Lord shall bring thee into the land . . . flowing with milk and honey." Exodus 13:5

123

Before Class

Materials

11's–15's flash cards

Large clock

Class Time

1. Call the children to the Number Line.
   a. **Count the odd numbers to 99.**
      1, 3, 5, . . .
   b. **Count by 100's to 1,000.**
   c. **We can count by 50's too.**
      50, 100, 150, 200 . . .
2. Stand near the clover patch.

   When King David was old, trouble came. He had to hurry away to the wilderness to be safe. Many people hurried away with him. They were all hungry and tired.

   Three kind men brought beds, wheat, corn, beans, cheese, __, and many other things to King David and his people.

   honey (2 Samuel 17–29)

3. | (15) 8 7 |
   |---|

   15 clovers in the patch;
   15 is the whole number.
   What part of the 15 has bees? 8
   What part of the 15 has no bees? 7

132

Answer these problems.
Carry *over* in some problems.

		159 − 87 = 72	158 − 73 = 85	85 + 73 = 158	159 − 82 = 77
78 + 37 = 115	158 − 86 = 72	74 + 83 = 157	159 − 74 = 85	80 + 70 = 150	156 − 85 = 71
68 + 87 = 155	155 − 72 = 83	157 − 83 = 74	158 − 77 = 81	157 − 84 = 73	77 + 48 = 125
159 − 88 = 71	74 + 76 = 150	157 − 72 = 85	85 + 72 = 157	157 − 85 = 72	67 + 48 = 115
155 − 73 = 82	68 + 67 = 135	157 − 80 = 77	70 + 88 = 158	159 − 74 = 85	158 − 86 = 72
68 + 57 = 125	156 − 83 = 73	155 − 74 = 81	156 − 82 = 74	158 − 75 = 83	77 + 78 = 155

124

15 is the whole number.
Its parts are 8 and 7.

a. **The triplet is (15) 8 7 . . .**
b. **The facts are 15−8, 7 . . .**

4. Drill the triplets on each Blossom Chart.
5. Double Drill: 11's–15's flash cards.
6. Hold the large clock. **Read the time as I set the clock. 12:30, 2:45, 4:15, 6:00, 7:15, 8:45 . . .**
7. **Name two fractions.** ½ and ¼
   2 halves make __. 1 whole
   4 fourths make __. 1 whole
8. Do the Speed Drill in Lesson 132.
9. Assign Lesson 132.

Note: If you are teaching multiplication and division, prepare Key #3 for Lesson 133.

Write the time.

Trace and copy.

12 inches = 1 foot

12 inches = 1 foot

3 feet = 1 yard

3 feet = 1 yard

125

Blacklines

Fact Hives #25

Missing Whole or Parts #15

Number Facts #15

Divide Form

Multiply/Divide #2

After Class

1. Ask individuals to give the triplets by memory.
2. Chalkboard Drill: **Change what I say to cents.**

   5 dimes (pause) 50¢
   1 quarter 25¢
   3 nickels 15¢
   Add to find the total. 90¢
   3 quarters 75¢
   12 pennies 12¢
   2 dimes 20¢
   Add to find the total. 107¢
   5 nickels 25¢
   6 dimes 60¢
   2 quarters 50¢
   Add to find the total. 135¢

*3. Have each child bring his keys to the teaching corner.
Say Key #2 together.

"Whatsoever thy hand findeth to do, do it with thy might." Ecclesiastes 9:10

126

133

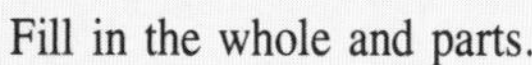

Fill in the whole and parts.

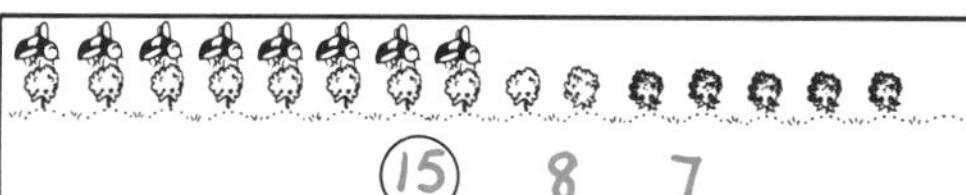

Write the facts.

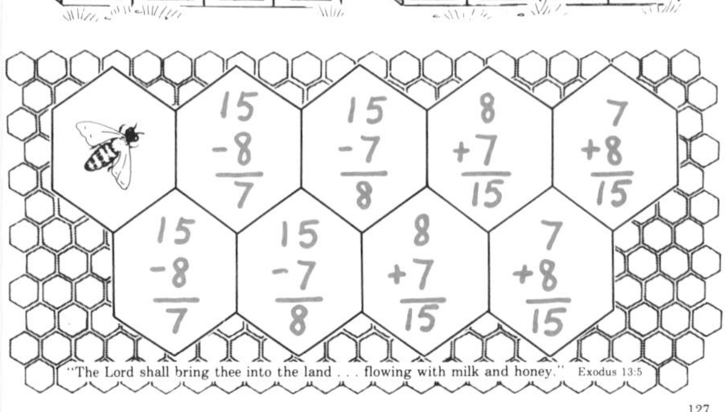

"The Lord shall bring thee into the land . . . flowing with milk and honey." Exodus 13:5
127

Before Class

Materials

11's–15's flash cards

1 half dollar

7's–10's flash cards

Chalkboard

95	58	94	76	75	69	85
−37	+87	−76	+58	−28	+76	−36

106¢
215¢
148¢
239¢

Class Time

1. Stand near the clover patch.

   (13) 8 5

   The whole number is __.
   Its parts are __ and __.
   a. **The triplet is (13) 8 5 . . .**
   b. **The facts are 13−8, 5 . . .**

2. (14) 8 6

   The whole number is __.
   Its parts are __ and __.
   a. **The triplet is (14) 8 6 . . .**
   b. **The facts are 14−8, 6 . . .**

3. (15) 8 7

   The whole number is __.
   Its parts are __ and __.
   a. **The triplet is (15) 8 7 . . .**
   b. **The facts are 15−8, 7 . . .**

133

Extra Activity

Count the first row.
Write the amount.
Count the second row.
Write the amount.
Add.
Then copy the answer into the dollar box.

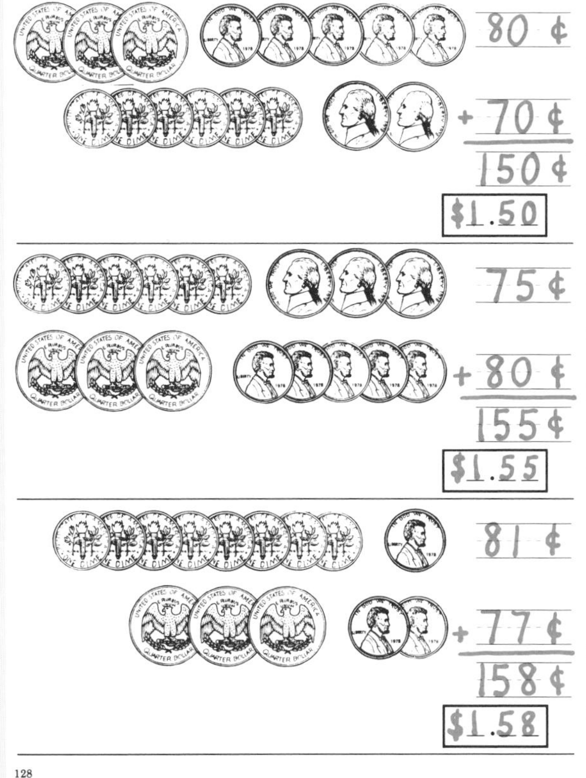

4. Point to the Blossom Charts.
   Drill all the triplets that have an 8.
   (11) 8 3
   (12) 8 4
   (13) 8 5
   (14) 8 6
   (15) 8 7 . . .
5. Flash the 11's–15's cards for 1 minute.
   Answer together.
6. Do the Computation samples.
7. Do the Money samples. Have a child change 106¢ to $1.06 and then read his answer.
8. **Answer together.**
   Half of 8 is __. Continue with half of 10, 14, 20, 60, 80, 100.
9. Assign Lesson 133.

Answer these problems; carry *over* or borrow *back*.

78 + 67 = 145	77 + 76 = 153	95 − 59 = 36	95 − 68 = 27	77 + 68 = 145	95 − 37 = 58
95 − 68 = 27	47 + 98 = 145	95 − 57 = 38	84 − 57 = 27	66 + 79 = 145	85 − 47 = 38
85 − 58 = 27	74 − 38 = 36	85 + 68 = 153	67 + 78 = 145	85 − 27 = 58	86 + 59 = 145

Trace and copy.

12 inches = 1 foot
12 inches = 1 foot

3 feet = 1 yard
3 feet = 1 yard

129

Blacklines

Fact Hives #25

Triplets With Facts #12

Number Facts #15

Multiply Form

After Class

1. Drill the 7's–10's flash cards.
2. Introduce the half dollar.
   a. **This coin is a half dollar. Can you guess how much it is worth?** 50¢
   b. **The man's name is John F. Kennedy. What bird is on the back of the coin?** An eagle with up-stretched wings

*3. Have each child bring his keys to the teaching corner.
   a. Review Keys #1 and #2.
   b. Give each child Key #3.
   Follow as I read.
   10 times 0=0
   10 times 1=10 . . .

134

Fill in the whole and parts.

Write the facts.

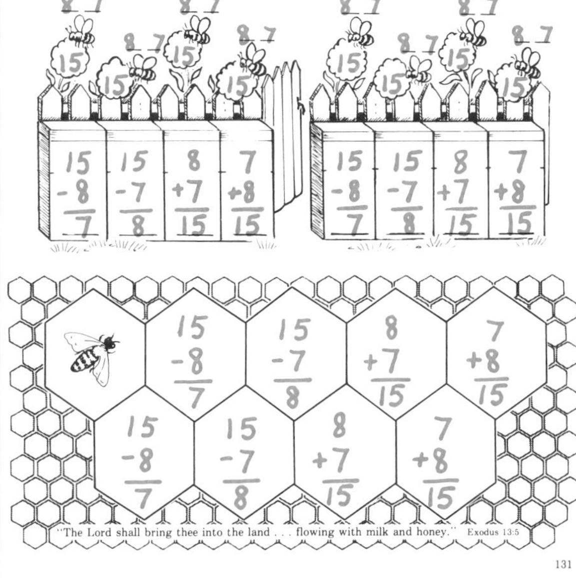

"The Lord shall bring thee into the land . . . flowing with milk and honey." Exodus 13:5
131

Before Class

Materials

Large coins: penny, nickel, dime, quarter, and half dollar

11's–15's flash cards

Chalkboard

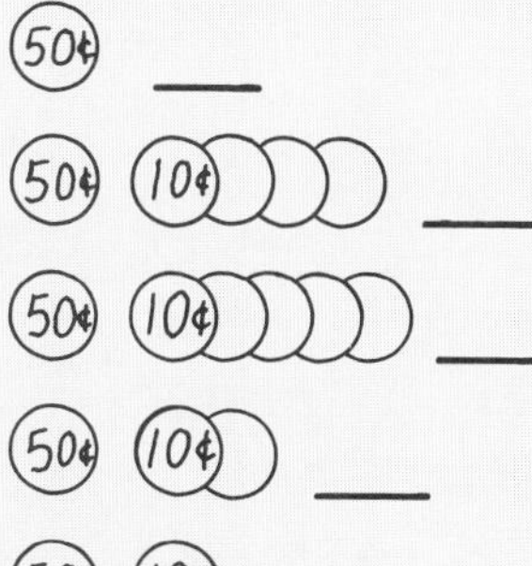

Class Time

1. Stand near the clover patch.

(15) 9 6

   The whole number is __.
   Its parts are __ and __.
   a. **The triplet is (15) 9 6 . . .**
   b. **The facts are 15−9, 6 . . .**

2. | (15) 8 7 |
   |---|

   The whole number is __.
   Its parts are __ and __.
   a. **The triplet is (15) 8 7 . . .**
   b. **The facts are 15−8, 7 . . .**

3. Point to the Blossom Charts.
   a. Drill the 13, 14, and 15 triplets 3 times.
   b. **Can we say all the triplets by memory? (11) 9 2 . . .**

4. **Who can give the whole problem?**
   a. **8 is how much less than 15?** 15−8=7
   6 . . . than 14? 14−6=8
   7 . . . than 13? 13−7=6

134

Fill in the missing whole or parts.

8 + 7 = 15	15 - 7 = 8	8 + 7 = 15
15 - 7 = 8	15 - 8 = 7	15 - 7 = 8
15 - 8 = 7	7 + 8 = 15	15 - 8 = 7
7 + 8 = 15	8 + 7 = 15	7 + 8 = 15
15 - 8 = 7	8 + 7 = 15	8 + 7 = 15
7 + 8 = 15	15 - 7 = 8	15 - 7 = 8

Speed Drill

Answer these problems.

4	7	4	2	3	7	2	7
4	2	3	6	5	2	6	0
+7	+5	+8	+7	+7	+4	+4	+8
15	14	15	15	15	13	12	15

5	3	6	6	3	5	1	3
4	4	2	1	3	3	6	5
+5	+8	+7	+8	+7	+7	+8	+4
14	15	15	15	13	15	15	12

132

b. **14 is how much more than 7?** 14−7=7
15 . . . than 9? 15−9=6
15 . . . than 7? 15−7=8

5. Hold the large half dollar.
   a. **This is a __.** half dollar
      It is worth __. 50¢
      The man's name is __. John F. Kennedy
      We count half dollars by __. 50's
   b. **Half dollar, 50¢; half dollar, 50¢** . . .
   c. Flash the coins. **Nickel, 5¢** . . .
   d. Stand near the Money samples.
      Count the half dollars and dimes with me. Write the answer.
6. Do the Speed Drill in Lesson 134.
7. Assign Lesson 134.

134

Answer these facts.

8 + 7 = 15	15 − 8 = 7	15 − 9 = 6	6 + 9 = 15	14 − 8 = 6	7 + 8 = 15	14 − 5 = 9	14 − 6 = 8
15 − 8 = 7	5 + 8 = 13	15 − 7 = 8	8 + 7 = 15	15 − 8 = 7	6 + 7 = 13	7 + 8 = 15	15 − 7 = 8
15 − 7 = 8	15 − 6 = 9	8 + 7 = 15	13 − 7 = 6	7 + 8 = 15	15 − 9 = 6	14 − 7 = 7	6 + 9 = 15

Trace and copy.

12 inches = 1 foot

12 inches = 1 foot

3 feet = 1 yard

3 feet = 1 yard

133

Blacklines

Fact Hives #25

Missing Whole or Parts #15

Fact Form VIII

Multiply Form

After Class

1. Double Drill: 11's–15's flash cards.
   Whoever says the correct answer first may have the card.
2. Call on individuals to answer.

50+10	**60−10**	**20−10**
80−10	**10+10**	**70+10**
100−10	**40−10**	**30−10**
30+10	**90+10**	**50−10**

*3. Ask the children to bring their keys to the teaching corner.
   a. **Read the 10 times table with me.**
   b. **Read only the answers.**

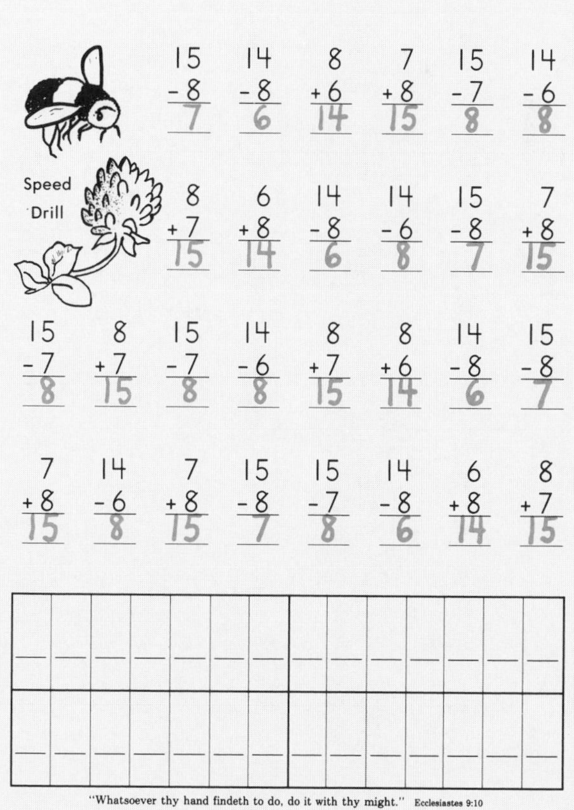
Speed Drill

		15 − 8 = 7	14 − 8 = 6	8 + 6 = 14	7 + 8 = 15	15 − 7 = 8	14 − 6 = 8
		8 + 7 = 15	6 + 8 = 14	14 − 8 = 6	14 − 6 = 8	15 − 8 = 7	7 + 8 = 15
15 − 7 = 8	8 + 7 = 15	15 − 7 = 8	14 − 6 = 8	8 + 7 = 15	8 + 6 = 14	14 − 8 = 6	15 − 8 = 7
7 + 8 = 15	14 − 6 = 8	7 + 8 = 15	15 − 8 = 7	15 − 7 = 8	14 − 8 = 6	6 + 8 = 14	8 + 7 = 15

"Whatsoever thy hand findeth to do, do it with thy might." Ecclesiastes 9:10

134

135

(15) 8 7

Fill in the whole and parts.

Write the facts.

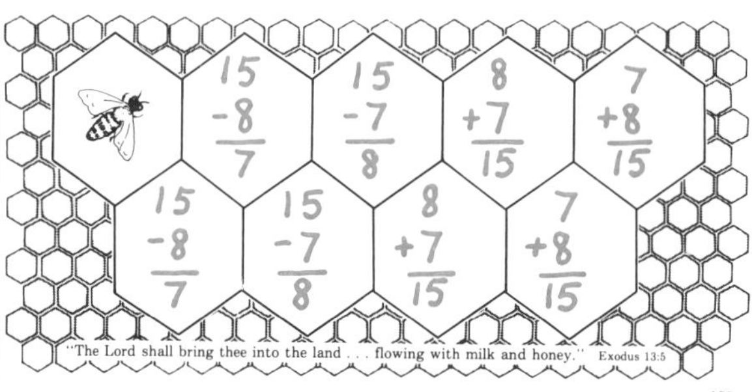

135

Before Class

Materials

12's–15's flash cards

Form C

Chalkboard

85	75	64	76	65	35	87
−76	+ 9	− 8	+ 8	−48	− 7	+56

(50¢) (10¢)( )( )( ) ____

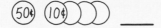

Class Time

1. Call the children to the clover patch.

   The queen bee pokes her head into an empty wax cell. Is the cell clean and strong? Will it make a good "cradle" for a baby bee? If the queen is not pleased, she will check the next cell. If the queen is pleased, she will lay one egg in the cell.

   How big is a bee egg? A bee egg is as big as a comma in your reading book.

2. (15) 8 7

   15 clovers in the patch;
   15 is the whole number.
   What part of the 15 has bees? 8
   What part of the 15 has no bees? 7
   15 is the whole number.
   Its parts are 8 and 7.

   a. **The triplet is (15) 8 7 . . .**
   b. **The facts are 15−8, 7 . . .**

135

Extra Activity

Read the story.
Write the numbers in the beehive.
Write the label words on the lines.
Answer the problem.

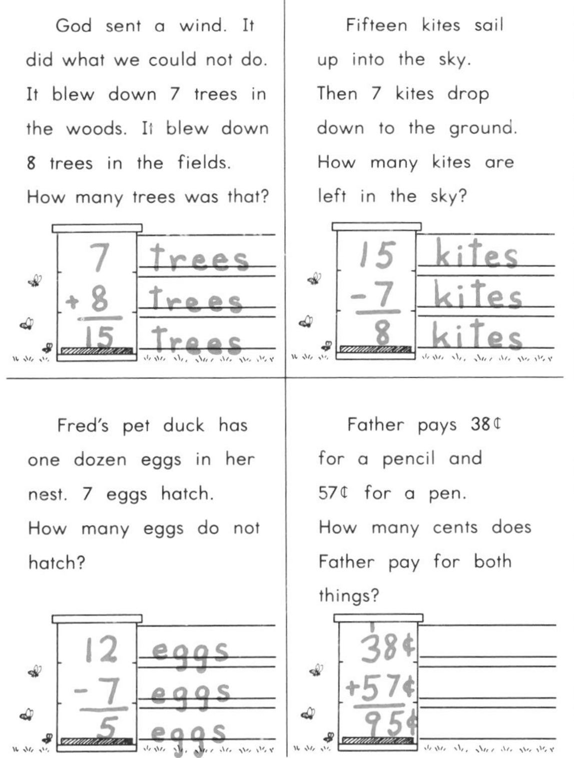

God sent a wind. It did what we could not do. It blew down 7 trees in the woods. It blew down 8 trees in the fields. How many trees was that?
7 trees
+8 trees
15 trees
Fifteen kites sail up into the sky. Then 7 kites drop down to the ground. How many kites are left in the sky?
15 kites
-7 kites
8 kites
Fred's pet duck has one dozen eggs in her nest. 7 eggs hatch. How many eggs do not hatch?
12 eggs
-7 eggs
5 eggs
Father pays 38¢ for a pencil and 57¢ for a pen. How many cents does Father pay for both things?
38¢
+57¢
95¢
136

3. Drill the triplets on each Blossom Chart.
4. Flash the 12's–15's cards for 1 minute. **Answer together.**
5. Flash Card Drill: 12's–15's flash cards. Use Form C. **Flower Row: Box 1 . . .**
6. Do the Computation samples.
7. Do the Money samples.
8. a. **12 inches=__.** 1 foot
   3 feet=__. 1 yard
   b. **If these things were real, would they measure *1 foot* or *1 yard*?**
   daffodils 1 foot
   beehive 1 yard
   feather 1 foot
   ball bat 1 yard
   table 1 yard
   hammer 1 foot
   book 1 foot
   cereal box 1 foot
   Grandfather's cane 1 yard
9. Assign Lesson 135.

Note: Are your children ready to borrow without shading the greater number in ones' place? Those who are at ease with the process, need not shade the greater number any longer.

If you detect **any** difficulty in a child's work, require him to shade the greater number.

Answer these problems; carry *over* or borrow *back*.

65 − 8 = 57	58 + 7 = 65	85 − 7 = 78	64 − 5 = 59	35 − 9 = 26	64 − 7 = 57
88 + 47 = 135	95 − 48 = 47	56 + 79 = 135	67 + 68 = 135	73 − 66 = 7	47 + 88 = 135
65 − 58 = 7	64 − 38 = 26	95 − 36 = 59	95 − 17 = 78	26 + 39 = 65	95 − 38 = 57

Count the half dollars and dimes.
Write the amount.

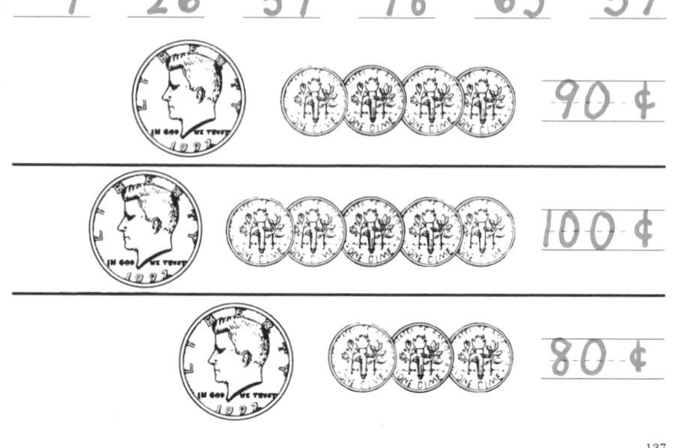

137

Blacklines

Form C (Class Time)
Triplets With Facts #12
Mixed Computation #5
Number Facts #15

Multiply Form

After Class

1. Ask individuals to give the triplets by memory.
2. Chalkboard Drill: **Write only the answer.**

76+10	**28+10**	**62+10**
56−10	**58+10**	**92−10**
36−10	**18−10**	**42−10**

*3. Ask each child to bring his keys to the teaching corner.
   a. Review Key #1.
   b. **Say Key #3 together.**

138

Fill in the whole and parts.

Write the facts.

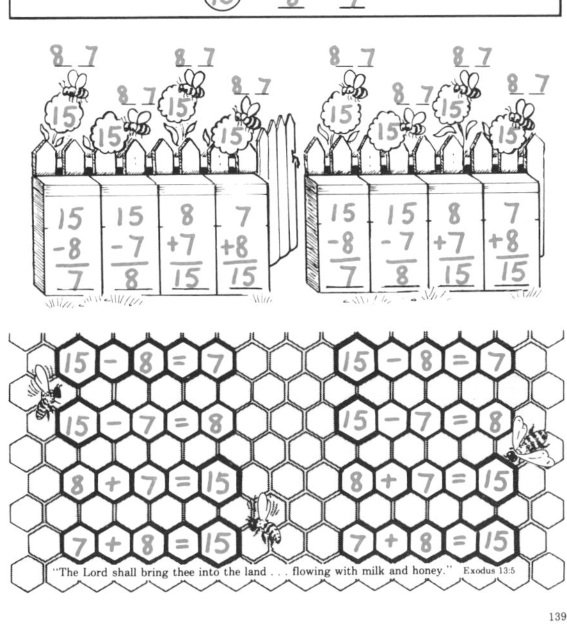

136
"The Lord shall bring thee into the land . . . flowing with milk and honey." Exodus 13:5
139

Before Class

Materials

13's–15's flash cards
Large coins
14's and 15's flash cards

Chalkboard

Class Time

1. Call the children to the beehives.
   Say the facts as I fill the hives. Begin with 13−9=4.
2. Circle Drill: 13's–15's flash cards.
3. Drill the triplets on the Blossom Charts. **Jump from chart to chart.**
   (11) 9 2; (12) 9 3 . . .
4. **What belongs on the blank?**
   (Say *blank* each time.)

15 __ 7	**13, 7 __**	**__ 8, 7**
14 __ 5	**15, 9 __**	**__ 9, 4**
15 __ 6	**14, 9 __**	**__ 9, 6**
14 __ 7	**14, 8 __**	**__ 7, 7**

5. **Who can give the whole problem?**
   a. **14 is how much more than 6?** 14−6=8
      15 . . . than 7? 15−7=8
      15 . . . than 9? 15−9=6
   b. **9 is how much less than 15?** 15−9=6
      8 . . . than 13? 13−8=5
      5 . . . than 14? 14−5=9

136

Answer these facts.

		15 - 8 = 7	14 - 6 = 8	7 + 8 = 15	15 - 8 = 7	15 - 7 = 8	8 + 7 = 15
7 + 8 = 15	14 - 8 = 6	6 + 8 = 14	7 + 8 = 15	15 - 7 = 8	8 + 6 = 14	14 - 8 = 6	15 - 8 = 7
14 - 8 = 6	15 - 7 = 8	7 + 8 = 15	14 - 6 = 8	6 + 8 = 14	7 + 8 = 15	14 - 6 = 8	6 + 8 = 14
8 + 6 = 14	7 + 8 = 15	15 - 8 = 7	8 + 6 = 14	15 - 7 = 8	15 - 8 = 7	8 + 7 = 15	14 - 8 = 6
14 - 8 = 6	15 - 7 = 8	15 - 8 = 7	14 - 6 = 8	8 + 7 = 15	15 - 8 = 7	15 - 7 = 8	15 - 8 = 7
15 - 8 = 7	15 - 7 = 8	8 + 6 = 14	7 + 8 = 15	15 - 7 = 8	6 + 8 = 14	14 - 6 = 8	14 - 8 = 6

140

Speed Drill

6. Display the large coins.
   a. **We count pennies by __, nickels by __, dimes by __, quarters by __, and half dollars by __.**
   b. **Name the coin that is worth the same as**
      10 pennies dime
      5 pennies nickel
      50 pennies half dollar
      25 pennies quarter
      5 nickels quarter
      2 nickels dime
      10 nickels half dollar
      5 dimes half dollar
      2 quarters half dollar
   c. Compare the quarter and half dollar.
      •The half dollar is larger.
      •The eagles are different.
      •There is a ring of fifty stars around the eagle on the half dollar (not for 50¢ but for fifty states in the U.S.).
7. Do the Speed Drill in Lesson 136.
8. Assign Lesson 136.

136

Answer these problems; carry *over* or borrow *back*.

45 − 8 = 37	78 + 7 = 85	85 − 6 = 79	65 − 7 = 58	35 − 9 = 26	24 − 7 = 17
78 + 47 = 125	55 − 47 = 8	56 + 89 = 145	57 + 68 = 125	74 − 56 = 18	57 + 88 = 145
65 − 38 = 27	64 − 38 = 26	95 − 37 = 58	95 − 16 = 79	46 + 39 = 85	85 − 78 = 7

Count the half dollars and dimes.
Write the amount.

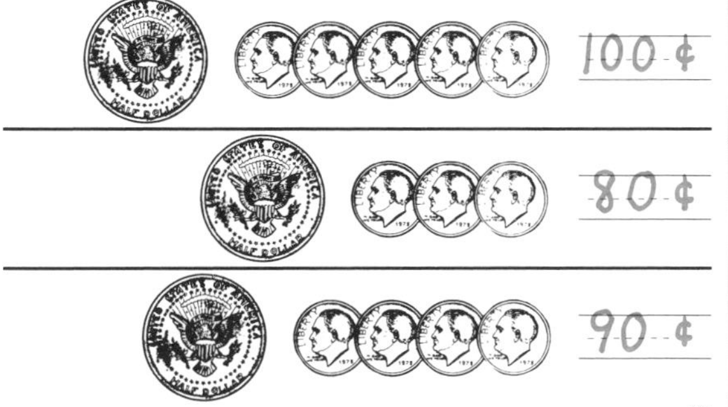

141

Blacklines

Missing Whole or Parts #15
2-Place Computation #10
Reading Problems #8

Multiply/Divide #3

After Class

1. Drill individuals with 14's and 15's flash cards.
2. **Count the odd numbers to 99.**

*3. Ask the children to bring their keys to the teaching corner.
   a. **I will say the problem on Key #2; you say the answer.**
   b. **Say the 10 times table together.**

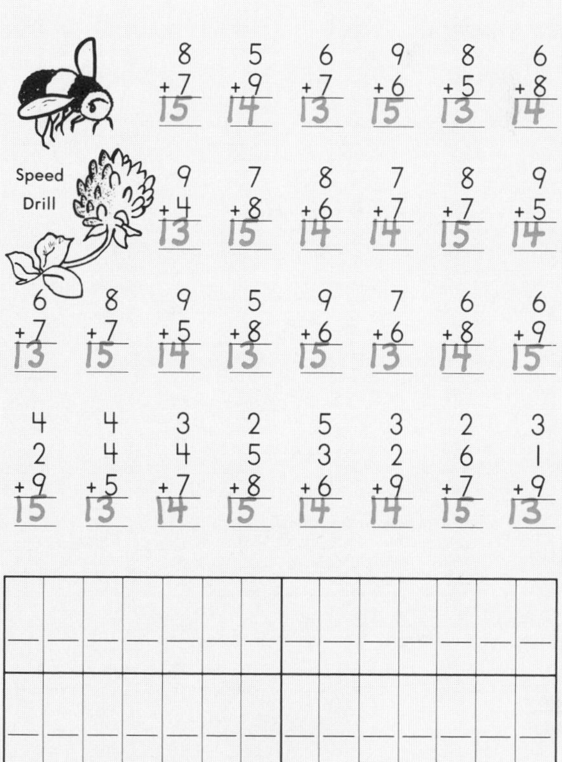

Speed Drill
8+7=15 5+9=14 6+7=13 9+6=15 8+5=13 6+8=14
9+4=13 7+8=15 8+6=14 7+7=14 8+7=15 9+5=14
6+7=13 8+7=15 9+5=14 5+8=13 9+6=15 7+6=13 6+8=14 6+9=15
4+2+9=15 4+4+5=13 3+4+7=14 2+5+8=15 5+3+6=14 3+2+9=14 2+6+7=15 3+1+9=13

"Whatsoever thy hand findeth to do, do it with thy might." Ecclesiastes 9:10

142

137

Fill in the whole and parts.

Write the facts.

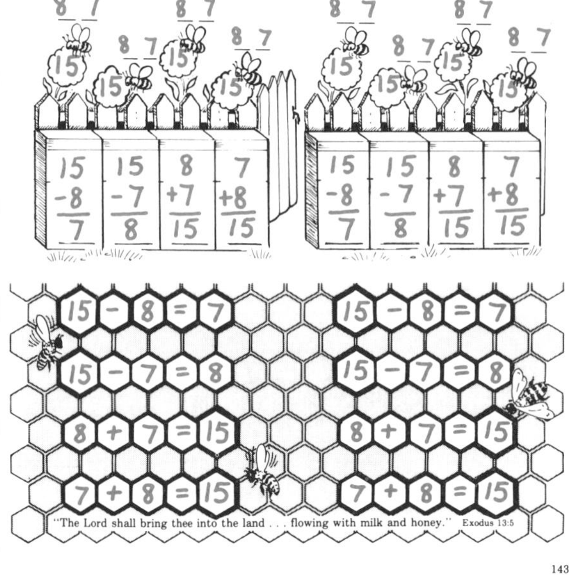

Before Class

Materials

14's and 15's flash cards

Chalkboard

(50¢) (1¢)(1¢)(1¢)(1¢) ____

(50¢) (1¢)(1¢)(1¢) ____

(50¢) (1¢)(1¢)(1¢)(1¢)(1¢)(1¢) ____

(50¢) (10¢)(10¢)(10¢) ____

(50¢) (10¢)(10¢)(10¢)(10¢)(10¢) ____

(50¢) (10¢)(10¢)(10¢)(10¢) ____

Class Time

1. Call the children to the clover patch.

(14) 9 5

   The whole number is __.
   Its parts are __ and __.
   The triplet is (14) 9 5 . . .

2. | (14) 8 6 |
   |---|

   The whole number is __.
   Its parts are __ and __.
   The triplet is (14) 8 6 . . .

3. | (14) 7 7 |
   |---|

   The whole number is __.
   Its parts are __ and __.
   The triplet is (14) 7 7 . . .

4. | (15) 9 6 |
   |---|

   The whole number is __.
   Its parts are __ and __.
   The triplet is (15) 9 6 . . .

137

Extra Activity

Answer these facts.

		15 − 7 = 8	15 − 8 = 7	7 + 6 = 13	15 − 8 = 7	15 − 7 = 8	15 − 9 = 6
14 − 8 = 6	15 − 8 = 7	8 + 7 = 15	5 + 8 = 13	15 − 8 = 7	7 + 8 = 15	14 − 7 = 7	15 − 7 = 8
15 − 8 = 7	13 − 4 = 9	5 + 7 = 12	15 − 6 = 9	6 + 7 = 13	4 + 8 = 12	15 − 6 = 9	6 + 8 = 14
5 + 9 = 14	9 + 4 = 13	15 − 8 = 7	5 + 8 = 13	14 − 5 = 9	13 − 6 = 7	8 + 5 = 13	15 − 8 = 7
14 − 6 = 8	14 − 9 = 5	13 − 5 = 8	15 − 8 = 7	6 + 9 = 15	15 − 7 = 8	13 − 8 = 5	7 + 7 = 14
9 + 5 = 14	13 − 7 = 6	7 + 8 = 15	9 + 6 = 15	15 − 8 = 7	8 + 7 = 15	15 − 9 = 6	15 − 7 = 8

144

5. (15) 8 7

   The whole number is __.
   Its parts are __ and __.
   The triplet is (15) 8 7 . . .

6. Flash the 14's and 15's cards for 1 minute.
   Answer together.

7. Point to the Blossom Charts.
   Say the 11 triplets 1 time.
   . . . 12 triplets 2 times.
   . . . 13 triplets 3 times.
   . . . 14 triplets 4 times.
   . . . 15 triplets 5 times.

8. Review
   60 minutes=__. 1 hour
   30 minutes=__. ½ hour
   12 things=__. 1 dozen
   6 things=__. ½ dozen
   7 days=__. 1 week
   12 months=__. 1 year
   12 inches=__. 1 foot
   3 feet=__. 1 yard.

9. Do the Money samples.

10. Assign Lesson 137.

Read the story.
Write the numbers in the beehive.
Write the label words on the lines.
Answer the problem.

137

Mother made one dozen pies. She took 8 pies to an all-day church meeting. How many pies did she have left?

12 pies
−8 pies
4 pies

Lois makes 18 cookies to look like rabbits. Fay makes 27 cookies to look like ducks. How many cookies do both girls make?

18 cookies
+27 cookies
45 cookies

70 ¢

100 ¢

90 ¢

145

Count the half dollars and dimes.
Write the amount.

Blacklines

Triplets With Facts #12
Number Triplets #5
Fact Form VIII

Multiply/Divide #3

After Class

1. Chalkboard Drill: **Write the answer as quickly as you can!**

6+9	**13−7**	**6+8**	**7+8**
14−8	**15−8**	**15−7**	**8+6**
15−9	**9+6**	**7+7**	**15−6**
8+7	**7+6**	**14−9**	**14−6**

*2. Ask each child to bring his keys to the teaching corner.
Review the 2 and 10 times tables.

Extra Activity

Job 28:10

If it's **1** child on a swing
Or **15** bees on wing,
"his eye seeth every precious thing."

If it's **300** busy ants
Or **400** tiny plants,
"his eye seeth every precious thing."

15 − 8 = 7   15 − 7 = 8   8 + 7 = 15   7 + 8 = 15

15 − 9 = 6   15 − 6 = 9   9 + 6 = 15   6 + 9 = 15

146

Unit 5

Lessons 138–170

138

Trace and write the whole and parts.

Trace, answer, and write the facts.

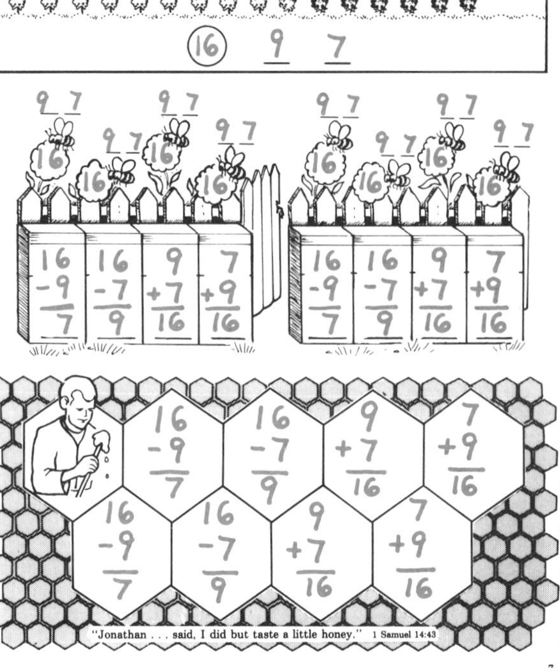
138
16 9 7
"Jonathan . . . said, I did but taste a little honey." 1 Samuel 14:43
7

Before Class

Make (16) 9 7 flash cards for each child.

Tack (16) 9 7 flash cards above the clover patch in this order:

16	16	9	7
−9	−7	+7	+9
7	9	16	16

Chalkboard

478	648	256	285	317	749
+276	+237	+539	+568	+478	+235

 ___

 ___

 ___

 ___

Class Time

1. Call the children to the Number Line.
   Count by 10's. Begin at
   •1 1, 11 . . .
   •2 2, 12 . . .
   •3 3, 13 . . .
   . . . 4 . . . 5 . . . 6 . . . 7 . . . 8 . . . 9
2. Stand near the clover patch.

(16) 9 7

   a. **How many pink clovers are in the patch?** 10
   We think—10 pink.
   6 more make __ altogether. 16
   We think—10 pink.
   1 less makes __ clovers with bees. 9

   b. **16 clovers in the patch;**
   16 is the whole number.
   What part of the 16 has bees? 9
   What part of the 16 has no bees? 7
   16 is the whole number.
   Its parts are 9 and 7.

138

Speed Drill

Answer these facts.

16 -9 7	16 -7 9	16 -9 7	9 +7 16	7 +9 16	16 -7 9	16 -9 7	9 +7 16
16 -7 9	16 -9 7	9 +7 16	16 -7 9	16 -9 7	7 +9 16	16 -7 9	9 +7 16
16 -7 9	16 -9 7	7 +9 16	16 -9 7	16 -7 9	9 +7 16	7 +9 16	16 -9 7
16 -9 7	16 -7 9	16 -7 9	7 +9 16	9 +7 16	16 -9 7	7 +9 16	16 -7 9
16 -9 7	16 -7 9	16 -9 7	16 -9 7	7 +9 16	16 -7 9	16 -9 7	7 +9 16
		16 -7 9	9 +7 16	16 -9 7	16 -9 7	16 -7 9	16 -9 7

8

c. **The triplet is (16) 9 7 . . .**

d. **The facts are 16−9, 7; 16−7, 9; 9+7, 16; 7+9, 16 . . .**

3. **Say the triplets as I fill the clover and bees.**
4. Point to the flash cards again. **Say the triplet and then the answer.**
5. Do the Addition samples.
6. Do the Money samples.
7. Do the Speed Drill in Lesson 138.
8. Assign Lesson 138.

Note: Make Blossom 16 Chart for Lesson 139.

Note: If you are teaching multiplication and division, prepare Key #4 for Lesson 139.

Answer these problems.
Carry *over* in one or two places.

138

578	328	247	486	157	458
+267	+596	+128	+369	+608	+184
845	924	375	855	765	642

463	475	246	357	157	138
+288	+169	+248	+394	+488	+356
751	644	494	751	645	494

259	228	579	127	266	459
+383	+537	+276	+248	+658	+386
642	765	855	375	924	845

Count the half dollars and pennies.
Write the amount.

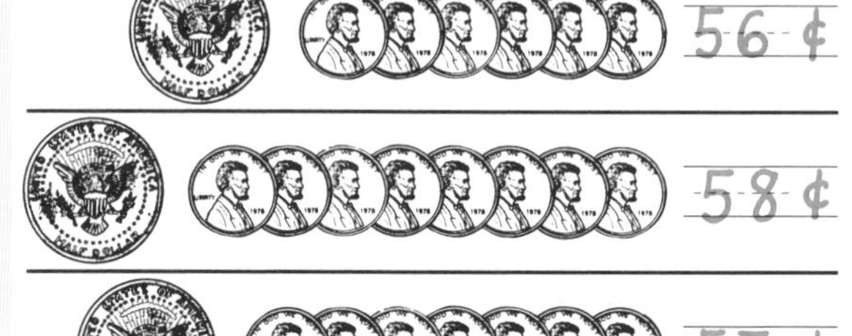

56¢

58¢

57¢

9

Blacklines

Fact Hives #26
Number Words #7
Fact Form VIII
Money Identification #7

Multiply/Divide #3

After Class

1. Give each child his (16) 9 7 flash cards.
2. Chalkboard Drill: **Write the three numbers I say.**

   524 542 452

   Circle the greatest number.

   609 601 610

   Circle the smallest number.

   1,450 1,504 1,540

   Circle the smallest number.

   1,800 1,080 1,808

   Circle the greatest number.

*3. a. **Say the 2 times table by memory.**
   b. **Say the 10 times table by memory.**

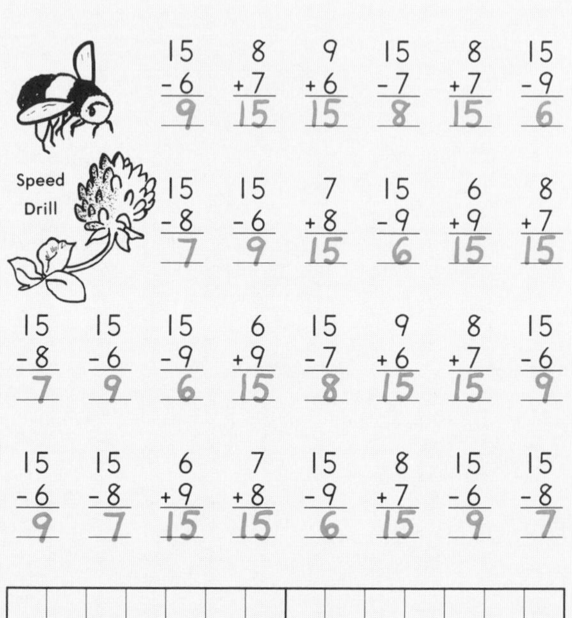

Speed Drill
15 − 6 = 9, 8 + 7 = 15, 9 + 6 = 15, 15 − 7 = 8, 8 + 7 = 15, 15 − 9 = 6
15 − 8 = 7, 15 − 6 = 9, 7 + 8 = 15, 15 − 9 = 6, 6 + 9 = 15, 8 + 7 = 15
15 − 8 = 7, 15 − 6 = 9, 15 − 9 = 6, 6 + 9 = 15, 15 − 7 = 8, 9 + 6 = 15, 8 + 7 = 15, 15 − 6 = 9
15 − 6 = 9, 15 − 8 = 7, 6 + 9 = 15, 7 + 8 = 15, 15 − 9 = 6, 8 + 7 = 15, 15 − 6 = 9, 15 − 8 = 7

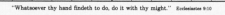

"Whatsoever thy hand findeth to do, do it with thy might." Ecclesiastes 9:10

10

139

Fill in the whole and parts.

Trace, answer, and write the facts.

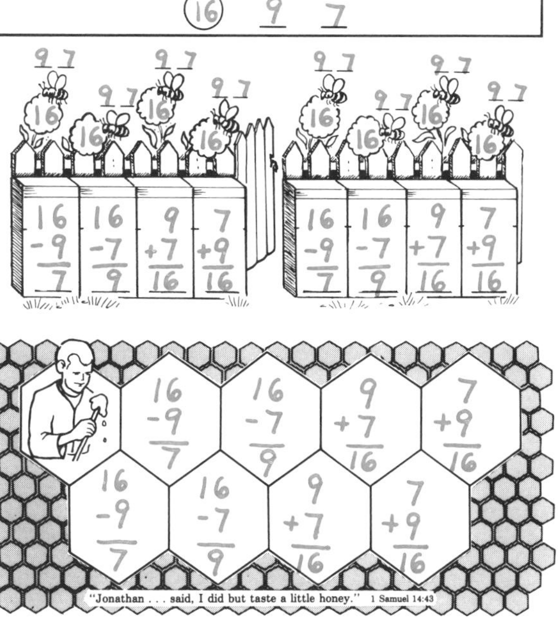
"Jonathan . . . said, I did but taste a little honey." 1 Samuel 14:43

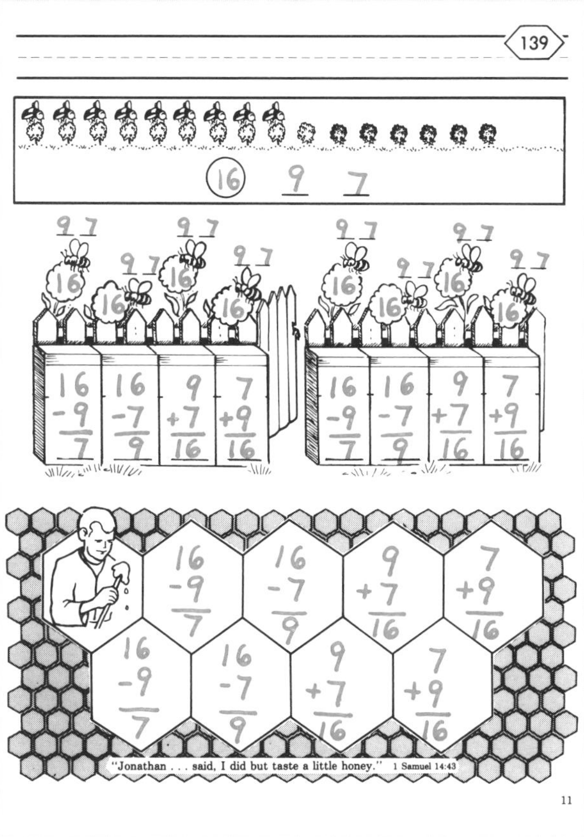

Before Class

Tack bee (16) 9 7 on Blossom 16 Chart. Mount it on the wall.

Materials

15's and 16's flash cards

11's–16's flash cards

Chalkboard

74	80	76	65	48	89	84
−27	−59	+79	−57	+97	+56	−58

50¢
1¢

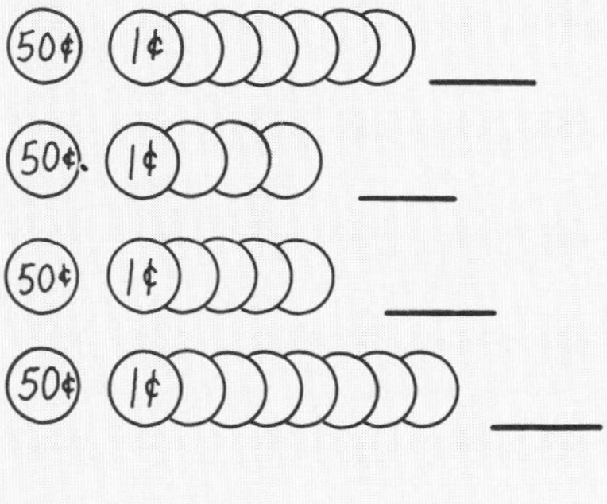

50¢ 1¢ ◯◯◯ ____

50¢ 1¢ ◯◯◯◯ ____

50¢ 1¢ ◯◯◯◯◯◯◯ ____

Class Time

1. Call the children to the clover patch.

(16) 9 7

   16 clovers in the patch;
   16 is the whole number.
   What part of the 16 has bees? 9
   What part of the 16 has no bees? 7
   16 is the whole number.
   Its parts are 9 and 7.

   a. **The triplet is (16) 9 7 . . .**
   b. **The facts are 16−9, 7 . . .**

2. Drill each triplet on the Blossom Charts.
3. **Can we say the triplets by memory?**
4. Flash the 15's and 16's cards. **Say the triplet and then the answer.**
5. Do the Computation samples.
6. Do the Money samples.

139

Answer these facts.

Extra Activity

16 -7 9	16 -9 7	16 -7 9	9 +7 16	7 +9 16	16 -7 9	16 -9 7	9 +7 16
16 -7 9	16 -9 7	7 +9 16	16 -7 9	16 -9 7	7 +9 16	16 -7 9	16 -9 7
16 -9 7	16 -7 9	9 +7 16	16 -7 9	16 -7 9	9 +7 16	7 +9 16	16 -9 7
16 -9 7	16 -7 9	16 -7 9	7 +9 16	9 +7 16	16 -9 7	16 -9 7	16 -7 9
16 -9 7	16 -7 9	16 -9 7	16 -9 7	7 +9 16	16 -7 9	16 -9 7	7 +9 16
		16 -7 9	9 +7 16	16 -9 7	16 -9 7	16 -7 9	16 -9 7

12

7. **Answer together.**
   Half of 2 is __. Continue with half of 8, 6, 10, 12, 14, 20, 40, 60, 100.
8. Assign Lesson 139.

139

Answer these problems; carry *over* or borrow *back*.

85 −28 = 57	56 +87 = 143	84 −56 = 28	84 −35 = 49	67 +78 = 145	85 −38 = 47
68 +85 = 153	95 −49 = 46	46 +79 = 125	74 −28 = 46	76 +77 = 153	87 +38 = 125
76 +67 = 143	94 −37 = 57	95 −46 = 49	95 −67 = 28	73 −26 = 47	76 +69 = 145

Count the half dollars and pennies.
Write the amount.

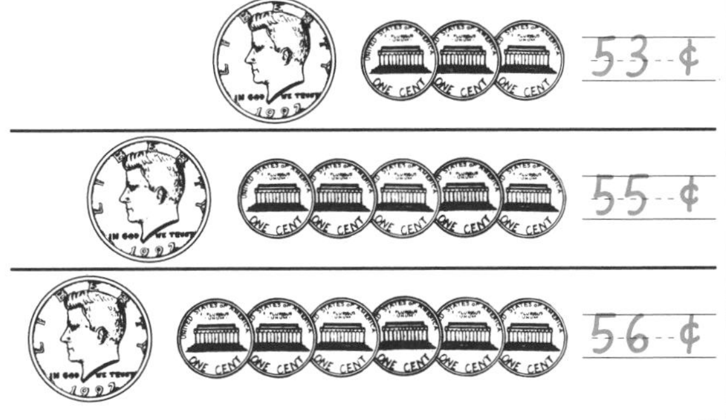

13

Blacklines

Fact Hives #26

Mixed Computation #5

2-Place Computation #10

Divide Form

After Class

__	124	126	__	__	__
35	__	__	__	75	__
__	600	__	800	__	__
48	__	68	__	__	__

1. Double Drill: 11's–16's flash cards. **Whoever says the answer first may have the card.**
2. Fill in the Missing Number samples.

*3. Have each child bring his keys to the teaching corner. Distribute Key #4.
   a. **Follow as I read the problems.**
   b. **Read the problems with me.**
   0 divided into 10=0
   10 divided into 10=1
   20 divided into 10=2 . . .

Extra Activity
If it's 1 child on a swing
Or 16 bees on wing,
"his eye seeth every precious thing."
Job 28:10
If it's 500 hives at night
Or 600 starbeams bright,
"his eye seeth every precious thing."
16 −9 = 7
16 −7 = 9
9 +7 = 16
7 +9 = 16
16

14

140

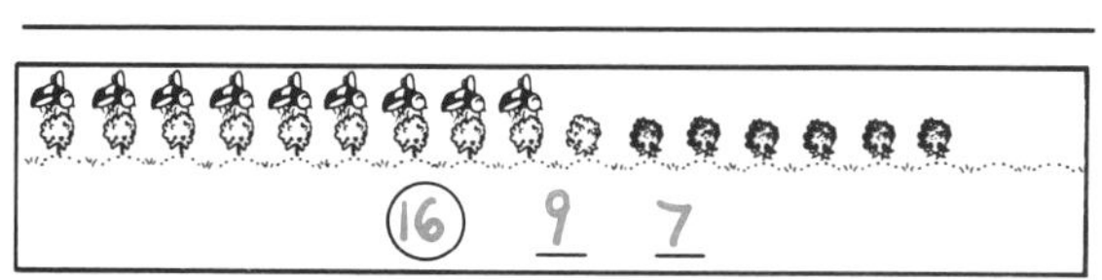
140
(16) 9 7

Fill in the whole and parts.

Trace, answer, and write the facts.

"Jonathan . . . said, I did but taste a little honey." 1 Samuel 14:43

15

Before Class

Materials

Large clock

Chalkboard

169	89	168	57	85	168	159
−72	+67	−95	+99	+78	−92	−87

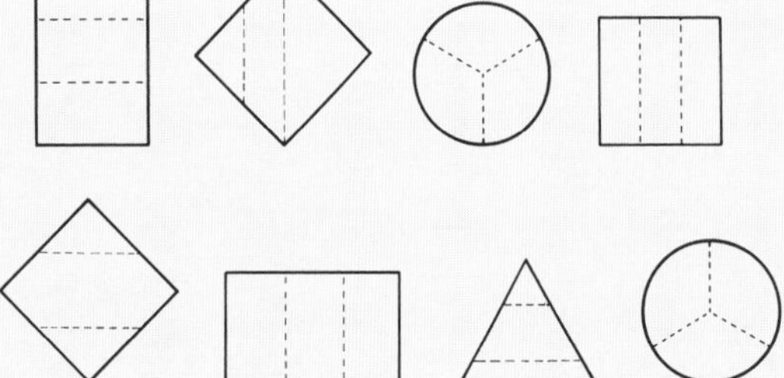

Class Time

1. Have each child bring *My 1,000 Book* to the teaching corner. Begin at 500.
   a. **Count by 5's to 700.**
   b. **Count on to 1,000 by 10's.**
2. Stand near the clover patch.

   (16) 9 7

   16 clovers in the patch;
   16 is the whole number.
   What part of the 16 has bees? 9
   What part of the 16 has no bees? 7
   16 is the whole number.
   Its parts are 9 and 7.
   a. **The triplet is (16) 9 7 . . .**
   b. **The facts are 16−9, 7 . . .**
3. Drill the 13, 14, 15, and 16 triplets.
4. Do the Computation samples.

140

Speed Drill

Answer these problems.
Carry *over* in some problems.

168 − 97 = 71	58 + 77 = 135	169 − 74 = 95	168 − 96 = 72	73 + 86 = 159	169 − 76 = 93
76 + 79 = 155	169 − 72 = 97	68 + 77 = 145	166 − 94 = 72	72 + 86 = 158	167 − 94 = 73
78 + 77 = 155	169 − 77 = 92	168 − 94 = 74	76 + 83 = 159	167 − 75 = 92	57 + 38 = 95
168 − 95 = 73	83 + 75 = 158	168 − 96 = 72	87 + 58 = 145	167 − 70 = 97	67 + 88 = 155
166 − 73 = 93	84 + 75 = 159	167 − 95 = 72	167 − 72 = 95	77 + 58 = 135	169 − 98 = 71
		75 + 84 = 159	169 − 95 = 74	167 − 75 = 92	67 + 88 = 155

16

5. Introduce ⅓.
   a. **Name two fractions.** ½ and ¼
   b. Write ⅓.
      One third is a __. fraction
      1 whole cut __. into 3 equal parts
   c. Have the children say ⅓ as they fill the shapes.
6. Hold the large clock.
   Read the time.
   5:45, 6:15, 7:30, 10:45, 12:45 . . .
7. Do the Speed Drill in Lesson 140.
8. Assign Lesson 140.

Write the time.

Read the story.
Write the numbers in the beehive.
Write the label words on the lines.
Answer the problem.

Lee has 37¢ in his bank. Grandfather gives him 58¢ for his birthday. How many cents does Lee have now?

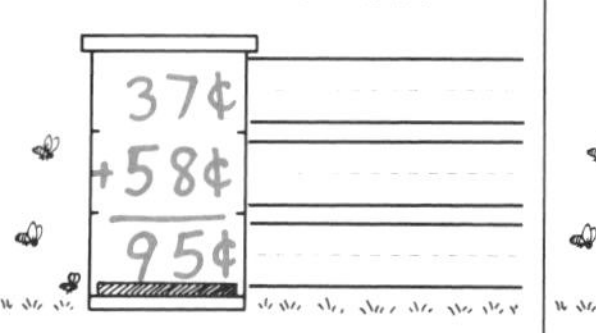

Fifteen children play tag. Eight children are on base. How many children are not on base?

17

Blacklines

Fact Hives #27

Missing Whole or Parts #16

Number Facts #16

Divide Form

Multiply/Divide #4

After Class

1. Have individuals say the triplets by memory.
2. Chalkboard Drill: **Listen. Then write the number that comes next.**

135, 140, 145, __
260, 270, 280, __
22, 32, 42, __
68, 78, 88, __
21, 23, 25, __
53, 55, 57, __
134, 133, 132, __
278, 277, 276, __

*3. Have each child bring his keys to the teaching corner. Practice Key #4.

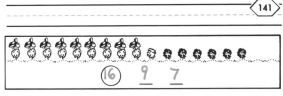

Fill in the whole and parts.

Write the facts.

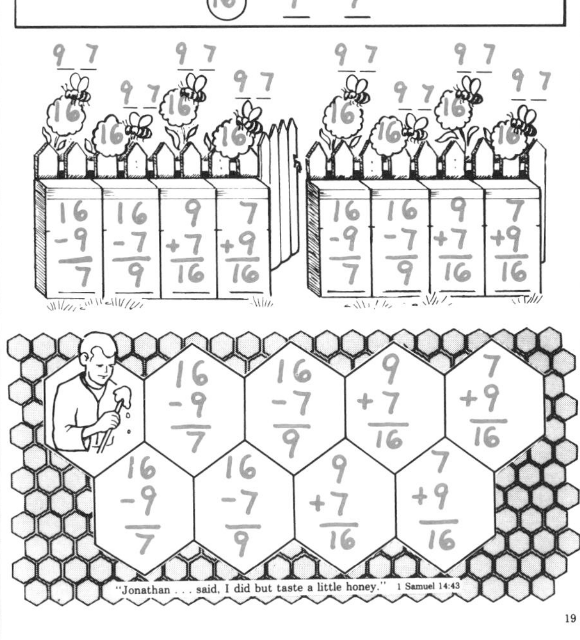

141
(16) 9 7
16 -9 7
16 -7 9
9 +7 16
7 +9 16
"Jonathan . . . said, I did but taste a little honey." 1 Samuel 14:43
19

Before Class

Materials

15's and 16's flash cards

Large coins

13's–16's flash cards

Chalkboard

50¢ 10¢ ◯ ◯ ____

25¢ ◯ ◯ 1¢ + ____

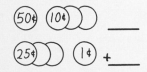

25¢ ◯ 10¢ ◯ ◯ ◯ ____

50¢ 1¢ ◯ ◯ ◯ ◯ ◯ ◯ ◯ ◯ ◯ + ____
(10)

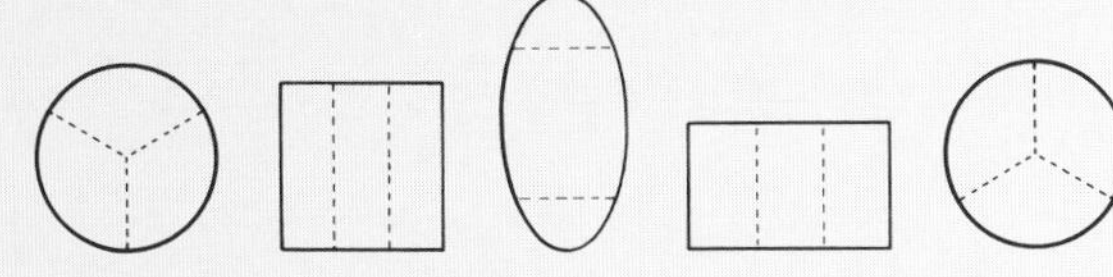

Class Time

1. Call the children to the clover patch.

(15) 9 6

   The whole number is __.
   Its parts are __ and __.
   a. **The triplet is (15) 9 6 . . .**
   b. **The facts are 15−9, 6 . . .**

2. | (15) 8 7 |
   |---|

   The whole number is __.
   Its parts are __ and __.
   a. **The triplet is (15) 8 7 . . .**
   b. **The facts are 15−8, 7 . . .**

3. | (16) 9 7 |
   |---|

   The whole number is __.
   Its parts are __ and __.
   a. **The triplet is (16) 9 7 . . .**
   b. **The facts are 16−9, 7 . . .**

141

Count the first row.
  Write the amount.
Count the second row.
  Write the amount.
Add.
Then copy the answer into
  the dollar box.

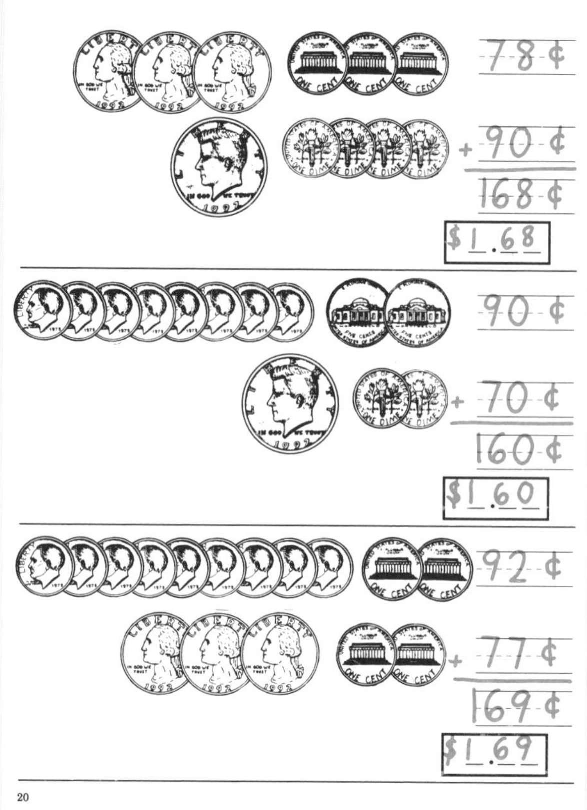

Extra Activity

4. Flash the 15's and 16's cards. **Say the triplet and then the answer.**
5. Point to the Blossom Charts. **Jump from chart to chart. (11) 9 2; (12) 9 3 . . .**
   Drill all the triplets.
6. Review Money.
   a. Flash the coins. **Dime, 10¢; half dollar, 50¢ . . .**
   b. **Can you name the man on each coin?**
   c. Do the Money samples.
7. a. **One-third is a __.** fraction
   One whole cut __. into 3 equal parts
   b. Do the samples.
8. Assign Lesson 141.

Note: If you are teaching multiplication and division, prepare Key #5 for Lesson 142.

Answer these problems.

Borrow *back* in some problems.

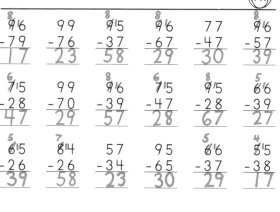

96 − 79 = 17	99 − 76 = 23	95 − 37 = 58	96 − 67 = 29	77 − 47 = 30	96 − 57 = 39
75 − 28 = 47	99 − 70 = 29	96 − 39 = 57	75 − 47 = 28	95 − 28 = 67	66 − 39 = 27
65 − 26 = 39	84 − 26 = 58	57 − 34 = 23	95 − 65 = 30	66 − 37 = 29	55 − 38 = 17

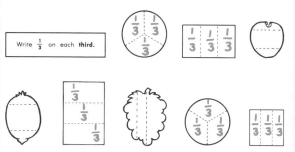

Write $\frac{1}{3}$ on each **third.**

21

Blacklines

Fact Hives #27

Triplets With Facts #13

Equations #1

Divide Form

Multiply/Divide #4

After Class

1. Circle Drill: 13's–16's flash cards.
2. Ask individuals to name the 12 months of the year. Begin at January, April, or September.

*3. Have each child bring his keys to the teaching corner.
   a. **Say the 10 times table together.**
   b. Key #4. **I will say the problem; you say the answer.**

Extra Activity
Job 28:10
If it's 1 child on a swing
Or 16 bees on wing,
"his eye seeth every precious thing."
If it's 500 hives at night
Or 600 starbeams bright,
"his eye seeth every precious thing."
16 − 9 = 7
16 − 7 = 9
9 + 7 = 16
7 + 9 = 16
16
22

142

Fill in the whole and parts.

16 9 7

Write the facts.

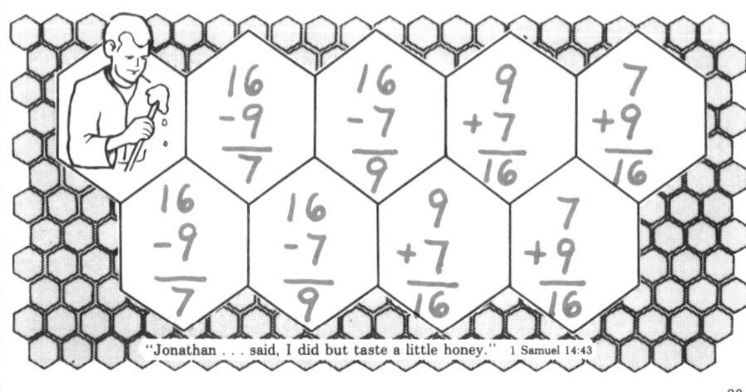
"Jonathan . . . said, I did but taste a little honey." 1 Samuel 14:43

23

Before Class

Materials

11's–16's flash cards

Chalkboard

53	74	36	65	67
24	55	43	93	12
+29	+ 7	+56	+ 7	+75

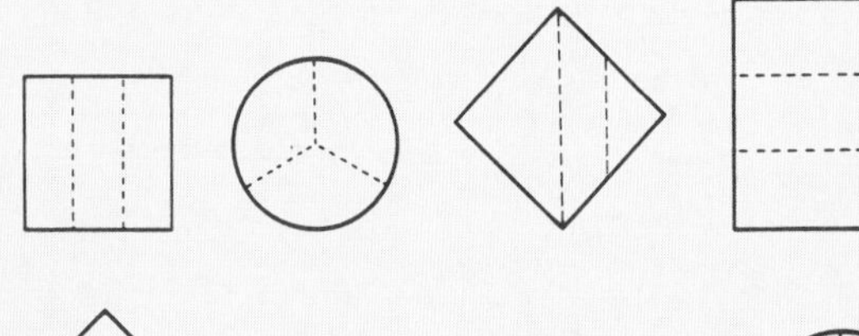

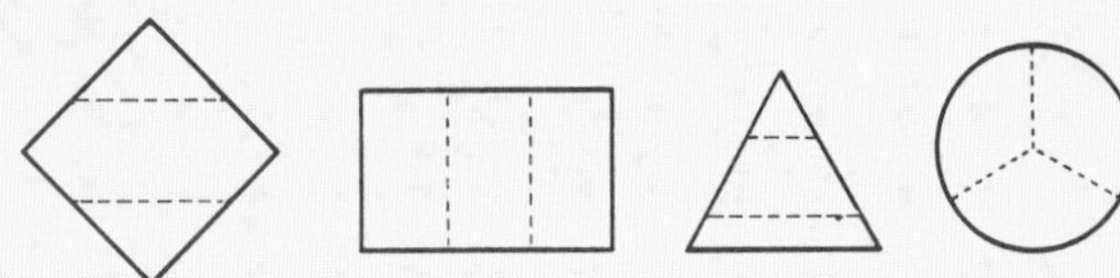

Class Time

1. Call the children to the Blossom Charts.

   When night comes, the clover blossoms close and the bees rest in the hive.

   But the skunk rested all day. When night comes, he is hungry for a tasty treat—honeybees. Quietly he walks to the hive. He stops and looks around. Is the beekeeper watching? Then up goes one front foot. Out come sharp claws. *Scratch, Scratch!* His claws scratch on the hive and waken the bees.

   ***Buzz-z-z!* Angry bees fly out.**

   ***Snap, smack!* The skunk catches the bees in his mouth and swallows them.**

2. Drill the triplets.
   a. 11 and 12 triplets 1 time
      13 and 14 triplets 2 times
      15 and 16 triplets 3 times
   b. **Say the triplets by memory.**

142

Speed Drill

Fill in the missing whole or parts.

9 + 7 = 16	16 - 9 = 7	16 - 7 = 9
7 + 9 = 16	7 + 9 = 16	7 + 9 = 16
16 - 9 = 7	16 - 9 = 7	16 - 9 = 7
16 - 7 = 9	16 - 7 = 9	16 - 7 = 9
7 + 9 = 16	7 + 9 = 16	7 + 9 = 16
16 - 9 = 7	9 + 7 = 16	16 - 9 = 7

Answer these problems.

5	4	2	4	5	1	1	2
4	3	7	2	3	8	6	5
+7	+9	+7	+7	+7	+7	+9	+9
16	16	16	13	15	16	16	16

6	7	6	4	3	5	7	4
3	2	3	5	4	2	2	4
+6	+5	+7	+7	+9	+9	+2	+6
15	14	16	16	16	16	11	14

24

3. Flash the 11's–16's cards.
   Answer together. Can you answer all of them in 1 minute?
4. Do the Column Addition samples.
5. a. **One-third is a __.** fraction
   One whole cut __. into 3 equal parts
   Three thirds make __. 1 whole.
   b. Do the samples.
6. Do the Speed Drill in Lesson 142.
7. Assign Lesson 142.

Answer these facts.

9	16	15	6	16	9	14	16
+7	-7	-9	+9	-9	+6	-5	-7
16	9	6	15	7	15	9	9

15	9	15	8	16	7	7	15
-8	+7	-7	+7	-9	+9	+8	-7
7	16	8	15	7	16	15	8

16	15	6	16	7	15	15	7
-7	-6	+9	-9	+8	-9	-6	+9
9	9	15	7	15	6	9	16

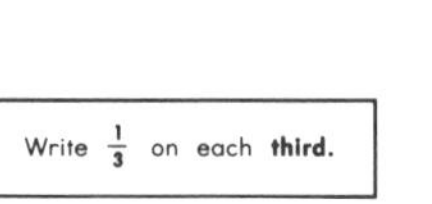

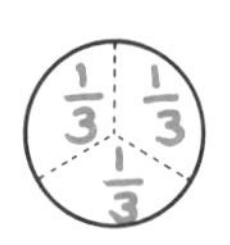
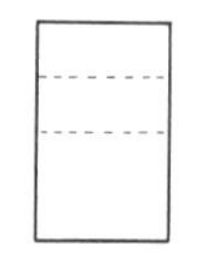

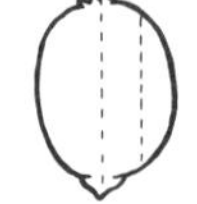
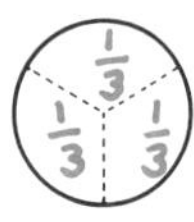

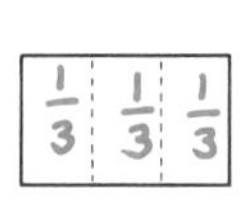

25

Blacklines

Fact Hives #27

Missing Whole or Parts #16

Number Facts #16

Multiply Form

After Class

What is the sum of 9 and 7?
What is the sum of 6 and 8?
What is the sum of 7 and 8?
What is the sum of 56 and 27?

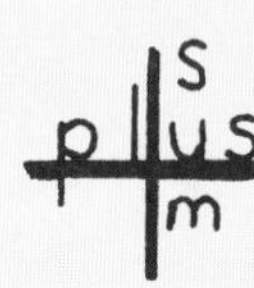

1. Review

53+10	36+10	68+10
83+10	76−10	28+10
43−10	16−10	98−10

2. Point to the questions on the board.
   a. **What is the sum of 9 and 7?**
      Write 9+7=16 (vertically).
   b. **9 plus 7 makes 16 in all.**
      16 is the answer.
      16 is the sum.
   c. Trace the "plus-sum" diagram as you say **We add to find the sum.**
   d. Have the children finish the samples.

*3. Give each child Key #5.
   Read the 5 times table with me.
   5 times 0=0 5 times 1=5 . . .

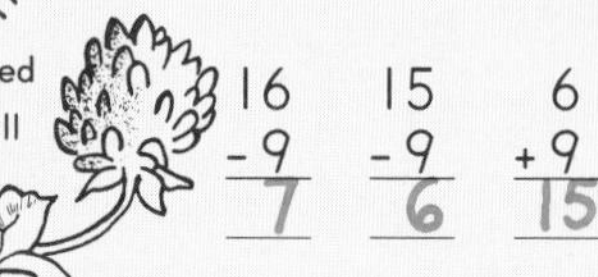

15	16	15	9	16	9
-6	-9	-9	+7	-7	+6
9	7	6	16	9	15

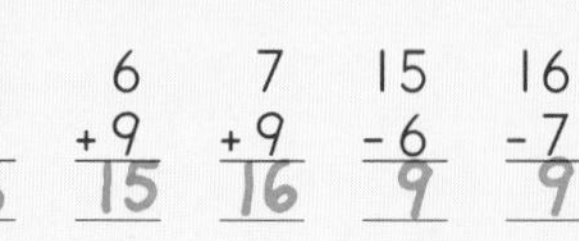

16	15	6	7	15	16
-9	-9	+9	+9	-6	-7
7	6	15	16	9	9

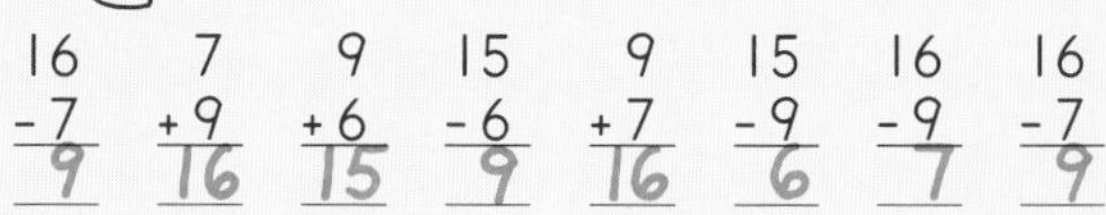

16	7	9	15	9	15	16	16
-7	+9	+6	-6	+7	-9	-9	-7
9	16	15	9	16	6	7	9

9	16	15	16	7	6	15	16
+7	-7	-6	-7	+9	+9	-9	-9
16	9	9	9	16	15	6	7

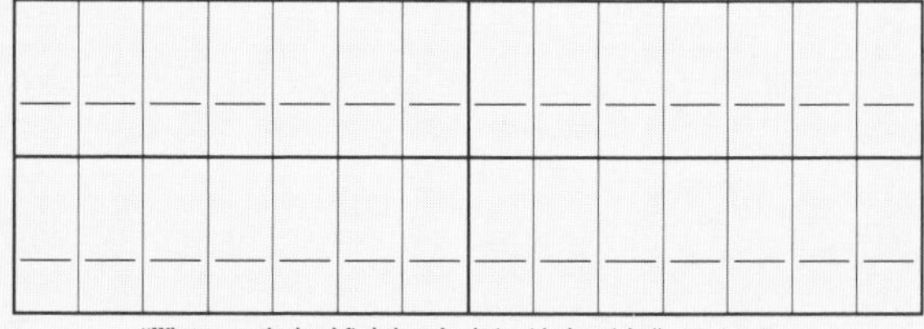

"Whatsoever thy hand findeth to do, do it with thy might." Ecclesiastes 9:10

26

143

Fill in the whole and parts.

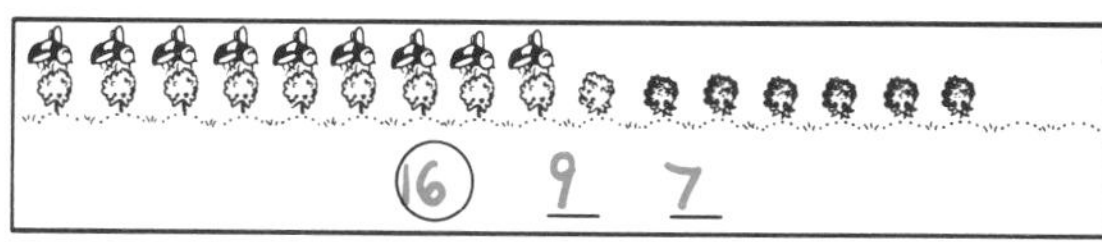

Write the facts.

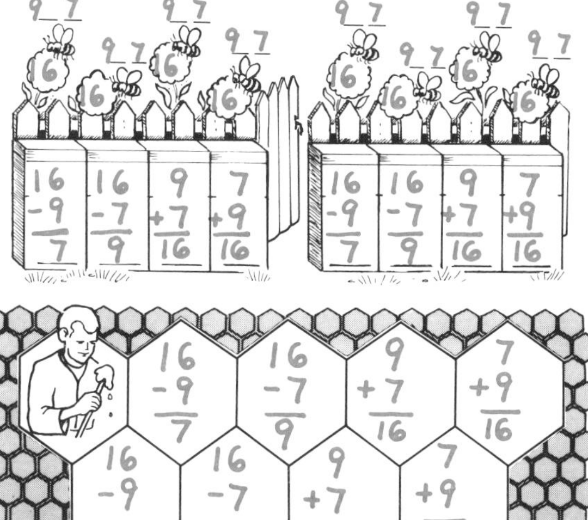

"Jonathan . . . said, I did but taste a little honey." 1 Samuel 14:43

27

Before Class

Chalkboard

45	66	58	86	86	95	59
−36	−29	+97	+79	− 7	−87	+87

Class Time

1. **Raise your hand to answer.**
   1 hour has __. 60 minutes
   ½ hour has __. 30 minutes
   1 dozen has __. 12 things
   ½ dozen has __. 6 things
   1 foot has __. 12 inches
   1 yard has __. 3 feet
   1 week has __. 7 days
   1 year has __. 12 months
2. Stand near the clover patch.
   (16) 9 7
   16 clovers in the patch;
   16 is the whole number.
   What part of the 16 has bees? 9
   What part of the 16 has no bees? 7
   16 is the whole number.
   Its parts are 9 and 7.
   a. **The triplet is (16) 9 7 . . .**
   b. Point to the first flash card.
      Close your eyes and say it 3 times.

143

Read the story.
Write the numbers in the beehive.
Write the label words on the lines.
Answer the problem.

Extra Activity

God made the sun to shine. Soon 16 buds opened. 7 buds were yellow. The rest were red. How many buds were red?

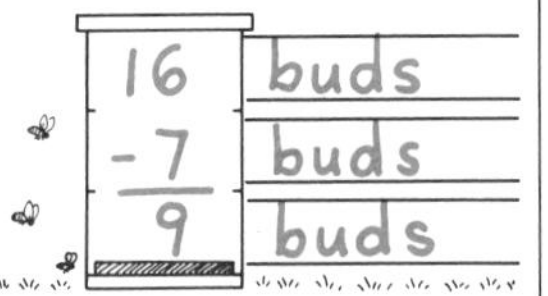

Father has one dozen stamps in his desk. He sticks 5 stamps on letters. How many stamps are left in his desk?

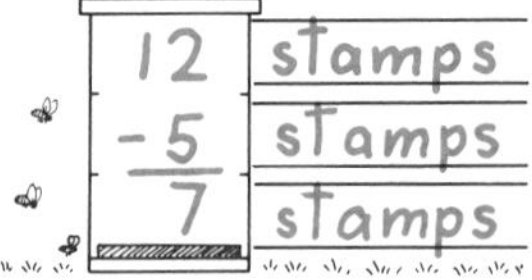

Mother pays 27¢ for a box of salt and 69¢ for a bag of nuts. How many cents does she pay for both things?

27¢
+69¢
96¢

A skunk scratched on a hive. 16 bees flew out. The skunk ate 9 of them. How many bees did the skunk not eat?

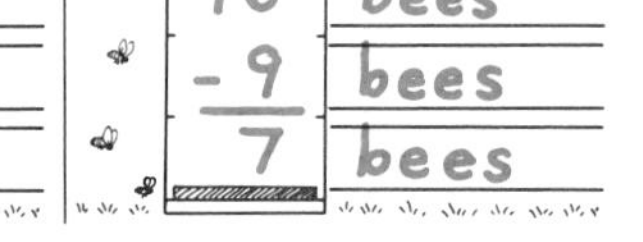

28

3. Stand near the Blossom Charts.
   Boys, say each triplet twice.
   Girls, say each triplet twice.
4. Do the Computation samples.
5. **Who can give the whole problem?**
   What is the sum of 6 and 8? 6+8=14
   What is the sum of 9 and 7? 9+7=16
   What . . . 8 and 5? 8+5=13
   What . . . 7 and 8? 7+8=15
   What . . . 9 and 6? 9+6=15
6. Assign Lesson 143.

Answer these problems; carry *over* or borrow *back*.

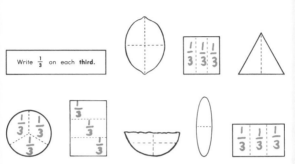

66 − 59 = 7	57 + 88 = 145	86 − 57 = 29	85 − 37 = 48	66 + 79 = 145	65 − 28 = 37
89 + 67 = 156	66 − 47 = 19	67 + 99 = 166	95 − 76 = 19	76 + 79 = 155	57 + 99 = 156
95 − 58 = 37	94 − 37 = 57	95 − 47 = 48	96 − 67 = 29	86 − 29 = 57	76 − 69 = 7

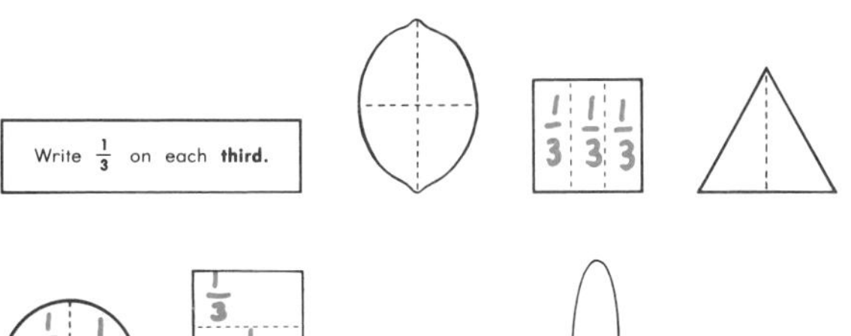

29

Blacklines

Triplets With Facts #13

Mixed Computation #5

Reading Problems #9

Multiply Form

After Class

6 +9	7 +7	15 −8	9 +6	8 +6
14 −8	16 −9	14 −5	7 +9	14 −7
9 +7	8 +7	15 −7	6 +8	14 −6
7 +8	15 −9	16 −7	9 +5	15 −6

1. Stand near the grid on the board. Drill the facts right and left, down and up. (You will use the grid in Lesson 144 too.)
2. **How many pennies are in $1.00?** Continue with nickels, dimes, quarters, and half dollars.

*3. Have each child bring his keys to the teaching corner.
   a. Review Keys #1 and #3.
   b. **Say Key #5 with me.**

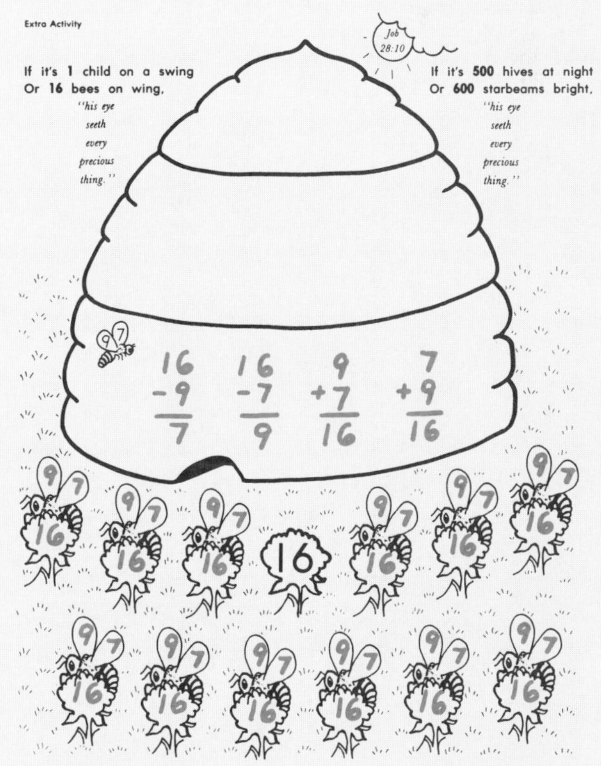

Extra Activity
Job 28:10
If it's **1** child on a swing
Or **16** bees on wing,
"his eye seeth every precious thing."
If it's **500** hives at night
Or **600** starbeams bright,
"his eye seeth every precious thing."
16 −9 = 7
16 −7 = 9
9 +7 = 16
7 +9 = 16
16
30

144

Fill in the whole and parts.

16 9 7

Write the facts.

16	16	9	7
-9	-7	+7	+9
7	9	16	16

16 - 9 = 7
16 - 7 = 9
9 + 7 = 16
7 + 9 = 16

"Jonathan . . . said, I did but taste a little honey." 1 Samuel 14:43

31

Before Class

Chalkboard

1,563	1,091
1,024	1,002
1,609	1,450
1,008	1,736
1,387	1,115

Class Time

1. Call the children to the Blossom Charts.

   In Bible times, bees did not live in hives. Sometimes they lived in hollow trees, or in holes in the ground, or in holes in the rocks.

   When Moses was old, he remembered how the Lord cared for the children of Israel. The Lord had given them butter and milk, wheat and grapes, and __ out of the rock. honey (Deuteronomy 32:13, 14)

2. Drill the triplets on the Blossom Charts.
   a. **Say each triplet once.**
   b. **Jump from chart to chart.**

3. **What belongs on the blank?**
   (Say *blank* each time.)

15, 9 __	**16 __ 7**	**__ 9, 6**
16, 9 __	**15 __ 6**	**__ 9, 7**
14, 8 __	**14 __ 5**	**__ 8, 7**
15, 8 __	**15 __ 7**	**__ 9, 5**

144

Speed Drill

Answer these facts.

16 -9 7	16 -7 9	15 -9 6	16 -7 9	9 +7 16	15 -9 6	15 -6 9	7 +9 16
9 +7 16	16 -7 9	9 +6 15	7 +9 16	15 -6 9	6 +9 15	15 -6 9	16 -9 7
16 -7 9	16 -9 7	7 +9 16	16 -9 7	6 +9 15	9 +7 16	16 -9 7	9 +6 15
6 +9 15	9 +7 16	15 -9 6	9 +6 15	16 -9 7	15 -9 6	7 +9 16	15 -6 9
16 -7 9	6 +9 15	15 -9 6	16 -9 7	9 +7 16	15 -6 9	16 -9 7	15 -9 6
		16 -7 9	7 +9 16	16 -9 7	15 -9 6	9 +6 15	15 -6 9

4. Stand near the grid on the board.
   a. **Girls, say the facts.**
      Boys, say the facts.
   b. **Answer together.**
5. Number places are **ones, tens, hundreds, (comma), thousands . . .**
   a. Read the numbers on the board.
   b. **Which number has 5 tens?** Continue with

      3 hundreds **7 hundreds**
      1 one **3 ones**
      2 tens **8 ones**
6. Do the Speed Drill in Lesson 144.
7. Assign Lesson 144.

Answer these problems.

74	52	56	24	43	45
15	37	12	44	34	32
+67	+76	+66	+97	+69	+79
156	165	134	165	146	156

35	44	61	35	54	34
43	23	95	63	43	93
+ 5	+ 9	+ 8	+ 7	+ 7	+ 9
83	76	164	105	104	136

Write $\frac{1}{3}$ on each **third.**

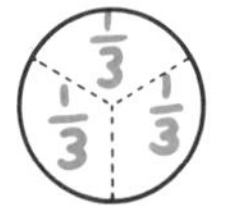

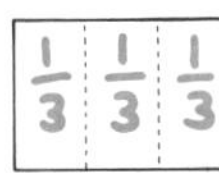

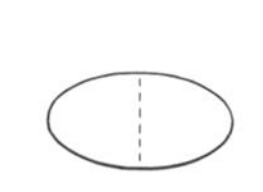

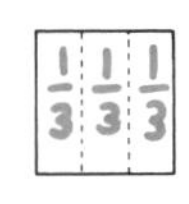

33

Blacklines

Missing Whole or Parts #16

Equations #1

Money Identification #8

Multiply Form

After Class

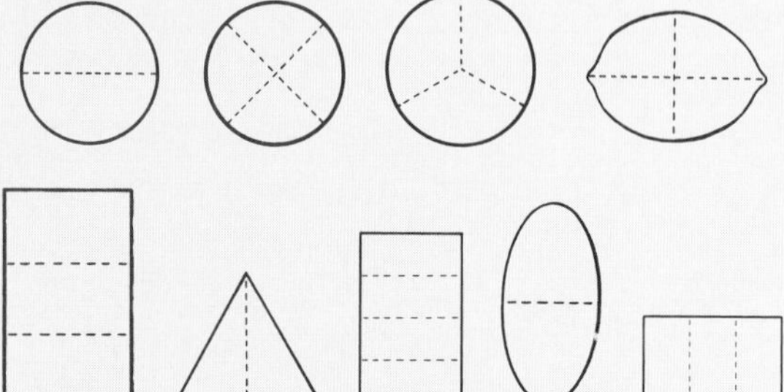

1. Drill individuals at the grid on the chalkboard.
2. Review fractions.
   a. **Give me three fractions.** ½, ¼, and ⅓
   b. Shade *one piece* in each of the first three pies as you say ½, ¼, ⅓.
   Which pie has the largest piece?
   Which pie has the smallest piece?
   c. Have the children write ½, ¼, or ⅓ in the shapes.

*3. Ask the children to bring their keys to the teaching corner.
Review Key #5.

Speed
Drill
7 +9 16
16 -7 9
15 -6 9
8 +7 15
15 -7 8
7 +9 16
7 +8 15
15 -9 6
16 -9 7
16 -7 9
15 -8 7
15 -6 9

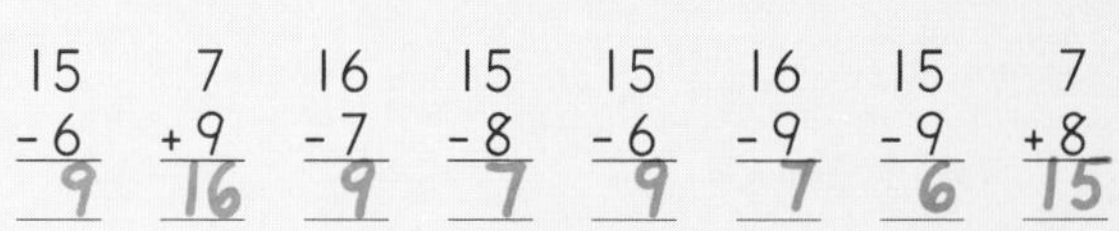

15 -6 9
7 +9 16
16 -7 9
15 -8 7
15 -6 9
16 -9 7
15 -9 6
7 +8 15

"Whatsoever thy hand findeth to do, do it with thy might." Ecclesiastes 9:10

34

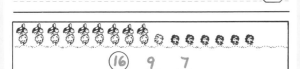

Fill in the whole and parts.

(16) 9 7

Write the facts.

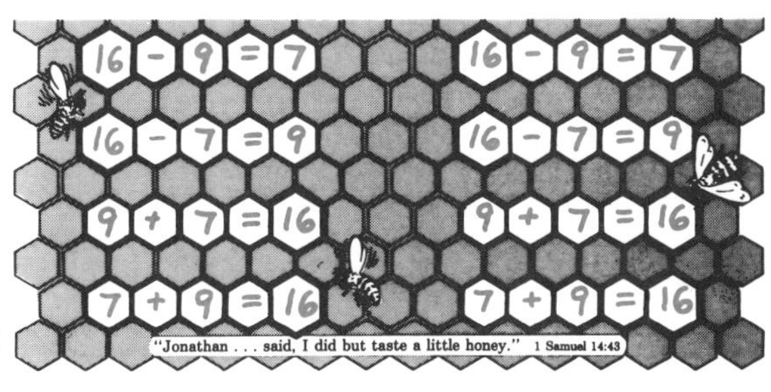

16 - 9 = 7
16 - 7 = 9
9 + 7 = 16
7 + 9 = 16
"Jonathan . . . said, I did but taste a little honey." 1 Samuel 14:43

35

Before Class

Materials

12's–16's flash cards
Form C
8's–10's flash cards

Chalkboard

259	369	285	258	346	167
+535	+557	+656	+327	+529	+479

Class Time

1. Call the children to the clover patch.

   (15) 9 6

   The whole number is __.
   Its parts are __ and __.
   The triplet is (15) 9 6 . . .

2. (15) 8 7

   The whole number is __.
   Its parts are __ and __.
   The triplet is (15) 8 7 . . .

3. (16) 9 7

   The whole number is __.
   Its parts are __ and __.
   The triplet is (16) 9 7 . . .

4. Drill the triplets on the Blossom Charts.
5. Flash the 12's–16's cards.
   Answer together.
6. Flash Card Drill: 12's–16's flash cards. Use Form C. **Flower Row: Box 1 . . .**

145

Answer these facts.

Extra Activity

16 -9 7	13 -4 9	14 -8 6	9 +7 16	9 +6 15	13 -8 5	15 -9 6	8 +6 14
14 -7 7	15 -7 8	5 +8 13	15 -6 9	13 -5 8	6 +9 15	13 -9 4	8 +5 13
16 -7 9	15 -8 7	7 +9 16	15 -9 6	14 -9 5	8 +7 15	7 +7 14	13 -7 6
14 -6 8	13 -6 7	14 -5 9	6 +7 13	7 +8 15	14 -6 8	7 +6 13	13 -9 4
16 -9 7	6 +8 14	15 -8 7	7 +9 16	9 +4 13	16 -7 9	16 -9 7	9 +5 14
		16 -7 9	4 +9 13	9 +7 16	16 -9 7	5 +9 14	16 -9 7

36

7. Do the Computation samples.
8. **If you want to find**
   - **the sum of 6 and 7, you __.**
     add
   - **how much more 15 is than 7, you __.**
     subtract
   - **how much less 6 is than 14, you __.**
     subtract
9. Assign Lesson 145.

Answer the problems.

Carry *over* in one or two places.

279	537	266	446	355	289
+367	+268	+529	+338	+449	+467
646	805	795	784	804	756
487	526	349	259	149	118
+269	+359	+355	+497	+736	+586
756	885	704	756	885	704
468	467	555	359	457	126
+337	+179	+229	+436	+299	+678
805	646	784	795	756	804

Write $\frac{1}{2}$ on each **half.**

Write $\frac{1}{4}$ on each **fourth.**

Write $\frac{1}{3}$ on each **third.**

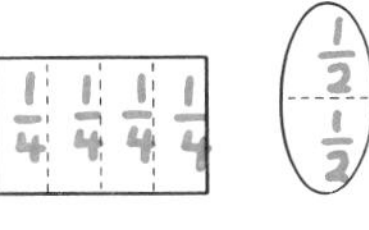

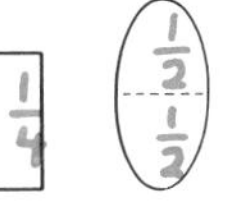

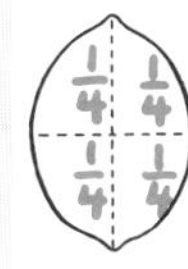

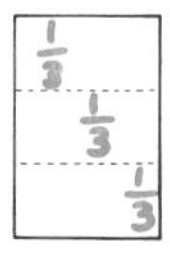

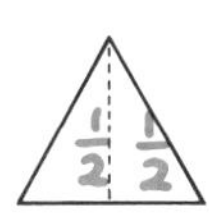

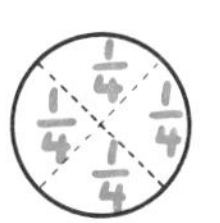

37

Blacklines

Form C (Class Time)

Triplets With Facts #13

Number Facts #16

Multiply/Divide #5

After Class

1. Review

10+3	**10+6**	**10+1**
10+9	**10+2**	**10+7**
10+4	**10+8**	**10+5**

2. Circle Drill: 8's–10's flash cards.

*3. Have each child bring his keys to the teaching corner.
   a. Review Keys #2 and #4.
   b. **Say Key #5 with me.**

Extra Activity
Job 28:10
If it's 1 child on a swing
Or 16 bees on wing,
"his eye seeth every precious thing."
If it's 500 hives at night
Or 600 starbeams bright,
"his eye seeth every precious thing."
16
-9
7
16
-7
9
9
+7
16
7
+9
16
16
38

146

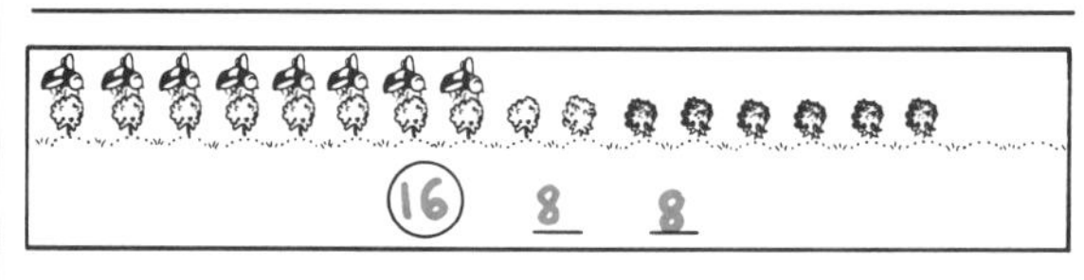

Trace and fill in the whole and parts.

Trace, answer, and write the facts.

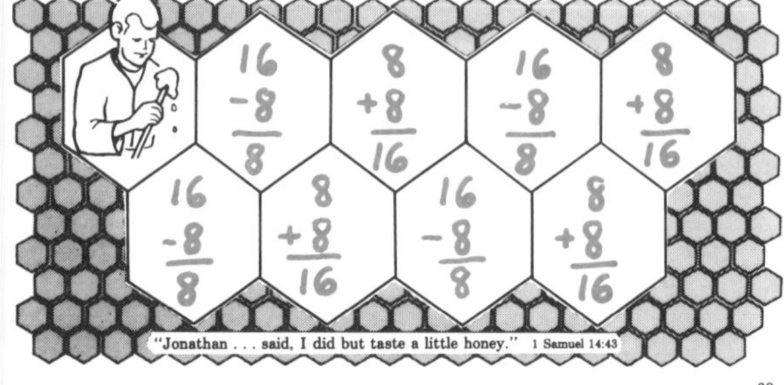

Before Class

Make (16) 8 8 flash cards for each child.

Tack (16) 8 8 flash cards above the clover patch in this order:

16	8
−8	+8
8	16

Chalkboard

59	86	95	67	96	85	87
+97	−57	−38	+78	−69	−36	+59

Class Time

1. Call the children to the Number Line for responsive counting.
   a. **Count the even numbers to 150.**
   b. **Count the odd numbers to 99.**
2. Stand near the clover patch.

   (16) 8 8

   a. **How many pink clovers are in the patch?** 10
   We think—10 pink.
   6 more make __ altogether. 16
   We think—10 pink.
   2 less make __ clovers with bees. 8
   b. **16 clovers in the patch;**
   16 is the whole number.
   What part of the 16 has bees? 8
   What part of the 16 has no bees? 8
   16 is the whole number.
   Its parts are 8 and 8.
   c. **The triplet is (16) 8 8 . . .**
   d. **The facts are 16−8, 8; 8+8, 16.**

146

Speed Drill

Answer these facts.

16 − 8 = 8	15 − 8 = 7	15 − 7 = 8	16 − 8 = 8	8 + 8 = 16	15 − 7 = 8	15 − 8 = 7	8 + 7 = 15
7 + 8 = 15	15 − 8 = 7	8 + 8 = 16	8 + 8 = 16	16 − 8 = 8	8 + 8 = 16	15 − 8 = 7	16 − 8 = 8
15 − 7 = 8	16 − 8 = 8	8 + 7 = 15	16 − 8 = 8	8 + 7 = 15	7 + 8 = 15	15 − 7 = 8	7 + 8 = 15
8 + 7 = 15	8 + 8 = 16	15 − 8 = 7	7 + 8 = 15	16 − 8 = 8	15 − 8 = 7	8 + 8 = 16	16 − 8 = 8
15 − 8 = 7	16 − 8 = 8	15 − 7 = 8	16 − 8 = 8	8 + 8 = 16	15 − 7 = 8	16 − 8 = 8	7 + 8 = 15
		8 + 7 = 15	8 + 8 = 16	16 − 8 = 8	15 − 7 = 8	16 − 8 = 8	15 − 8 = 7

40

3. **Say the triplet as I fill the clover and bees.**
4. **Say the facts as I fill the beehive.**
5. a. **Say the 13–16 triplets twice.**
   b. **Say all the triplets by memory.**
6. Do the Computation samples.
7. **Name three fractions.** ½, ¼, ⅓
   a. **One-half is 1 whole cut __.**
      into 2 equal parts
      One-fourth is 1 whole cut __.
      into 4 equal parts
      One-third is 1 whole cut __.
      into 3 equal parts
   b. **2 halves make __.** 1 whole
      4 fourths make __. 1 whole
      3 thirds make __. 1 whole
8. Do the Speed Drill in Lesson 146.
9. Assign Lesson 146.

Note: You need 1 cup and 1 pint for Lesson 147. Label each container like this:

1 cup | 1 pint

Carry *over* or borrow *back* in these problems.

86 − 48 = 38	78 + 78 = 156	95 − 88 = 7	86 − 58 = 28	67 + 89 = 156	75 − 48 = 27
88 + 58 = 146	96 − 38 = 58	96 − 29 = 67	85 − 27 = 58	57 + 89 = 146	95 − 19 = 76
66 − 39 = 27	76 + 89 = 165	96 − 68 = 28	54 − 47 = 7	87 + 78 = 165	66 − 28 = 38

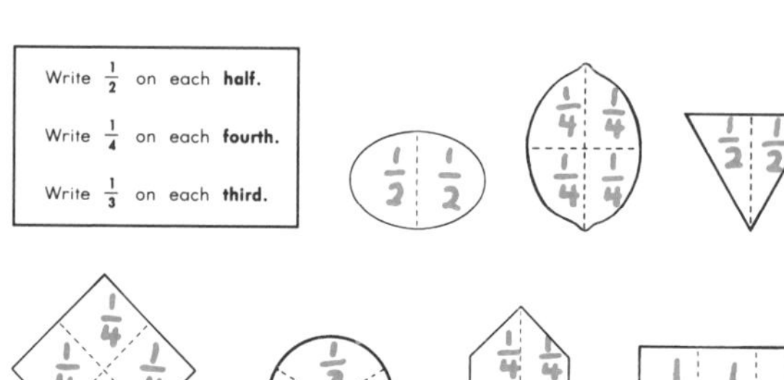

Write 1/2 on each half.
Write 1/4 on each fourth.
Write 1/3 on each third.

41

Blacklines

Fact Hives #28

Fact Form VIII

Number Words #8

Multiply/Divide #5

After Class

1. Give each child his (16) 8 8 flash cards.
2. Review
   60 minutes=__. 1 hour
   30 minutes=__. ½ hour
   12 things=__. 1 dozen
   6 things=__. ½ dozen
   7 days=__. 1 week
   12 months=__. 1 year
   12 inches=__. 1 foot
   3 feet=__. 1 yard

*3. Call the children to the teaching corner.
   a. **I will say the 10 times table; you say the answer.**
   b. **Say the 5 times table with me.**

Speed Drill
16 − 7 = 9, 15 − 9 = 6, 6 + 9 = 15, 15 − 6 = 9, 9 + 7 = 16, 14 − 9 = 5
9 + 7 = 16, 5 + 9 = 14, 16 − 9 = 7, 9 + 6 = 15, 7 + 9 = 16, 14 − 5 = 9
16 − 7 = 9, 16 − 9 = 7, 14 − 9 = 5, 7 + 9 = 16, 16 − 7 = 9, 6 + 9 = 15, 15 − 9 = 6, 15 − 6 = 9
16 − 9 = 7, 15 − 6 = 9, 16 − 7 = 9, 9 + 7 = 16, 9 + 6 = 15, 16 − 9 = 7, 9 + 5 = 14, 7 + 9 = 16

"Whatsoever thy hand findeth to do, do it with thy might." Ecclesiastes 9:10

42

147

Fill in the whole and parts.

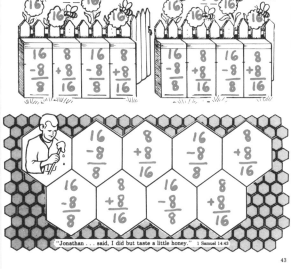

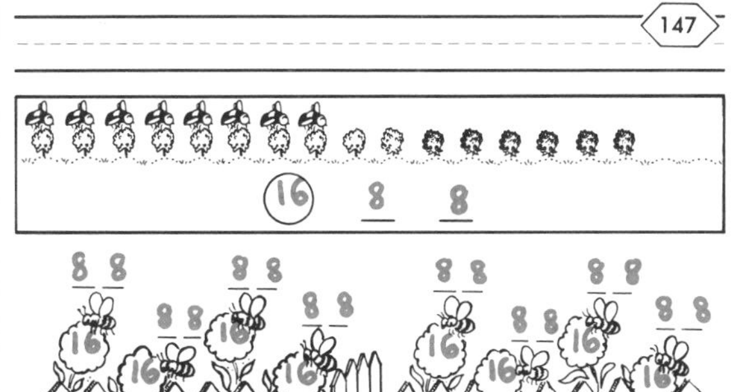

Trace, answer, and write the facts.

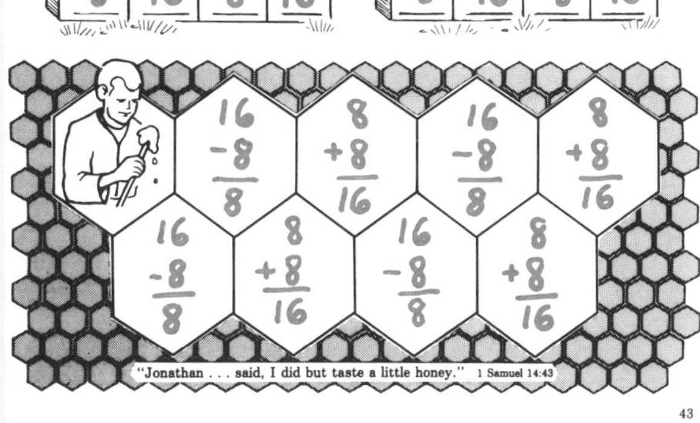

16 − 8 = 8   8 + 8 = 16   16 − 8 = 8   8 + 8 = 16

16 − 8 = 8   8 + 8 = 16   16 − 8 = 8   8 + 8 = 16

"Jonathan . . . said, I did but taste a little honey." 1 Samuel 14:43

43

Before Class

Add bee (16) 8 8 to Blossom 16 Chart.

Materials

15's and 16's flash cards

Large clock

14's–16's flash cards

1 eight-ounce cup and 1 pint

Chalkboard

77	78	169	158	59	167	76
+89	+68	−75	−93	+87	−84	+79

Class Time

1. Call the children to the clover patch.

   The twinkling stars fade when the golden sun brings daylight. The beekeeper comes to check his hive. Some bees dart out. Some bees dart in. "Where are all the bees?" he asks.

   Ah! What does he spy? Is it claw scratches on the hive? Is an enemy coming at night to feast on bees? Yes, here are his tracks in the soil. "A __ is eating the bees," says the beekeeper. skunk

2. | (16) 8 8 |
   |---|

   16 clovers in the patch;
   16 is the whole number.
   What part of the 16 has bees? 8
   What part of the 16 has no bees? 8
   16 is the whole number.
   Its parts are 8 and 8.

   a. **The triplet is (16) 8 8 . . .**

   b. **The facts are 16−8, 8 . . .**

147

Answer these problems.
Carry *over* in some problems.

169 − 87 = 82	78 + 87 = 165	169 − 84 = 85	157 − 85 = 72	73 + 86 = 159	166 − 86 = 80
78 + 78 = 156	169 − 82 = 87	83 + 85 = 168	156 − 74 = 82	72 + 86 = 158	167 − 84 = 83
78 + 78 = 156	169 − 87 = 82	158 − 84 = 74	86 + 83 = 169	167 − 85 = 82	58 + 38 = 96
168 − 85 = 83	83 + 75 = 158	158 − 76 = 82	84 + 84 = 168	167 − 80 = 87	68 + 88 = 156
164 − 84 = 80	84 + 75 = 159	158 − 86 = 72	167 − 82 = 85	77 + 88 = 165	166 − 84 = 82
		85 + 84 = 169	159 − 85 = 74	167 − 85 = 82	68 + 88 = 156

44

3. Point to the Blossom Charts.
   a. **Say each triplet once.**
   b. **Jump from chart to chart.**
   (11) 9 2; (12) 9 3 . . .
4. Flash the 15's and 16's cards. **Say the triplet; then say the answer.**
5. Do the Computation samples.
6. Hold the large clock. **Read the time. 12:15, 1:30, 2:45, 4:00, 5:15, 6:30, 7:45 . . .**
7. Assign Lesson 147.

Note: If you are teaching multiplication and division, prepare Key #6 for Lesson 148.

Write the time.

Write $\frac{1}{2}$ on each **half.**

Write $\frac{1}{4}$ on each **fourth.**

Write $\frac{1}{3}$ on each **third.**

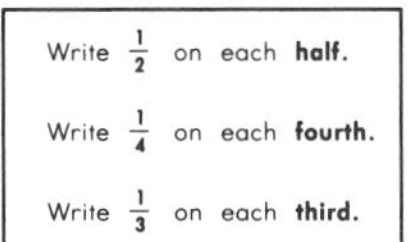

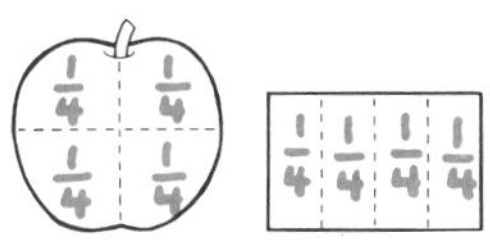

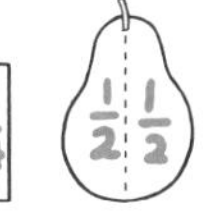

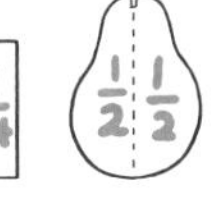

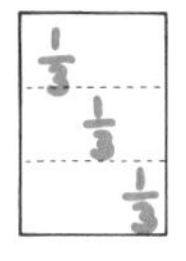

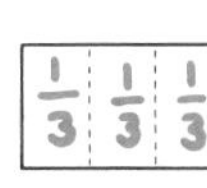

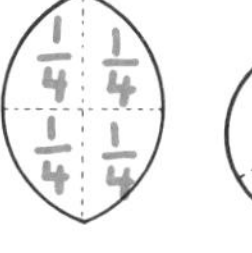

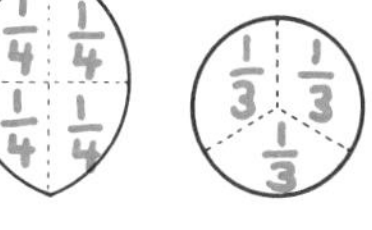

45

Blacklines

Fact Hives #28

Fact Form IX

Money Identification #8

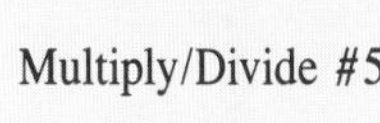

Multiply/Divide #5

After Class

1. Double Drill: 14's and 16's flash cards.
2. Introduce liquid measures.
   a. Hold the cup. **This is __.** 1 cup
      Hold the pint. **This is __.** 1 pint
      Which holds more?
   b. **2 cups fill 1 pint, or**
      2 cups=1 pint.

*3. Ask each child to bring his keys to the teaching corner.
Review the 10 and 5 times tables.

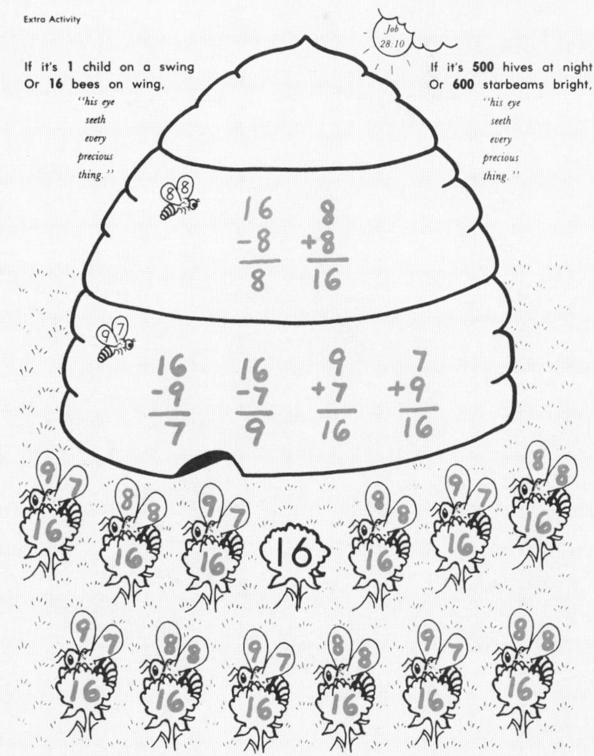

148

Fill in the whole and parts.

Trace, answer, and write the facts.

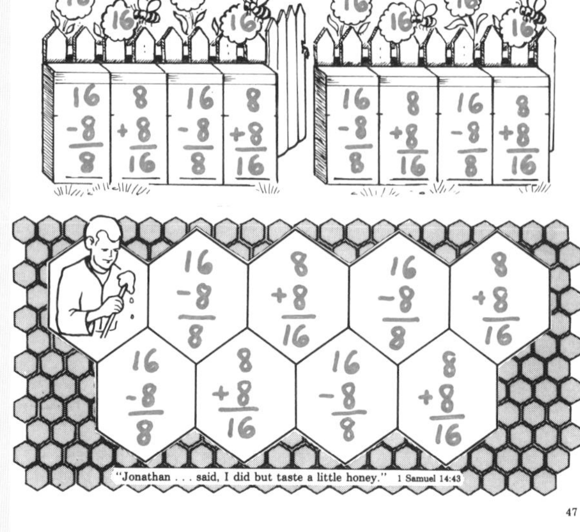
148
16 8 8
"Jonathan . . . said, I did but taste a little honey." 1 Samuel 14:43
47

Before Class

Materials

11's–16's flash cards

Cup, pint

Chalkboard

Class Time

1. Stand near the clover patch.

(16) 9 7

   The whole number is __.
   Its parts are __ and __.
   a. **The triplet is (16) 9 7 . . .**
   b. **The facts are 16−9, 7 . . .**

2. | (16) 8 8 |
   |---|

   The whole number is __.
   Its parts are __ and __.
   a. **The triplet is (16) 8 8 . . .**
   b. **The facts are 16−8, 8 . . .**

3. **Say the facts as I fill the beehives.** Begin with 15−9=6.

4. Flash the 11's–16's cards. **Can we answer these in 1 minute?**

148

Speed Drill

Read the story.
Write the numbers in the beehive.
Write the label words on the lines.
Answer the problem.

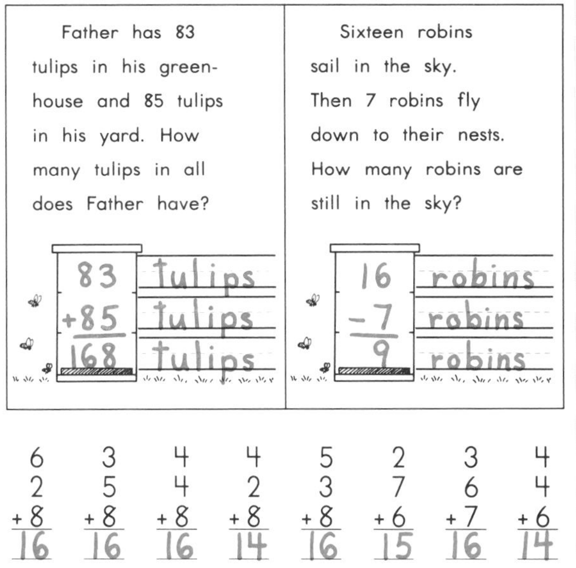

Father has 83 tulips in his greenhouse and 85 tulips in his yard. How many tulips in all does Father have?

83	tulips
+85	tulips
168	tulips

Sixteen robins sail in the sky. Then 7 robins fly down to their nests. How many robins are still in the sky?

16	robins
−7	robins
9	robins

Answer these problems.

6	3	4	4	5	2	3	4
2	5	4	2	3	7	6	4
+8	+8	+8	+8	+8	+6	+7	+6
16	16	16	14	16	15	16	14

7	2	6	1	4	7	8	6
2	6	3	7	5	1	0	3
+5	+8	+6	+8	+5	+8	+8	+7
14	16	15	16	14	16	16	16

48

5. Story Problems
   a. **Mother bought 9 tomato plants and 6 pepper plants. How many plants is that in all?**
      9 plants + 6 plants = 15 plants.
   b. **Hold that answer in your mind. Mother gave Grandmother ½ dozen of the plants. How many plants does Mother have left?**
      15 plants − 6 plants = 9 plants.
6. **Can you give the whole problem?**
   What is the sum of 8 and 7? 8 + 7 = 15
   What . . . 6 and 8? 6 + 8 = 14
   What . . . 8 and 8? 8 + 8 = 16
   What . . . 9 and 5? 9 + 5 = 14
   What . . . 9 and 6? 9 + 6 = 15
7. Hold the cup and pint.
   a. **This is __.** 1 cup
      This is __. 1 pint
   b. **2 cups fill __.** 1 pint
      or 2 cups = __. 1 pint
   c. **If you drink 2 cups of milk and I drink 1 pint of milk, who drinks more?**
8. Do the Speed Drill in Lesson 148.
9. Assign Lesson 148.

Carry *over* in one or two places.

578	378	486	488	705	458
+268	+586	+309	+358	+208	+346
846	964	795	846	913	804

547	335	458	607	275	567
+248	+578	+388	+197	+689	+279
795	913	846	804	964	846

Answer these facts.

8	16	6	9	15	5	15	15
+8	-8	+9	+7	-8	+9	-9	-6
16	8	15	16	7	14	6	9

16	14	6	16	8	7	15	7
-7	-8	+8	-9	+8	+8	-7	+9
9	6	14	7	16	15	8	16

9	7	16	7	15	16	8	15
+7	+8	-8	+9	-7	-9	+7	-8
16	15	8	16	8	7	15	7

49

Blacklines

Fact Hives #28

Mixed Computation #6

Number Triplets #6

Divide Form

After Class

1. Ask individuals to give the triplets by memory.
2. Chalkboard Drill: **Change what I say to cents.**

   3 quarters 75¢
   2 nickels 10¢
   8 dimes 80¢
   Add. Can you change your answer to $1.65?
   56 pennies 56¢
   3 nickels 15¢
   1 half dollar 50¢
   Add. Can you change your answer to $1.21?
   8 nickels 40¢
   1 half dollar 50¢
   6 dimes 60¢
   Add. Can you change your answer to $1.50?

*3. Give each child Key #6.
   Follow as I read.
   0 divided into 5=0
   5 divided into 5=1 . . .

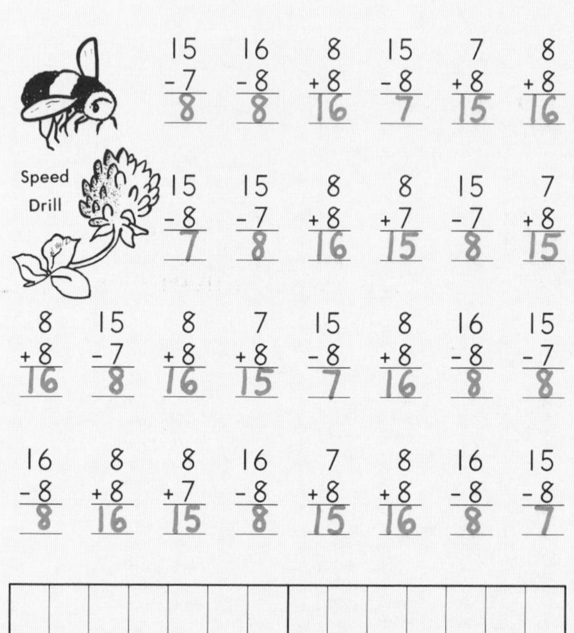

15	16	8	15	7	8
-7	-8	+8	-8	+8	+8
8	8	16	7	15	16

15	15	8	8	15	7
-8	-7	+8	+7	-7	+8
7	8	16	15	8	15

8	15	8	7	15	8	16	15
+8	-7	+8	+8	-8	+8	-8	-7
16	8	16	15	7	16	8	8

16	8	8	16	7	8	16	15
-8	+8	+7	-8	+8	+8	-8	-8
8	16	15	8	15	16	8	7

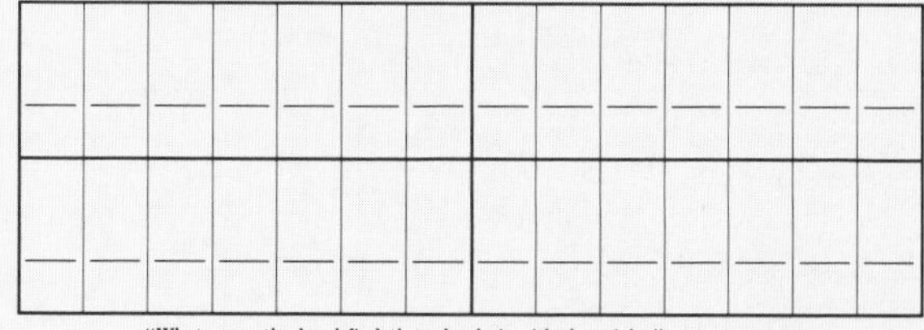

"Whatsoever thy hand findeth to do, do it with thy might." Ecclesiastes 9:10

50

Trace and fill in the whole and parts.

Trace, answer, and write the facts.

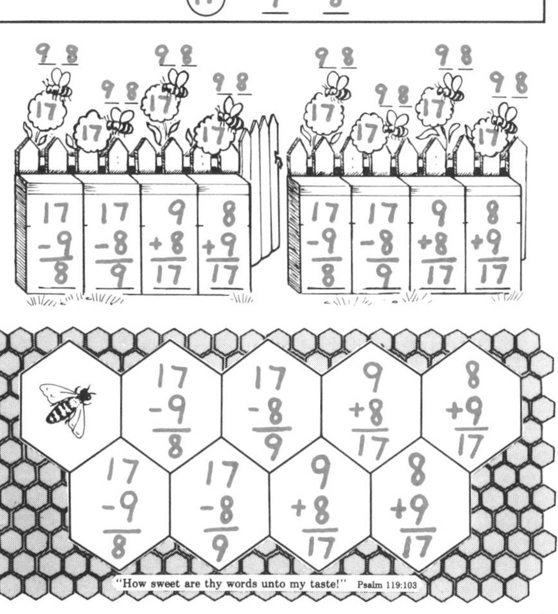
149
(17) 9 8
"How sweet are thy words unto my taste!" Psalm 119:103
51

Before Class

Make (17) 9 8 flash cards for each child.

Tack (17) 9 8 flash cards above the clover patch in this order:

17	17	9	8
−9	−8	+8	+9
8	9	17	17

Materials

13's–16's flash cards

Chalkboard

16	8	8	15	9	17	16	9	9
7	7	9	7	7	9	8	6	8
9	15	17	8	16	8	8	15	17

Class Time

1. Call the children to the Number Line.
   Count backwards by 10's.
   •90, 80 . . . 10
   •93, 83 . . . 3
   •96, 86 . . . 6
   •99, 89 . . . 9

2. **Answer together.**

73−10	**46−10**	**10+5**	**10+9**
56−10	**33−10**	**10+8**	**10+3**
29−10	**76−10**	**10+4**	**10+7**
89−10	**69−10**	**10+6**	**10+2**

3. Stand near the clover patch.

   (17) 9 8

   a. **How many pink clovers are in the patch?** 10
      We think—10 pink.
      7 more makes __ altogether. 17
      We think—10 pink.
      1 less makes __ clovers with bees. 9

149

Answer these facts.

17 − 9 = 8; 9 + 8 = 17; 17 − 8 = 9; 17 − 9 = 8; 9 + 8 = 17; 17 − 9 = 8
8 + 9 = 17; 9 + 8 = 17; 17 − 9 = 8; 8 + 9 = 17; 17 − 9 = 8; 17 − 8 = 9; 8 + 9 = 17; 17 − 9 = 8
17 − 8 = 9; 9 + 8 = 17; 17 − 9 = 8; 8 + 9 = 17; 9 + 8 = 17; 8 + 9 = 17; 17 − 8 = 9; 17 − 9 = 8
8 + 9 = 17; 17 − 8 = 9; 17 − 9 = 8; 8 + 9 = 17; 17 − 8 = 9; 17 − 9 = 8; 8 + 9 = 17; 17 − 8 = 9
9 + 8 = 17; 17 − 8 = 9; 8 + 9 = 17; 17 − 9 = 8; 9 + 8 = 17; 9 + 8 = 17; 17 − 9 = 8; 17 − 8 = 9
17 − 8 = 9; 9 + 8 = 17; 9 + 8 = 17; 17 − 9 = 8; 17 − 9 = 8; 17 − 8 = 9; 17 − 8 = 9; 9 + 8 = 17

52

Extra Activity

b. **17 clovers in the patch;**
   17 is the whole number.
   What part of the 17 has bees? 9
   What part of the 17 has no bees? 8
   17 is the whole number.
   Its parts are 9 and 8.

c. **The triplet is (17) 9 8 . . .**

d. **The facts are 17−9, 8; 17−8, 9; 9+8, 17; 8+9, 17 . . .**

4. **Say the triplets as I fill the clover and bees.**
5. **Say the facts as I fill the beehive.**
6. Point to the flash cards again. **Say the triplet; then say the answer.**
7. Fill in the missing sign at the Chalkboard samples.
8. **If you want to find**
   - **the sum of 8 and 8, you __.** add
   - **how much more 16 is than 9, you __.** subtract
   - **how much less 9 is than 15, you __.** subtract
9. Assign Lesson 149.

Note: Make Blossom 17 Chart for Lesson 150.
Bring 1 quart jar for Lesson 150. Label it like this:

1 quart

149

Borrow *back* in some problems.

56 − 8 = 48	55 − 8 = 47	38 − 2 = 36	56 − 7 = 49	34 − 7 = 27	28 − 4 = 24
94 − 56 = 38	96 − 28 = 68	76 − 69 = 7	98 − 28 = 70	83 − 15 = 68	85 − 47 = 38
75 − 39 = 36	83 − 56 = 27	95 − 47 = 48	79 − 55 = 24	86 − 39 = 47	65 − 16 = 49

Trace and copy.

2 cups = 1 pint

2 cups = 1 pint

2 cups = 1 pint

2 cups = 1 pint

53

Blacklines

Fact Hives #29

Reading Problems #10

Number Words #8

Divide Form

Multiply/Divide #6

After Class

1. Give each child his (17) 9 8 flash cards.
2. Flash the 13's–16's cards.
   Answer together.
3. Review
   7 days=__. 1 week
   12 months=__. 1 year
   12 inches=__. 1 foot
   3 feet=__. 1 yard
   2 cups=__. 1 pint

*4. Have each child bring his keys to the teaching corner.
Say Key #6 together 2 times.

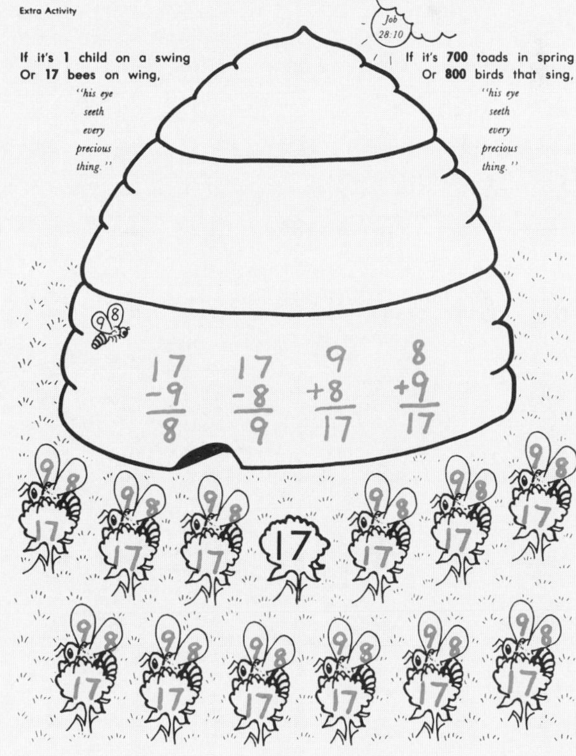

Extra Activity
Job 28:10
If it's 1 child on a swing
Or 17 bees on wing,
"his eye seeth every precious thing."
If it's 700 toads in spring
Or 800 birds that sing,
"his eye seeth every precious thing."
17 − 9 = 8
17 − 8 = 9
9 + 8 = 17
8 + 9 = 17
17
54

150

150

(17) 9 8

Fill in the whole and parts.

9 8 9 8 9 8 9 8 9 8 9 8 9 8 9 8

17 17 17 17 17 17 17 17

Trace, answer, and write the facts.

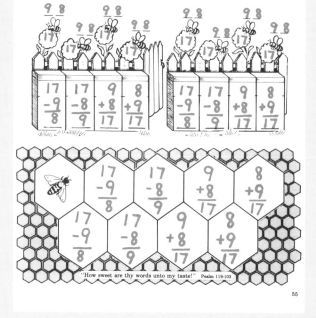

17 − 9 = 8　17 − 8 = 9　9 + 8 = 17　8 + 9 = 17　17 − 9 = 8　17 − 8 = 9　9 + 8 = 17　8 + 9 = 17

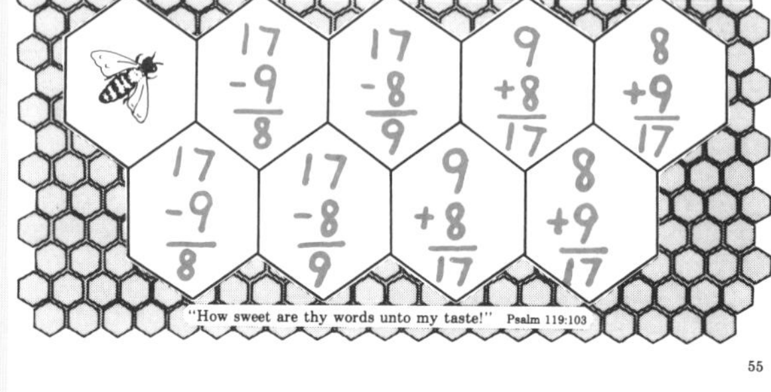

55

Before Class

Tack bee (17) 9 8 on Blossom 17 Chart. Mount it on the wall.

Materials

13's–16's flash cards
Cup, pint, quart
16's and 17's flash cards

Chalkboard

(ones)	1063	842	59	1605	7	938
(tens)	700	1535	8	491	1284	1003
(hundreds)	32	1374	1010	712	1605	1026

Class Time

1. Circle Drill 13's–16's flash cards.
2. Call the children to the clover patch.

(17) 9 8

   17 clovers in the patch;
   17 is the whole number.
   What part of the 17 has bees? 9
   What part of the 17 has no bees? 8
   17 is the whole number.
   Its parts are 9 and 8.
   a. **The triplet is (17) 9 8 . . .**
   b. **The facts are 17−9, 8 . . .**
3. Drill the triplets.
   11 and 12 triplets 1 time
   13 and 14 triplets 2 times
   15, 16, 17 triplets 3 times
4. Stand near the Place Value samples.
   a. Add the missing commas.
   b. Circle the correct numeral.
   c. **Read the numbers with me.**

150

Speed Drill

Answer these facts.

		17 − 9 = 8	8 + 9 = 17	17 − 9 = 8	8 + 9 = 17	17 − 8 = 9	9 + 8 = 17
17 − 8 = 9	17 − 8 = 9	8 + 9 = 17	17 − 8 = 9	9 + 8 = 17	17 − 9 = 8	9 + 8 = 17	17 − 9 = 8
8 + 9 = 17	17 − 8 = 9	17 − 9 = 8	17 − 9 = 8	8 + 9 = 17	17 − 9 = 8	17 − 8 = 9	17 − 8 = 9
17 − 8 = 9	8 + 9 = 17	17 − 8 = 9	9 + 8 = 17	17 − 9 = 8	17 − 8 = 9	9 + 8 = 17	9 + 8 = 17
17 − 9 = 8	17 − 8 = 9	17 − 9 = 8	8 + 9 = 17	17 − 8 = 9	17 − 9 = 8	17 − 8 = 9	9 + 8 = 17
8 + 9 = 17	9 + 8 = 17	17 − 9 = 8	17 − 8 = 9	8 + 9 = 17	17 − 9 = 8	8 + 9 = 17	17 − 9 = 8

56

5. Introduce 1 quart.
    a. Hold the quart. **This is __.**
    b. **Name each container.**
       1 quart, 1 cup, 1 pint . . .
    c. Point to the labels.
       Cup, pint, quart—
       3 letters, 4 letters, 5 letters; as the word becomes longer, the container becomes larger.
    d. **2 cups fill __.** 1 pint
       2 pints fill __. 1 quart
       2 cups=__. 1 pint
       2 pints=__. 1 quart
6. Do the Speed Drill in Lesson 150.
7. Assign Lesson 150.

Note: If you are teaching multiplication and division, prepare Key #7 for Lesson 151.

Answer these problems.

34 + 23 + 79 = 136	44 + 34 + 48 = 126	25 + 43 + 37 = 105	53 + 32 + 69 = 154	35 + 22 + 28 = 85	61 + 25 + 78 = 164
32 + 43 + 68 = 143	45 + 22 + 33 = 100	33 + 55 + 28 = 116	54 + 12 + 95 = 161	40 + 25 + 78 = 143	36 + 53 + 45 = 134
24 + 53 + 28 = 105	35 + 23 + 27 = 85	45 + 12 + 79 = 136	63 + 22 + 79 = 164	21 + 48 + 57 = 126	23 + 34 + 97 = 154

Trace and copy.

2 cups = 1 pint

2 cups = 1 pint

2 cups = 1 pint

2 cups = 1 pint

57

Blacklines

Fact Hives #29

Number Facts #17

Mixed Computation #6

Divide Form

Multiply/Divide #6

After Class

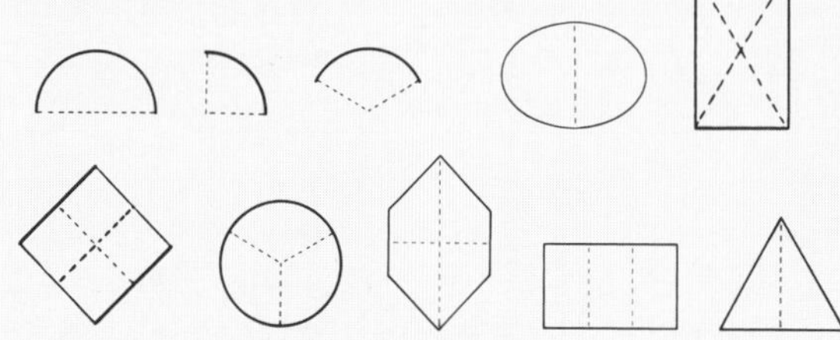

1. Drill the 16's and 17's flash cards. **Say the triplet; then say the answer.**
2. **Name three fractions.** ½, ¼, ⅓
   a. **One-half is 1 whole cut __.**
      into 2 equal parts
      One-fourth is 1 whole cut __.
      into 4 equal parts
      One-third is 1 whole cut __.
      into 3 equal parts
   b. Point to the first shape. **Is this ½, ¼, or ⅓ of a pie?** Write ½.
      Do the first three samples together.
   c. Have the children finish the samples.

*3. Have each child bring his keys to the teaching corner.
Review Keys #2, #4, and #6 together.

Speed Drill

		9 + 8 = 17	17 − 9 = 8	8 + 9 = 17	17 − 8 = 9	17 − 8 = 9	17 − 9 = 8
		17 − 9 = 8	9 + 8 = 17	8 + 9 = 17	17 − 8 = 9	9 + 8 = 17	17 − 8 = 9
17 − 9 = 8	9 + 8 = 17	17 − 9 = 8	17 − 8 = 9	17 − 8 = 9	8 + 9 = 17	17 − 9 = 8	9 + 8 = 17
8 + 9 = 17	17 − 9 = 8	17 − 8 = 9	8 + 9 = 17	17 − 8 = 9	9 + 8 = 17	8 + 9 = 17	17 − 9 = 8

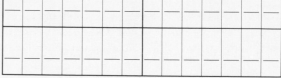

"Whatsoever thy hand findeth to do, do it with thy might." Ecclesiastes 9:10

58

Fill in the whole and parts.

Trace, answer, and write the facts.

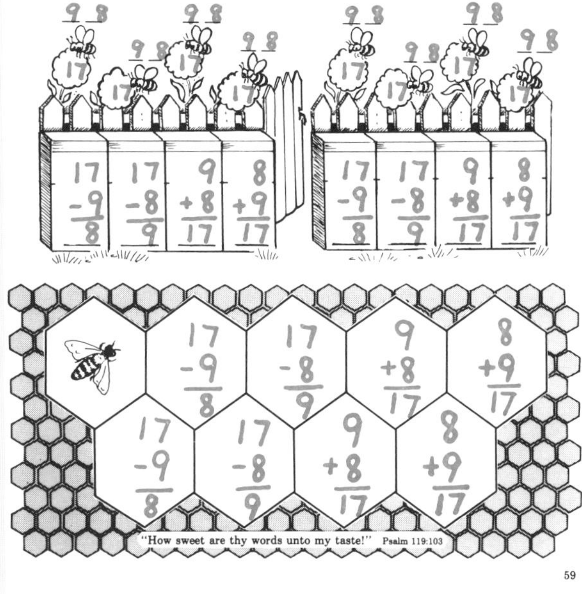
151
(17) 9 8
"How sweet are thy words unto my taste!" Psalm 119:103
59

Before Class

Chalkboard

56	78	86	97	79	97	59
−48	+99	−29	−38	+87	−69	+98

243¢
316¢
108¢
450¢

Class Time

1. Call the children to the clover patch.

   The children of Israel brought their best things to the tabernacle as an offering to God. Sometimes they brought sheep, goats, or doves. Sometimes they brought grain or cakes.

   But they did not bring __. honey. **God did not want them to offer honey.**

   (Leviticus 2:11)

2. (17) 9 8

   17 clovers in the patch;
   17 is the whole number.
   What part of the 17 has bees? 9
   What part of the 17 has no bees? 8
   17 is the whole number.
   Its parts are 9 and 8.

   a. **The triplet is (17) 9 8 . . .**
   b. **The facts are 17−9, 8 . . .**

151

Answer these problems.
Carry *over* in some problems.

		179 -94 85	178 -86 92	83 +96 179	179 -86 93
78 +79 157	179 -82 97	69 +78 147	176 -94 82	92 +86 178	177 -84 93
78 +99 177	179 -87 92	178 -94 84	96 +83 179	177 -85 92	58 +39 97
178 -85 93	93 +85 178	178 -96 82	88 +59 147	177 -80 97	69 +88 157
176 -83 93	94 +85 179	177 -85 92	177 -92 85	77 +98 175	179 -98 81
69 +28 97	179 -87 92	95 +84 179	179 -95 84	177 -85 92	79 +98 177

60

3. Point to the Blossom Charts.
   a. **Say the 13–17 triplets each 3 times.**
   b. **Say all the triplets by memory.**
4. Do the Computation samples.
5. Review money.
   a. **We count pennies by __, nickels by __, dimes by __, quarters by __, and half dollars by __.**
   b. **How many half dollars are in $1.00?** Continue with quarters, dimes, nickels, and pennies.
   c. Change the Money samples to dollars and cents.
6. Review
   12 inches=__. 1 foot
   3 feet=__. 1 yard
   2 cups=__. 1 pint
   2 pints=__. 1 quart
7. Assign Lesson 151.

Read the story.
Write the numbers in the beehive.
Write the label words on the lines.
Answer the problem.

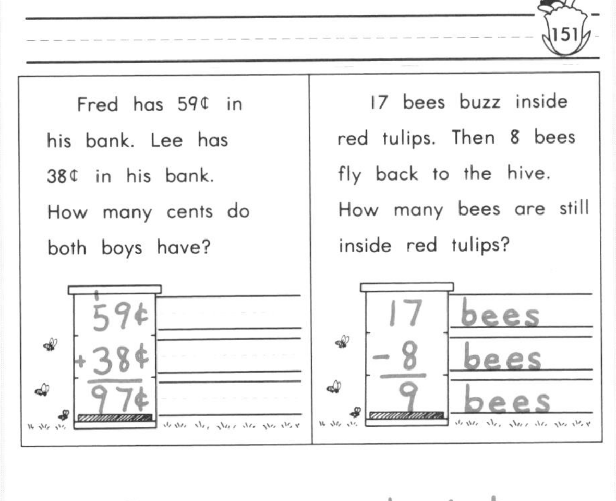

Fred has 59¢ in his bank. Lee has 38¢ in his bank. How many cents do both boys have?
59¢
+38¢
97¢
17 bees buzz inside red tulips. Then 8 bees fly back to the hive. How many bees are still inside red tulips?
17 bees
-8 bees
9 bees

Trace and copy.

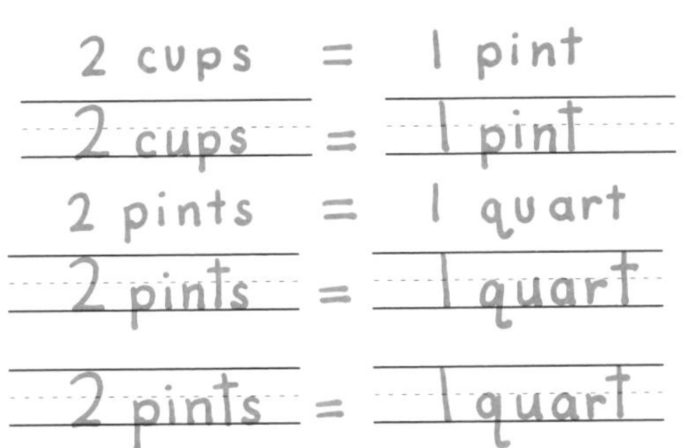

Blacklines

Fact Hives #30
Missing Whole or Parts #17
Fact Form IX

Multiply Form

After Class

1. Oral Drill: **Whoever says the correct answer first may go to the back of his line.**

9+7	13−7	16−9	9+6
8+9	7+8	14−7	8+7
16−8	9+5	13−9	17−8
15−9	6+8	7+9	16−7
15−8	8+8	9+8	7+8

2. Review liquid measures.
   a. **Which is more:**
      - **1 quart or 1 pint?** 1 quart
      - **2 cups or 2 pints?** 2 pints
      - **2 cups or 1 quart?** 1 quart
      - **1 pint or 3 cups?** 3 cups

   b. Have each child name some things that Mother measures with a cup . . . pint . . . quart.

*3. Have the children bring their keys to the teaching corner.
   a. Review Keys #5 and #6 together.
   b. Give each child Key #7. **Read it with me. 1 times 0=0 1 times 1=1 . . .**

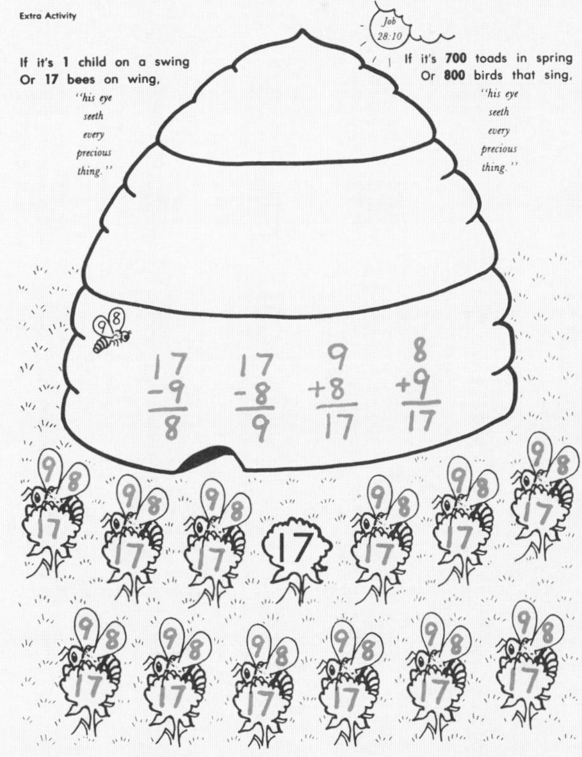

Extra Activity
Job 28:10
If it's 1 child on a swing
Or 17 bees on wing,
"his eye seeth every precious thing."
If it's 700 toads in spring
Or 800 birds that sing,
"his eye seeth every precious thing."
17
-9
8
17
-8
9
9
+8
17
8
+9
17
62

152

Fill in the whole and parts.

Write the facts.

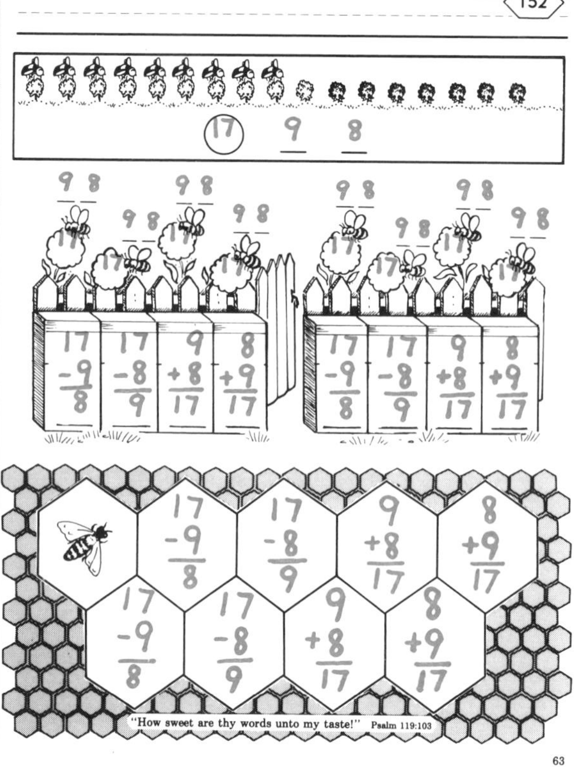
152
17 9 8
"How sweet are thy words unto my taste!" Psalm 119:103
63

Before Class

Materials

Large coins

15's–17's flash cards

Class Time

1. Call the children to the clover patch.

(15) 9 6

   The whole number is __.
   Its parts are __ and __.
   The triplet is (15) 9 6 . . .

2. | (16) 9 7 |
   |---|

   The whole number is __.
   Its parts are __ and __.
   The triplet is (16) 9 7 . . .

3. | (17) 9 8 |
   |---|

   The whole number is __.
   Its parts are __ and __.
   The triplet is (17) 9 8 . . .

4. Point to the Blossom Charts.
   a. Drill each triplet that has a 9.
   b. **Say the triplets by memory.**

Count the first row.
Write the amount.
Count the second row.
Write the amount.
Add.
Then copy the answer into the dollar box.

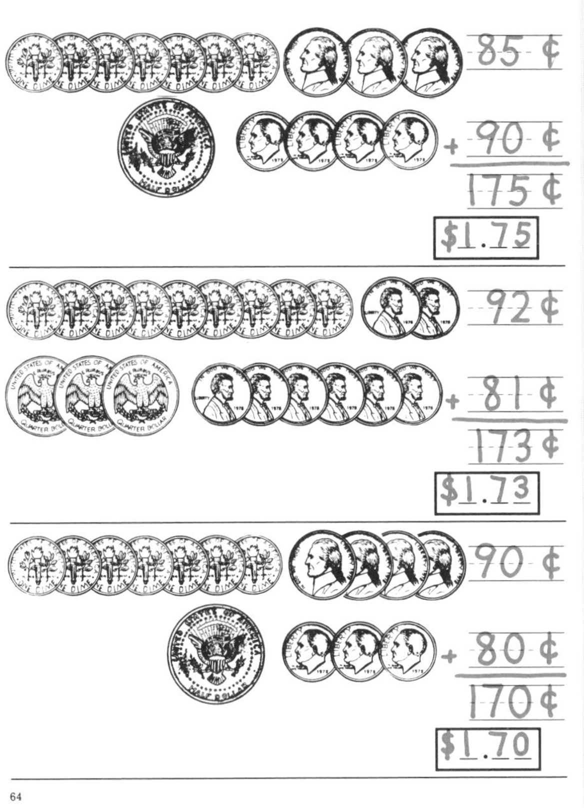

Speed Drill

5. **Answer together.**
   a. **When we add, we may have to __.**
      carry *over*
      When we subtract, we may have to __.
      borrow *back*
   b. **If you want to find**
      •**the sum of 9 and 8, you __.** add
      •**how much more 16 is than 7, you __.** subtract
      •**how much less 9 is than 15, you __.** subtract
6. Flash the large coins. **Nickel, 5¢ . . .**
7. **2 cups=__.** 1 pint
   2 pints=__. 1 quart
8. **Half of 6 is __.** Continue with half of 14, 10, 8, 12, 20, 40, 60, 100, 80.
9. Do the Speed Drill in Lesson 152.
10. Assign Lesson 152.

Note: You need 1 gallon jar for Lesson 153. Label it like this:

1 gallon

Carry *over* or borrow *back*.

152

97	76	88	88	97	95
-79	-27	+79	+88	-69	-56
18	49	167	176	28	39
68	76	89	87	76	97
+99	-49	+77	-59	+89	-68
167	27	166	28	165	29
87	86	67	89	87	85
-68	-38	+99	+88	-58	-47
19	48	166	177	29	38

Trace and copy.

2 cups = 1 pint

2 cups = 1 pint

2 pints = 1 quart

2 pints = 1 quart

2 pints = 1 quart

65

Blacklines

Fact Hives #30

Triplets With Facts #14

Mixed Computation #7

Multiply Form

After Class

1. Flash the 15's–17's cards. **Say the triplet; then say the answer.**
2. Chalkboard Drill: **Write the three numbers I say.**

   1,562 1,625 1,256

   Circle the number with the greatest tens.

   1,037 1,307 1,073

   Circle the number with the greatest hundreds.

   1,812 1,128 1,821

   Circle the number with the least ones.

   1,950 1,095 1,509

   Circle the number with the least tens.

*3. Drill Key #7 together.

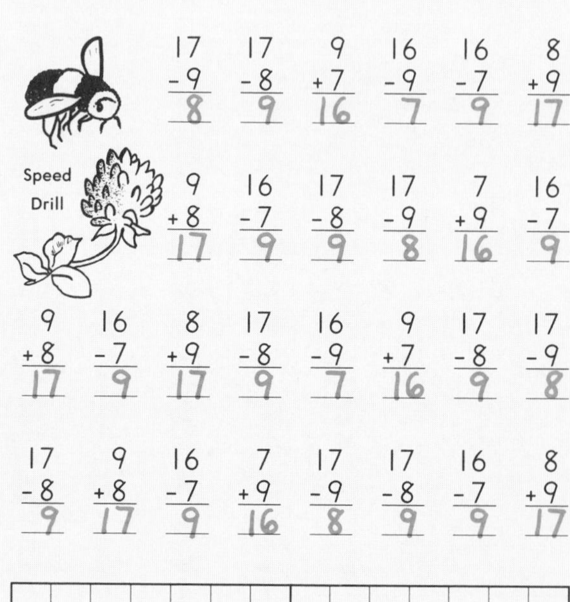

"Whatsoever thy hand findeth to do, do it with thy might." Ecclesiastes 9:10

66

Fill in the whole and parts.

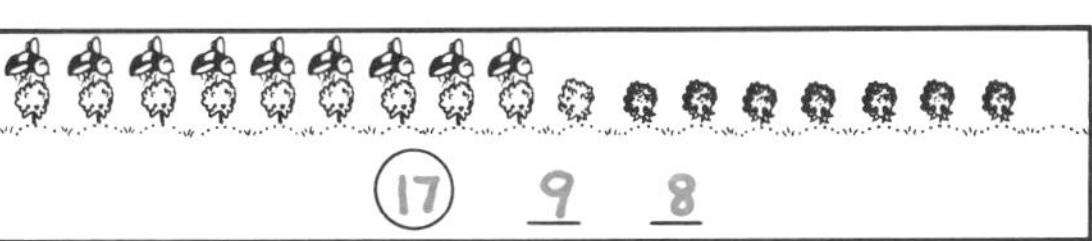

Write the facts.

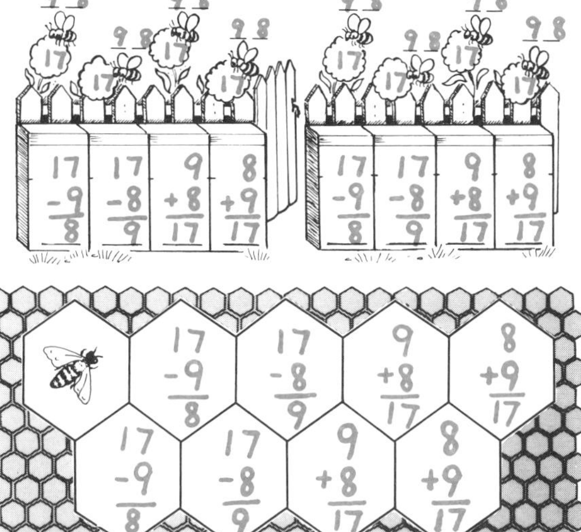

Before Class

Materials

13's–17's flash cards
Form C
14's–17's flash cards
1 gallon

Chalkboard

What is the difference between 16 and 7? What is the difference between 15 and 8? What is the difference between 60 and 20? What is the difference between 98 and 72? What is the difference between 87 and 40?

Class Time

1. Call the children to the clover patch.

(17) 9 8

   17 clovers in the patch;
   17 is the whole number.
   What part of the 17 has bees? 9
   What part of the 17 has no bees? 8
   17 is the whole number.
   Its parts are 9 and 8.
   a. **The triplet is (17) 9 8 . . .**
   b. **The facts are 17−9, 8 . . .**
2. Point to the Blossom Charts.
   a. Drill the triplets.
      11 and 12 triplets 1 time
      13 and 14 triplets 2 times
      15, 16, and 17 triplets 3 times
   b. **Say the triplets by memory.**

Extra Activity

Fill in the missing whole or parts.

9 + 8 = 17	17 - 9 = 8	17 - 8 = 9
8 + 9 = 17	8 + 9 = 17	8 + 9 = 17
17 - 8 = 9	17 - 9 = 8	17 - 9 = 8
17 - 9 = 8	17 - 8 = 9	17 - 8 = 9
8 + 9 = 17	8 + 9 = 17	8 + 9 = 17
17 - 9 = 8	9 + 8 = 17	17 - 9 = 8

Answer these problems.

6	7	1	4	8	5	7	6
3	2	7	5	1	2	2	2
+8	+5	+9	+8	+7	+8	+8	+9
17	14	17	17	16	15	17	17

5	2	2	4	5	1	1	4
4	6	7	3	3	8	6	4
+8	+9	+6	+9	+9	+8	+7	+9
17	17	15	16	17	17	14	17

68

3. Flash the 13's–17's cards.
   Answer together.
4. Flash Card Drill: 13's–17's flash cards. Use Form C. **Flower Row: Box 1 . . .**
5. Stand near the questions on the board.
   a. **What is the difference between 16 and 7?** Trace *difference* as you say **We subtract to find the difference.**
   b. Have individuals read the questions and write the problems.
6. **Answer together.**
   60 minutes=__. 1 hour
   30 minutes=__. ½ hour
   12 things=__. 1 dozen
   6 things=__. ½ dozen
   7 days=__. 1 week
   12 months=__. 1 year
   2 cups=__. 1 pint
   2 pints=__. 1 quart
7. Assign Lesson 153.

153

Carry *over* or borrow *back*.

39	97	99	76	97	66
+38	−78	+67	+99	−59	−58
77	19	166	175	38	8
88	97	77	95	89	96
+89	−19	+99	−27	+86	−38
177	78	176	68	175	58
96	86	78	87	77	95
−17	−69	+87	+89	−39	−87
79	17	165	176	38	8

Trace and copy.

2 cups = 1 pint

2 cups = 1 pint

2 pints = 1 quart

2 pints = 1 quart

2 pints = 1 quart

69

Blacklines

Form C (Class Time)

Fact Hives #30

Missing Whole or Parts #17

2-Place Computation #11

Multiply Form

After Class

1. Drill individuals with 14's–17's flash cards.
2. Introduce 1 gallon.
   a. Hold the gallon. **This is __.**
   b. **2 cups=__.** 1 pint
   2 pints=__. 1 quart
   Will 2 quarts fill 1 gallon? No, it takes *4* quarts to fill 1 gallon.
   Write *4 quarts=1 gallon.*

*3. Review Keys #5 and #7 together.

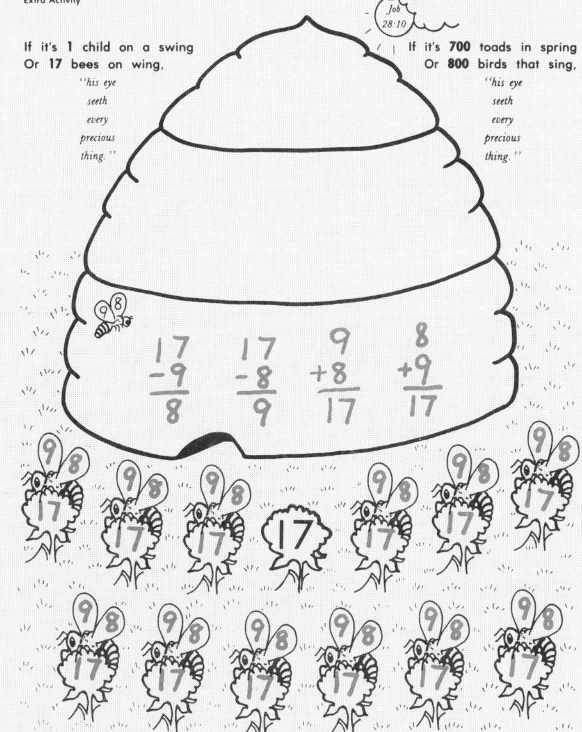

Extra Activity
Job 28:10
If it's 1 child on a swing
Or 17 bees on wing,
"his eye seeth every precious thing."
If it's 700 toads in spring
Or 800 birds that sing,
"his eye seeth every precious thing."
17 −9 = 8
17 −8 = 9
9 +8 = 17
8 +9 = 17
17
70

154

154

Fill in the whole or parts.

(17) 9 8

Write the facts.

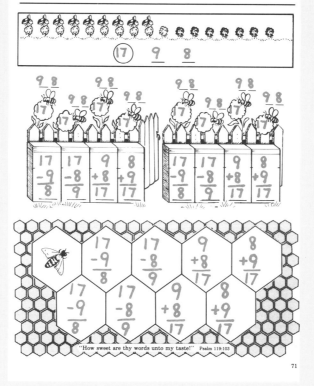

17	17	9	8	17	17	9	8
−9	−8	+8	+9	−9	−8	+8	+9
8	9	17	17	8	9	17	17

71

Before Class

Materials

14's–17's flash cards

14's–17's flash cards

Gallon, quart, pint, cup

Chalkboard

98	67	96	89	87	98	96
−58	−59	−58	−37	− 8	−46	− 9

Class Time

1. Call the children to the clover patch.

   The quiet toad sits near the beehive as the bees fly home for the night. Suddenly he shoots out his long, sticky tongue. *Zip!* He catches a bee and swallows it. *Zip, zip!* He catches bee after bee. Then he hops away as quietly as he came.

2. (17) 9 8

   17 clovers in the patch;
   17 is the whole number.
   What part of the 17 has bees? 9
   What part of the 17 has no bees? 8
   17 is the whole number.
   Its parts are 9 and 8.

   a. **The triplet is (17) 9 8 . . .**
   b. **The facts are 17−9, 8 . . .**

3. Drill the triplets on each Blossom Chart.

4. Flash the 14's–17's cards for 1 minute.

154

Speed Drill

Read the story.
Write the numbers in the beehive.
Write the label words on the lines.
Answer the problem.

Seventeen children are in Ray's Sunday school class. Nine children are boys. How many children are girls?
17 children
-9 children
8 children
Little lambs run and skip. 19 lambs are black. 18 lambs are white. How many lambs is that altogether?
19 lambs
+18 lambs
37 lambs
Mother plants one dozen plants in the garden and 29 plants in the flower bed. How many plants is that?
12 plants
+29 plants
41 plants
Seventeen bees buzz. Then a toad eats 8 of them. How many bees are left?
17 bees
-8 bees
9 bees
72

5. Do the Computation samples.
   When we add, we may have to __.
   carry *over*
   When we subtract, we may have to __.
   borrow *back*
6. **Who can give the whole problem?**
   What is the difference between 16 and 9? 16−9=7
   What . . . 17 and 8? 17−8=9
   What . . . 15 and 7? 15−7=8
   What . . . 16 and 8? 16−8=8
7. Review
   2 cups=__. 1 pint
   2 pints=__. 1 quart
   4 quarts=__. 1 gallon
8. Do the Speed Drill in Lesson 154.
9. Assign Lesson 154.

Borrow *back* in some problems.

154

97	95	96	99	76	95
-79	-78	-38	-56	-49	-56
18	17	58	43	27	39
97	86	87	96	77	77
-67	-39	-58	-48	-49	-28
30	47	29	48	28	49
67	84	54	96	78	55
-28	-26	-37	-69	-35	-37
39	58	17	27	43	18

Trace and copy.

4 quarts = 1 gallon

4 quarts = 1 gallon

4 quarts = 1 gallon

4 quarts = 1 gallon

73

Blacklines

Triplets With Facts #14

Mixed Computation #7

Multiply/Divide #7

After Class

1. Circle Drill: 14's–17's flash cards.
2. Review liquid measures.
   a. **Name the containers as I point to them.**
   1 gallon, 1 pint . . .
   b. **Which is more:**
   - **1 pint or 1 quart?** 1 quart
   - **1 pint or 1 cup?** 1 pint
   - **2 quarts or 1 gallon?** 1 gallon
   - **2 pints or 2 cups?** 2 pints
   - **1 quart or 2 cups?** 1 quart
   - **1 gallon or 3 quarts?** 1 gallon

*3. Ask individuals to say the 1 times table by memory.

Speed Drill

7	9	17	16	8	17		
+9	+8	-8	-7	+8	-9		
16	17	9	9	16	8		
16	17	9	8	16	16		
-7	-9	+7	+9	-8	-7		
9	8	16	17	8	9		
17	9	17	8	16	17	9	9
-9	+8	-9	+8	-7	-8	+8	+7
8	17	8	16	9	9	17	16
8	16	17	17	8	7	17	16
+9	-8	-8	-9	+9	+9	-9	-7
17	8	9	8	17	16	8	9

"Whatsoever thy hand findeth to do, do it with thy might." Ecclesiastes 9:10

74

Fill in the whole and parts.

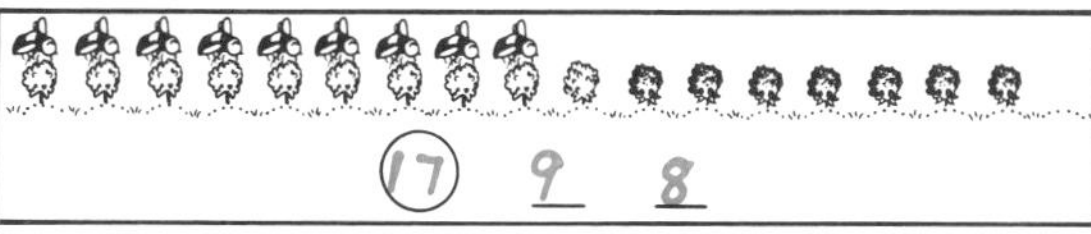

Write the facts.

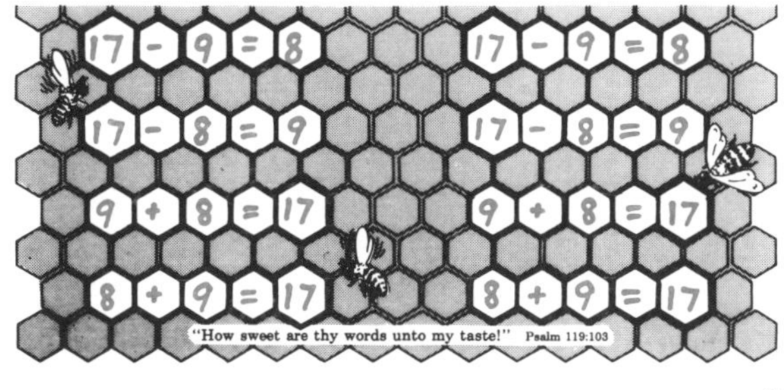

"How sweet are thy words unto my taste!" Psalm 119:103

75

Before Class

Materials

11's–17's flash cards

Large coins

Chalkboard

8 9=17	17 9=8
9 7=16	9 8=17
15 8=7	15 9=6
16 9=7	17 8=9

Class Time

1. Stand near the Number Line.
   Count backwards by 10's.
   •94, 84 . . . 4
   •97, 87 . . . 7
   •92, 82 . . . 2

2. **Answer together.**

74−10	**68+10**	**10+6**	**20+5**
38−10	**17+10**	**10+3**	**20+7**
92−10	**50+10**	**10+8**	**20+9**
55−10	**21+10**	**10+4**	**20+6**

3. Call the children to the Blossom Charts.
   a. **Say each triplet once.**
   b. **Jump from chart to chart.**

4. **What belongs on the blank?**
   (Say *blank* each time.)

16, 9 __	**15 __ 7**	**__ 9, 8**
17, 9 __	**16 __ 8**	**__ 9, 7**
15, 9 __	**17 __ 8**	**__ 8, 7**
16, 8 __	**15 __ 6**	**__ 8, 8**

155

Answer these facts.

Extra Activity

		17 − 9 = 8	9 + 8 = 17	17 − 8 = 9	8 + 9 = 17	16 − 9 = 7	16 − 7 = 9
17 − 8 = 9	17 − 9 = 8	7 + 9 = 16	16 − 7 = 9	8 + 9 = 17	9 + 7 = 16	17 − 9 = 8	17 − 9 = 8
7 + 9 = 16	17 − 9 = 8	16 − 7 = 9	16 − 9 = 7	8 + 9 = 17	16 − 7 = 9	17 − 9 = 8	17 − 8 = 9
17 − 8 = 9	8 + 9 = 17	16 − 7 = 9	9 + 8 = 17	16 − 9 = 7	16 − 7 = 9	9 + 8 = 17	9 + 7 = 16
17 − 8 = 9	17 − 9 = 8	16 − 9 = 7	7 + 9 = 16	17 − 9 = 8	16 − 9 = 7	17 − 9 = 8	9 + 8 = 17
8 + 9 = 17	7 + 9 = 16	17 − 8 = 9	17 − 9 = 8	9 + 7 = 16	17 − 8 = 9	9 + 7 = 16	17 − 8 = 9

76

5. Flash the 11's–17's cards.
   Boys, answer the addition facts.
   Girls, answer the subtraction facts.
6. Fill in the missing signs at the Computation samples.
7. Review
   2 cups=__. 1 pint
   2 pints=__. 1 quart
   4 quarts=__. 1 gallon
8. Assign Lesson 155.

155

155

Answer the problems.

35	47	15	64	45	63
43	31	63	23	22	23
+79	+69	+96	+69	+78	+78
157	147	174	156	145	164
65	45	32	53	40	36
24	22	56	22	49	53
+78	+93	+28	+95	+78	+28
167	160	116	170	167	117
24	35	45	63	43	23
54	23	34	22	45	34
+96	+87	+78	+79	+59	+99
174	145	157	164	147	156

Trace and copy.

4 quarts = 1 gallon

4 quarts = 1 gallon

4 quarts = 1 gallon

4 quarts = 1 gallon

77

Blacklines

Number Facts #17

Missing Whole or Parts #17

Equations #2

Multiply/Divide #7

After Class

1. Have individuals give the 14–17 triplets by memory.
2. a. Flash the large coins. **Dime, 10¢; half dollar, 50¢ . . .**
   b. Set the coins on the chalk tray.
   Which coin is worth the same as
   - **•2 nickels?** dime
   - **•5 dimes?** half dollar
   - **•25 pennies?** quarter
   - **•10 nickels?** half dollar
   - **•50 pennies?** half dollar
   - **•5 nickels?** quarter
   - **•1 nickel and 5 pennies?** dime
   - **•2 dimes and 1 nickel?** quarter

*3. Review Keys #5 and #7.

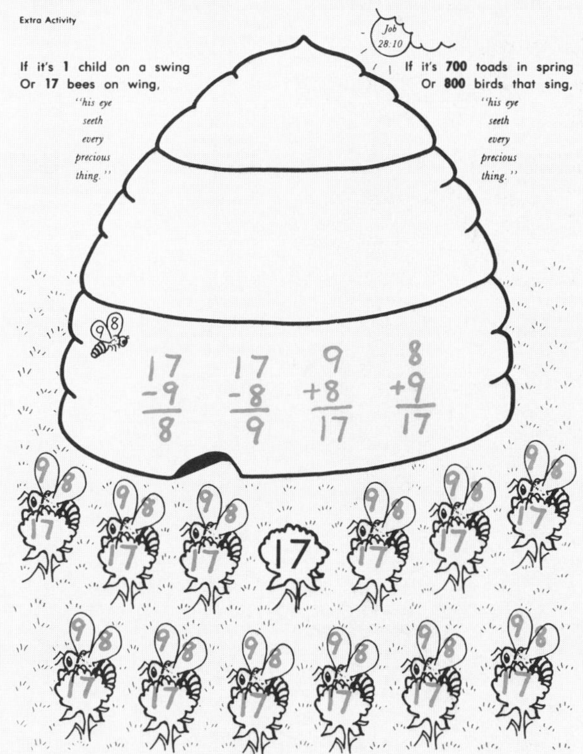
Extra Activity
Job 28:10
If it's 1 child on a swing
Or 17 bees on wing,
"his eye seeth every precious thing."
If it's 700 toads in spring
Or 800 birds that sing,
"his eye seeth every precious thing."
17 −9 8
17 −8 9
9 +8 17
8 +9 17
17
78

156

Fill in the whole and parts.

Write the facts.

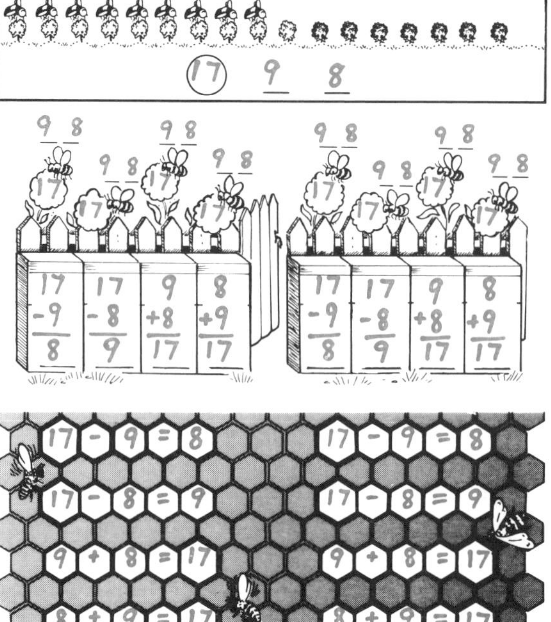

Before Class

Materials

15's–17's flash cards

Class Time

1. Call the children to the clover patch.

    The queen bee lays a tiny white egg in a wax "cradle." Three days later the egg hatches. Worker bees feed the bee baby more than 1,000 times each day. The bee grows and grows. Then a worker bee covers the cradle with a wax lid. Slowly the bee in the cradle changes. At last he pokes his head up through the lid and crawls out.

    In 21 days God makes a tiny white egg into a beautiful brown and yellow honeybee.

2. | (16) 9 7 |
   |---|

    The whole number is __.
    Its parts are __ and __.

    a. **The triplet is (16) 9 7 . . .**
    b. **The facts are 16−9, 7 . . .**

156

Speed Drill

Answer these facts.

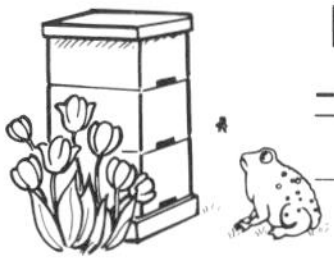

		17 − 8 = 9	9 + 8 = 17	15 − 6 = 9	8 + 9 = 17	14 − 5 = 9	9 + 7 = 16
8 + 8 = 16	6 + 9 = 15	7 + 7 = 14	14 − 5 = 9	8 + 9 = 17	6 + 8 = 14	7 + 8 = 15	16 − 7 = 9
7 + 9 = 16	16 − 8 = 8	15 − 6 = 9	15 − 9 = 6	8 + 7 = 15	17 − 8 = 9	14 − 6 = 8	17 − 9 = 8
15 − 7 = 8	8 + 6 = 14	16 − 9 = 7	9 + 6 = 15	14 − 8 = 6	15 − 8 = 7	9 + 5 = 14	9 + 7 = 16
16 − 9 = 7	17 − 9 = 8	17 − 8 = 9	6 + 8 = 14	15 − 7 = 8	16 − 7 = 9	16 − 8 = 8	6 + 9 = 15
7 + 8 = 15	9 + 8 = 17	14 − 7 = 7	17 − 9 = 8	5 + 9 = 14	16 − 9 = 7	8 + 9 = 17	15 − 8 = 7

80

3. (16) 8 8

   The whole number is __.
   Its parts are __ and __.

   a. **The triplet is (16) 8 8 . . .**
   b. **The facts are 16−8, 8 . . .**

4. (17) 9 8

   The whole number is __.
   Its parts are __ and __.

   a. **The triplet is (17) 9 8 . . .**
   b. **The facts are 17−9, 8 . . .**

5. **Say the triplets by memory.**

6. Flash the 15's–17's cards. **Say the triplet; then say the answer.**

7. **Who can give the whole problem?**

   a. **What is the sum of 6 and 9?** 6+9=15
      What . . . 7 and 8? 7+8=15
      What . . . 8 and 8? 8+8=16
      What . . . 9 and 6? 9+6=15

   b. **What is the difference between 17 and 9?** 17−9=8
      What . . . 16 and 9? 16−9=7
      What . . . 14 and 6? 14−6=8
      What . . . 15 and 8? 15−8=7

8. Do the Speed Drill in Lesson 156.

9. Assign Lesson 156.

Note: If you are teaching multiplication and division, prepare Key #8 for Lesson 157.

Carry *over* or borrow *back*.

97 − 58 = 39	76 − 58 = 18	78 + 89 = 167	77 + 69 = 146	95 − 48 = 47	97 − 69 = 28
58 + 99 = 157	86 − 79 = 7	87 + 69 = 156	94 − 77 = 17	58 + 97 = 155	76 − 49 = 27
85 − 47 = 38	95 − 76 = 19	68 + 98 = 166	59 + 88 = 147	87 − 39 = 48	85 − 58 = 27

Trace and copy.

4 quarts = 1 gallon

4 quarts = 1 gallon

4 quarts = 1 gallon

4 quarts = 1 gallon

81

Blacklines

Number Facts #17

Triplets With Facts #14

Reading Problems #11

Multiply/Divide #7

After Class

1. Chalkboard Drill: **Write only the answer.**

15−6+5=	14	**15−7+3=**	11
16−8+5=	13	**14−6+9=**	17
17−9+8=	16	**16−9+7=**	14
17−8+6=	15	**16−7+4=**	13
15−9+8=	14		

2. Have individuals say the months of the year.

*3. Review Keys #1 and #3.

Speed Drill
9+8=17 7+9=16 9+6=15 8+9=17 8+9=17 8+8=16
8+7=15 8+9=17 8+8=16 6+8=14 9+8=17 9+7=16
7+8=15 8+9=17 7+9=16 9+8=17 8+9=17 9+6=15 7+9=16 9+8=17
3+5+9=17 4+2+9=15 6+2+8=16 4+5+8=17 3+4+7=14 7+2+7=16 4+4+9=17 5+3+7=15
"Whatsoever thy hand findeth to do, do it with thy might." Ecclesiastes 9:10
82

Trace and fill in the whole and parts.

Trace, answer, and write the facts.

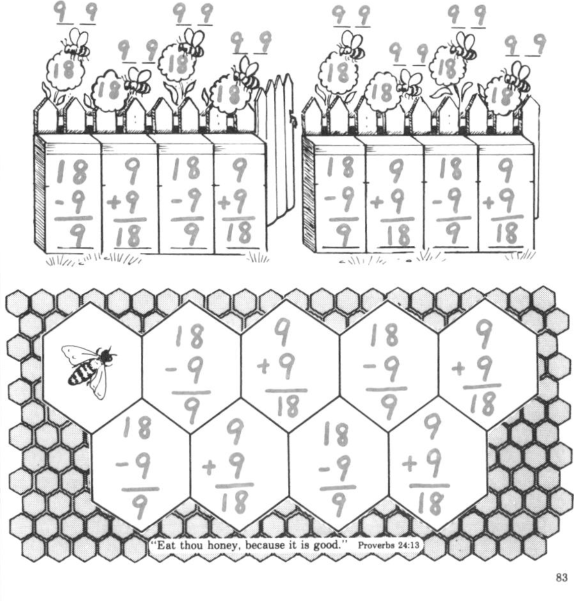

Before Class

Make (18) 9 9 flash cards for each child.

Tack (18) 9 9 flash cards above the clover patch in this order:

18	9
−9	+9
9	18

Materials

Select one of these ways to make a 1-ounce bundle. Put a rubber band around

- 4 new pencils
- 5 new crayons
- 3 sticks of chalk

15's–17's flash cards

Chalkboard

80	38	77	68	98	89	79
−56	+98	−49	−40	−87	+88	−54

16 ounces = 1 pound

Class Time

1. Call the children to the Number Line.
   a. **Count the odd numbers to 99.**
   b. **Count by 10's.**
      - **6, 16 . . .**
      - **3, 13 . . .**
      - **91, 81 . . .**
      - **95, 85 . . .**

2. Stand near the clover patch.
   a. **How many pink clovers are in the patch?** 10
      We think—10 pink.
      8 more make __ altogether. 18
      We think—10 pink.
      1 less makes __ clovers with bees. 9
   b. **18 clovers in the patch;**
      18 is the whole number.
      What part of the 18 has bees? 9
      What part of the 18 has no bees? 9
      18 is the whole number.
      Its parts are 9 and 9.

157

Answer these facts.

18 -9 9	9 +9 18	17 -8 9	9 +8 17			18 -9 9	17 -9 8
9 +9 18	9 +9 18	17 -9 8	18 -9 9	8 +9 17	17 -8 9	9 +9 18	18 -9 9
8 +9 17	17 -9 8	18 -9 9	18 -9 9	9 +9 18	9 +8 17	18 -9 9	17 -8 9
17 -8 9	18 -9 9	9 +8 17	9 +9 18	18 -9 9	18 -9 9	17 -9 8	8 +9 17
18 -9 9	17 -8 9	18 -9 9			18 -9 9	17 -9 8	9 +9 18
17 -8 9	8 +9 17	9 +9 18	17 -9 8	18 -9 9	18 -9 9	17 -8 9	18 -9 9

84

Extra Activity

c. **The triplet is (18) 9 9 . . .**
d. **The facts are 18−9, 9; 9+9, 18.**

3. **Say the triplet as I fill the clover and bees.**
4. **Say the facts as I fill the beehive.**
5. Do the Computation samples.
6. **Answer together.**
   1 hour has __. 60 minutes
   ½ hour has __. 30 minutes
   1 dozen has __. 12 things
   ½ dozen has __. 6 things
   1 foot has __. 12 inches
   1 yard has __. 3 feet
   1 week has __. 7 days
   1 year has __. 12 months
   1 pint has __. 2 cups
   1 quart has __. 2 pints
   1 gallon has __. 4 quarts
7. Introduce 16 ounces=1 pound.
   a. Hold your 1-ounce bundle.
   These four pencils (5 crayons, 3 sticks of chalk) **weigh about 1 ounce.** Allow each child to hold the bundle.
   b. **One ounce is light.**
   Point to the 16 on the chalkboard.
   Count the circles with me.
   1, 2 . . . 16 ounces make 1 pound.
   16 ounces=1 pound. . . .
8. Assign Lesson 157.

Note: Make Blossom 18 Chart for Lesson 158.

Carry *over* in one or two places.

183 +597 = 780	368 +526 = 894	259 +179 = 438	468 +399 = 867	149 +629 = 778	487 +198 = 685
438 +267 = 705	317 +659 = 976	558 +148 = 706	448 +529 = 977	318 +389 = 707	649 +329 = 978
286 +399 = 685	229 +549 = 778	589 +278 = 867	149 +289 = 438	276 +618 = 894	586 +194 = 780

Trace and copy.

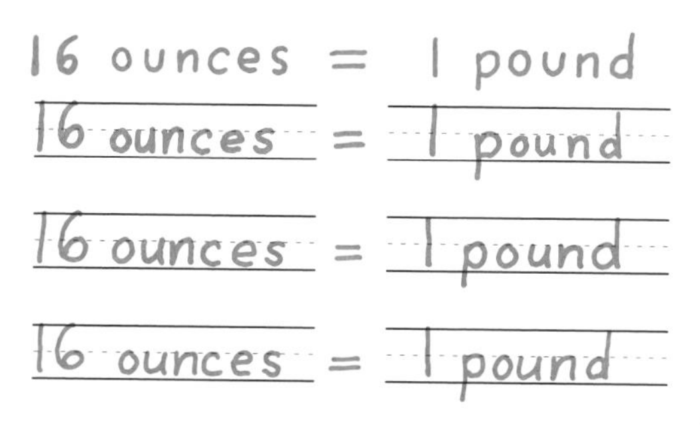

Blacklines

Fact Hives #31

2-Place Computation #11

Equations #2

Divide Form

After Class

1. Give each child his (18) 9 9 flash cards.
2. Double Drill: 15's–17's flash cards.

*3. Have the children bring their keys to the teaching corner.
   a. Give each child Key #8.
   b. **Read the problems with me.**
      0 divided into 1=0
      1 divided into 1=1 . . .

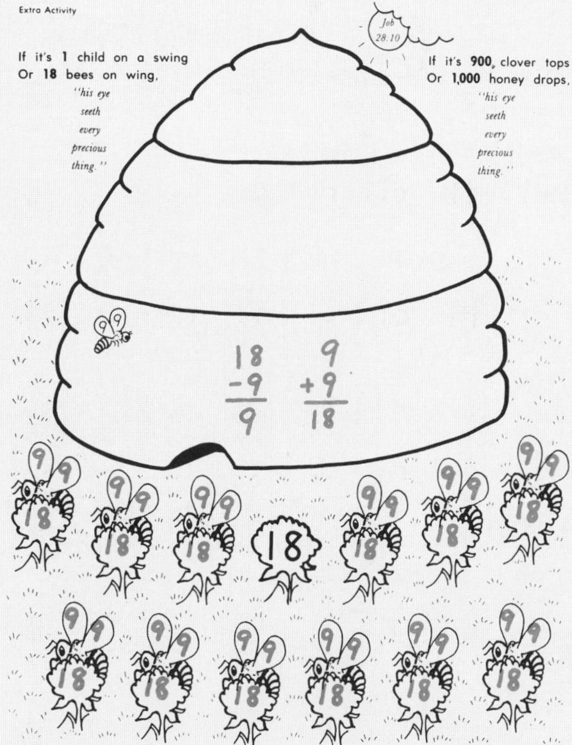

Extra Activity
If it's 1 child on a swing
Or 18 bees on wing,
''his eye seeth every precious thing.''
Job 28:10
If it's 900, clover tops
Or 1,000 honey drops,
''his eye seeth every precious thing.''
18 −9 = 9
9 +9 = 18
18
86

158

Fill in the whole and parts.

(18) 9 9

Trace, answer, and write the facts.

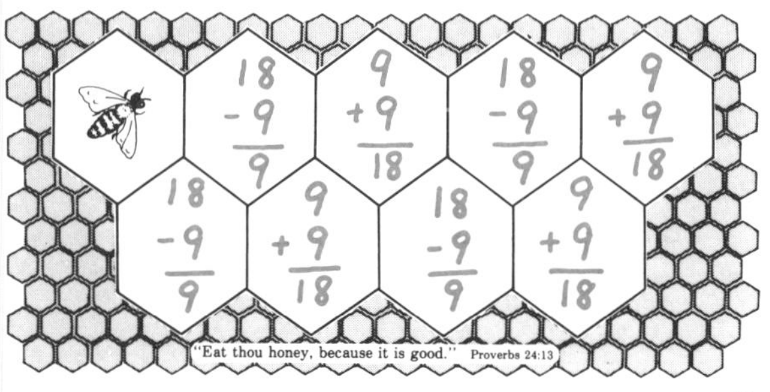

"Eat thou honey, because it is good." Proverbs 24:13

87

Before Class

Tack bee (18) 9 9 on Blossom 18 Chart. Mount it on the wall.

Materials

15's–18's flash cards

15's–18's flash cards

Select one of these ways to make a 1-pound bundle. Put a rubber band around

- 6 boxes of one dozen pencils
- 5 boxes of sixteen crayons
- 4 boxes of one dozen chalk sticks

Class Time

1. Call the children to the clover patch.

   Suppose Mother makes fresh buns for dinner. You help yourself to a bun. You spread a dab of butter on it. Then you reach for the honey bear. *Drop, drip!* As the golden honey drops on the bun, you think, "How long does it take one bee to make enough honey for my bun?"

   It takes one bee's whole lifetime to make enough honey for your bun.

2. (18) 9 9

   18 clovers in the patch;
   18 is the whole number.
   What part of the 18 has bees? 9
   What part of the 18 has no bees? 9
   18 is the whole number.
   Its parts are 9 and 9.

   a. **The triplet is (18) 9 9 . . .**
   b. **Say each fact 3 times. 18–9, 9 . . .**

158

Speed Drill

Answer these problems.
Carry *over* in some problems.

91 + 92 = 183	183 − 92 = 91	83 + 94 = 177			58 + 39 = 97
179 − 87 = 92	189 − 93 = 96	49 + 39 = 88	178 − 94 = 84	96 + 80 = 176	189 − 95 = 94
95 + 94 = 189	184 − 94 = 90	68 + 29 = 97	95 + 82 = 177	189 − 98 = 91	93 + 90 = 183
188 − 95 = 93	177 − 94 = 83	188 − 97 = 91	81 + 97 = 178	189 − 97 = 92	86 + 93 = 179
178 − 94 = 84	29 + 59 = 88			178 − 82 = 96	189 − 97 = 92
91 + 88 = 179	187 − 95 = 92	89 + 89 = 178	189 − 98 = 91	179 − 96 = 83	185 − 92 = 93

88

3. Point to the Blossom Charts.
   a. **Say each triplet once.**
   b. **Jump from chart to chart.**
   c. Drill 15–18 triplets 3 times.
4. Flash 15's–18's cards for 1 minute.
5. **Answer together.**
   a. **Amy wants to find the sum of 8 and 9. She should __.** add
   b. **Michael wants to find the difference between 52 and 21. He should __.** subtract
   c. **When Susan adds, she may have to __.** carry *over*
   d. **When Marlin subtracts, he may have to __.** borrow *back*
6. Review: 16 ounces = 1 pound.
   a. **Describe an ounce.** It is light. 4 pencils (5 crayons, 3 sticks of chalk) weigh 1 ounce.
   b. Hold your 1-pound bundle.
      This bundle weighs about 16 ounces or __. 1 pound. Allow each child to handle the bundle.
   c. **16 ounces = 1 pound. . . .**
7. Do the Speed Drill in Lesson 158.
8. Assign Lesson 158.

Answer these facts.

18	9	17	7	9	8	15	16
-9	+9	-9	+9	+8	+7	-6	-7
9	18	8	16	17	15	9	9

8	15	16	9	18	17	7	15
+9	-6	-8	+8	-9	-9	+8	-8
17	9	8	17	9	8	15	7

9	18	9	15	6	8	15	16
+9	-9	+7	-7	+9	+9	-6	-7
18	9	16	8	15	17	9	9

Trace and copy.

16 ounces = 1 pound

16 ounces = 1 pound

16 ounces = 1 pound

16 ounces = 1 pound

89

Blacklines

Fact Hives #31

Number Facts #18

Number Triplets #7

Missing Whole or Parts #18

Divide Form

Multiply/Divide #8

After Class

1. Flash the 17's and 18's cards. **Say the triplet; then say the answer.**
2. Have the children stand in a circle. **We will race around the circle saying our triplets by memory. When it is your turn, say one triplet.** (Pupil) **may begin.**

*3. Review Key #8 together.

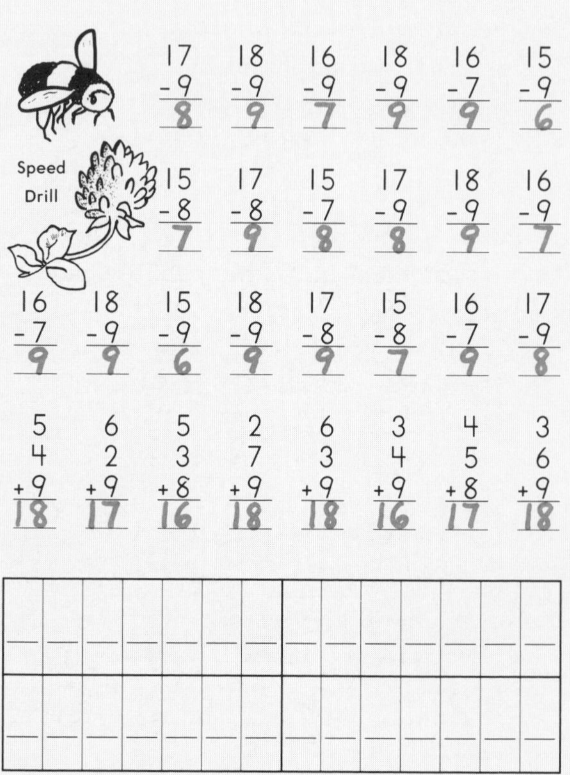

17	18	16	18	16	15
-9	-9	-9	-9	-7	-9
8	9	7	9	9	6

15	17	15	17	18	16
-8	-8	-7	-9	-9	-9
7	9	8	8	9	7

16	18	15	18	17	15	16	17
-7	-9	-9	-9	-8	-8	-7	-9
9	9	6	9	9	7	9	8

5	6	5	2	6	3	4	3
4	2	3	7	3	4	5	6
+9	+9	+8	+9	+9	+9	+8	+9
18	17	16	18	18	16	17	18

"Whatsoever thy hand findeth to do, do it with thy might." Ecclesiastes 9:10

90

159

Fill in the whole and parts.

Trace, answer, and write the facts.

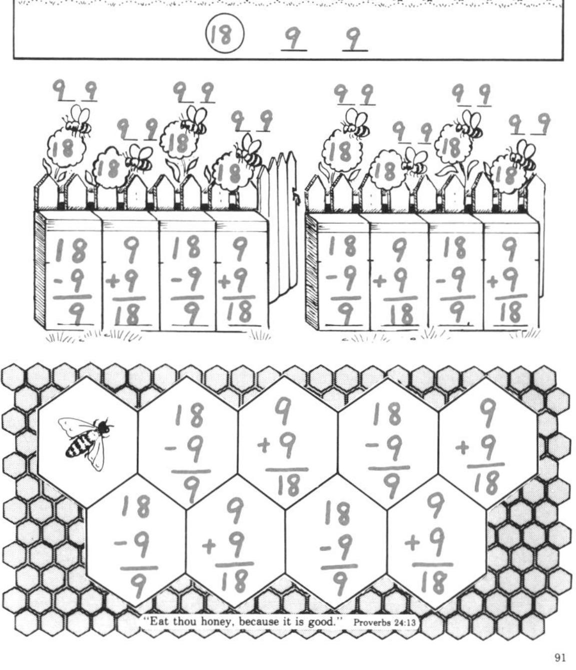
159
18 9 9
"Eat thou honey, because it is good." Proverbs 24:13
91

Before Class

Materials

10's–18's flash cards
Large coins
1-ounce bundle
1-pound bundle

Class Time

1. Stand near the clover patch.

(17) 9 8

   The whole number is __.
   Its parts are __ and __.
   a. **The triplet is (17) 9 8 . . .**
   b. **The facts are 17−9, 8 . . .**

2. | (18) 9 9 |
   |---|

   The whole number is __.
   Its parts are __ and __.
   a. **The triplet is (18) 9 9 . . .**
   b. **The facts are 18−9, 9 . . .**

3. Drill the triplets.
   11 and 12 triplets 1 time
   13 and 14 triplets 2 times
   15, 16, 17, 18 triplets 3 times

159

Read the story.
Write the numbers in the beehive.
Write the label words on the lines.
Answer the problem.

Mae and Fay played store. Mae sold a cup for 59¢ and a bell for 39¢. How many cents was that altogether?

59¢
+39¢
98¢

Mother made one dozen muffins. She gave seven muffins to Grandmother and kept the rest. How many did she keep?

12 muffins
− 7 muffins
5 muffins

Extra Activity

Answer these problems.

6	7	3	8	2	4	3	6
3	2	5	1	4	5	4	1
+9	+6	+8	+9	+9	+6	+9	+7
18	15	16	18	15	15	16	14

7	2	2	4	2	6	4	1
2	6	4	5	5	1	2	5
+9	+8	+9	+9	+7	+9	+9	+9
18	16	15	18	14	16	15	15

92

4. **What belongs on the blank?**
   (Say *blank* each time.)
   17, 9 __ 18 __ 9 __ 9, 8
   18, 9 __ 16 __ 8 __ 9, 9
   16, 9 __ 17 __ 8 __ 9, 7
   16, 8 __ 16 __ 7 __ 8, 8
5. Double Drill: 10's–18's flash cards.
   Whoever answers first may have the card.
6. Review: 16 ounces = 1 pound.
   a. Hold the two bundles of pencils (crayons, chalk). **How much does the small bundle weigh? the large bundle?**
   b. **16 small bundles weigh as much as this large bundle.**
   c. **16 ounces make 1 pound.**
   16 ounces = 1 pound. . . .
7. Display the large coins.
   a. **We count pennies by __, nickels by __, dimes by __, quarters by __, and half dollars by __.**
   b. **Which coin is worth the same as**
   - **5 dimes?** half dollar
   - **5 nickels?** quarter
   - **2 quarters?** half dollar
   - **10 nickels?** half dollar
   - **10 pennies?** dime
   - **2 nickels?** dime
   - **1 nickel and 5 pennies?** dime
   - **2 dimes and 5 pennies?** quarter
   - **4 dimes and 2 nickels?** half dollar
8. Assign Lesson 159.

Note: If you have taught multiplication and division since Lesson 124, this is your last lesson. Take the keys from the children and store them for second grade next year.
Spend the remaining days of this term drilling addition and subtraction.

159

Carry *over* or borrow *back*.

159

98 − 59 = 39	39 + 47 = 86	87 − 48 = 39	85 − 28 = 57	49 + 58 = 107	98 − 69 = 29
57 − 19 = 38	37 + 59 = 96	76 − 39 = 37	95 − 58 = 37	27 + 69 = 96	86 − 48 = 38
28 + 58 = 86	78 − 39 = 39	96 − 39 = 57	96 − 57 = 39	88 − 59 = 29	38 + 69 = 107

Trace and copy.

16 ounces = 1 pound

16 ounces = 1 pound

16 ounces = 1 pound

16 ounces = 1 pound

93

Blacklines

Fact Hives #31

Number Facts #18

Number Triplets #7

Triplets With Facts #15

Multiply/Divide #8

After Class

1. Ask individuals to name the months of the year.
2. Chalkboard Drill: **Change what I say to cents.**

6 nickels	30¢
24 pennies	24¢
3 quarters	75¢

Add. Now change the total to $1.29.

7 dimes	70¢
1 quarter	25¢
1 half dollar	50¢

Add. Now change the total to $1.45.

8 nickels	40¢
1 half dollar	50¢
2 quarters	50¢

Add. Now change the total to $1.40.

*3. Review Key #7 and Key #8.

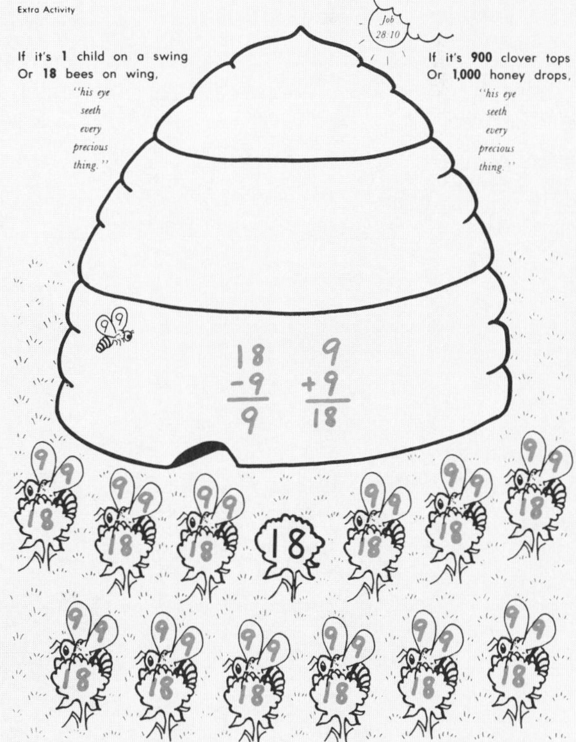

Extra Activity
Job 28:10
If it's 1 child on a swing
Or 18 bees on wing,
"his eye seeth every precious thing."
If it's 900 clover tops
Or 1,000 honey drops,
"his eye seeth every precious thing."
18 −9 9
9 +9 18
18
94

160

Answer these facts.

160

9 + 2 = 11	11 − 6 = 5	8 + 7 = 15	18 − 9 = 9	11 − 9 = 2	17 − 8 = 9	9 + 7 = 16	16 − 8 = 8
8 + 9 = 17	11 − 2 = 9	9 + 9 = 18	16 − 7 = 9	15 − 8 = 7	2 + 9 = 11	16 − 9 = 7	17 − 9 = 8
15 − 6 = 9	9 + 9 = 18	17 − 8 = 9	9 + 8 = 17	15 − 7 = 8	11 − 4 = 7	8 + 3 = 11	15 − 8 = 7
11 − 8 = 3	17 − 9 = 8	11 − 8 = 3	16 − 8 = 8	9 + 6 = 15	16 − 9 = 7	6 + 9 = 15	15 − 8 = 7
	11 − 6 = 5	7 + 8 = 15	18 − 9 = 9	11 − 9 = 2	16 − 7 = 9	8 + 8 = 16	11 − 3 = 8
	7 + 4 = 11	15 − 9 = 6	5 + 6 = 11	11 − 5 = 6	11 − 7 = 4	6 + 5 = 11	11 − 7 = 4

95

Before Class

Materials

11's–18's flash cards
Large clock

Chalkboard

1,615	1,093
1,223	1,007
1,740	1,036
1,852	1,989

Class Time

1. Stand near the blossoms and blanks on the chalkboard.
   a. **Say the triplets as I fill the blossoms. (11) 9 2 . . .** Do the blossoms clockwise, using 11–15 triplets.
   b. **Say the facts as I fill the hive. 16−9, 7 . . .** Fill the hive with 16's–18's.
2. Point to the Blossom Charts.
   Jump from chart to chart.
3. Flash the 11's–18's cards.
   Answer together.
4. **Number places are ones, tens, hundreds, (comma), thousands . . .**
   a. Read the numbers on the board.
   b. **Which number has 9 tens?**
   Continue with

7 ones	**9 hundreds**
6 hundreds	**0 ones**
4 tens	**2 ones**

160

Speed Drill

Answer these problems.
Carry *over* in some problems.

114 − 93 = 21	93 + 22 = 115	156 − 94 = 62	175 − 91 = 84	86 + 84 = 170	118 − 66 = 52
36 + 83 = 119	169 − 98 = 71	92 + 75 = 167	187 − 94 = 93	35 + 66 = 101	167 − 82 = 85
24 + 91 = 115	118 − 97 = 21	117 − 33 = 84	117 − 55 = 62	119 − 67 = 52	83 + 87 = 170
117 − 46 = 71	47 + 72 = 119	158 − 65 = 93	74 + 93 = 167	159 − 74 = 85	27 + 74 = 101
	89 + 86 = 175	158 − 88 = 70	78 + 37 = 115	77 + 88 = 165	178 − 83 = 95
	165 − 70 = 95	69 + 96 = 165	66 + 49 = 115	165 − 95 = 70	77 + 98 = 175

96

5. Hold the large clock.
   a. **Name the hands.**
   b. **60 minutes=__.**
      30 minutes=__.
   c. Set the hands at **9:30.**
      In ½ hour it will be __.
      In 1 hour it will be __.
      ½ hour ago it was __.
      1 hour ago it was __.
   d. **Read the time together.**
      11:15, 1:45, 3:45, 6:15 . . .
6. Review
   2 cups=__. 1 pint
   2 pints=__. 1 quart
   4 quarts=__. 1 gallon
   16 ounces=__. 1 pound
7. Do the Speed Drill in Lesson 160.
8. Assign Lesson 160.

Write the numbers in the correct places.
Add a comma where needed.

	thousands	hundreds	tens	ones			thousands	hundreds	tens	ones
1583	1,	5	8	3		1639	1,	6	3	9
1815	1,	8	1	5		1298	1,	2	9	8
80			8	0		20			2	0
293		2	9	3		1315	1,	3	1	5
1325	1,	3	2	5		290		2	9	0
1324	1,	3	2	4		1784	1,	7	8	4
1623	1,	6	2	3		1816	1,	8	1	6

Write the time.

97

Blacklines

Missing Whole or Parts #18

Reading Problems #12

Number Facts #18

Fact Form III

Number Words #9

After Class

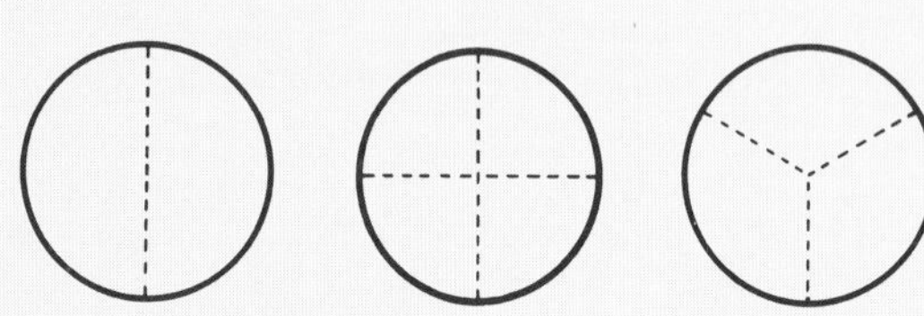

1. Have the children stand in a circle. **Race around the circle, saying the triplets.** (Pupil) **may begin.**
2. **Give me three fractions.**
   Write ½, ¼, ⅓.
   a. **One-half is 1 whole cut __.**
   One-fourth is 1 whole cut __.
   One-third is 1 whole cut __.
   b. **2 halves make __.** 1 whole
   4 fourths make __. 1 whole
   3 thirds make __. 1 whole
   c. **Which fraction is the largest?**
   Which fraction is the smallest?

"Whatsoever thy hand findeth to do, do it with thy might." Ecclesiastes 9:10

98

Answer these facts.

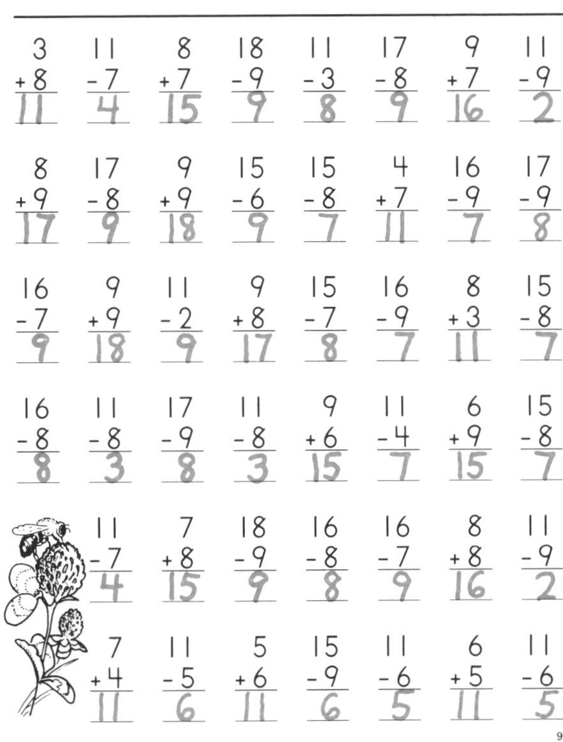

Before Class

Materials

14's–18's flash cards

Cup, pint, quart, gallon

Chalkboard

87	98	89	97	87	79	88
+99	−29	+79	−36	−58	+79	+89

147¢
330¢
289¢
400¢

Class Time

1. Have each child bring *My 1,000 Book* to the teaching corner.
   a. **Begin at 400. Count by 10's to 800.**
   b. **Count on to 1,000 by 5's.**
2. Stand near the Blossom Charts.
   a. Drill the triplets.
      11 and 12 triplets 1 time
      13 and 14 triplets 2 times
      15, 16, 17, and 18 triplets 3 times
   b. **Say the triplets by memory.**
3. Circle Drill: 14's–18's flash cards.
4. a. **What is the difference between 18 and 9?** 18−9=9
      What . . . 17 and 8? 17−8=9
      What . . . 16 and 7? 16−7=9
      What . . . 17 and 9? 17−9=8
   b. **What is the sum of 9 and 7?** 9+7=16
      What . . . 8 and 7? 8+7=15
      What . . . 9 and 8? 9+8=17
      What . . . 9 and 9? 9+9=18

Count the first row.
Write the amount.
Count the second row.
Write the amount.
Add.
Then copy the answer into the dollar box.

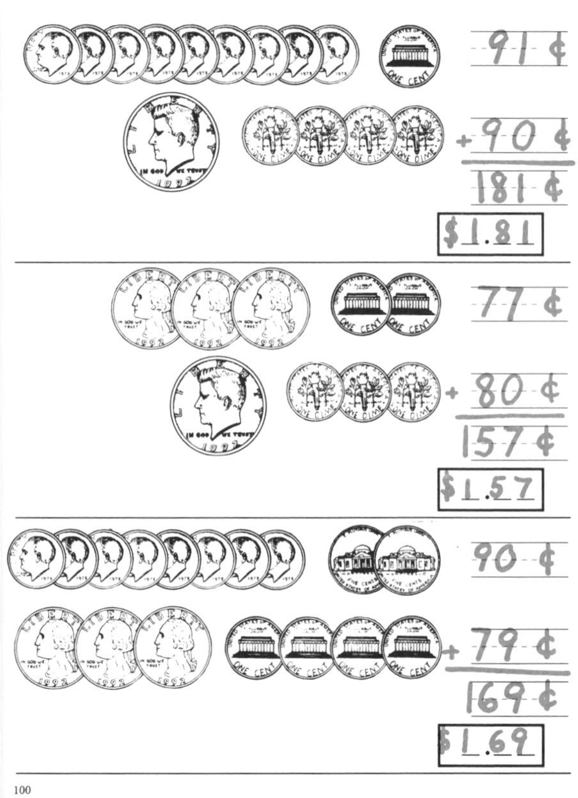

Extra Activity

5. **When you add, you may have to __.** carry *over*
   When you subtract, you may have to __. borrow *back*
6. Do the Compuation samples.
7. Review money.
   a. **We count nickels by __, quarters by __, pennies by __, dimes by __, and half dollars by __.**
   b. **How many pennies make 50¢?** Continue with nickels, dimes, quarters, and half dollars.
   c. Point to the Money samples.
   Read together as I change it.
   147¢=$1.47 (one dollar and forty-seven cents).
8. Assign Lesson 161.

Carry *over* or borrow *back*.

80	97	59	58	68	71
−54	−78	+48	+38	−49	−45
26	19	107	96	19	26

28	85	27	88	97	36
+77	−27	+69	+19	−39	+69
105	58	96	107	58	105

Answer these facts.

16	9	17	7	9	8	15	17
−7	+9	−9	+9	+8	+7	−6	−8
9	18	8	16	17	15	9	9

8	17	18	9	16	15	7	15
+9	−9	−9	+8	−8	−6	+8	−8
17	8	9	17	8	9	15	7

9	18	9	15	6	8	15	16
+9	−9	+7	−7	+9	+9	−6	−7
18	9	16	8	15	17	9	9

101

Blacklines

Triplets With Facts #15

2-Place Computation #12

Fact Form X

Equations #3

After Class

1. Oral Drill: **Whoever says the correct answer first may go to the back of his line.**

18−9	**16−8**	**17−9**	**9+6**
6+9	**7+8**	**8+8**	**16−9**
7+9	**8+9**	**16−7**	**15−7**
8+7	**9+7**	**9+9**	**9+8**
15−6	**17−8**	**15−8**	**15−9**

2. Display the cup, pint, quart, and gallon.
   a. **Name them.**
   b. **As the container becomes larger, the word becomes __.** longer
   c. **Which container**
      - **is less than 1 pint?** cup
      - **is more than 1 quart?** gallon
      - **is half of a pint?** cup
      - **is half of a quart?** pint
      - **holds 2 cups?** pint
      - **holds 4 cups?** quart

Extra Activity

102

162

Answer these facts.

162

5 + 7 = 12	12 − 7 = 5	17 − 8 = 9	9 + 9 = 18	12 − 8 = 4	8 + 9 = 17	12 − 5 = 7	12 − 9 = 3
17 − 8 = 9	6 + 6 = 12	18 − 9 = 9	9 + 3 = 12	16 − 8 = 8	8 + 9 = 17	9 + 8 = 17	17 − 9 = 8
12 − 9 = 3	15 − 8 = 7	9 + 8 = 17	12 − 8 = 4	9 + 9 = 18	15 − 6 = 9	12 − 7 = 5	8 + 4 = 12
12 − 6 = 6	3 + 9 = 12	16 − 8 = 8	17 − 9 = 8	12 − 4 = 8	16 − 9 = 7	4 + 8 = 12	16 − 7 = 9
7 + 8 = 15	15 − 6 = 9	6 + 9 = 15	16 − 7 = 9	9 + 6 = 15	7 + 9 = 16	8 + 8 = 16	8 + 7 = 15
		16 − 9 = 7	15 − 7 = 8	17 − 9 = 8	12 − 4 = 8	7 + 5 = 12	15 − 9 = 6

103

Before Class

Materials

12's–18's flash cards

Chalkboard

Class Time

1. Flash the 12's–18's cards.
   Boys, answer the addition facts.
   Girls, answer the subtraction facts.
2. Stand near the blossoms and blanks on the board.
   a. Have individuals fill them as everyone says the triplets together. Do the blossoms clockwise, using 11–15 triplets.
   b. **Say the facts as I fill the hive.**
   16−9, 7 . . . Fill the hive with 16's–18's.
3. Drill 15–18 triplets on the Blossom Charts.
4. **What belongs on the blank?**
   (Say *blank* each time.)

17, 9 __	**18 __ 9**	**__ 9, 9**
18, 9 __	**16 __ 7**	**__ 8, 8**
16, 9 __	**17 __ 8**	**__ 9, 7**
16, 8 __	**16 __ 8**	**__ 9, 8**

162

Speed Drill

Answer these problems.
Carry *over* in some problems.

126 - 95 = 31	88 + 37 = 125	166 - 94 = 72	158 - 65 = 93	66 + 96 = 162	168 - 86 = 82
86 + 83 = 169	179 - 88 = 91	88 + 64 = 152	127 - 84 = 43	93 + 75 = 168	189 - 96 = 93
47 + 78 = 125	129 - 98 = 31	127 - 34 = 93	159 - 87 = 72	156 - 74 = 82	67 + 95 = 162
167 - 76 = 91	95 + 74 = 169	128 - 85 = 43	84 + 68 = 152	187 - 94 = 93	73 + 95 = 168
129 - 65 = 64	26 + 99 = 125	128 - 48 = 80	88 + 69 = 157	69 + 98 = 167	128 - 63 = 65
		79 + 78 = 157	163 - 83 = 80	47 + 78 = 125	158 - 94 = 64

104

5. Review
   60 minutes=__. 1 hour
   30 minutes=__. ½ hour
   12 things=__. 1 dozen
   6 things=__. ½ dozen
   7 days=__. 1 week
   12 months=__. 1 year
   12 inches=__. 1 foot
   3 feet=__. 1 yard
   2 cups=__. 1 pint
   2 pints=__. 1 quart
   4 quarts=__. 1 gallon
   16 ounces=__. 1 pound
6. Do the Speed Drill in Lesson 162.
7. Assign Lesson 162.

Answer these problems.

34	44	25	53	35	64
43	30	43	33	22	25
+79	+98	+99	+99	+28	+78
156	172	167	185	85	167

46	39	33	54	43	36
43	50	54	34	25	53
+68	+86	+78	+99	+14	+77
157	175	165	187	82	166

Trace and copy.

12 inches = 1 foot

12 inches = 1 foot

3 feet = 1 yard

3 feet = 1 yard

16 ounces = 1 pound

16 ounces = 1 pound

105

Blacklines

Missing Whole or Parts #18

Fact Form X

Number Words #9

Equations #3

After Class

1. Have the children stand in a circle.
   Race around the circle, saying the triplets.
2. Chalkboard Drill: **Write the three numbers I say.**

   1,155 1,055 1,515

   Circle the number with the greatest hundreds.

   1,280 1,208 1,802

   Circle . . . the greatest tens.

   1,063 1,630 1,360

   Circle . . . the smallest tens.

   1,791 1,719 1,079

   Circle . . . the smallest ones.

   1,406 1,809 1,100

   Circle . . . the greatest hundreds.

Speed Drill

9	17	9	16	9	7
+7	-9	+9	-9	+8	+9
16	8	18	7	17	16

17	8	16	18	9	17
-9	+9	-7	-9	+8	-9
8	17	9	9	17	8

7	8	16	9	17	9	9	18
+9	+9	-9	+9	-9	+7	+8	-9
16	17	7	18	8	16	17	9

6	3	5	4	7	8	4	5
2	6	4	4	2	1	3	3
+9	+7	+9	+9	+8	+9	+9	+9
17	16	18	17	17	18	16	17

"Whatsoever thy hand findeth to do, do it with thy might." Ecclesiastes 9:10

106

163

Answer these facts.

8 +4 12	12 -9 3	15 -6 9	9 +9 18	12 -8 4	8 +9 17	15 -8 7	12 -7 5
18 -9 9	9 +3 12	17 -8 9	6 +6 12	16 -8 8	8 +9 17	9 +8 17	17 -9 8
12 -7 5	12 -5 7	9 +8 17	12 -8 4	9 +9 18	17 -8 9	12 -9 3	5 +7 12
15 -9 6	7 +5 12	16 -8 8	17 -9 8	15 -7 8	16 -9 7	4 +8 12	16 -7 9
6 +9 15	15 -6 9	8 +7 15	16 -7 9	9 +6 15	7 +9 16	8 +8 16	8 +7 15
		16 -9 7	12 -4 8	17 -9 8	12 -4 8	3 +9 12	12 -6 6

Before Class

Chalkboard

87	98	89	88	67	89	98
−49	−76	−35	−59	−28	−56	−29

Class Time

1. Call the children to your teaching corner.

   King Solomon had gardens and orchards. He often talked about trees and birds, animals and insects.

   He may have talked about bees too. I am sure that the bees visited his gardens and orchards.

   King Solomon did enjoy honey. In Proverbs, he said, "Eat . . . __ (honey), because it is good." (Proverbs 24:13)

2. Point to the Number Line.
   a. **Count the even numbers from 50 to 150.**
   b. **Count the odd numbers to 99.**
   c. **Count by 10's.**
      - **7, 17 . . .**
      - **4, 14 . . .**
      - **8, 18 . . .**
      - **96, 86 . . .**
      - **92, 82 . . .**
      - **99, 89 . . .**

163

Fill in the missing whole or parts.

9 + 9 = 18	16 - 7 = 9	15 - 7 = 8
9 + 8 = 17	7 + 8 = 15	9 + 9 = 18
16 - 8 = 8	18 - 9 = 9	15 - 7 = 8
15 - 6 = 9	17 - 8 = 9	17 - 8 = 9
7 + 9 = 16	9 + 9 = 18	8 + 8 = 16
15 - 9 = 6	9 + 7 = 16	16 - 9 = 7

Extra Activity

Answer these problems.

6	3	4	3	8	2	4	7
3	5	5	5	1	7	3	1
+7	+7	+9	+9	+8	+7	+8	+8
16	15	18	17	17	16	15	16

5	3	7	3	5	2	1	4
4	6	2	6	3	5	6	4
+8	+9	+6	+7	+8	+8	+9	+9
17	18	15	16	16	15	16	17

108

3. **Raise your hand to answer.**

50+10	**29−10**	**45+10**
61+10	**54+10**	**90−10**
32−10	**78−10**	**33+10**
87−10	**66+10**	**72−10**

4. Stand near the Blossom Charts.
   a. **Jump from chart to chart.**
   b. Drill the 14–18 triplets.
5. Do the Subtraction samples.
6. Review fractions.
   a. **Name three fractions.**
   Write ½, ¼, ⅓.
   b. **Ray ate ¼ of a cantaloupe. Nevin ate ⅓ of a cantaloupe. Who ate more?**
   c. **How many halves make 1 whole?**
   Continue with thirds and fourths.
7. Assign Lesson 163.

Carry *over* or borrow *back*.

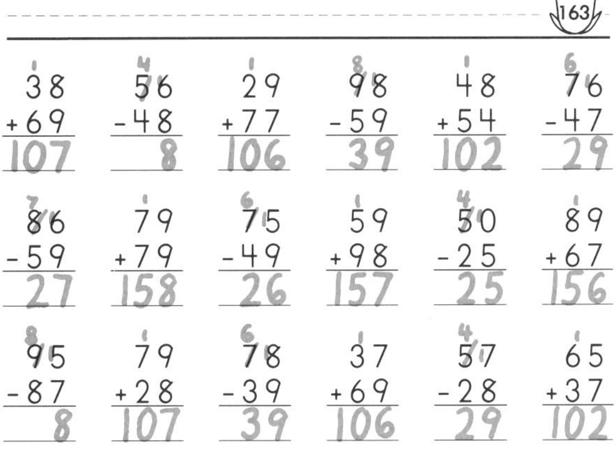

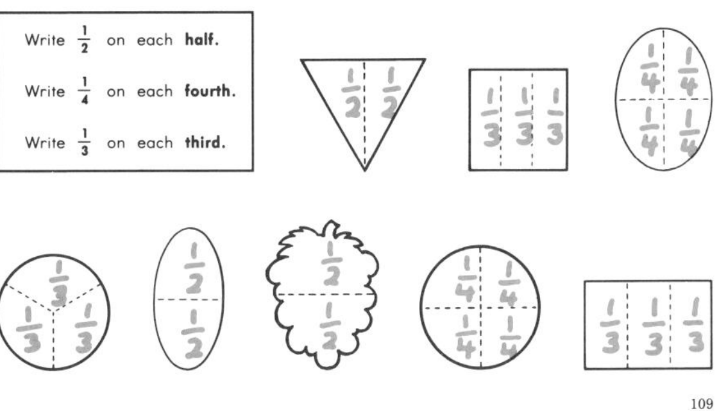

Blacklines

- Triplets With Facts #15
- Reading Problems #13
- 2-Place Computation #12
- Fact Form X

After Class

1. **Answer together.**

10+3	**10+9**	**10+5**
10+6	**10+4**	**10+8**
10+2	**10+1**	**10+7**

2. Chalkboard Drill

8 nickels=__. 40¢
2 quarters=__. 50¢
7 dimes=__. 70¢
38 pennies=__. 38¢
1 half dollar=__. 50¢
3 quarters=__. 75¢
9 dimes=__. 90¢
2 half dollars=__. 100¢ or $1.00
10 nickels=__. 50¢
4 quarters=__. 100¢ or $1.00
3 dimes + 2 pennies= __. 32¢
1 quarter + 3pennies= __. 28¢
4 nickels + 4 pennies= __. 24¢
1 half dollar + 1 dime= __. 60¢
2 quarters + 2 nickels= __. 60¢

164

Answer these facts.

164

13 -9 4	13 -4 9	15 -8 7	13 -7 6	7 +6 13	16 -9 7	17 -8 9	5 +8 13
4 +9 13	17 -9 8	9 +8 17	6 +7 13	15 -9 6	8 +9 17	16 -8 8	13 -9 4
17 -9 8	15 -7 8	9 +6 15	13 -8 5	7 +9 16	7 +8 15	13 -5 8	8 +5 13
9 +4 13	8 +8 16	13 -6 7	9 +7 16	13 -8 5	16 -9 7	7 +9 16	17 -9 8
18 -9 9	16 -8 8	17 -9 8	18 -9 9	15 -6 9	15 -7 8	17 -9 8	6 +9 15
		8 +7 15	15 -6 9	16 -7 9	16 -7 9	9 +9 18	16 -7 9

111

Before Class

Materials

13's–18's flash cards

11's–18's flash cards

Chalkboard

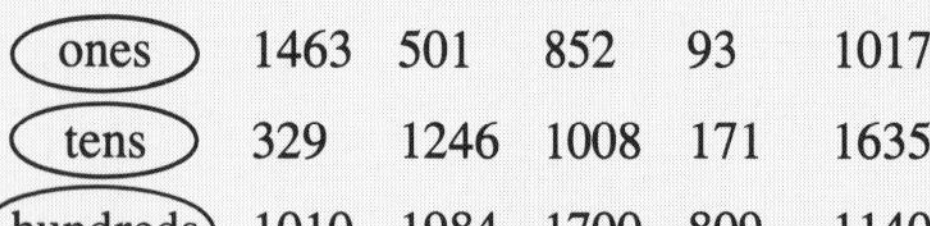

ones	1463	501	852	93	1017
tens	329	1246	1008	171	1635
hundreds	1010	1984	1700	809	1140

Class Time

1. Call the children to the blossoms and blanks on the board.
   a. **Say the triplets as I fill the blossoms.**
   b. **What shall I write in the hive?**
   16−9, 7 . . .
2. Flash the 13's–18's cards.
   Girls, answer the addition facts.
   Boys, answer the subtraction facts.
3. **To find**
   - **how much more 56 is than 18,**
   we __. subtract
   - **how much less 12 is than 43,**
   we __. subtract
   - **the sum of 25 and 69, we __.** add
   - **the difference between 70 and 20,**
   we __. subtract
4. **Half of 4 is __.** Continue with half of 10, 14, 6, 18, 20, 16, 40, 12, 60, 100.

164

Speed Drill

Answer these problems.
Carry *over* in some problems.

136 -86 50	38 +45 83	167 -85 82	156 -94 62	56 +83 139	138 -46 92
38 +69 107	179 -96 83	65 +85 150	179 -84 95	37 +26 63	159 -81 78
56 +27 83	138 -88 50	135 -73 62	135 -53 82	189 -97 92	44 +95 139
158 -75 83	59 +48 107	157 -62 95	56 +94 150	168 -90 78	39 +24 63
168 -73 95	82 +82 164	178 -94 84	79 +26 105	64 +96 160	139 -98 41
		88 +17 105	167 -83 84	91 +73 164	187 -92 95

112

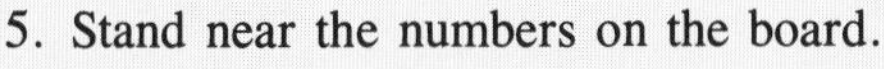

5. Stand near the numbers on the board.
   a. Add the missing commas.
   b. Circle the correct numeral.
   c. **Read the numbers with me.**
6. Do the Speed Drill in Lesson 164.
7. Assign Lesson 164.

Read the story.
Write the numbers
in the beehive.
Write the label words
on the lines.
Answer the problem.

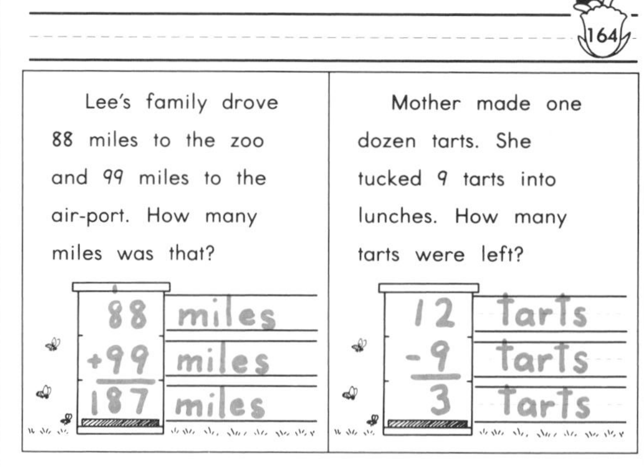

164

Lee's family drove 88 miles to the zoo and 99 miles to the air-port. How many miles was that?

88	miles
+99	miles
187	miles

Mother made one dozen tarts. She tucked 9 tarts into lunches. How many tarts were left?

12	tarts
-9	tarts
3	tarts

Trace and copy.

2 cups = 1 pint
2 cups = 1 pint
2 pints = 1 quart
2 pints = 1 quart
4 quarts = 1 gallon
4 quarts = 1 gallon

113

Blacklines

Missing Whole or Parts #19
Fact Form XI
Fact Form III
Number Words #10

After Class

1. Have individuals give the triplets by memory.
2. Double Drill: 11's–18's flash cards. **Whoever says the correct answer first may have the card.**
3. **16 ounces=__.**
   a. **Which of these things weigh more than 1 pound? dictionary, feather, tulip, brick, rooster, father's shoes, light bulb**
   b. **Which of these things weigh less than 1 pound? eraser, thimble, ironing board, marble, lollipop, sewing machine, turkey**

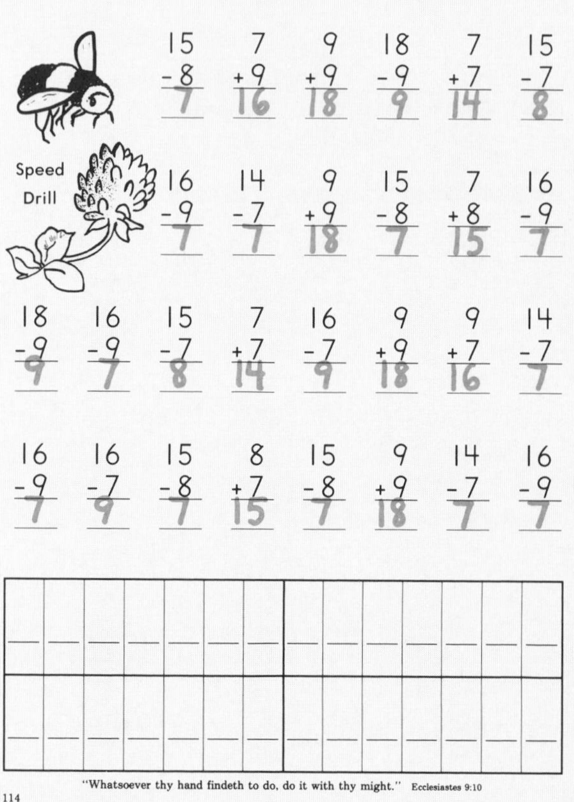

Speed Drill

15 - 8 = 7	7 + 9 = 16	9 + 9 = 18	18 - 9 = 9	7 + 7 = 14	15 - 7 = 8
16 - 9 = 7	14 - 7 = 7	9 + 9 = 18	15 - 8 = 7	7 + 8 = 15	16 - 9 = 7

18 - 9 = 9	16 - 9 = 7	15 - 7 = 8	7 + 7 = 14	16 - 7 = 9	9 + 9 = 18	9 + 7 = 16	14 - 7 = 7
16 - 9 = 7	16 - 7 = 9	15 - 8 = 7	8 + 7 = 15	15 - 8 = 7	9 + 9 = 18	14 - 7 = 7	16 - 9 = 7

"Whatsoever thy hand findeth to do, do it with thy might." Ecclesiastes 9:10

114

165

Answer the facts.

Before Class

Materials

13's–18's flash cards

Form C

Chalkboard

97	86	80	98	97	97	70
−39	−49	−57	−76	−88	−35	−24

8+9=	6+8=	16−7=	7+8=	16−8=
7+7=	9+7=	6+9=	9+9=	14−6=
14−5=	18−9=	15−7=	7+9=	15−6=
16−9=	14−7=	8+8=	14−9=	17−9=
14−8=	8+7=	17−8=	15−9=	5+9=
9+8=	9+6=	9+5=	8+6=	15−8=

Note: You will use the grid in Lesson 166 too.

Class Time

1. Call the children to the Blossom Charts.

   A honeybee buzzes to the clover patch to gather nectar. Will one blossom have enough nectar to fill its honey stomach?

   Once a man followed a honeybee to count how many blossoms the bee would visit to get one load of nectar. The bee visited 585 blossoms. Then the bee made a beeline back to the hive with its load.

   How many nectar loads can a bee gather in one hour? It may gather 30 loads! Now we know what people mean when they say, "Be as busy as bee!"

2. Drill the triplets.
3. Stand near the grid on the board.

   Answer together.

4. Flash Card Drill: 13's–18's flash cards. Use Form C. **Flower Row: Box 1 . . .**
5. Do the Subtraction samples.

Extra Activity

Read the story.
Write the numbers in the beehive.
Write the label words on the lines.
Answer the problem.

Father cut grass. The boys raked it into 17 heaps. They dumped 8 heaps on the garden. How many heaps were left?

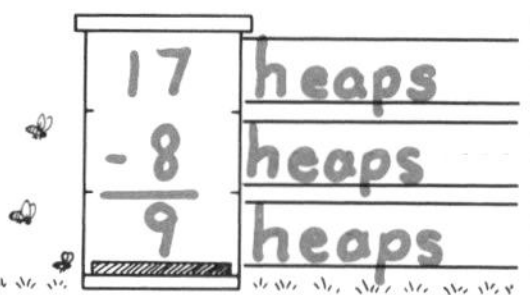

Fred and Fay played church. Fred preached for five minutes. They sang for nine minutes. How many minutes was that?

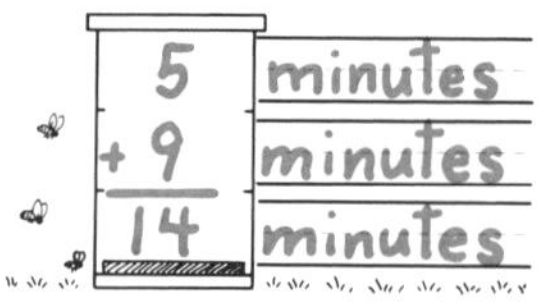

Grandfather had seventeen kids in his flock of goats. He sold eight kids. How many kids did he have then?

Mother has one dozen buttons in a jar and 88 buttons in a box. How many buttons does Mother have altogether?

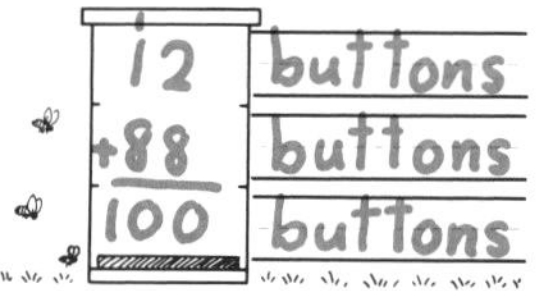

116

6. Review
   60 minutes=__. 1 hour
   30 minutes=__. ½ hour
   12 things=__. 1 dozen
   6 things=__. ½ dozen
   12 inches=__. 1 foot
   3 feet=__. 1 yard
   7 days=__. 1 week
   12 months=__. 1 year
   2 cups=__. 1 pint
   2 pints=__. 1 quart
   4 quarts=__. 1 gallon
   16 ounces=__. 1 pound
7. Assign Lesson 165.

Carry *over* or borrow *back*.

Write the time.

Blacklines

Form C (Class Time)

2-Place Computation #13

Fact Form XI

Mixed Computation #8

Equations #4

After Class

1. Drill each child at the grid on the chalkboard. Can he answer all the facts in 40 seconds?
2. Ask individuals to name the 12 months of the year.
3. Fill in the shapes with *T, R, S,* or *C.*

166

Answer these facts.

166

14 -5 9	15 -7 8	14 -9 5	16 -7 9	9 +5 14	14 -9 5	16 -8 8	7 +7 14
5 +9 14	14 -7 7	9 +5 14	8 +6 14	14 -5 9	5 +9 14	15 -8 7	16 -7 9
14 -8 6	16 -9 7	7 +9 16	18 -9 9	9 +8 17	9 +7 16	15 -8 7	9 +4 13
4 +9 13	6 +8 14	14 -7 7	8 +9 17	17 -8 9	16 -9 7	7 +7 14	15 -9 6
17 -9 8	14 -8 6	9 +6 15	17 -8 9	17 -9 8	6 +9 15	15 -9 6	8 +6 14
		6 +8 14	15 -7 8	18 -9 9	14 -5 9	8 +8 16	14 -6 8

119

Before Class

Materials

Cup, pint, quart, gallon
Half dollar

Chalkboard

__	41	__	__	__	81	__
8	__	__	__	48	__	__
__	29	31	__	__	__	__
350	__	__	500	__	__	__

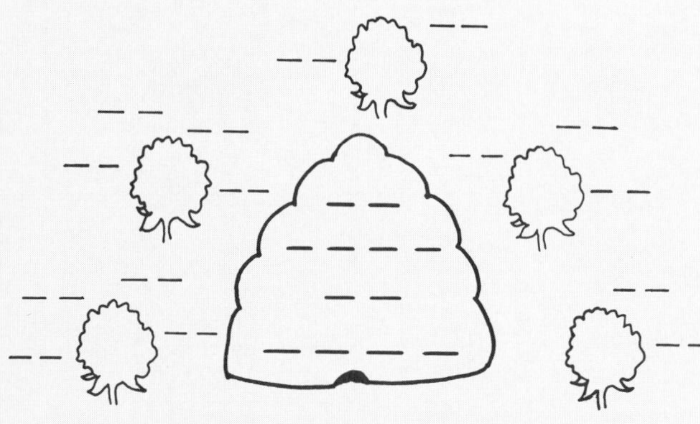

Class Time

1. Call the children to the Number Line.
   a. **Count backwards by 10's.**
      •100, 90 . . .
      •93, 83 . . .
      •97, 87 . . .
2. Have responsive counting. **I will say the first number; you say the next number.**
   a. **Count by 100's to 1,000.**
   b. **Count by 50's to 1,000.**
   c. **Count the odd numbers to 99.**
3. Fill in the Missing Number samples.
4. Stand near the blossoms and blanks on the board.
   a. **Give me triplets for the blossoms.**
   b. **Give me facts for the beehive.**
5. **What belongs on the blank?**
   (Say *blank* each time.)

15, 8 __	**16 __ 7**	**__ 9, 9**
17, 9 __	**15 __ 6**	**__ 8, 7**
16, 8 __	**14 __ 6**	**__ 8, 8**
18, 9 __	**17 __ 8**	**__ 9, 8**

166

Speed Drill

Answer these problems.
Carry *over* in some problems.

144 − 93 = 51	35 + 49 = 84	177 − 95 = 82	146 − 54 = 92	96 + 53 = 149	168 − 86 = 82
38 + 67 = 105	159 − 96 = 63	75 + 85 = 160	179 − 84 = 95	69 + 37 = 106	157 − 84 = 73
56 + 28 = 84	149 − 98 = 51	154 − 62 = 92	145 − 63 = 82	159 − 77 = 82	74 + 75 = 149
148 − 85 = 63	57 + 48 = 105	187 − 92 = 95	60 + 90 = 150	146 − 73 = 73	77 + 29 = 106
145 − 95 = 50	96 + 83 = 179	168 − 74 = 94	79 + 28 = 107	74 + 66 = 140	149 − 58 = 91
		88 + 19 = 107	167 − 73 = 94	84 + 95 = 179	147 − 97 = 50

120

6. Stand near the grid on the board. Drill the facts down and up, left and right.
7. Display the liquid measures.
   a. **2 cups=__.** 1 pint
      2 pints=__. 1 quart
      4 quarts=__. 1 gallon
   b. **Which is smaller:**
      •**2 pints or 2 cups?** 2 cups
      •**1 gallon or 1 quart?** 1 quart
      •**1 pint or 1 quart?** 1 pint
      •**1 cup or 1 pint?** 1 cup
      •**3 cups or 1 pint?** 1 pint
      •**3 cups or 1 quart?** 3 cups
      •**2 quarts or 1 gallon?** 2 quarts
8. Do the Speed Drill in Lesson 166.
9. Assign Lesson 166.

Carry *over* in one or two places.

289	549	259	477	177	628
+686	+249	+508	+379	+588	+239
975	798	767	856	765	867

489	357	358	269	167	528
+269	+529	+399	+607	+589	+338
758	886	757	876	756	866

459	576	587	328	359	777
+408	+189	+269	+439	+439	+198
867	765	856	767	798	975

Write $\frac{1}{2}$ on each **half.**

Write $\frac{1}{4}$ on each **fourth.**

Write $\frac{1}{3}$ on each **third.**

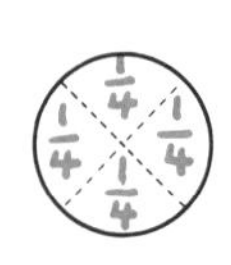

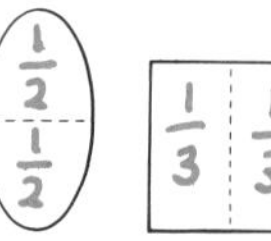

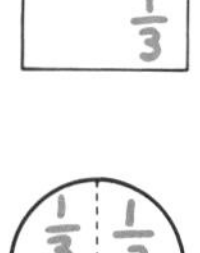

121

Blacklines

Reading Problems #14

Fact Form XI

Mixed Computation #9

Fact Form III

Number Words #10

After Class

1. Stand in a circle. **Race around the circle, saying the triplets.**
2. **How many pieces would you have if you cut**
   - **a pie into fourths?**
   - **an apple into halves?**
   - **a banana into thirds?**
3. Hold the half dollar. **How many pennies are in a half dollar?** Continue with nickels, dimes, quarters, and half dollars.

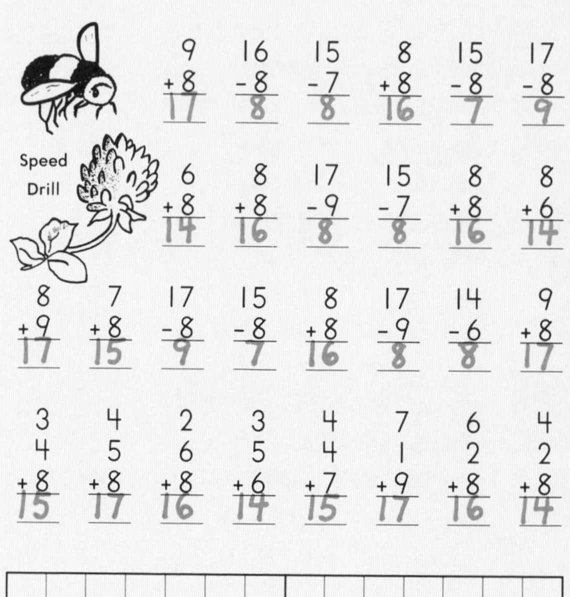

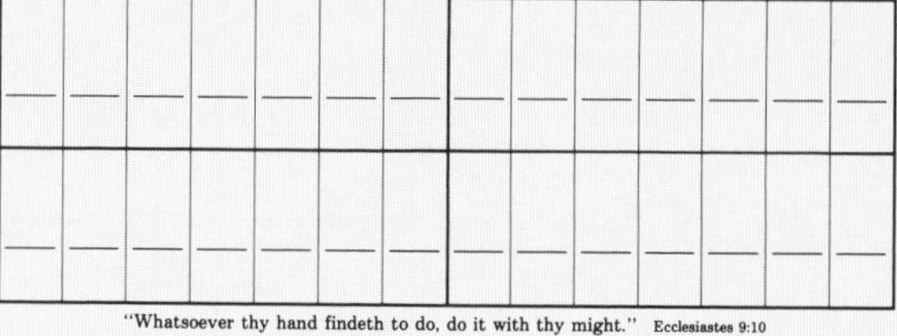

"Whatsoever thy hand findeth to do, do it with thy might." Ecclesiastes 9:10

122

167

Answer these facts.

167

		15 − 9 = 6	14 − 5 = 9	6 + 9 = 15	14 − 7 = 7	16 − 9 = 7	8 + 7 = 15
9 + 6 = 15	18 − 9 = 9	7 + 9 = 16	7 + 8 = 15	17 − 8 = 9	8 + 8 = 16	15 − 6 = 9	15 − 9 = 6
17 − 9 = 8	16 − 7 = 9	8 + 7 = 15	17 − 9 = 8	8 + 6 = 14	7 + 8 = 15	14 − 5 = 9	6 + 8 = 14
7 + 7 = 14	9 + 7 = 16	15 − 8 = 7	5 + 9 = 14	14 − 6 = 8	15 − 8 = 7	7 + 9 = 16	15 − 7 = 8
14 − 8 = 6	15 − 7 = 8	15 − 6 = 9	14 − 9 = 5	9 + 5 = 14	15 − 6 = 9	15 − 7 = 8	14 − 6 = 8
16 − 8 = 8	9 + 9 = 18	9 + 8 = 17	6 + 8 = 14	14 − 9 = 5	8 + 9 = 17	9 + 9 = 18	15 − 9 = 6

123

Before Class

Materials

14's–18's flash cards

Large coins

Chalkboard

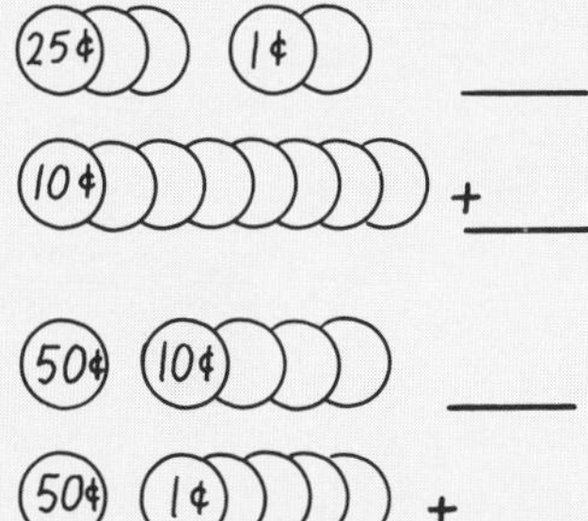

Class Time

1. Circle Drill: 14's–18's flash cards.
2. Stand near the Blossom Charts.
   a. **Jump from chart to chart.**
   b. **Boys, say the triplets by memory.**
   Girls, say the triplets by memory.
3. Chalkboard Drill: **Write the whole problem.**
   a. **What is the difference between 17 and 8?** 17−8=9
   What . . . 93 and 48? 93−48=45
   What . . . 89 and 56? 89−56=33
   What . . . 90 and 34? 90−34=56
   b. **What is the sum of 9 and 9?** 9+9=18
   What . . . 80 and 54? 80+54=134
   What . . . 38 and 26? 38+26=64
   What . . . 79 and 29? 79+29=108

167

Count the first row.
Write the amount.
Count the second row.
Write the amount.
Add.
Then copy the answer into the dollar box.

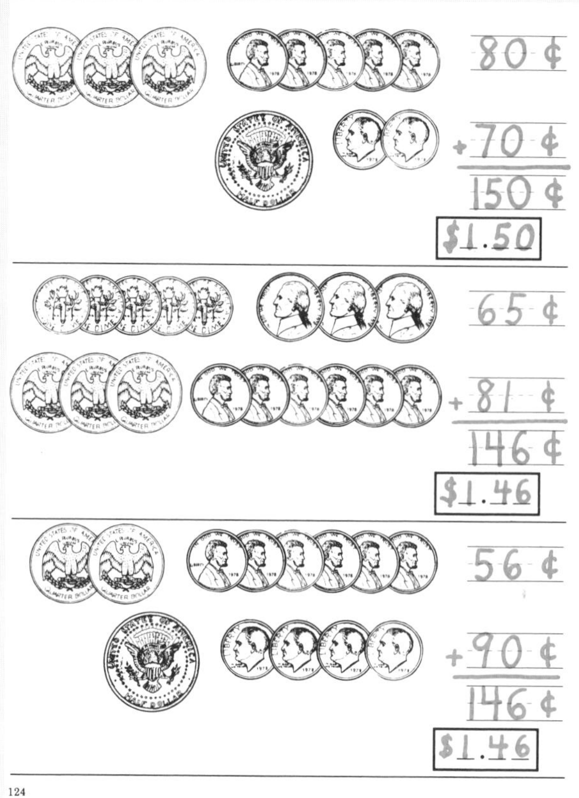

Extra Activity

4. Flash the large coins. **5¢, 50¢** . . .
   a. **We count dimes by __, pennies by __, quarters by __, nickels by __, and half dollars by __.**
   b. **Count the money problems with me.**
5. Review
   2 cups=__. 1 pint
   2 pints=__. 1 quart
   4 quarts=__. 1 gallon
   16 ounces=__. 1 pound
6. Assign Lesson 167.

After Class

1,260	1,001
1,100	1,428
1,743	1,090
1,012	1,574
1,685	1,810

167

167

Carry *over* or borrow *back*.

94	38	87	55	39	94
-55	+46	-48	-28	+68	-28
39	84	39	27	107	66

55	28	74	96	47	88
-19	+59	-37	-67	+57	-19
36	87	37	29	104	69

75	86	97	94	85	27
+29	-38	-39	-46	-27	+78
104	48	58	48	58	105

Answer these facts.

18	15	9	15	8	5	17	9
-9	-8	+6	-7	+8	+9	-8	+8
9	7	15	8	16	14	9	17

8	15	9	7	14	8	16	14
+9	-6	+5	+9	-6	+7	-9	-5
17	9	14	16	8	15	7	9

125

Blacklines

Triplets With Facts #16

2-Place Computation #13

Fact Form XII

Mixed Computation #10

Equations #4

1. Call the children to the numbers on the board.
   a. **Number places are ones, tens, hundreds . . .**
   b. **Which number has 6 hundreds?**
      Continue with **3 ones**
      2 tens **7 tens**
      2 hundreds **9 tens**
   c. **Six of the numbers have 0. Read those with me.**
   d. Ask individuals to read the number you point to.
2. **16 ounces=__.**
   a. **Name something that weighs about 1 pound.** (Accept reasonable answers.) a box of butter, a loaf of bread, a box of cereal . . .
   b. **Name something that weighs less than 1 pound.** washcloth, pen, pair of socks . . .

126

168

Answer these facts.

168

16	15	18	9	8	16	15	9
-9	-6	-9	+7	+6	-7	-9	+7
7	9	9	16	14	9	6	16
16	17	8	16	15	9	14	6
-8	-9	+8	-7	-8	+6	-9	+8
8	8	16	9	7	15	5	14
16	16	8	14	16	5	7	14
-7	-9	+8	-5	-7	+9	+9	-8
9	7	16	9	9	14	16	6
15	14	17	7	8	14	7	14
-7	-6	-8	+9	+7	-7	+7	-9
8	8	9	16	15	7	14	5
16	17	16	7	8	15	16	9
-8	-8	-7	+8	+9	-7	-9	+9
8	9	9	15	17	8	7	18
		16	9	6	15	18	17
		-8	+8	+9	-6	-9	-9
		8	17	15	9	9	8

127

Before Class

Materials

10's–18's flash cards

Chalkboard

79	70	99	95	87	89	90	89
−27	−66	−46	−78	−59	−39	−67	−25

Class Time

1. Call the children to the Blossom Charts.

   God gave honeybees a work that no other animal or insect can do. They stick to their work as if there is not a minute to lose. No mouse or bear, no ants or skunk or toad can stop a hiveful of busy bees.

   In the fields they buzz from blossom to blossom; then they make a beeline to their little city of wax cells inside the hive.

   There the nectar is changed into honey—sweet honey for you and me.

2. Drill the triplets on the Blossom Charts.
   11 and 12 triplets 1 time
   13 and 14 triplets 2 times
   15, 16, 17, and 18 triplets 3 times

3. Double Drill: 10's–18's flash cards.
   Whoever says it first may have it.

168

Speed Drill

Answer these problems.
Carry *over* in some problems.

169 -87 82	68 +27 95	179 -94 85	157 -85 72	73 +86 159	166 -76 90
72 +74 146	159 -62 97	93 +85 178	156 -94 62	82 +66 148	177 -84 93
39 +67 106	149 -87 62	148 -74 74	96 +63 159	187 -95 92	57 +39 96
188 -95 93	63 +85 148	148 -86 62	84 +94 178	167 -70 97	53 +93 146
144 -54 90	84 +75 159	168 -96 72	147 -62 85	66 +29 95	156 -74 82
		75 +84 159	169 -95 74	147 -85 62	68 +38 106

4. **When you add, you may have to __.**
   carry *over*
   When you subtract, you may have to __. borrow *back*
5. Do the Subtraction samples.
6. **Raise your hand to answer.**
   (Speak slowly.)

6+9−8=	7	**16−8+7=**	15
8+8−7=	9	**17−8+6=**	15
5+9−6=	8	**15−7+8=**	16
9+9−9=	9	**18−9+5=**	14
7+9−8=	8	**15−6+8=**	17
8+7−9=	6	**17−9+7=**	15

7. Do the Speed Drill in Lesson 168.
8. Assign Lesson 168.

Answer these problems.

35	46	15	64	45	63
43	31	63	23	22	26
+79	+69	+96	+69	+78	+78
157	146	174	156	145	167

55	45	32	54	23	36
24	22	56	25	45	53
+78	+78	+88	+75	+78	+78
157	145	176	154	146	167

Trace and copy.

12 inches = 1 foot
12 inches = 1 foot
3 feet = 1 yard
3 feet = 1 yard
16 ounces = 1 pound
16 ounces = 1 pound

129

Blacklines

- Missing Whole or Parts #19
- Fact Form XII
- Mixed Computation #8
- Fact Form III
- Equations #4

After Class

1. Chalkboard Drill: **Write the number that comes next.**

   38, 48, 58, __ **11, 13, 15, __**
   62, 72, 82, __ **59, 61, 63, __**
   51, 41, 31, __ **520, 525, 530, __**
   75, 65, 55, __ **785, 790, 795, __**

2. **Which is more:**
   - **3 dimes or 1 quarter?** 3 dimes
   - **35 pennies or 6 nickels?** 35 pennies
   - **1 half dollar or 6 dimes?** 6 dimes
   - **3 quarters or 8 dimes?** 8 dimes
   - **5 nickels or 2 dimes?** 5 nickels
   - **2 half dollars or 9 dimes?** 2 half dollars

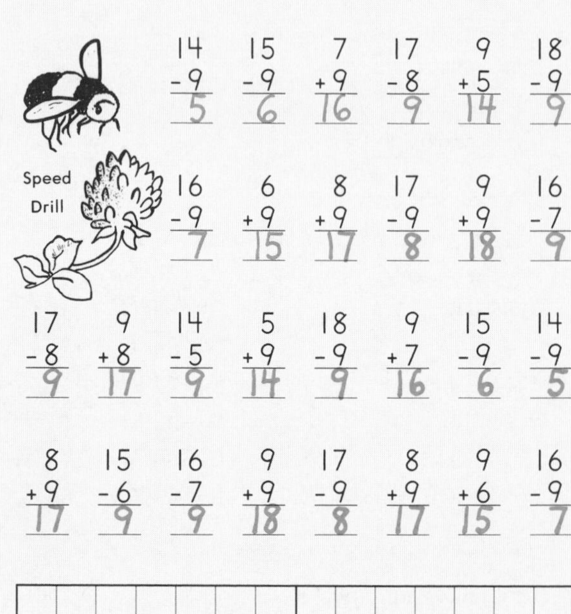
Speed Drill

14	15	7	17	9	18
-9	-9	+9	-8	+5	-9
5	6	16	9	14	9

16	6	8	17	9	16
-9	+9	+9	-9	+9	-7
7	15	17	8	18	9

17	9	14	5	18	9	15	14
-8	+8	-5	+9	-9	+7	-9	-9
9	17	9	14	9	16	6	5

8	15	16	9	17	8	9	16
+9	-6	-7	+9	-9	+9	+6	-9
17	9	9	18	8	17	15	7

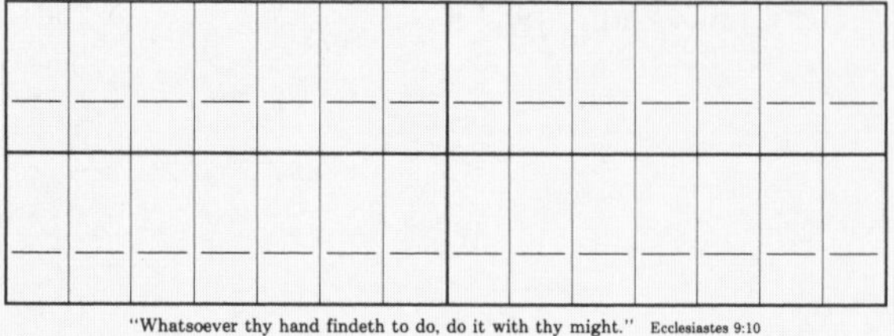

"Whatsoever thy hand findeth to do, do it with thy might." Ecclesiastes 9:10

130

169

Answer these facts.

169

		17	9	16	17	9	16
		−9	+8	−8	−8	+8	−9
		8	17	8	9	17	7

7	7	14	8	14	15	8	17
+7	+9	−7	+9	−5	−7	+9	−9
14	16	7	17	9	8	17	8
14	6	15	9	5	9	15	17
−8	+9	−8	+7	+9	+9	−6	−8
6	15	7	16	14	18	9	9
8	14	17	7	15	17	9	15
+6	−9	−9	+8	−7	−9	+7	−6
14	5	8	15	8	8	16	9
9	15	8	16	9	6	16	18
+6	−9	+8	−9	+9	+8	−7	−9
15	6	16	7	18	14	9	9
14	9	8	14	16	14	16	7
−9	+5	+7	−6	−8	−6	−7	+9
5	14	15	8	8	8	9	16

131

Before Class

Materials

14's–18's flash cards

Large clock

Chalkboard

3 quarters + 2 pennies =
4 dimes + 2 nickels =
1 half dollar + 2 dimes =
8 nickels + 4 pennies =
2 quarters + 3 dimes =
9 nickels + 1 penny =

156¢
173¢
206¢
250¢
300¢

Class Time

1. Call the children to the Blossom Charts.
   a. **I will say the whole number, you say the parts.**
   b. Drill the 14–18 triplets three times.
2. Flash the 14's–18's cards for 1 minute.
3. **Answer together.**
   a. **18 is how much more than 9?** 18−9=9
      16 . . . than 7? 16−7=9
      17 . . . than 8? 17−8=9
      16 . . . than 8? 16−8=8
   b. **9 is how much less than 17?** 17−9=8
      8 . . . than 15? 15−8=7
      9 . . . than 16? 16−9=7
      6 . . . than 15? 15−6=9
4. Do the Money samples.

169

Fill in the missing whole or part.

8 + 9 = 17	15 - 6 = 9	8 + 9 = 17
15 - 6 = 9	17 - 8 = 9	18 - 9 = 9
18 - 9 = 9	8 + 8 = 16	15 - 6 = 9
7 + 8 = 15	9 + 8 = 17	7 + 9 = 16
15 - 8 = 7	9 + 6 = 15	8 + 8 = 16
9 + 7 = 16	16 - 8 = 8	15 - 7 = 8

Extra Activity

Answer these problems.

4	7	4	2	4	8	3	6
4	2	3	6	5	0	3	3
+7	+9	+8	+8	+7	+9	+9	+8
15	18	15	16	16	17	15	17

8	3	6	6	5	1	3	3
1	4	3	1	3	8	6	5
+7	+8	+9	+8	+9	+6	+8	+8
16	15	18	15	17	15	17	16

132

5. **Answer together.**
   1 hour has __. 60 minutes
   ½ hour has __. 30 minutes
   1 dozen has __. 12 things
   ½ dozen has __. 6 things
   1 week has __. 7 days
   1 year has __. 12 months
   1 foot has __. 12 inches
   1 yard has __. 3 feet
   1 pint has __. 2 cups
   1 quart has __. 2 pints
   1 gallon has __. 4 quarts
   1 pound has __. 16 ounces
6. Assign Lesson 169.

169

Carry *over* or borrow *back*.

35 + 69 = 104	95 − 58 = 37	27 + 78 = 105	86 − 48 = 38	49 + 57 = 106	76 − 37 = 39
98 − 79 = 19	76 + 94 = 170	66 − 59 = 7	48 + 56 = 104	29 + 78 = 107	98 − 39 = 59
88 − 29 = 59	78 + 29 = 107	36 + 68 = 104	94 − 87 = 7	83 + 87 = 170	74 − 55 = 19

Write the time.

9:30	7:15	11:30	2:00	1:45
6:15	10:30	8:15	12:45	3:00

133

Blacklines

2-Place Computation #14

Fact Form XII

Mixed Computation #9

Equations #4

After Class

1. Ask individuals to give the triplets by memory.
2. Hold the large clock.
   a. Set the hands at 6:30.
   Two hours ago it was __.
   In two hours it will be __.
   In 30 minutes it will be __.
   b. Ask similar questions with the clock set at 8:00, 10:30, 1:30, 3:00.

170

Answer these facts.

170

18 − 9 = 9	9 + 9 = 18	17 − 8 = 9	9 + 8 = 17			15 − 9 = 6	17 − 9 = 8
8 + 6 = 14	7 + 7 = 14	15 − 7 = 8	14 − 8 = 6	8 + 9 = 17	16 − 7 = 9	9 + 9 = 18	14 − 5 = 9
9 + 7 = 16	16 − 8 = 8	16 − 9 = 7	15 − 6 = 9	9 + 6 = 15	6 + 8 = 14	15 − 8 = 7	17 − 9 = 8
16 − 8 = 8	16 − 9 = 7	9 + 5 = 14	7 + 8 = 15	18 − 9 = 9	14 − 7 = 7	14 − 6 = 8	7 + 9 = 16
18 − 9 = 9	14 − 9 = 5	6 + 9 = 15			18 − 9 = 9	17 − 9 = 8	8 + 8 = 16
17 − 8 = 9	5 + 9 = 14	7 + 9 = 16	17 − 9 = 8	18 − 9 = 9	8 + 7 = 15	14 − 9 = 5	18 − 9 = 9

135

Before Class

Materials

14's–18's flash cards

Chalkboard

Class Time

1. Call the children to the Blossom Charts.

   God promised King Ahaz that someday a special child would be given to special parents. God said the child would eat butter and __. (honey) (Isaiah 7:14, 15)

   After many years the child came. He was given the sweetest name on earth. Yes, it is a name that is sweeter than honey. Do you know the child's name? Jesus

2. Drill the triplets.
   a. **Say each triplet 3 times.**
   b. **Jump from chart to chart.**

3. Have the children fill in the blossoms and blanks on the chalkboard.

170

Speed Drill

Answer these problems.
Carry *over* in some problems.

97 +90 = 187	189 −96 = 93	28 +49 = 77			58 +38 = 96
169 −77 = 92	159 −83 = 76	28 +36 = 64	179 −96 = 83	76 +80 = 156	189 −95 = 94
95 +74 = 169	164 −84 = 80	67 +29 = 96	39 +38 = 77	187 −94 = 93	92 +95 = 187
178 −95 = 83	157 −94 = 63	188 −97 = 91	26 +39 = 65	149 −77 = 72	66 +83 = 149
146 −63 = 83	35 +29 = 64			168 −92 = 76	159 −67 = 92
91 +58 = 149	157 −85 = 72	39 +26 = 65	149 −58 = 91	149 −86 = 63	155 −72 = 83

136

4. Flash the 14's–18's cards.
   Answer together.
5. **Name the coin.**
   - **5¢** nickel
   - **1¢** penny
   - **50¢** half dollar
   - **10¢** dime
   - **25¢** quarter
6. **Name the fraction.**
   a. **Mother cut a peach into 2 equal parts. Each piece is __.**
   b. **Father cut a watermelon into 4 equal parts. Each piece is __.**
   c. **Matthew cut his candy bar into 3 equal parts. Each piece is __.**
7. **Name the shape.**
   - **It has no corners.** circle
   - **It has 3 corners.** triangle
   - **It has 4 equal sides.** square
   - **It has 2 long sides and 2 short sides.** rectangle
8. Do the Speed Drill in Lesson 170.
9. Assign Lesson 170.

Read the story.
Write the numbers in the beehive.
Write the label words on the lines.
Answer the problem.

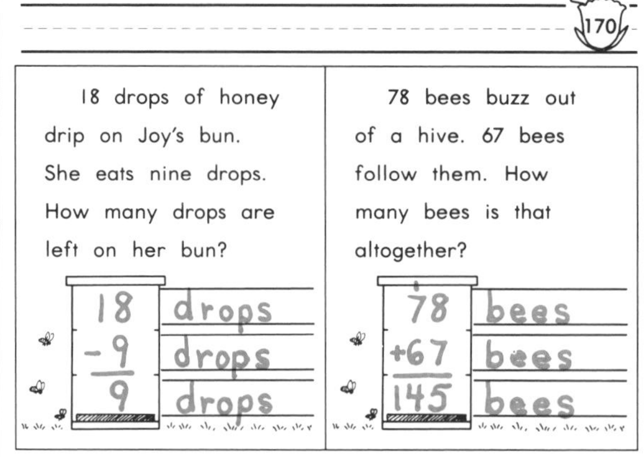

170

18 drops of honey drip on Joy's bun. She eats nine drops. How many drops are left on her bun?

18	drops
−9	drops
9	drops

78 bees buzz out of a hive. 67 bees follow them. How many bees is that altogether?

78	bees
+67	bees
145	bees

Trace and copy.

2 cups = 1 pint
2 cups = 1 pint
2 pints = 1 quart
2 pints = 1 quart
4 quarts = 1 gallon
4 quarts = 1 gallon

137

Blacklines

- 2-Place Computation #14
- Triplets With Facts #16
- Fact Form XII
- Mixed Computation #10

After Class

1. Circle Drill: 14's–18's flash cards.
2. Ask individuals to give the triplets by memory.
3. Review
   a. **Mother made 4 quarts of lemonade or __ of lemonade.** 1 gallon
   b. **Nathan's hamster weighs 16 ounces or __.** 1 pound
   c. **The doctor told Grandfather to stay in bed for 7 days or __.** 1 week
   d. **Brother Paul helped the Christians in Guatemala for 12 months or for __.** 1 year

Speed Drill

9 + 7 = 16; 17 − 9 = 8; 17 − 8 = 9; 16 − 9 = 7; 9 + 9 = 18; 16 − 7 = 9

18 − 9 = 9; 8 + 9 = 17; 16 − 7 = 9; 15 − 6 = 9; 9 + 8 = 17; 17 − 8 = 9

8 + 9 = 17; 6 + 9 = 15; 14 − 5 = 9; 9 + 9 = 18; 16 − 9 = 7; 18 − 9 = 9; 17 − 9 = 8; 7 + 9 = 16

2 + 4 + 9 = 15; 2 + 7 + 8 = 17; 3 + 4 + 9 = 16; 5 + 4 + 9 = 18; 3 + 6 + 9 = 18; 7 + 2 + 7 = 16; 4 + 5 + 8 = 17; 6 + 3 + 9 = 18

"Whatsoever thy hand findeth to do, do it with thy might." Ecclesiastes 9:10

138

Appendix

Patterns

Boat Poster
Number Line Markers
Clover Patch Poster
Blossom Chart
Place Value Chart

These patterns are repeated on loose sheets with the set of blacklines for this course.

Patterns for individual flash cards and *My 1,000 Book* are provided with the blacklines for this course.

Boat Poster

See page 12 for instructions.

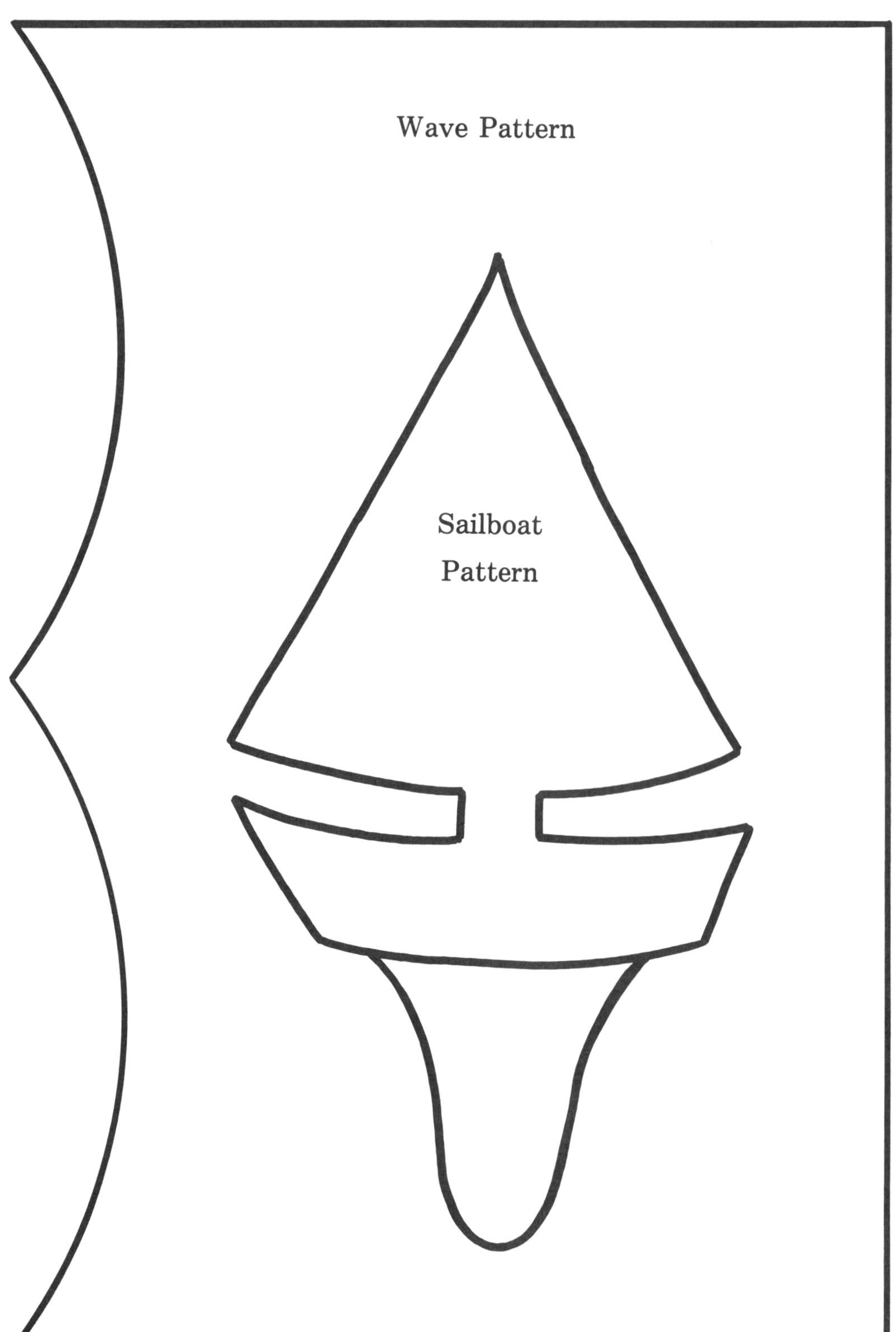

Boat Poster patterns are repeated on loose sheets with the blacklines.

These patterns are repeated on loose sheets with the blacklines.

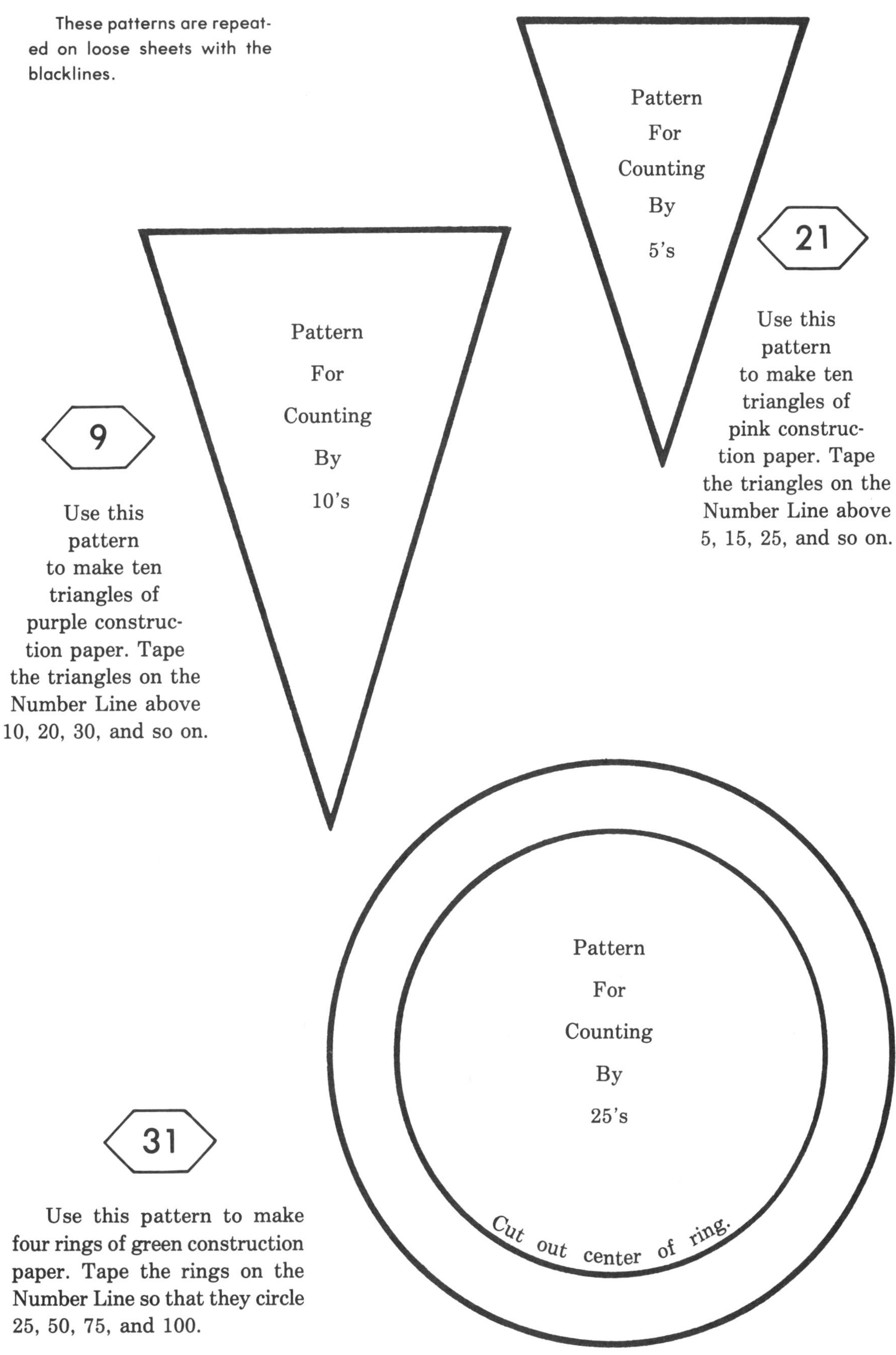
Pattern
For
Counting
By
5's
21
Use this pattern to make ten triangles of pink construction paper. Tape the triangles on the Number Line above 5, 15, 25, and so on.
Pattern
For
Counting
By
10's
9
Use this pattern to make ten triangles of purple construction paper. Tape the triangles on the Number Line above 10, 20, 30, and so on.
Pattern
For
Counting
By
25's
Cut out center of ring.
31

Use this pattern to make four rings of green construction paper. Tape the rings on the Number Line so that they circle 25, 50, 75, and 100.

Clover Patch Poster

See page 13 for instructions.

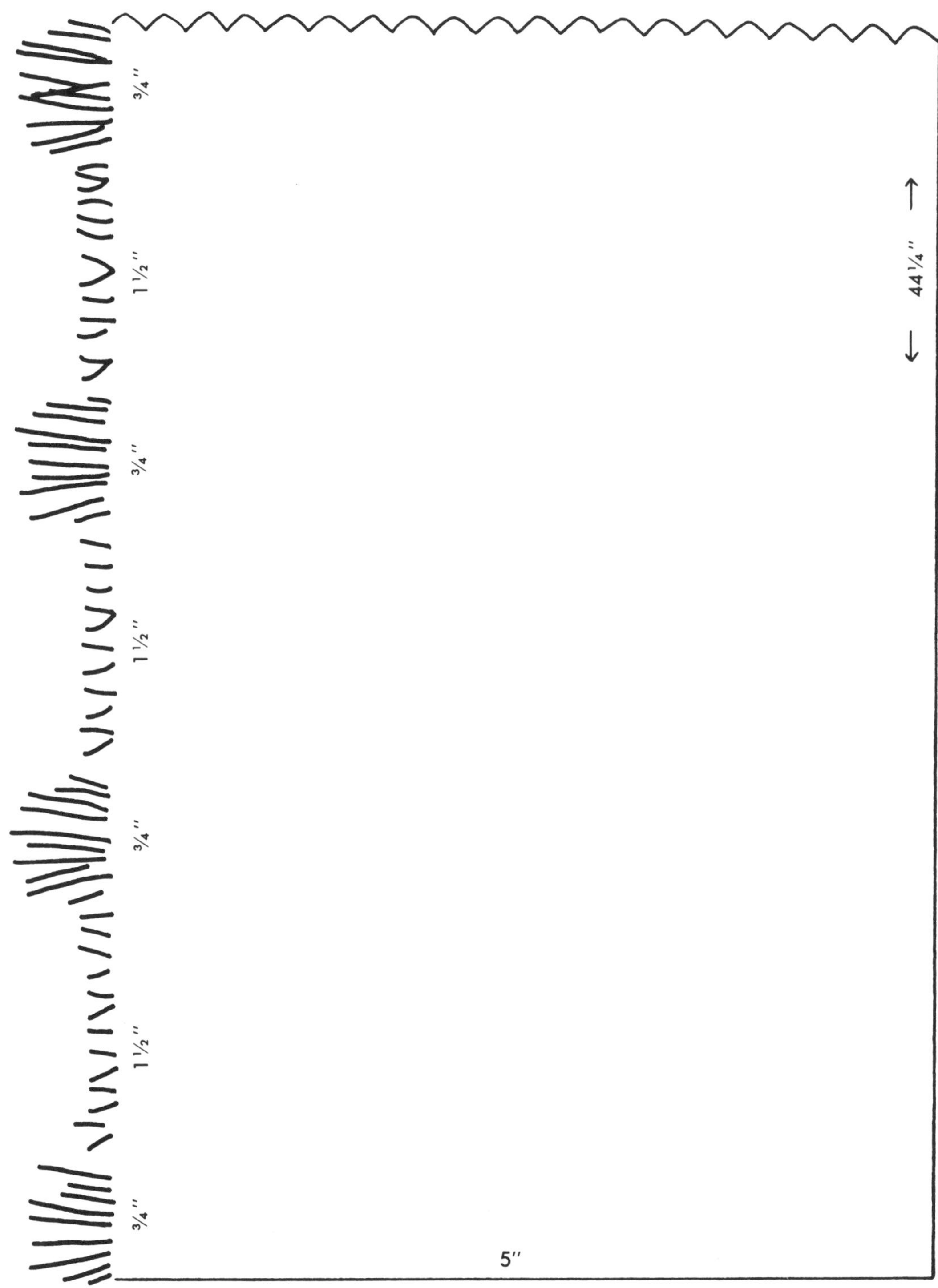

Draw this grass pattern 5" from the bottom of your poster. The clover blossoms will slip into the slots when the poster is made.

Clover Patch Poster

Make nine
of this pattern.
Color the clover
blossoms pink.
Color the bees'
body yellow.

Clover Patch Poster patterns are repeated on loose sheets with the blacklines.

Make eighteen
of this pattern.
Color ten clover
blossoms pink.
Color eight clover
blossoms red-violet.

46

Blossom Chart

See page 14 for instructions.

Make ten of this pattern.

Color the bees yellow and brown.
Do not color the wings.
Write the *2 parts* on the wings with a broad-tipped green marker.
Make the numbers as large and bold as possible.

With each new triplet, add another bee to the chart.

1. Arrange the bees clockwise around the clover blossom.
2. Mount the bees with reusable adhesive.
3. When the school year closes, remove the bees. Store the blossom charts for use next year.

Make ten of this pattern.

Blossom Chart

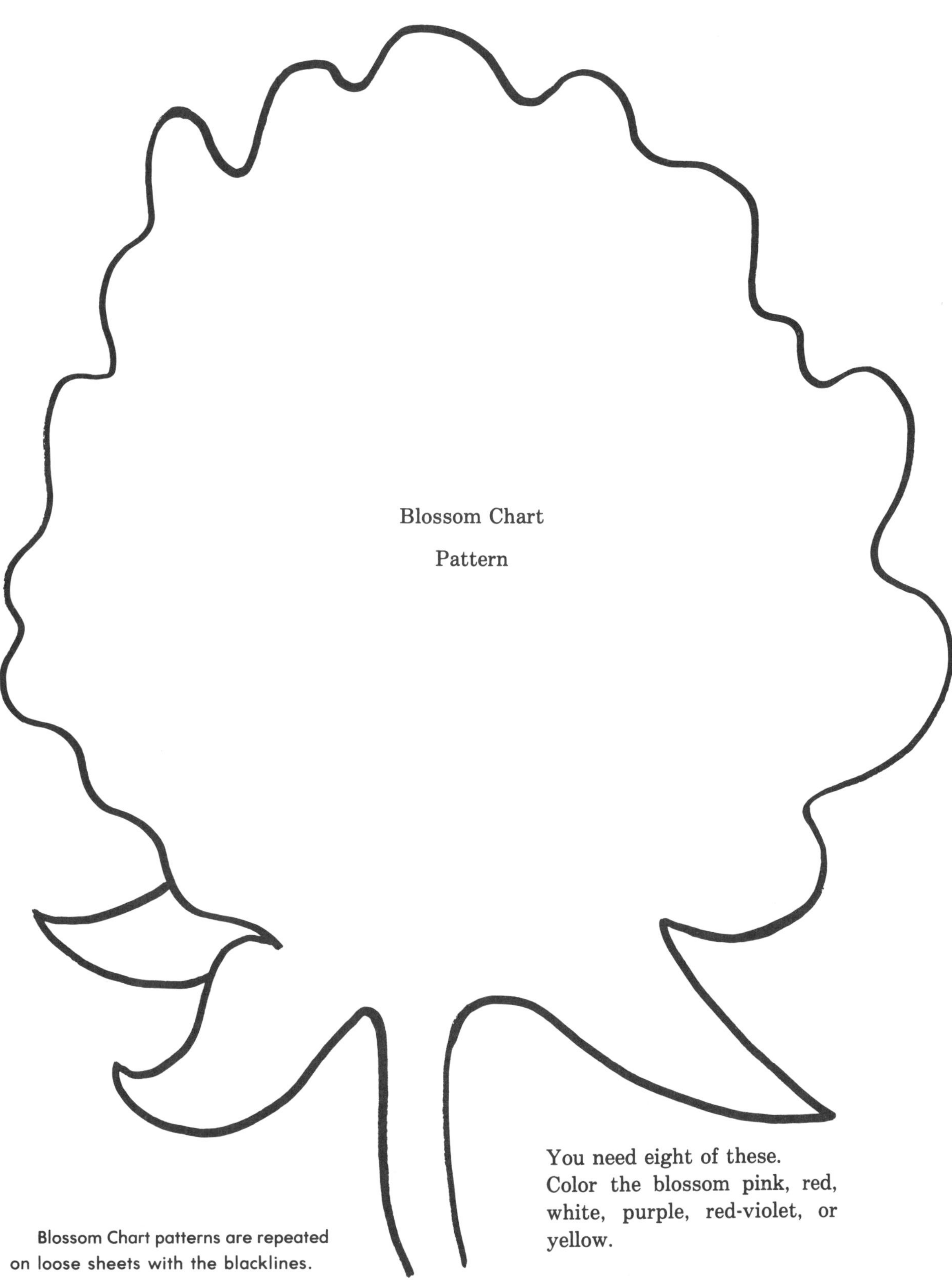

You need eight of these.
Color the blossom pink, red, white, purple, red-violet, or yellow.

Blossom Chart patterns are repeated on loose sheets with the blacklines.

Place Value Chart

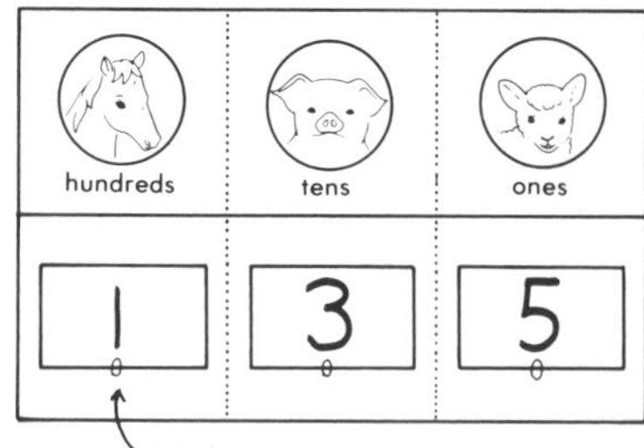

A place value chart can help the children learn and remember the names of the places. Draw a grid on a large white poster board. Reproduce and color the pictures of these three animals. Paste the lamb in ones' place, the pig in tens' place, and the pony in hundreds' place.

Write numerals 0–9 on 3×5 index cards. Make three cards of each numeral for working with numbers like 111.

Press an E-Z Clip at the bottom of each number place to hold the card.

Use the chart for handy reference during seatwork and for working with numbers that switch digits (127 and 172, 105 and 150).

Place Value Chart patterns are repeated on loose sheets with the blacklines.

Index of New Skills—Where They Are First Introduced

COMPUTATION	Teacher's Manual Lesson Number	Pupil's Book Lesson Number	Blacklines Lesson Number		Skill Number
Addition Families 2 and 3	1	1			
Addition Family 4	2	2			
Addition Family 5	3	3			
Addition Family 6	4	4	5	Number Facts	#1
2 digits + 2 digits	6	8			
Addition Family 7	7	7	8	Number Facts	#2
2 digits + 1 digit	8	10	10	Adding 2-Place Nos.	#1
Subtraction Families 2 and 3	11	11			
Subtraction Family 4	12	12			
Subtraction Family 5	13	13			
2 digits−2 digits	13	15			
Subtraction Family 6	14	14	15	Number Facts	#3
2 digits−1 digit	15	17	18	Subtracting 2-Place Nos.	#2

Index of New Skills—Where They Are First Introduced

COMPUTATION	Teacher's Manual Lesson Number	Pupil's Book Lesson Number	Blacklines Lesson Number		Skill Number
Subtraction Family 7	17	17	18	Number Facts	#4
Addition Family 8	21	21	22	Number Facts	#5
Addition Family 9	24	24	25	Number Facts	#6
3 digits + 3 digits	25	27			
Addition Family 10	27	27	28	Fact Form I	
3 digits + 2 digits	28	29			
Subtraction Family 8	31	31			
Subtraction Family 9	34	34	35	Number Facts	#7
3 digits − 3 digits	35	36			
Subtraction Family 10	37	37	38	Fact Form II	
3 digits − 2 digits	37	38			
1 digit + 1 digit + 1 digit	38	44			
(11) 9 2 triplet and facts	41	41	41 43	Fact Hives Missing Whole or Part	#1 #1

Index of New Skills—Where They Are First Introduced

COMPUTATION	Teacher's Manual Lesson Number	Pupil's Book Lesson Number	Blacklines Lesson Number		Skill Number
(11) 8 3 triplet and facts	46	46	46 48	Fact Hives Missing Whole or Part	#2 #2
(11) 7 4 triplet and facts	51	51	51 51 53	Fact Hives Triplets With Facts Missing Whole or Part	#4 #1 #3
2 digits + 2 digits + 2 digits	53	55			
(11) 6 5 triplet and facts	56	56	56 56 58 64	Fact Hives Triplets With Facts Missing Whole or Part Fact Form IV	#6 #2 #4
2 digits + 2 digits + 1 digit	56	61			
(12) 9 3 triplet and facts	61	61	61 61 63	Fact Hives Triplets With Facts Missing Whole or Part	#8 #3 #5
Carrying: 2 digits + 2 digits	65	67			
(12) 8 4 triplet and facts	66	66	66 66 66 68	Fact Hives Triplets With Facts Number Facts Missing Whole or Part	#9 #4 #8 #6
(12) 7 5 triplet and facts	71	71	71 71 72 73	Fact Hives Triplets With Facts Number Facts Missing Whole or Part	#11 #5 #9 #7
(12) 6 6 triplet and facts	76	76	76 76 79	Fact Hives Missing Whole or Part Fact Form V	#13 #8
(13) 9 4 triplet and facts	79	79	79 81 82 84	Fact Hives Missing Whole or Part Number Facts Triplets With Facts	#14 #9 #10 #6
Column addition—carrying	84	84			

Index of New Skills—Where They Are First Introduced

COMPUTATION	Teacher's Manual Lesson Number	Pupil's Book Lesson Number	Blacklines Lesson Number		Skill Number
(13) 8 5 triplet and facts	87	87	87 88 89 92	Fact Hives Number Facts Missing Whole or Part Triplets With Facts	#15 #11 #10 #7
Borrowing: 2 digits − 2 digits	88	90			
(13) 7 6 triplet and facts	95	95	95 96 97 98 100 106	Fact Hives Number Facts Missing Whole or Part Triplets With Facts Fact Form VI Subtracting 2-Place Nos.	#17 #12 #11 #8 #7
(14) 9 5 triplet and facts	103	103	103 105 106	Fact Hives Missing Whole or Part Triplets With Facts	#19 #12 #9
(14) 8 6 triplet and facts	111	111	111 112 113 114	Fact Hives Number Facts Missing Whole or Part Triplets With Facts	#20 #13 #13 #10
Carrying twice: 3 digits + 3 digits	114	115			
(14) 7 7 triplet and facts	119	119	119 119 125	Fact Hives Fact Form VII Triplets With Facts	#22 #11
(15) 9 6 triplet and facts	122	122	122 123 124	Fact Hives Number Facts Missing Whole or Part	#23 #14 #14
2× table (optional)	124				
Divide by 2 (optional)	130				
(15) 8 7 triplet and facts	130	130	130 132 132 133 134	Fact Hives Missing Whole or Part Number Facts Triplets With Facts Fact Form VIII	#24 #15 #15 #12

Index of New Skills—Where They Are First Introduced

COMPUTATION	Teacher's Manual Lesson Number	Pupil's Book Lesson Number	Blacklines Lesson Number		Skill Number
10× table (optional)	133				
(16) 9 7 triplet and facts	138	138	138 140 140 141	Fact Hives Missing Whole or Part Number Facts Triplets With Facts	#26 #16 #16 #13
Divide by 10 (optional)	139				
5× table (optional)	142				
(16) 8 8 triplet and facts	146	146	146 147	Fact Hives Fact Form IX	#28
Divide by 5 (optional)	148				
(17) 9 8 triplet and facts	149	149	149 150 151 152	Fact Hives Number Facts Missing Whole or Part Triplets With Facts	#29 #17 #17 #14
1× table (optional)	151				
(18) 9 9 triplet and facts	157	157	157 158 158 159 161	Fact Hives Missing Whole or Part Number Facts Triplets With Facts Fact Form X	#31 #18 #18 #15

Index of New Skills—Where They Are First Introduced

EQUATIONS	Teacher's Manual Lesson Number	Pupil's Book Lesson Number	Blacklines Lesson Number		Blacklines Skill Number
60 minutes = 1 hour	48				
30 minutes = ½ hour	55				
12 things = 1 dozen	115	117			
6 things = ½ dozen	115	117			
7 days = 1 week	117				
12 months = 1 year	119				
12 inches = 1 foot	125	127			
3 feet = 1 yard	128	129	141	Equations	#1
2 cups = 1 pint	147	149			
2 pints = 1 quart	150	151	155	Equations	#2
4 quarts = 1 gallon	153	154	161	Equations	#3
16 ounces = 1 pound	157	157	165	Equations	#4

FRACTIONS	Teacher's Manual Lesson Number	Pupil's Book Lesson Number	Blacklines Lesson Number	Blacklines Skill Number
1/2	98	100		
1/4	106	108		
1/2 of a number	108			
1/3	140	141		

Index of New Skills—Where They Are First Introduced

MONEY	Teacher's Manual Lesson Number	Pupil's Book Lesson Number	Blacklines Lesson Number		Skill Number
Penny	7	8			
Dime	14	16	17	Money Identification	#1
Dimes + pennies	19	19			
Nickel	22	24	27	Money Identification	#3
Nickels + pennies	27	29			
Quarter	32	34	41	Money Identification	#5
Quarters + pennies	36	37			
Dimes + nickels	49	50			
$ sign and decimal point	97	98			
Half dollar	133	135	138	Money Identification	#7
Half dollar + dimes	134	135			
Half dollar + pennies	138	138			

NUMBER COMPARISON	Teacher's Manual Lesson Number	Pupil's Book Lesson Number	Blacklines Lesson Number	Skill Number
Largest number	1	3		
Smallest number	11	13		

NUMBER ORDER	Teacher's Manual Lesson Number	Pupil's Book Lesson Number	Blacklines Lesson Number	Skill Number
After numbers	3	1		
Before numbers	4	6		
Before and After numbers	12	21		

Index of New Skills—Where They Are First Introduced

PLACE VALUE	Teacher's Manual Lesson Number	Pupil's Book Lesson Number	Blacklines Lesson Number	Blacklines Skill Number
up to 100's place	5	6		
up to 1000's place	62	64		

READING PROBLEMS	Teacher's Manual Lesson Number	Pupil's Book Lesson Number	Blacklines Lesson Number	Blacklines Skill Number
Key word: in all	6	8	22	Reading Problems #1
Key word: left	14	19	39	Reading Problems #3
Key word: altogether	23	52		
Key word: both	30	78		
No key word	33	50		
Finding a missing part	44	100		
2-digit computation	64	112		
Using ¢	64	116		
Key word: how much more	100		106	Reading Problems #4
Key word: less	113		116	Reading Problems #6
Using 1 dozen	117	127		
Key word: sum	142		143	Reading Problems #9
Key word: difference	153		156	Reading Problems #11

Index of New Skills—Where They Are First Introduced

SHAPES	Teacher's Manual Lesson Number	Pupil's Book Lesson Number	Blacklines Lesson Number	Blacklines Skill Number
Circle	83	84		
Square	83	84		
Triangle	84	85		
Rectangle	87	87		

SKIP COUNTING	Teacher's Manual Lesson Number	Pupil's Book Lesson Number	Blacklines Lesson Number	Blacklines Skill Number
Counting by 10's	9	11	11 Skip Counting	#1
Counting by 5's	21	23	24 Skip Counting	#2
Counting by 25's	31	33	33 Skip Counting	#3
Counting by 2's	39	41	44 Skip Counting	#4
Counting by 100's	61			
Counting by 50's	132			

TELLING TIME	Teacher's Manual Lesson Number	Pupil's Book Lesson Number	Blacklines Lesson Number	Blacklines Skill Number
:00	43	44		
:30	56	57		
:15	72	74		
:45	79	81		

Teaching Aids—Where They Are First Used

DRILLS	Teacher's Manual Lesson Number
Chalkboard Drill	2
Speed Drill	6
Double Drill	9
Flash Card Drill	26
Circle Drill	28
Oral Drill	46

FACT FORMS	Teacher's Manual Lesson Number
I	28
II	38
III	46
IV	64
V	79
VI	100
VII	119
VIII	134
IX	147
X	161
XI	164
XII	167

FORMS	Teacher's Manual Lesson Number
A	2
B	6
C	26
D	

VISUAL AIDS	**Teacher's Manual** Lesson Number
Number line	1
Boat Poster	1
My 1,000 Book	3
Real pennies (one for each child)	7
Large penny	9
10 purple triangles	9
Real dimes (one for each child)	14
Large dime	16
10 pink triangles	21
Real nickels (one for each child)	22
Large nickel	25
4 green rings	31
Real quarters (one for each child)	32
Large quarter	34
Clover Patch Poster	41
Large clock	43
Blossom Charts	47
Large classroom calendar	117
12″ ruler	125
36″ yardstick	128
Real half dollar	133
Large half dollar	134
Cup	147
Pint jar	147
Quart jar	150
Gallon jar	153
1 ounce bundle of 4 new pencils (5 new crayons, 3 sticks of chalk)	157
1 pound bundle of 6 boxes of 1 dozen pencils (5 boxes of sixteen crayons, 4 boxes of one dozen chalk sticks)	158
Place Value Chart